Taking SIDES

Clashing Views on Controversial Issues in Crime and Criminology

Fourth Edition

Taking
SIDES

Clashing Views on
Controversial Issues in
Crime and
Criminology

Fourth Edition

Edited, Selected, and with Introductions by

Richard C. Monk
Coppin State College

Dushkin Publishing Group/Brown & Benchmark Publishers
A Times Mirror Higher Education Group Company

364
T136
1996

To the memory of my father, Daniel R. Monk (April 29, 1913–March 17, 1995), and to my mother, Elsie M. Monk, who first taught me the importance of debating controversial issues.

Photo Acknowledgments

Part 1   EPA Documerica
Part 2   Baker/DPG
Part 3   DPG
Part 4   Drug Enforcement Agency

Cover Art Acknowledgment

Charles Vitelli

Library of Congress Cataloging-in-Publication Data

Main entry under title:
    Taking sides: clashing views on controversial issues in crime and criminology/edited, selected, and with introductions by Richard C. Monk.—4th ed.
    Includes bibliographical references and index.
    1. Crime and criminals. I. Monk, Richard C., *comp.*

1-56134-446-X

364
95-74671

Printed on Recycled Paper

PREFACE

To those who share the age-old hope that man's inhumanity to man can be diminished.

—Harry Elmer Barnes and Howard Becker

Comprehension without critical evaluation is impossible.

—Hegel

It was my fate to be a scholar for a while.

—Nietzsche

This volume contains 38 essays presented in a pro and con format. A total of 19 different clashing issues within crime and criminology are debated. The issues are arranged in four broad topical areas that touch upon some of the most important and interesting aspects of criminology and criminal justice.

I have included a mix of fundamental issues and newly emerging ones. Some of the authors unabashedly write for a popular audience primarily to grind their own axes or to arouse public sentiment. Other selections are written by some of the most profound thinkers within the social sciences and deal with vital theoretical issues in crime and criminology (for example, the functionality of crime). I have not shirked my obligation to provide you with the best discussions on relevant issues available, even if the discussions are sometimes technical or theoretical and require you to think deeply about the issue at hand before making up your mind.

In order to assist you in your voyage into controversial criminological issues, I have supplied you with an *introduction* to each issue and an issue *postscript*, which follows the "yes" and "no" readings. All the postscripts have detailed suggestions for further reading should you want to pursue the topics raised in an issue. While my primary concern was to get the authors' ideas up front so that you could be immersed in them, fight with them, embrace some of them, than make your own decisions, I have not been averse to "editorializing." Now and then my own disdain (or support) for certain ideas will be more manifest than on other occasions. Do not be bashful about debating the authors and their ideas, or your editor as well. I definitely could be wrong and may need your critical evaluation!

I feel strongly that the only way that irrationalities and cruelties among men and women can be reduced is through critical evaluation of the issues at hand. I hope that this volume can assist you and your generation in keeping criminology and criminal justice vital areas of study. I feel that one realistic way to achieve this goal is through reintroducing the necessary art of systematic and informed debate over clashing issues in crime and criminology.

Changes to this edition In response to the rapidly changing world of crime and criminal justice, and on the strength of the recommendations that have come from professors who have used the book, I have made considerable changes to this edition. There are 10 completely new issues: *Does Rap Music Contribute to Violent Crime?* (Issue 3); *Is the War on Black Criminals Misguided?* (Issue 6); *Is the Death Penalty Racially Discriminatory?* (Issue 7); *Should Pornography Be Banned as a Threat to Women?* (Issue 8); *Is Waiver to Adult Courts a Solution to Juvenile Crime?* (Issue 11); *Are Violent Criminals and Delinquents Treated Too Leniently?* (Issue 12); *Should Drugs Be Legalized?* (Issue 14); *Should Euthanasia Be a Crime?* (Issue 16); *Will Community Policing Be the Answer to Crime Control?* (Issue 17); and *Should We Get Even Tougher on Criminals?* (Issue 19). In addition, for three of the issues retained from the previous edition, the issue question has been significantly modified and one of the selections has been replaced in order to focus the debate more sharply and to bring it up to date: Issue 1 on the functionality of crime; Issue 5 on general theories of crime; and Issue 13 on capital punishment. For the issues on street crime versus white-collar crime (Issue 4) and gun control (Issue 15), one of the selections has been replaced to provide new points of view. In all, there are 25 new readings in this edition. Issue introductions and postscripts have been revised and updated where necessary.

A word to the instructor An *Instructor's Manual With Test Questions* (multiple-choice and essay) is available through the publisher for the instructor using *Taking Sides* in the classroom. And a general guidebook, *Using Taking Sides in the Classroom*, which discusses methods and techniques for integrating the pro-con approach into any classroom setting, is also available.

Acknowledgments Many people contribute to any worthwhile project. Among those more directly involved in this project whom I would like to thank are the authors of these excellent and stimulating selections. Also, my thanks to my many students over the years who have contributed to the criminological dialogue. At Coppin State College, these students include Maxima Shay, Sandra Ben-Avraham, Ken Toppin, and Daphne Snowden. I remain honored to have been the teacher of the brave writers and researchers of the student journal *Kaleidoscope*, now no longer published, at Valdosta State University. Their courageous work remains a beacon illuminating the surrounding land.

Several colleagues, scholars, and administrators provided comments and support that were immensely helpful and greatly appreciated. Thanks are extended to T. J. Bryan, dean of Arts and Sciences at Coppin State College; Elizabeth Gray, Elmer Polk, and Ronnie Salahu-Din of the Department of Criminal Justice at Coppin State College; Kurt Finsterbusch of the University of Maryland; Alex Hooke of Villa Julie College; Ben Wright, Fred Cheesman, and Nijole V. Benokraitis of the University of Baltimore; Joel Henderson and Tom Gitchoff of San Diego State University; George Rush of California State University, Long Beach; Paul A. Wortman of New York City Public School 252; Rudy Faller of the Inter-American Development Bank; Horst Senger of Simi Valley, California; Harv Greisman of West Chester State University; Harvey W. Kushner of Long Island University–C. W. Post Center; Erich Goode of the State University of New York at Stony Brook; Steve Steele of Applied Data Associates, Inc.; Natalie J. Sokoloff of John Jay College and Towson State University; Thomas R. O'Connor of Southeastern Louisiana University; Daniel B. Monk of Arlington, Virginia; and Vincent Schiraldi, executive director of the Center on Juvenile and Criminal Justice.

I also received many helpful comments and suggestions from professors across the United States and Canada. Their suggestions have markedly enhanced the quality of this edition. Special thanks to those professors who responded to the questionnaire with specific suggestions for the fourth edition:

Bryan Byers
Valparaiso University

William P. Collins
Mater Dei College

James W. Cox
West Georgia College

Randy Eastep
Brevard Community College

Joseph R. Garvey
Community College of Rhode Island

David M. Horton
Saint Edwards University

Lin Huff-Corzine
Kansas State University

Leslie W. Kennedy
University of Alberta

Michael Klausner
University of Pittsburgh

Jerry Lane
Central Virginia Community College

Meneleo D. Litonjua
College of Mount St. Joseph

Evelyn Mercer
Southwest Baptist University

Patricia Narciso
Illinois Benedictine College

Lewis I. Nicholson
Christopher Newport University

Thomas O'Connor
Southeastern Louisiana University

John R. Poindexter
East Georgia College

Michael D. Reisig
Washington State University

Richard Stempien
Syracuse University

Mark A. Winton
University of Central Florida

Finally, someone must have once said that an author or an editor is only as good as his or her publisher. Without doubt, this *Taking Sides* would not have seen the light of day without the professional assistance and ingenious prodding of Mimi Egan, publisher for the Taking Sides series, and the work of the staff at Dushkin Publishing Group/Brown & Benchmark Publishers. Naturally, I remain solely responsible for errors.

Richard C. Monk
Coppin State College

CONTENTS IN BRIEF

CONTENTS

Classic sociologist Emile Durkheim (1858–1917) theorizes that crime reaffirms moral boundaries and helps bring about needed social changes. U.S. senator Daniel Patrick Moynihan (D-New York) argues that Durkheim does not address deviancy as a serious societal problem and that modern crime has gone way beyond the point of being functional.

Criminologist C. R. Jeffery argues that physiological and chemical imbalances are frequently precipitants of criminal behavior. *Crime and Social Justice* editors Tony Platt and Paul Takagi contend that Jeffery's ideas suffer from a poor understanding of biology, history, and criminology.

Dennis R. Martin, president of the National Association of Chiefs of Police, theorizes that rising racial tensions and violence can be attributed to rock music's promotion of "vile, deviant, and sociopathic behaviors." Criminologists Mark S. Hamm and Jeff Ferrell charge that Martin's theory is based on racism and ignorance of both music and broader cultural forces.

Professor of management and public policy James Q. Wilson and psychologist Richard J. Herrnstein argue that the focus of crime study ought to be on street criminals. Professor of philosophy Jeffrey Reiman contends that pollution, medical malpractice, and dangerous working conditions that go uncorrected are far more serious than street crime.

Criminologist Charles R. Tittle insists that criminology will remain stagnant unless it promotes general theory building. Professors Michael J. Lynch and W. Byron Groves argue that it is better to develop specific, grounded theories and to engage in careful comparative criminology.

Journalist Jeremy Seabrook argues that capitalism and increasing economic expansion based on greed leads to crime. Former New York City mayor Ed Koch maintains that it is unreasonable to blame a racist system for violent crime.

Sociology professors Adalberto Aguirre, Jr., and David V. Baker contend that
racial discrimination remains a fact of life in America with regard to the death
penalty. Social scientists Stanley Rothman and Stephen Powers argue that
when researchers control for type of crime, they find that capital punishment
is not at all discriminatory.

Freelance writer Alice Leuchtag contends that pornography should be banned
as a threat to women and humanity. Professor of law Nadine Strossen argues
that misguided feminist assaults on pornography have led to censorship that
ranges from the silly to the barbaric.

Professors Alfred Blumstein and Jacqueline Cohen declare that criminal career studies are far more helpful than traditional criminological knowledge
of the correlates of crime. Professor of management and policy Michael Gottfredson and professor of sociology Travis Hirschi charge that research on
criminal careers is pretentious, ignores counterevidence, and is conceptually
and methodologically unsound.

Lawrence W. Sherman, a professor of criminology and president of the Crime Control Institute, maintains that studies of arrests for misdemeanor domestic assault can be fundamental for understanding and reducing domestic violence. Law professor Cynthia Grant Bowman argues that current research on domestic violence is badly flawed and that it does not address vital social factors.

Henry Sontheimer, a contributing author to *Juvenile Justice Update,* supports waiving to adult courts juveniles charged with serious crimes, which, he suggests, will help reduce crime. Writer and activist Jennifer Vogel contends that placing juveniles into adult courts and prisons is a tragic part of the increasing abuse of America's young.

Albert Shanker, president of the American Federation of Teachers, argues that the system should quit coddling troublemakers who are ruining the system. D. Stanley Eitzen, a professor emeritus of sociology at Colorado State University, argues that the idea that America has been too lenient on violent criminals and delinquents is a myth.

David Von Drehle, a writer and the arts editor for the *Washington Post*, examines specific capital punishment cases and statistics and concludes that capital punishment is bad policy. Ernest van den Haag, a professor (now retired) and a psychoanalyst, rejects claims that capital punishment is unfair and barbaric, and he insists that the death penalty is just retribution for terrible crimes.

Arnold S. Trebach, president of the Drug Policy Foundation in Washington, D.C., argues for the immediate removal of all legal prohibitions against the use of any drug. James A. Inciardi, director of the Center for Drug and Alcohol Studies at the University of Delaware, asserts that laws against drugs must be maintained.

Josh Sugarmann, formerly with the National Coalition to Ban Handguns, identifies several problems with legal handguns. Sociologist James D. Wright concludes that most gun control laws are unfair and ineffective.

George Allen, governor of Virginia, insists that getting tougher on criminals reduces crime, serves justice, and is economically a bargain. Professor of criminology John Irwin and James Austin, executive vice president of the National Council on Crime and Delinquency, argue that getting tougher on criminals results in more petty offenders being locked up for longer periods of time, which increases racial discrimination and threatens to bankrupt state budgets.

INTRODUCTION

The Changing Study of Crime and Criminology

Richard C. Monk

By almost any measurement of "what is important," crime continues to rank at or near the top of America's priorities and concerns. Local, state, and federal crime fighting and crime control budgets often involve the highest expenditures—typically numbering in the billions of dollars—for the police, courts, and prisons. The losses from crime in lives and in dollars are equally high. The perception of crime expressed as fear is very high among most Americans. For instance, a recent Gallup Poll reveals that some 62 percent of all women and over 25 percent of all men state that there are areas within a mile of their home in which they would be afraid to walk at night.

Since the 1960s, following the Omnibus Safe Streets Act, billions of federal dollars have been spent to create law enforcement training programs, to buy equipment for local police, to fund hundreds of massive research studies, and to create new state and federal crime control agencies and research centers (for example, the Bureau of Justice Statistics). Unfortunately, many politicians and criminal justice administrators, most of the public, and a growing number of criminologists view these efforts as dismal failures.

Intellectually, one can also discern a definite shift in scholarly attitudes toward crime, criminals, and crime control. In the early years of the twentieth century, criminologists registered optimism about conquering crime. The assumption was that if we simply started to research crime systematically, utilizing the cognitive tools of science, based upon rationality and empirical investigations free of sensationalism and biases, then significant advances would follow.

John Lewis Gillin, in his popular 1926 criminology text, said:

> Criminal statistics are becoming more reliable every year.... It is time that calm, scientific study, rather than sensational journalistic methods be devoted to the problem of crime and criminals. Only so can popular fallacies concerning what makes the criminal and how to treat him be exploded, and a sound program for the treatment and the prevention of crime be established.

A short time later, the preeminent criminologist Thorsten Sellin, as cited by F. Zimring and G. Hawkins in *Capital Punishment and the American Agenda* (Cambridge University Press, 1986), wrote what might be considered the basis of the modern scientific research approach to crime:

> [It] is characteristic of modern man, reared in an age of scientific orientation, that he wishes to use scientific thoughtways in the approach to his problems. He

does not like to be considered irrational. When he formulates public policies, he wants to think that such policies are based on scientific facts.

It appears that current criminologists are imbued with a more realistic understanding of both the complexities of the twentieth century and crime and criminals. In the words of noted sociologist Peter Berger, in his book *The Heretical Imperative* (Doubleday, 1979), current academic thinking is probably more likely to be influenced by an awareness that

> the institutional pluralization that marks modernity affects not only human ac-
> tions but also human consciousness: Modern men and women find themselves
> confronted not only by multiple options of possible courses of action but also by
> multiple options of possible ways of thinking about the world.

This volume attempts to assist you in examining both possible options for action and possible ways of thinking about crime, criminals, and criminology. I am not particularly optimistic, however, that the problems of the twentieth century will be solved by the twenty-first century.

CRIME: DEFINITIONS AND CAUSES

Ideological Issues

Any theory or explanation of crime obviously has several dimensions built into it from the start. First, even the most "scientific" or "neutral" theory will reflect to some extent the existing ideological or political sentiments of the day. At the very least, most criminological theories can be classified as conservative, radical, or liberal, or some analytical combination of these three political perspectives.

In theory, a scientific explanation of some phenomenon, including one of crime and criminals, is supposed to be value-free, uncontaminated by emotions and political circumstances. Yet funding decisions are often based on prevailing political concerns with public demands, and consequently the formulation of theory and the pursuits of research programs for scholars are affected. For instance, the disciplinary area of criminal justice administration, which has rapidly matured since the 1960s largely as a direct result of the massive infusion of federal funds, reflects concerns quite different from those of traditional criminology. Basically, criminal justice eschews any search for *causes* of criminal behavior. Instead, it tends to serve the needs of political funding agencies, which respond to the public's demand for solutions to the crime problem, and is therefore an atheoretical, applied academic discipline. The focus is on the development of strategies for administering more effectively the courts, the police, and the prisons.

Images of Society

A second dimension of any theory of crime causation, which also sometimes overlaps with ideological issues, is the image of society and of men and women contained within the theory. If criminals are seen as evil men and women contaminating an otherwise "pure" and "perfectable" society, then the explanation of crime that follows from this thinking will probably be a conservative one. That is, crime is a consequence of the individual offender's pathology.

By contrast, if crime is seen as a reaction against the inequities of the capitalist society or system, then the system, according to a crude variant of radical or Marxist criminology, is exclusively to blame. This theory's image of men and women is that they are inherently good but the system is bad and, through oppression, drives many to commit crimes.

The liberal image of men and women is that they are potentially good but that, through a combination of factors ranging from socialization to unfortunate circumstances, they can make mistakes. Reform of certain aspects of either society or individuals, or both, is suggested by this theoretical perspective.

Theory and Treatment

A third dimension of any theory of crime is an inherent treatment modality. The conservative explanation of crime would recommend punishment. As noted, the liberal perspective would recommend "treatment" or "rehabilitation" as well as possible economic reforms in society. A biological theory would have as part of its implicit treatment modality either sterilization, chemical therapy, or some kind of medical remedies directed at the individual offender.

Research Programs

A fourth dimension of criminological theories is that, in addition to having built-in ideological biases, however implicit, images of society and of men and women, and a concomitant treatment modality, they will have a specific research program. That is, each contains a particular methodological agenda. This, along with the other dimensions of a theory, is influenced by and influences the conceptualization of key theoretic concepts such as "crime" and "criminal." The exact scope of a theory is largely a result of how the element that the theory purports to explain is specifically defined. For instance, noted criminologist Edwin H. Sutherland's (1883–1950) classic definition of criminology is the study of the making of laws, the breaking of laws, and society's responses to these processes. This is a very comprehensive approach to criminology and technically includes both criminology and criminal justice. In actuality, criminologists have traditionally focused more heavily on studying the causes, rates, and distributions of crime. Criminal justice scholars have focused almost exclusively on society's responses to lawbreaking; that is, the criminal justice system. However, this historical distinction between the two has recently shown signs of collapse.

Other definitions and their theoretic frames of reference have been more narrow in scope. As a consequence, their research methodologies have also been more narrow than those working within Sutherland's tradition. For instance, a legalistic approach to criminology might emphasize simply the passage of laws. European criminologists, for example, for generations have emphasized the study of laws. American criminologists, by contrast, have studied criminals, crime, and prisons far more extensively.

A LOOK AT SOME THEORIES

Some criminologists develop novel definitions of crime. James Q. Wilson, for instance (see Issue 4), centers his theory of crime around predatory street crimes and ignores all other types. His work, to some extent, is reminiscent of the Italian jurist Garofalo, who in 1914 defined crimes as offenses against society's ideas of "pity" and "probity." The offense also has to be injurious to society, Garofalo wrote.

The acts of defining and explaining some phenomenon, then, automatically set the boundaries for both the discipline itself and what is to be researched in that discipline (what kinds of crimes, who commits crime, etc.). For example, both formally and informally, rape was not considered a crime in many parts of the world. Informally, in the United States, it was often not treated as a crime, or at least not as a serious crime, although laws were always on the books against it. Until the past several years, it was not considered possible for a man to rape his wife. Indeed, in some states it was assumed that if a woman had invited a man to her home, then rape could not have occurred (only voluntary sexual intercourse). Thus, what your theory of crime consists of, how it defines crime, and what acts are included as crimes will all have a tremendous impact on your research and policy recommendations. That is why it is very important to inquire about a scholar's particular theoretic frame of reference.

Criminology in the United States grew up in the late 1800s basically as an applied study of the effects of prisons on criminals. It later received "academic respectability" through its inclusion within sociology departments at the turn of the century (for example, the University of Chicago). Almost from the very beginning, criminology as a subdiscipline of sociology emphasized a reformist, scientific orientation. It was assumed that, by scientifically understanding crime, criminals could be better controlled and helped. Thus, crime would be reduced. Most of the early theories, though, were a grab bag of different superstitions, Protestant reform sentiments, and pop biology and psychology, with some vague sociological or structural ideas thrown in. Generally, the sociological aspects of criminological theorizing were restricted to a focus upon the organization (or more typically, the perceived disorganization) of the family, the community, and the school. (See, for instance, Gillin's *Criminology and Penology* [1926]).

Throughout the 1940s and 1950s, the dominant theory within American criminology, by far, was that of Sutherland and later Sutherland and Donald R. Cressey. This perspective, though vast and complicated in many ways, is usually reduced to representing the symbolic interactionist sociological frame of reference. Within American sociology since the 1960s, there have been three dominant paradigms, or theories, explaining social behavior. These are the symbolic interactionist, the structural functional, and the conflict, or radical, perspectives.

As indicated, most criminological work was set within the symbolic interactionist frame of reference for several years. The emphasis was placed on how criminals were socialized into a world of crime through their interactions with criminal others. The importance of learning symbols, attitudes, and values conducive of crime commission from knowledgeable, experienced criminals was stressed. Later, the role (sometimes a fatal role) of labeling was incorporated into this perspective. The interaction between the police and alleged criminals, as well as between the courts and alleged criminals, was emphasized. However, economic factors as well as political ones were generally ignored by this perspective.

The structural functional perspective derives its thinking largely from the sociology of Emile Durkheim (see Issue 1). It has been elaborated on by a number of American sociologists. The most important bearer of Durkheim's tradition has been Robert Merton, whose elaborations upon Durkheim's work include his famous means-end scheme approach to explaining deviant behavior (first published in 1938). Later theorists writing in this tradition include Kingsley Davis and, more recently, Kai T. Erikson.

Structural functionalists attempt to determine what patterns of interaction or structures exist in various groups. They investigate what these patterns contribute to the maintenance of that group and of the society to which the group belongs. In the United States, for example, dating patterns and their relation to marriage are studied. Marriage patterns and their relation to the economy, to religion, and so on are traced. In addition, structural functionalists want to know about what consequences patterns of behavior have for groups, for members of groups, and for society as a whole. Such consequences can be both positive and negative, intentional and unintentional.

Radical or Marxist sociologists are similar to structural functionalists in that they frequently look at the entire society and try to determine how its various component parts interrelate. However, the radical or conflict theorist (these terms are often used interchangeably) generally sees as the core definers of society's interests those who dominate the economy. By contrast, structural functionalists seem to assume core values that are shared by members of society regardless of their position vis-à-vis the economy (whether they are workers, managers, or owners).

For the structural functionalist, crime results from people having their goals or values blocked. An example would be poor teenagers who share the American goal of material success but through lack of education, discrimination, and so on are not able to achieve success through the prescribed channels. Therefore, they commit crimes as a "short cut."

The Marxist would argue, by contrast, that often the system itself through oppression pressures the criminal to commit crimes. There are many variants of radical criminology. However, earlier variants insisted that criminals were often guilty only of political acts. The radical criminologists would also emphasize the unfair treatment society's disadvantaged are subjected to by agents of the criminal justice system, such as the police on the beat harassing the poor, the courts' unfair sentencing of them, and the prison's mistreatment of its inmates, usually poorer citizens. To the radical criminologist, the criminal justice system is little more than a handmaiden serving to protect the interests of the rich. The structural functionalists, then, obviously view crime in a very different way.

As a point of interest, an intellectual contradiction within criminology that parallels contradictions within broader institutional and cultural structures is the continued appeal of radical criminology. Logically, one might have predicted that, since the demise of the Soviet Union revealed the many sharp political and economic contradictions inherent in that former system's application of Marxian ideas, intellectuals in the West would have radically changed their perceptions of the relevancy of Marx. Within the social sciences, at least so far, this has not happened. Although many novel variants of criminological theory are rapidly emerging—including postmodernism, deconstructionism, feminist theory, and even applications of chaos theory— none of them can be seen as consistently Marxist. Yet a hard core of Marxist criminologists remains alive and well, threatened neither by the extremely punitive mood reflected by politicians and the public nor by the rapidlv splintering groups developing within the social sciences.

SOME FINAL THOUGHTS

In the years between the publication of the first edition of this book in 1988 and now, there have been some noticeable changes on the crime scene, including the types of crime receiving public attention, the public perception of crime, how crime is depicted in the mass media, and, to some extent, changes within the criminal justice system itself. In the United States, a slightly more conservative cast has been evident in recent Supreme Court rulings due to the appointment of new justices. There have been sensational new trials, allegations of police brutality at the highest levels, the most lethal terrorist acts ever seen on U.S. soil, charges of corruption and cover-ups reaching as high as the White House, and overwhelming citizen support of a draconian punishment that was meted out to a teenager in Singapore. Specifically, the 1995 O. J. Simpson murder trial and its media coverage dwarfed the 1992 Mike Tyson rape trial, the 1991 William Kennedy Smith rape trial, and the 1992 Jeffrey Dahmer murder trial combined. Ignoring the sensationalism and brutality of the double murders, the trial made "legal history" through its jurors' "going on strike." Many insist that regardless of the verdict of not guilty, and many more *because* of the verdict, the obvious inefficiency of the police and courts have further eroded Americans' faith in the criminal justice system.

Both the 1993 bombing of the World Trade Center in New York City and that of a federal building in Oklahoma City in 1995 are feared to be an indication of things to come. In addition to the horror of the acts, one aspect of Oklahoma that caught many by surprise, including criminologists, is the revelation of powerful, well-armed militia groups reflecting deep disenchantment with what they see their country becoming. Prominent politicians and members of the public, though condemning the bombing, have openly defended militant groups who claim that federal agents' acts in areas in which shoot-outs have occurred are responsible for the unrest. The congressional investigations and criticisms that arose after a federal assault on the Branch Davidian religious cult in Waco, Texas, resulted in the deaths of 28 members, including many children, is possibly seen more as proof of government cover-ups and brutality than as a democratic system correcting itself.

In recent years a get-tough-on-crime mood has been increasingly reflected in public opinion and policy. This is seen in the "three strikes and you're out" sentencing policy (i.e., three arrests for violent or other serious crimes equals a mandatory life sentence), the phenomenal increase in state and federal prisons, the swelling of death row inmate numbers, the growing practice of waiving juvenile offenders to adult courts, and the termination of inmate privileges such as educational grants (for some of these changes, see Issues 6, 7, 11, 13, and 19). However, even the most cynical observers were surprised at the generally widespread support of Singapore's decision in 1994 to cane American teenager Michael Fay for vandalism. Lawmakers in several states such as California, Maryland, and Tennessee immediately called for similar punishment in the United States. Although it is unlikely that caning can be defended legally in the United States, it is ironic that with the doubling of inmate populations and crackdowns on crime and criminals, many serious offenses, especially of a violent nature, continue to rise.

Crime, the fear of it and the anxiety it provokes, seems to permeate all layers of American society and has assumed a permanent place on the cultural landscape. Even when the shared interpretations of crime and its dimensions are based upon inaccurate perceptions (for example, women, children, and the elderly are generally far *less* likely to be homicide victims than young males), the public nonetheless "knows" that there is a serious crime problem eroding communities.

Whether or not criminologists, criminal justice practitioners, and other scholars and writers have anything meaningful to say about the current malaise, it is up to you and your generation to decide.

Meanwhile, it is interesting to note that the public, the police, and sometimes the courts often find scientific explanations threatening. Many police officers feel that criminologists in searching for structural causes of crime attempt to "excuse" delinquents, who the police may feel deserve a "good kick in the ass" along with jail instead of "help" and "treatment." The public and the police currently are more comfortable with explanations of crime that assume individual responsibility for criminal acts. The courts, too, may object to studies that show racial patterns in sentencing and possibly expose prejudice. To judges and other officials, the "causes" of their sentencing and processing of criminals are a result of legal factors, not racial or economic ones.

Thus, as you begin your voyage into academic criminology and criminal justice, you should be aware of the fact that there are many scientific explanations of crime, some of which are politically and even morally threatening to various interest groups. At the same time, though, for you and your generation to have the capacity to help solve the crime problem, you will have to be able to sort out the competing explanations with their respective images of human beings and resulting crime treatment models. To ignore rationally assessing these controversial issues is to risk perpetuating the ignorance and myths that characterize many of the current crime theories and policies—the unanticipated and unintended consequence of which is frequently to magnify the crime problem instead of solving it.

PART 1

Crime: Definitions and Causes

Exactly what is crime, who commits crime, and why, where, when, and how crimes are committed remain core questions for the public, criminal justice practitioners, and scholars alike. It would seem that defining crime, as well as explaining crime, is a straightforward matter. In reality, definitions, explanations, and even assessments of the harm that criminals do is problematic. Some experts, for instance, claim that crime is necessary and functional in all societies. Others say that society is concerned about the wrong kinds of crime. These questions are important for criminologists and policymakers.

- ■ Is Crime Always Functional?
- ■ Is Criminal Behavior Biologically Determined?
- ■ Does Rap Music Contribute to Violent Crime?
- ■ Is Street Crime More Serious than White-Collar Crime?
- ■ Are General Theories of Crime Useful?

ISSUE 1

Is Crime Always Functional?

YES: Emile Durkheim, from *Rules of Sociological Method* (Free Press, 1938)

NO: Daniel Patrick Moynihan, from "Defining Deviancy Down," *The American Scholar* (Winter 1993)

ISSUE SUMMARY

YES: Classic sociologist Emile Durkheim (1858–1917) theorizes that crime exists in all societies because it reaffirms moral boundaries and at times assists needed social changes.

NO: U.S. senator (D-New York) and former Harvard professor Daniel Patrick Moynihan worries that Durkheim's thinking omits the possibility of "too much crime," especially violent crime, so that deviancy as a serious societal problem is not addressed.

What is crime? Who commits it? And why? The importance given to these questions, and their answers, varies among different categories of people, although there is little certainty that any one group's meanings and interpretations are superior to those of another.

For example, younger and older people have different perceptions of crime (older people are more likely to fear crime, even though younger people are far more likely to be victims of crime). Public officials also disagree about crime. During election years many politicians have inflated the number of crimes committed and have attributed crime to forces and influences that only the politicians, if elected, can combat.

Criminological and criminal justice scholars, although generally slightly less shrill and self-serving than politicians in their definitions and explanations of crime, are also very likely to disagree among themselves about what crime is and its causes. Unlike politicians, they do not follow four-year cycles in their crime conceptualizations, but they do reflect trends. For example, 20 years ago most criminologists probably reflected a "liberal ideology" in their crime explanations and suggested treatments. Today some are more likely to reflect an ideologically "conservative" scholarly bias. Radical or Marxist criminologists continue to have a marginal position within the discipline.

The seminal essay by Emile Durkheim, excerpted here, argues that deviancy, including crime, is functional and exists in all societies because it is needed to establish moral boundaries and to distinguish between those who obey and those who disobey society's rules. Although it was written almost 100 years ago, Durkheim's original structural or sociological approach continues to be relied on by criminological and criminal justice scholars.

There are, of course, many variants of the sociological approach to crime, its definitions, and its causes. However, Durkheim's approach is central for many criminologists and especially *structural functionalists*. Structural functionalists attempt to determine what patterns of interaction or structures exist in various groups. They investigate what these patterns contribute to the maintenance of a group and of the society to which the group belongs. In the United States, for example, dating patterns and their relation to marriage are studied. Marriage patterns and their relation to the economy, to religion, and so on are traced. In addition, structural functionalists want to know about the consequences of patterns of behavior for groups, for members of groups, and for society as a whole. Such consequences can be both positive and negative, intentional and unintentional.

Durkheim selects a pattern of behavior, in this case deviant acts, and attempts to determine what it contributes to the maintenance of society and what its consequences might be, including intended and unintended ones. Durkheim asserts that crime is functional (not necessarily good and certainly not to be encouraged) and helps to establish moral boundaries. Deviant acts also provide a sense of propriety and a feeling of righteousness for those who do not commit crimes, as they share sentiments of moral indignation about those who do violate society's norms. Durkheim says that crime also allows for a social change. It prevents a society from having too much rigidity and from becoming too slavish in its obedience to norms.

Politician and sociologist Daniel Patrick Moynihan acknowledges his debt to Durkheim and to sociologist Kai T. Erikson, a follower of some of Durkheim's ideas. But he questions the soundness of Durkheim's contention that crime is functional for societies, especially in the context of violence-ridden 1990s America. Moynihan argues that on the one hand, certain classes of relatively harmless behavior are nowadays being defined as deviant, if not criminal (dysfunctional contraction of moral boundaries). On the other hand, and far more serious to Moynihan, moral boundaries are becoming too elastic as society expands its tolerance for serious crime. He asks, How can deviancy be said to be functional if citizens are no longer shocked by outrageous violence?

As you read the selections by Durkheim and Moynihan, consider examples from your life in which a type of deviancy might be functional, or an act that might have been viewed as criminal a generation ago but that is no longer viewed that way. In addition, what types of acts do you tolerate today that would have been morally outrageous to your grandparents? Have society's legal and ethical boundaries become "too elastic"?

YES   Emile Durkheim

THE NORMAL AND THE PATHOLOGICAL

Crime is present not only in the majority of societies of one particular species but in all societies of all types. There is no society that is not confronted with the problem of criminality. Its form changes; the acts thus characterized are not the same everywhere; but, everywhere and always, there have been men who have behaved in such a way as to draw upon themselves penal repression. If, in proportion as societies pass from the lower to the higher types, the rate of criminality, i.e., the relation between the yearly number of crimes and the population, tended to decline, it might be believed that crime, while still normal, is tending to lose this character of normality. But we have no reason to believe that such a regression is substantiated. Many facts would seem rather to indicate a movement in the opposite direction. From the beginning of the [nineteenth] century, statistics enable us to follow the course of criminality. It has everywhere increased. In France the increase is nearly 300 percent. There is, then, no phenomenon that presents more indisputably all the symptoms of normality, since it appears closely connected with the conditions of all collective life. To make of crime a form of social morbidity would be to admit that morbidity is not something accidental, but, on the contrary, that in certain cases it grows out of the fundamental constitution of the living organism; it would result in wiping out all distinction between the physiological and the pathological. No doubt it is possible that crime itself will have abnormal forms, as, for example, when its rate is unusually high. This excess is, indeed, undoubtedly morbid in nature. What is normal, simply, is the existence of criminality, provided that it attains and does not exceed, for each social type, a certain level, which it is perhaps not impossible to fix in conformity with the preceding rules.[1]

Here we are, then, in the presence of a conclusion in appearance quite paradoxical. Let us make no mistake. To classify crime among the phenomena of normal sociology is not to say merely that it is an inevitable, although regrettable phenomenon, due to the incorrigible wickedness of men; it is to affirm that it is a factor in public health, an integral part of all healthy societies. This result is, at first glance, surprising enough to have puzzled even ourselves for a long time. Once this first surprise has been overcome,

From Emile Durkheim, *Rules of Sociological Method* (Free Press, 1938). Translated by Sarah A. Solovay and John H. Mueller. Edited by George E. G. Catlin. Copyright © 1938 by George E. G. Catlin. Copyright renewed 1966 by Sarah A. Solovay, John H. Mueller, and George E. G. Catlin. Reprinted by permission of The Free Press, an imprint of Simon & Schuster, Inc.

however, it is not difficult to find reasons explaining this normality and at the same time confirming it.

In the first place crime is normal because a society exempt from it is utterly impossible. Crime, we have shown elsewhere, consists of an act that offends certain very strong collective sentiments. In a society in which criminal acts are no longer committed, the sentiments they offend would have to be found without exception in all individual consciousnesses, and they must be found to exist with the same degree as sentiments contrary to them. Assuming that this condition could actually be realized, crime would not thereby disappear; it would only change its form, for the very cause which would thus dry up the sources of criminality would immediately open up new ones.

Indeed, for the collective sentiments which are protected by the penal law of a people at a specified moment of its history to take possession of the public conscience or for them to acquire a stronger hold where they have an insufficient grip, they must acquire an intensity greater than that which they had hitherto had. The community as a whole must experience them more vividly, for it can acquire from no other source the greater force necessary to control these individuals who formerly were the most refractory. For murderers to disappear, the horror of bloodshed must become greater in those social strata from which murderers are recruited; but, first it must become greater throughout the entire society. Moreover, the very absence of crime would directly contribute to produce this horror; because any sentiment seems much more respectable when it is always and uniformly respected.

One easily overlooks the consideration that these strong states of the common consciousness cannot be thus reinforced without reinforcing at the same time the more feeble states, whose violation previously gave birth to mere infraction of convention—since the weaker ones are only the prolongation, the attenuated form, of the stronger. Thus robbery and simple bad taste injure the same single altruistic sentiment, the respect for that which is another's. However, this same sentiment is less grievously offended by bad taste than by robbery; and since, in addition, the average consciousness had not sufficient intensity to react keenly to the bad taste, it is treated with greater tolerance. That is why the person guilty of bad taste is merely blamed, whereas the thief is punished. But, if this sentiment grows stronger, to the point of silencing in all consciousnesses the inclination which disposes man to steal, he will become more sensitive to the offenses which, until then, touched him but lightly. He will react against them, then, with more energy; they will be the object of greater opprobrium, which will transform certain of them from the simple moral faults that they were and give them the quality of crimes. For example, improper contracts, or contracts improperly executed, which only incur public blame or civil damages, will become offenses in law.

Imagine a society of saints, a perfect cloister of exemplary individuals. Crimes, properly so called, will there be unknown; but faults which appear venial to the layman will create there the same scandal that the ordinary offense does in ordinary consciousnesses. If, then, this society has the power to judge and punish, it will define these acts as criminal and will treat them as such. For the same reason, the perfect and upright man judges his smallest failings with a severity that the majority reserve for acts more truly in the nature of an offense. Formerly, acts of violence against persons were more frequent than they are today, because respect for individual dignity was less strong. As this has increased, these crimes have become more rare; and also, many acts violating this sentiment have been introduced into the penal law which were not included there in primitive times.[2]

In order to exhaust all the hypotheses logically possible, it will perhaps be asked why this unanimity does not extend to all collective sentiments without exception. Why should not even the most feeble sentiment gather enough energy to prevent all dissent? The moral consciousness of the society would be present in its entirety in all the individuals, with a vitality sufficient to prevent all acts offending it—the purely conventional faults as well as the crimes. But a uniformity so universal and absolute is utterly impossible; for the immediate physical milieu in which each one of us is placed, the hereditary antecedents, and the social influences vary from one individual to the next, and consequently diversify consciousnesses. It is impossible for all to be alike, if only because each one has his own organism and that these organisms occupy different areas in space. That is why, even among the lower peoples, where individual originality is very little developed, it nevertheless does exist.

Thus, since there cannot be a society in which the individuals do not differ more or less from the collective type, it is also inevitable that, among these divergences, there are some with a criminal character. What confers this character upon them is not the intrinsic quality of a given act but that definition which the collective conscience lends them. If the collective conscience is stronger, if it has enough authority practically to suppress these divergences, it will also be more sensitive, more exacting; and, reacting against the slightest deviations with the energy it otherwise displays only against more considerable infractions, it will attribute to them the same gravity as formerly to crimes. In other words, it will designate them as criminal.

Crime is, then, necessary; it is bound up with fundamental conditions of all social life, and by that very fact it is useful, because these conditions of which it is a part are themselves indispensable to the normal evolution of morality and law.

Indeed, it is no longer possible today to dispute the fact that law and morality vary from one social type to the next, nor that they change within the same type if the conditions of life are modified. But, in order that these transformations may be possible, the collective sentiments at the basis of morality must not be hostile to change, and consequently must have but moderate energy. If they were too strong, they would no longer be plastic. Every pattern is an obstacle to new patterns, to the extent that the first pattern is inflexible. The better a structure is articulated, the more it offers a healthy resistance to all modification; and this is equally true of functional, as of anatomical, organization. If there were no crimes, this condition could not have been fulfilled; for such a hypothesis presupposes that collective sentiments have arrived at a degree of intensity unexampled in history. Nothing is good indefinitely and to an unlimited extent. The authority which the moral conscience enjoys must not be excessive;

otherwise no one would dare criticize it, and it would too easily congeal into an immutable form. To make progress, individual originality must be able to express itself. In order that the originality of the idealist whose dreams transcend this century may find expression, it is necessary that the originality of the criminal, who is below the level of his time, shall also be possible. One does not occur without the other.

Nor is this all. Aside from this indirect utility, it happens that crime itself plays a useful role in this evolution. Crime implies not only that the way remains open to necessary changes but that in certain cases it directly prepares these changes. Where crime exists, collective sentiments are sufficiently flexible to take on a new form, and crime sometimes helps to determine the form they will take. How many times, indeed, it is only an anticipation of future morality—a step toward what will be! According to Athenian law, Socrates was a criminal, and his condemnation was no more than just. However, his crime, namely, the independence of his thought, rendered a service not only to humanity but to his country. It served to prepare a new morality and faith which the Athenians needed, since the traditions by which they had lived until then were no longer in harmony with the current conditions of life. Nor is the case of Socrates unique; it is reproduced periodically in history. It would never have been possible to establish the freedom of thought we now enjoy if the regulations prohibiting it had not been violated before being solemnly abrogated. At that time, however, the violation was a crime, since it was an offense against sentiments still very keen in the average conscience. And yet this crime was useful as a prelude to reforms which daily become more necessary. Liberal philosophy had as its precursors the heretics of all kinds who were justly punished by secular authorities during the entire course of the Middle Ages and until the eve of modern times.

From this point of view the fundamental facts of criminality present themselves to us in an entirely new light. Contrary to current ideas, the criminal no longer seems a totally unsociable being, a sort of parasitic element, a strange and unassimilable body, introduced into the midst of society.[3] On the contrary, he plays a definite role in social life. Crime, for its part, must no longer be conceived as an evil that cannot be too much suppressed. There is no occasion for self-congratulation when the crime rate drops noticeably below the average level, for we may be certain that this apparent progress is associated with some social disorder. Thus, the number of assault cases never falls so low as in times of want.[4] With the drop in the crime rate, and as a reaction to it, comes a revision, or the need of a revision in the theory of punishment. If, indeed, crime is a disease, its punishment is its remedy and cannot be otherwise conceived; thus, all the discussions it arouses bear on the point of determining what the punishment must be in order to fulfil this role of remedy. If crime is not pathological at all, the object of punishment cannot be to cure it, and its true function must be sought elsewhere.

NOTES

1. From the fact that crime is a phenomenon of normal sociology, it does not follow that the criminal is an individual normally constituted from the biological and psychological points of view. The two questions are independent of each other. This independence will be better understood when

we have shown, later on, the difference between psychological and sociological facts.

2. Calumny, insults, slander, fraud, etc.

3. We have ourselves committed the error of speaking thus of the criminal, because of a failure to apply our rule (*Division du travail social*, pp. 395–96).

4. Although crime is a fact of normal sociology, it does not follow that we must not abhor it. Pain itself has nothing desirable about it; the individual dislikes it as society does crime, and yet it is a function of normal physiology. Not only is it necessarily derived from the very constitution of every living organism, but it plays a useful role in life, for which reason it cannot be replaced. It would, then, be a singular distortion of our thought to present it as an apology for crime. We would not even think of protesting against such an interpretation, did we not know to what strange accusations and misunderstandings one exposes oneself when one undertakes to study moral facts objectively and to speak of them in a different language from that of the layman.

NO

Daniel Patrick Moynihan

DEFINING DEVIANCY DOWN

In one of the founding texts of sociology, *The Rules of Sociological Method* (1895), Emile Durkheim set it down that "crime is normal." "It is," he wrote, "completely impossible for any society entirely free of it to exist." By defining what is deviant, we are enabled to know what is not, and hence to live by shared standards.... Durkheim writes:

> From this viewpoint the fundamental facts of criminology appear to us in an entirely new light.... [T]he criminal no longer appears as an utterly unsociable creature, a sort of parasitic element, a foreign, inassimilable body introduced into the bosom of society. He plays a normal role in social life. For its part, crime must no longer be conceived of as an evil which cannot be circumscribed closely enough. Far from there being cause for congratulation when it drops too noticeably below the normal level, this apparent progress assuredly coincides with and is linked to some social disturbance.

Durkheim suggests, for example, that "in times of scarcity" crimes of assault drop off. He does not imply that we ought to approve of crime—"[p]ain has likewise nothing desirable about it"—but we need to understand its function. He saw religion, in the sociologist Randall Collins's terms, as "fundamentally a set of ceremonial actions, assembling the group, heightening its emotions, and focusing its members on symbols of their common belongingness." In this context "a punishment ceremony creates social solidarity."

The matter was pretty much left at that until seventy years later when, in 1965, Kai T. Erikson published *Wayward Puritans*, a study of "crime rates" in the Massachusetts Bay Colony. The plan behind the book, as Erikson put it, was "to test [Durkheim's] notion that the number of deviant offenders a community can afford to recognize is likely to remain stable over time." The notion proved out very well indeed. Despite occasional crime waves, as when itinerant Quakers refused to take off their hats in the presence of magistrates, the amount of deviance in this corner of seventeenth-century New England fitted nicely with the supply of stocks and shipping posts. Erikson remarks:

> It is one of the arguments of the... study that the amount of deviation a community encounters is apt to remain fairly constant over time. To start at the beginning, it is a simple logistic fact that the number of deviancies which come

to a community's attention are limited by the kinds of equipment it uses to detect and handle them, and to that extent the rate of deviation found in a community is a least in part a function of the size and complexity of its social control apparatus. A community's capacity for handling deviance, let us say, can be roughly estimated by counting its prison cells and hospital beds, its policemen and psychiatrists, its courts and clinics. Most communities, it would seem, operate with the expectation that a relatively constant number of control agents is necessary to cope with a relatively constant number of offenders. The amount of men, money, and material assigned by society to "do something" about deviant behavior does not vary appreciably over time, and the implicit logic which governs the community's efforts to man a police force or maintain suitable facilities for the mentally ill seems to be that there is a fairly stable quota of trouble which should be anticipated.

In this sense, the agencies of control often seem to define their job as that of keeping deviance within bounds rather than that of obliterating it altogether. Many judges, for example, assume that severe punishments are a greater deterrent to crime than moderate ones, and so it is important to note that many of them are apt to impose harder penalties when crime seems to be on the increase and more lenient ones when it does not, almost as if the power of the bench were being used to keep the crime rate from getting out of hand.

Erikson was taking issue with what he described as "a dominant strain in sociological thinking" that took for granted that a well-structured society "is somehow designed to prevent deviant behavior from occurring." In both authors, Durkheim and Erikson, there is an undertone that suggests that, with deviancy, as with most social goods, there is the continuing problem of demand exceeding supply. Durkheim invites us to

imagine a society of saints, a perfect cloister of exemplary individuals. Crimes, properly so called, will there be unknown; but faults which appear venial to the layman will create there the same scandal that the ordinary offense does in ordinary consciousness. If, then, this society has the power to judge and punish, it will define these acts as criminal and will treat them as such.

Recall Durkheim's comment that there need be no cause for congratulations should the amount of crime drop "too noticeably below the normal level." It would not appear that Durkheim anywhere contemplates the possibility of too much crime. Clearly his theory would have required him to deplore such a development, but the possibility seems never to have occurred to him.

Erikson, writing much later in the twentieth century, contemplates both possibilities. "Deviant persons can be said to supply needed services to society." There is no doubt a tendency for the supply of any needed thing to run short. But he is consistent. There can, he believes, be *too much* of a good thing. Hence "the number of deviant offenders a community can *afford* to recognize is likely to remain stable over time." [My emphasis]

Social scientists are said to be on the lookout for poor fellows getting a bum rap. But here is a theory that clearly implies that there are circumstances in which society will choose *not* to notice behavior that would be otherwise controlled, or disapproved, or even punished.

It appears to me that this is in fact what we in the United States have been doing of late. I proffer the thesis that, over the past generation, since the time Erikson wrote, the amount of deviant behavior in American society has increased beyond the levels the community can "afford to recognize" and that, accordingly, we have been re-defining deviancy so as to exempt much conduct previously stigmatized, and also quietly raising the "normal" level in categories where behavior is now abnormal by any earlier standard. This redefining has evoked fierce resistance from defenders of "old" standards, and accounts for much of the present "cultural war" such as proclaimed by many at the 1992 Republican National Convention.

Let me, then, offer three categories of redefinition in these regards: the *altruistic*, the *opportunistic*, and the *normalizing*.

The first category, the *altruistic*, may be illustrated by the deinstitutionalization movement within the mental health profession that appeared in the 1950s. The second category, the *opportunistic*, seen in the interest group rewards derived from the acceptance of "alternative" family structures. The third category, the *normalizing*, is to be observed in the growing acceptance of unprecedented levels of violent crime....

Our *normalizing* category most directly corresponds to Erikson's proposition that "the number of deviant offenders a community can afford to recognize is likely to remain stable over time." Here we are dealing with the popular psychological notion of "denial." In 1965, having reached the conclusion that there would be a dramatic increase in single-parent families, I reached the further conclusion that this would in turn lead to a dramatic increase in crime. In an article in *America*, I wrote:

> From the wild Irish slums of the 19th century Eastern seaboard to the riot-torn suburbs of Los Angeles, there is one unmistakable lesson in American history: a community that allows a large number of young men to grow up in broken families, dominated by women, never acquiring any stable relationship to male authority, never acquiring any set of rational expectations about the future—that community asks for and gets chaos. Crime, violence, unrest, unrestrained lashing out at the whole social structure—that is not only to be expected; it is very near to inevitable.

The inevitable, as we now know, has come to pass, but here again our response is curiously passive. Crime is a more or less continuous subject of political pronouncement, and from time to time it will be at or near the top of opinion polls as a matter of public concern. But it never gets much further than that. In the words spoken from the bench, Judge Edwin Torres of the New York State Supreme Court, Twelfth Judicial District, described how "the slaughter of the innocent marches unabated: subway riders, bodega owners, cab drivers, babies; in laundromats, at cash machines, on elevators, in hallways." In personal communication, he writes: "This numbness, this near narcoleptic state can diminish the human condition to the level of combat infantrymen, who, in protracted campaigns, can eat their battlefield rations seated on the bodies of the fallen, friend and foe alike. A society that loses its sense of outrage is doomed to extinction." There is no expectation that this will change, nor any efficacious public insistence that it do so. The crime level has been *normalized*.

Consider the St. Valentine's Day Massacre. In 1929 in Chicago during Prohibition, four gangsters killed seven gangsters on February 14. The nation was shocked. The event became legend. It merits not one but two entries in the *World Book Encyclopedia*. I leave it to others to judge, but it would appear that the society in the 1920s was simply not willing to put up with this degree of deviancy. In the end, the Constitution was amended, and Prohibition, which lay behind so much gangster violence, ended.

In recent years, again in the context of illegal traffic in controlled substances, this form of murder has returned. But it has done so at a level that induces denial. James Q. Wilson comments that Los Angeles has the equivalent of a St. Valentine's Day Massacre every weekend. Even the most ghastly reenactments of such human slaughter produce only moderate responses. On the morning after the close of the Democratic National Convention in New York City in July, there was such an account in the second section of the *New York Times*. It was not a big story; bottom of the page, but with a headline that got your attention. "3 Slain in Bronx Apartment, but a Baby is Saved." A subhead continued: "A mother's last act was to hide her little girl under the bed." The article described a drug execution; the now-routine blindfolds made from duct tape; a man and a woman and a teenager involved. "Each had been shot once in the head." The police had found them a day later. They also found, under a bed, a three-month-old baby, dehydrated but alive. A lieutenant remarked of the mother, "In her last dying act she protected her baby. She probably knew she was going to die, so she stuffed the baby where she knew it would be safe." But the matter was left there. The police would do their best. But the event passed quickly; forgotten by the next day, it will never make *World Book*.

Nor is it likely that any great heed will be paid to an uncanny reenactment of the Prohibition drama a few months later, also in the Bronx. The *Times* story, page B3, reported:

9 Men Posing as Police

Are Indicted in 3 Murders

Drug Dealers Were Kidnapped for Ransom

The *Daily News* story, same day, page 17, made it *four* murders, adding nice details about torture techniques. The gang members posed as federal Drug Enforcement Administration agents, real badges and all. The victims were drug dealers, whose families were uneasy about calling the police. Ransom seems generally to have been set in the $650,000 range. Some paid. Some got it in the back of the head. So it goes.

Yet, violent killings, often random, go on unabated. Peaks continue to attract some notice. But these are peaks above "average" levels that thirty years ago would have been thought epidemic.

LOS ANGELES, AUG. 24. (Reuters) Twenty-two people were killed in Los Angeles over the weekend, the worst period of violence in the city since it was ravaged by riots earlier this year, the police said today.

Twenty-four others were wounded by gunfire or stabbings, including a 19-year old woman in a wheelchair who was shot in the back when she failed to respond to a motorist who asked for directions in south Los Angeles.

["The guy stuck a gun out of the window and just fired at her," said a police spokesman, Lieut. David Rock. The woman was later described as being in stable condition.

Among those who died was an off-duty officer, shot while investigating reports of a prowler in a neighbor's yard, and a Little League baseball coach who had argued with the father of a boy he was coaching.]

The police said at least nine of the deaths were gang-related, including that of a 14-year old girl killed in a fight between rival gangs.

Fifty-one people were killed in three days of rioting that started April 29 after the acquittal of four police officers in the beating of Rodney G. King.

Los Angeles usually has above-average violence during August, but the police were at a loss to explain the sudden rise. On an average weekend in August, 14 fatalities occur.

Not to be outdone, two days later the poor Bronx came up with a near record, as reported in *New York Newsday*:

Armed with 9-mm. pistols, shotguns and M-16 rifles, a group of masked men and women poured out of two vehicles in the South Bronx early yesterday and sprayed a stretch of Longwood Avenue with a fustillade of bullets, injuring 12 people.

A Kai Erikson of the future will surely need to know that the Department of Justice in 1990 found that Americans reported only about 38 percent of all crimes and 48 percent of violent crimes. This, too, can be seen as a means of *normalizing* crime. In much the same way, the vocabulary of crime reporting can be seen to move toward the normal-seeming. A teacher is shot on her way to class. The *Times* subhead reads: "Struck in

the Shoulder in the Year's First Shooting Inside a School." First of the season.

It is too early, however, to know how to regard the arrival of the doctors on the scene declaring crime a "public health emergency." The June 10, 1992, issue of the *Journal of the American Medical Association* was devoted entirely to papers on the subject of violence, principally violence associated with firearms. An editorial in the issue signed by former Surgeon General C. Everett Koop and Dr. George D. Lundberg is entitled: "Violence in America: A Public Health Emergency." Their proposition is admirably succinct.

Regarding violence in our society as purely a sociological matter, or one of law enforcement, has led to unmitigated failure. It is time to test further whether violence can be amenable to medical/public health interventions.

We believe violence in America to be a public health emergency, largely unresponsive to methods thus far used in its control. The solutions are very complex, but possible.

The authors cited the relative success of epidemiologists in gaining some jurisdiction in the area of motor vehicle casualties by re-defining what had been seen as a law enforcement issue into a public health issue. Again, this process began during the Harriman administration in New York in the 1950s. In the 1960s the morbidity and mortality associated with automobile crashes was, it could be argued, a major public health problem; the public health strategy, it could also be argued, brought the problem under a measure of control. Not in "the 1970s and 1980s," as the *Journal of the American Medical Association* would have us think: the federal legislation involved was signed in 1965. Such a strategy would surely produce insights into the control of violence that elude law enforcement professionals, but whether it would change anything is another question.

For some years now I have had legislation in the Senate that would prohibit the manufacture of .25 and .32 caliber bullets. These are the two calibers most typically used with the guns known as Saturday Night Specials. "Guns don't kill people," I argue, "bullets do."

Moreover, we have a two-century supply of handguns but only a four-year supply of ammunition. A public health official would immediately see the logic of trying to control the supply of bullets rather than of guns.

Even so, now that the doctor has come, it is important that criminal violence not be defined down by epidemiologists. Doctors Koop and Lundberg note that in 1990 in the state of Texas "deaths from firearms, for the first time in many decades, surpassed deaths from motor vehicles, by 3,443 to 3,309." A good comparison. And yet keep in mind that the number of motor vehicle deaths, having leveled off since the 1960s, is now pretty well accepted as normal at somewhat less then 50,000 a year, which is somewhat less than the level of the 1960s—the "carnage," as it once was thought to be, is now accepted as normal. This is the price we pay for high-speed transportation: there is a benefit associated with it. But there is no benefit associated with homicide, and no good in getting used to it. Epidemiologists have powerful insights that can contribute to lessening the medical trauma, but they must be wary of normalizing the social pathology that leads to such trauma.

The hope—if there be such—of this essay has been twofold. It is, first, to suggest that the Durkheim constant, as I put it, is maintained by a dynamic process which adjusts upwards and *downwards*. Liberals have traditionally been alert for upward redefining that does injustice to individuals. Conservatives have been correspondingly sensitive to downward redefining that weakens societal standards. Might it not help if we could all agree that there is a dynamic at work here? It is not revealed truth, nor yet a scientifically derived formula. It is simply a pattern we observe in ourselves. Nor is it rigid. There may once have been an unchanging supply of jail cells which more or less determined the number of prisoners. No longer. We are building new prisons at a prodigious rate. Similarly, the executioner is back. There is something of a competition in Congress to think up new offenses for which the death penalty is seemed the only available deterrent. Possibly also modes of execution, as in "fry the kingpins." Even so, we are getting used to a lot of behavior that is not good for us.

As noted earlier, Durkheim states that there is "nothing desirable" about pain. Surely what he meant was that there is nothing pleasurable. Pain, even so, is an indispensable warning signal. But societies under stress, much like individuals, will turn to pain killers of various kinds that end up concealing real damage. There is surely nothing desirable about *this*. If our analysis wins general acceptance, if, for example, more of us came to share Judge Torres's genuine alarm at "the trivialization of the lunatic crime rate" in his city (and mine), we might surprise ourselves how well we respond to the manifest decline of the American civic order. Might.

POSTSCRIPT

Is Crime Always Functional?

One of the first American sociologists to attempt to use the insights of Durkheim was Robert Merton in his classic article "Social Structure and Anomie," *American Sociological Review* (1938). Merton attempted to show the bearing that culturally established goals and legitimate means for achieving them or their absence has upon criminogenic behavior. For an excellent recent consideration of continuities between Merton and Durkheim, see N. Passas, "Continuities in the Anomie Tradition," in F. Adler and W. Laufer, eds., *The Legacy of Anomie Theory* (Transaction Publishers, 1995). In it, Passas briefly challenges Moynihan's contention that Durkheim neglected problems of "too much crime." A provocative interpretation of Durkheim's intellectual demise that is quite different from Moynihan's is C. Sumner's *The Sociology of Deviance: An Obituary* (Continuum, 1994).

Moynihan himself is a well-known "cognitive deviant" or intellectual gadfly. Although his 1965 work *The Negro Family: The Case for National Action* predicted many of the problems of the 1980s and 1990s, liberals and radicals accused him of racism and insensitivity. Moynihan prevailed and remains an important political and intellectual figure. One of his most recent books is *Pandaemonium: Ethnicity in International Politics* (Oxford University Press, 1993).

Note that Moynihan argues roughly from the same theoretic tradition as Durkheim: structural functionalism. Their disagreement centers around when deviancy becomes dysfunctional. A third argument would be that of some Marxists who see crime, including violent crime, as *functional* but only for the *elite* because it deflects society's concerns away from their own corporate crimes. For an outstanding presentation of this view, see J. Reiman's *The Rich Get Richer and the Poor Get Prison: Ideology, Class, and Criminal Justice*, 4th ed. (Allyn & Bacon, 1995).

An excellent work that sets up clearly the distinction within the social sciences between the Marxist perspective and the structural functional perspective and their concomitant approaches to social issues, ranging from accounting for social order to crime and deviance, is *Class and Class Conflict in Industrial Societies* by Ralph Dahrendorf (Stanford University Press, 1959).

Among the many rapidly emerging feminist perspectives that are situated outside of both Durkheim and Marx is *Feminist Perspectives in Criminology* edited by Loraine Gelsthorpe and Allison Morris (Open University Press, 1990). One of the most insightful articles on the conservative-liberal ideological bias within criminal justice is Walter Miller's "Ideology and Criminal Justice Policy," *Journal of Criminal Law and Criminology* (vol. 64, 1973).

ISSUE 2

Is Criminal Behavior Biologically Determined?

YES: C. R. Jeffery, from "Criminology as an Interdisciplinary Behavioral Science," *Criminology* (August 1978)

NO: Tony Platt and Paul Takagi, from "Biosocial Criminology: A Critique," *Crime and Social Justice* (Spring/Summer 1979)

ISSUE SUMMARY

YES: Criminologist C. R. Jeffery argues that physiological and chemical imbalances are frequently precipitants of criminal behavior. Therefore, research into causes and possible cures might be better placed in the hands of medical researchers.

NO: *Crime and Social Justice* editors Tony Platt and Paul Takagi characterize Jeffery's proposals as ridiculous and dangerous and contend that his ideas suffer from a poor understanding of biology, history, and criminology.

The "bad blood" theory of crime has held appeal for both the public and experts alike. What could be more logical than "like father, like son," or "like mother, like daughter"? According to this thinking, criminal traits *must* be genetic since so many criminals have relatives who are also criminals. The origins of crime have been attributed biologically to flawed genes, physiological deficiencies, and other inherited defects. Experts have argued that particular ethnic groups and/or races have a "predominance" of such criminogenic traits.

Proponents of this biological theory, which accounts for both general and criminal behavior, often ignore socioeconomic factors—race, discrimination, and the like; late-nineteenth-century criminologists took for granted that biology contributed to criminal behavior. In the 1920s the field of *eugenics*, or "good genes," became very popular. Within this field it was assumed that some groups were biologically superior to others. Therefore, "imbeciles" and the like ought to be controlled, and "controls" at that time included involuntary sterilization.

The inherent irrationalities and cruelties within the eugenics movement were generally overlooked until the 1940s, when one logical consequence, or so some contended, was manifested in Hitler's Germany and the Nazis' attempt to build a "master race" through the annihilation of the *untermenschen* (inferior people), based on their assumption of Aryan racial superiority.

After the horrors of the Holocaust, explanations of human behavior that drew on genetic origins were labeled racist and have since been unacceptable scientifically and politically to most social scientists until the past 10 years or so.

C. R. Jeffery contends that just as scientists are about to make major breakthroughs in understanding human behavior (including criminal behavior), and possibly changing it through their new understanding, we are returning to an irrational, punitive, "lock them up and hang them high" mentality. For Jeffery, a former president of the American Society of Criminology, the focus should be on the biological, physiological, and medical aspects of human behavior in order to understand better why criminals are as they are.

Continuing a long-standing and acrimonious debate with Jeffery, radical criminologists Tony Platt and Paul Takagi assert that in spite of his claims to being a nonconformist, Jeffery's ideas frequently fit into mainstream criminology. Platt and Takagi have dismissed current criminology, which they argue Jeffery is representative of, as "new realism." In essence, to them this means an applied, atheoretical criminology that supports the state in its efforts of repression. They contend that Jeffery's variant of conservative criminology reflects just such an applied, funded, policy-oriented approach that serves to legitimize state repression of the poor and oppressed.

Platt and Takagi claim that it is not just coincidence that Jeffery's biological criminology control strategies apply only to street criminals, who consist mainly of poor and minority groups, and they argue that he purposely ignores white-collar crimes, organized crimes, and political crimes.

YES

C. R. Jeffery

CRIMINOLOGY AS AN INTERDISCIPLINARY BEHAVIORAL SCIENCE

As Radzinowicz (1977) reminds us, the failures of criminology and criminal justice are found in such facts as (a) we have more people in custody in the United States than any other country reporting, (b) we have more people in custody than at any time in history, (c) we are experiencing a 60%–70% recidivism rate, (d) we have no evidence that punishment and deterrence are solutions to the crime problem, and (e) we have no theory of behavior in criminology that stands close scrutiny.

The growth of a psychological model of treatment a la Freud resulted in the failure of psychology and psychiatry to help the crime problem (Lewis and Balla, 1976). At the same time, there were many violations of the legal rights of those supposedly in treatment (Kittrie, 1971). The merger of law and psychiatry created such tragic problems as exemplified by the Patuxent Institution. When Patuxent was closed in 1976, many criminologists regarded it as the end of a bold experiment in the use of psychology as a rehabilitative tool (American Academy, 1977).

The failure of psychiatry and psychology during the 1920–1950 era is matched by the failure of the sociological model as found in the war against poverty in the 1960 era. The notion that the opportunity structure could be altered through education and job training, thus altering poverty and delinquency, was also a total disaster (Jeffery, 1977; Radzinowicz, 1977). The failure of criminology as a science of the individual offender was matched by its failure as a science of the social offender.

The failure of the treatment model in criminology—that is, the failure of criminology—led to the LEAA[1] program of the 1970s with an emphasis on law and order, punishment, and bigger and better prisons. We are told we cannot know the causes of criminal behavior. We are told we cannot prevent crime. This is the Martinson "nothing works" era. The experts of the 1970s, such as Wilson, Morris, Fogel, and Von Hirsch, are advocating a return to punishment and prisons, to the use of fixed sentences, to sentences based on the crime and not the criminal. This philosophy does not allow for discretion, and it depends on larger police departments and more prisons to solve the crime problem (Jeffery, 1977; Serrill, 1976a). Involuntary treatment is not allowed, but we do allow the executions of criminals or their confinement to snake pits for life. In the 1970s the legal view that man cannot be treated but must be punished comes once again into full bloom.

We have given up the treatment model at a time when the behavioral sciences are about to make a major contribution to our knowledge of human behavior. It is ironic that in the 1970s, when we are returning to an eighteenth-century punishment model of crime control, twenty-first century breakthroughs are occurring in our understanding of human behavior.

A NEW MODEL: BIOSOCIAL CRIMINOLOGY

Elements of the New Model
The new model must contain several basic elements now absent in criminology: (1) It must move from deterrence, punishment, and treatment to *prevention*. (2) It must move from a social to a *physical environment*. (3) It must move from a social to a *biosocial* model of learning.

Crime Prevention
By crime prevention we mean those actions taken before a crime is committed to reduce or eliminate the crime rate. The public health model of medical care is a prevention model. Today medicine is more concerned with the prevention of heart disease and cancer than with the treatment and institutionalization of those already afflicted.

The present criminal justice model waits for the crime to occur before responding. The LEAA and federal government response has been to increase the capacity of the criminal justice system. The more police we have, the more arrests: the more arrests, the more courts and lawyers; the more courts, the more prisons; the more prisons, the more people who will return to prisons.

Behavior is the product of two sets of variables: a physical environment and a physical organism in interaction. Crime prevention must be based on a social ecology which recognizes the interaction of man and environment as complementary physical systems in interactions.

On January 3, 1978, there was a special on medicine in America on NBC news. In this program the Delta Health Center in Mississippi was discussed in detail. The Delta project was established by a community health group at Tufts University to prevent disease among the rural poor of the Delta. They were concerned with such variables as diet, sanitary conditions, food supplies, inoculations, preventive physical care, and preventive medicine in general. The disease rate dropped immediately, and the clinics and hospitals for the sick were almost empty. Then Washington and the federal government decided that monies would not be available for disease control, but only for the treatment of those already diseased. Payments were made for X-rays, surgery, medications, hospital costs, and other expenses connected with being ill. Within a few months the hospitals in the Delta were again filled with sick people, with people standing in long lines all day long in hope of getting some medical care.

The more hospitals and mental institutions we build, the more sick people we have. The more prisons and courts we build, the more criminals we have. We have made the "Delta Plan" national policy.

The Physical Environment

Criminology must move from Sutherland, Shaw, and McKay, from the cultural conflict perspective, to a physical environment perspective (Jeffery, 1976). Crime rates are highly correlated with the physical features of the environment, such as buildings, streets, parks, automobiles, and highways. Most areas of the urban environment are crime-free; crime is very selective in where it occurs. Some blocks have many murders and robberies, others have none. Crime prevention involves the design of physical space. This is a joining of urban design, environmental psychology, and social ecology into a meaningful relationship.

Last year I was in a gymnasium on the Florida State campus to watch a dance review, and my daughter had to use the bathroom facilities which were located in the basement. At that time I remarked how this was a perfect environment for a mugging and/or rape. Within a month a rape occurred there, one of many on the campus. On January 15, 1978 two coeds were murdered and three brutally attacked on the campus. The intruder gained entrance to a sorority house by means of an unlocked door. The police are now spending thousands of dollars and thousands of man-hours on the case, the politicians want to execute the bastard, and yet this predictable response has not helped the dead girls or their families and friends, nor has it reduced the level of hysteria and fear on this campus. As I am writing this article, there is another radio account of an attempted rape on campus over the weekend.

Biosocial Criminology

The new criminology must represent a merging of biology, psychology, and sociology. It must reflect the hierarchies of sciences as found in systems analysis.

Behavior reflects both genetic and environmental variables. The equipotentiality environmentalism of the past must be replaced with a model which clearly recognizes that each and every individual is different genetically (except perhaps for MZ [identical] twins). Williams (1967), a biochemist and past president of the American Chemical Society, argues that only 15% of the population has what is termed normal anatomical features. If our noses varied as much as our hearts and kidneys and hormonal systems, some of us would have noses the size of beans, others would have noses the size of watermelons.

The sociologist/criminologist often assumes that if behavior is learned, then learning in no way involves biology or psychology. This argument ignores the fact that learning is a psychobiological process involving changes in the biochemistry and cell structure of the brain. Learning can only occur if there are physical changes in the brain. The process is best summarized as a system of information flow from environment to organism:

Genetic code $\times$ Environment $=$ Brain code $\times$ Environment $=$ Behavior

Genetic codes and brain codes are of a biochemical nature, involving the biochemical structure of genes and of neural transmission in the brain. The types of behavior (response) exhibited by an organism depends on the nature of the environment (stimulus) and the way in which the stimulus is coded, transmitted, and decoded by the brain and nervous system. This is what is meant by the biological limitations on learning (Jeffery, 1977).

We do not inherit behavior any more than we inherit height or intelligence. We do inherit a capacity for interaction with the environment. Sociopathy and alcoholism are not inherited, but a biochemical preparedness for such behaviors are present in the brain, which, if given a certain type of environment, will produce sociopathy or alcoholism.

The brain contains a center for emotion and motivation, based on pleasure and pain, a center for reason and thought, and a center for the processing of information from the environment. This is almost a Freudian model put within the context of modern psychobiology, as suggested by Pribram and Gill (1976) in their work on the new Freud. The concept of social control is a neglected theory in criminology, although it is to be found in Reckless, Nye, Hirschi, and others. Certainly biosocial learning theory, as I have presented it, is control theory. In summary, what biosocial control theory holds is that behavior is controlled by the brain. Behavior involves biochemical changes in the neurons which then activate muscles and glands. An incoming impulse or experience from the social environment must be encoded, stored, acted upon, and decoded by the brain before it comes out as social behavior. Social behavior, be it conforming or deviant, must go into a brain and come out of a brain. G. H. Mead made this a basic part of his social behaviorism, but this has been totally neglected by the symbolic interactionists.

Emerging Issues in Criminology

If one regards behavior as a product of the interaction of a physical organism with a physical environment, then one must be prepared to find different sorts of things in criminology in the near future, assuming the courage to look for them. Gordon (1976) and Hirschi and Hindeland (1977) have in recent articles suggested a link between low intelligence and delinquency. Mednick and his associates found that 41.7% of the XYY[2] cases identified in Denmark had a history of criminal careers, compared to 9% of the XY population. They also found that the link between XYY and criminality was not aggression and high testosterone but rather low intelligence. They also found that criminals from the XY population had low intelligence. Since genes interact with one another, this suggests the possibility that the Y chromosome is involved in those biochemical processes labeled intelligence (Mednick and Christiansen, 1977).

Intelligence is related to both genetics and environment (Oliverio, 1977; Halsey, 1977; Stine, 1977). This means the impact of poverty and social class on crime rates must be reinterpreted in terms of intelligence, as well as influencing intelligence. To take one example, protein intake is a crucial variable in brain development and thus intelligence. Protein intake is also very dependent on the educational and socioeconomic background of the parents. The link between poverty and crime is intelligence and protein intake, at least as one of several interacting variables.

Criminal and delinquent behaviors have also been related to learning disabilities, hypoglycemia, epilepsy, perceptual difficulties, and sociopathy (Hippchen, 1978; Lewis and Balla, 1976; and Kalita, 1977).

The new model of treatment emerging in biological psychiatry is one involving the biochemistry of the brain (Rosenthal and Kety, 1968; Brady, et al., 1977; Maser and Seligman, 1977; Van Praag and Bruinvels, 1977; Hamburg and Brodie, 1975). The genetic factor in mental disorders is now well recognized. Dopamine and norepinephrine levels in the brain are related to behavioral disorders; the more norepinephrine, the greater the level of excitation, as in schizophrenia; the lower the norepinephrine level, the lower the level of excitation, as in sociopathy and depression.

The use of drugs in the treatment of behavioral disorders has resulted in a dramatic decrease in institutionalization for schizophrenics. Chlorpromazine (thorazine) is the major drug used in the United States (Julien, 1975). Lithium to treat depression has received widespread publicity because of its use in the case of Tony Orlando, the popular television star. Lithium and thorazine act to block the norepinephrine postsynaptic sites, thus reducing the amount of norepinephrine available for the neurochemical transmission of information. As noted, behavior depends on the encoding and decoding of information by the brain.

A Private Criminal Justice System

The future of crime control must depend on the development of a crime prevention program involving both the physical organism and the physical environment. The environmental design aspects of crime control must be addressed within the structure of federal policy concerning housing and urban design. The more crucial issue, as far as implementation of policy is concerned, is at the level of the individual offender.

In order to implement a biosocial approach to crime prevention, we must have early diagnosis and treatment of neurological disorders. This means experimentation and research. It will mean brain scans and blood tests. It will mean tests for learning disabilities and hypoglycemia. All of this involves medical examinations, intrusions into the privacy of the individual, and controversial and experimental surgeries and/or drug therapies. Under such circumstances, and with as much opposition as exists today to the control of human behavior by the state system, it will be difficult if not impossible to turn biomedical research over to a federal agency.

Because of the major failures of the federal government with health, education, and welfare problems, including crime, and because of the great dangers attendant upon the use of behavioral control systems by the state, it is recommended that a private treatment system be set up to parallel or to replace the present criminal justice system. The treatment of behavioral disorders, including those labeled as crime, must be removed *from the political arena*. The lawyer and politician are so committed to a given view of human nature and justice that an impossible gap has been created between the behavioral sciences and the criminal justice system. The administration of LEAA in the Department of Justice is a beautiful example of what happens to crime control policy in the political arena.

A private treatment system would be established at two or three major research centers, hopefully associated with major medical research centers. At such a clinic a complete medical and behavioral history would be taken, including a complete neurological workup as described by Lewis in her book on the New Haven clinic. Treatment would flow from a total assessment of the behavioral state of the individual. Such services would be on a voluntary basis, as it is for cancer, kidney disorders, and heart disease.

Since such clinics would be expensive, private funds must be sought. A new policy must be established wherein public funds could be transferred to such clinics if they accept cases from the current criminal justice system. The state would save a great deal of money by transferring cases to the private sector. This would be established as a part of the existing legal doctrine of "right to treatment." Under such a doctrine no one would be denied needed medical care, including medical attention for brain disorders. Mental illness has been redefined as physical illness by biological psychiatry, and it should have the same legal status as a heart attack or cancer of colon. We worry about not providing counsel for a defendant before we send him to the electric chair or to prison, but we do not show the same amount of concern for placing neurologically disordered people in prison. We worry about the insanity defense and all the nonsense it has produced about behavioral disorders, but we do not ask why the definitions of insanity do not include those found today in biological psychiatry. We would rather put Charles Manson in prison or Gary Gilmore before a firing squad than spend the time and money needed to find out why they become what they became.

It has been proposed for years that a voucher system be created by the state for its educational system. Such a system would allow students to select the elementary or high schools they want to attend, and they would then buy their education. In this way the school becomes directly responsible to the client. In the same way I propose a voucher system for criminal justice.

Each defendant could spend his voucher where he wanted. If he was not helped by the clinic, then the clinic would have failed him. Unsuccessful treatments would be driven out of existence once we make those engaged in treatment responsible for the outcome of the treatment.

It goes without saying that a major research effort is needed to join biology, medicine, psychology, criminology, and criminal law into a new crime prevention model. We must approach the crime problem as a behavioral problem and not as a political problem. We must recognize that the police, courts, and corrections cannot handle a genetic defect, hypoglycemia, or learning disabilities any more than they can handle cancer or heart disease.

I realize that this paper is caught in the winds of an era powered by fixed sentencing and punishment with justice. The denial of the rehabilitative and medical model for criminology is such today that my plea for a behavioral criminology is unlikely to receive a very warm reception. However, this is nothing new to me, and I have patience and faith in history and in the human animal.

For those who insist on being on the stormy water of criminology, as I do, I offer the following:

A Ship in Harbor is Safe
But That is Not What
A Ship is Made For

NOTES

1. Law Enforcement Assistance Administration, an important provision of the Omnibus Crime Control and Safe Streets Act, passed by Congress in 1968 to curb crime. It was heavily criticized for misuse of funds by various police agencies that received LEAA monies.—Ed.

2. Chromosomal abnormality has been researched as a cause of crime, especially crimes of violence. Males are a combination of XY, and females are XX. A male with a surplus chromosome is XYY.—Ed.

REFERENCES

American Academy of Psychiatry and the Law (1977). "Patuxent Institution." Bulletin 5: 116–271.

Bell, G. (1977). "Memorandum for the President: the Law Enforcement Assistance Administration." November 21.

Brady, J. P. (1977). Psychiatry. New York: Spectrum.

Gordon, R. (1976). "Prevalence: the rare datum in delinquency," in M. Klein (ed.) The Juvenile Justice System. Beverly Hills, CA: Sage.

Halsey, A. H. (1977). Heredity and Environment. New York: Free Press.

Hamburg, D. and H. Brodie (1975). American Handbook of Psychiatry, Vol. 6: New Psychiatric Frontiers. New York: Basic Books.

Hippchen, L. (1978). The Ecologic-Biochemical Approaches to Treatment of Delinquents and Criminals. New York: Van Nostrand Reinhold.

Hirschi, T. (1969). The Causes of Delinquency. Berkeley: Univ. of California Press.

—— and M. Hindelang (1977). "Intelligence and delinquency." Amer. Soc. Rev. 42: 571–586. Behav. Scientist 20: 149–174.

Jeffery, C. R. (1977). Crime Prevention Through Environmental Design. Beverly Hills, CA: Sage.

—— (1976). "Criminal behavior and the physical environment." Amer. Behav. Scientist 20: 149–174.

—— (1967). Criminal Responsibility and Mental Disease. Springfield, IL: Thomas.

—— (1965). "Criminal behavior and learning theory." J. of Criminal Law, Criminology, and Police Sci. 56: 294–300.

—— (1956). "The structure of American criminological thinking." J. of Criminal Law, Criminology, and Police Sci. 46: 658–672.

Julien, R. (1975). A Primer of Drug Action. San Francisco: Freeman.

Kitterie, N. (1971). The Right To Be Different. Baltimore: Johns Hopkins Press.

Klein, M., K. Teilmann Styles, S. Lincoln, and Labin-Rosensweig (1976). "The explosion of police diversion programs," in M. Klein (ed.) The Juvenile Justice System. Beverly Hills, CA: Sage.

Klir, G. (1972). Trends in General Systems Theory. New York: John Wiley.

Kuhn, A. (1975). Unified Social Science. Homewood, IL: Dorsey.

Lewis, D. and D. Balla (1976). Delinquency and Psychopathology. New York: Grune & Stratton.

Loehlin, J., G. Lindzey, and J. Spuhler (1975). Race Differences in Intelligence. San Francisco: Freeman.

Maser, J. and M. Seligman (1977). Psychopathology: Experimental Models. San Francisco: Freeman.

Mednick, S. and K. O. Christiansen (1977). Biosocial Bases of Criminal Behavior. New York: Gardner.

Michael, J. and M. J. Adler (1933). Crime, Law and Social Structure. New York: Harcourt, Brace.

Mueller, G. O. W. (1969). Crime, Law and the Scholars. Seattle: Univ. of Washington Press.

Nettler, G. (1978). Explaining Crime. New York: McGraw-Hill.

Newman, G. (1978). The Punishment Response. Philadelphia: Lippincott.

Oliverio, A. (1977). Genetics, Environment, and Intelligence. New York: Elsevier.

Packer, H. L. (1968). The Limits of the Criminal Sanction. Stanford, CA: Stanford Univ. Press.

Pribram, K. and M. Gill (1976). Freud's Project Re-Assessed. New York: Basic Books.

Radzinowicz, L. (1977). The Growth of Crime. New York: Basic Books.

NO
Tony Platt and Paul Takagi

BIOSOCIAL CRIMINOLOGY: A CRITIQUE

The sharp polarization in criminology has recently taken a new twist with the revival of biological and sociobiological theories. There is of course a long and notorious history of biologically-oriented theory in criminology. Though such a perspective had its heyday in the late nineteenth and early twentieth centuries, (Fink, 1962), it has always retained a respectable foothold in academic circles from Ernest Hooton's anthropological treatise on "criminal stock" in the 1930's, to chromosomal research on the XYY syndrome and studies on the relationship between criminal violence and brain damage in the 1960's, to the investigations by Jose Delgado and Ralph Switzgebel into psychosurgery and biotechnology in the 1970's (Moran, 1978). In Europe, the theoretical expression of this "school" is centered around the work of Eysenck in England and Mednick and Christiansen (1977) in Denmark.

Biological research on criminality is increasingly acceptable in the United States. The 1979 Southern Conference on Corrections, for example, included a whole panel on "A Biological Perspective on the Criminal Justice System," as well as other papers on XYY research and a "psychobiological analysis" of Synanon and People's Temple. The "biosocial" perspective on crime has received a new impetus and respectability in this country from the recent writings of C. Ray Jeffery. For a long time a major figure in American criminology, with a prolific list of publications and awards, Jeffery was president of the American Society of Criminology in 1977–78 and he made full use of this platform to advocate the development of a "biosocial criminology."

In his lead article for the special issue of *Criminology*, (devoted to "Criminology: New Concerns and New Directions," 1978), Jeffery argues that a "new criminology," a *biosocial* criminology must be articulated as the first priority of research. As the title of his article indicates, he believes that criminology must be an interdisciplinary behavioral science, representing a merger of biology, psychology and sociology, as well as reflect the hierarchies of sciences as found in "systems analysis."

Critical of the present clamor by the leading "experts" for more prisons and fixed sentences, Jeffery instead calls for a major research effort intended to [bring] biology, medicine, psychology, criminology and criminal law into a

From Tony Platt and Paul Takagi, "Biosocial Criminology: A Critique," *Crime and Social Justice*, vol. 11 (Spring/Summer 1979). Copyright © 1979 by *Crime and Social Justice*, P.O. Box 40601, San Francisco, CA 94140. Reprinted by permission.

new crime control model. Prevention techniques, starting at the prenatal period, not punishment and deterrence after the fact, is Jeffery's departure point. Biosocial criminology, not criminal justice, must be turned to for solutions.

Jeffery argues that since criminality involves behavior, the scientific understanding of "deviance" and "norm violations" first requires the articulation of a basic theory of behavior, in particular learning theory as derived from biology and psychology. He rejects the argument that every individual possesses the same potentiality for learning behavior in a given environment and proposes instead that genetic differences must be recognized: not the social environment, but the physical one is the primary determinant.

In support of this perspective, Jeffery points to recent studies which claim that a linkage exists between low intelligence, the XYY chromosome, and criminality. Hence "the impact of poverty and social class on crime rates must be reinterpreted in terms of intelligence"; and "the link between poverty and crime is intelligence and protein intake, at least as one of several interacting variables." Criminal and delinquent behavior is also said to be related to learning disabilities, hypoglycemia, epilepsy, etc.

While Jeffery's work departs in some important respects from the typical concerns of the new "realists," we think that he shares a great deal of political and scientific unity with his leading criminological colleagues. Despite his self-assessment as a renegade and his relentless and somewhat unique emphasis on *biosocial* criminology, his political ideology is very much in the mainstream of the new conservative tendency.

Jeffery is motivated like the "realists," by the crisis in liberal penology and the ineffectiveness of the criminal justice apparatus in controlling crime. He supports their proposals which call for "target hardening," "defensible space," and the use of experimental psychology to test the deterrent effects of specific punishments. But while he shares the "realists'" emphasis on utilitarian models of penal discipline he argues that crime can only be fully controlled through *preventive strategies*. Jeffery's solution is crime prevention through a combination of environmental design and a "biosocial model of learning." By crime prevention, he says, "we mean those actions taken before a crime is committed to reduce or eliminate the crime rate." The way to control crime is to regulate the environment by the "science and technology of behavior," especially physiology and psychopharmacology (Jeffery, 1971: 184).

Jeffery's model of crime control assumes that people are not purposeful, conscious, and self-actualizing social beings. Since there are no criminals, only criminogenic conditions, people are not accountable or responsible for their actions. Aside from this mechanistic and static view of social relations, Jeffery at least implies that "scientists" are not only capable of being effective "environmental engineers," but also that they are above and beyond the law. With prevention the goal, the adversary system and the niceties of due process are simply abandoned. While we of course recognize that bourgeois justice is an imperfect instrument—to say the least—for protecting the rights of working people, we do however think that it provides some measure of defense against arbitrary actions by the state. Constitutional rights represent hard-won concessions to the working class, as well as a practical weapon to defend political and labor organizing. Under Jeffery's proposal, as under fascism, such rights would apparently not exist.

As we noted earlier, the "realists" focus "almost exclusively on those crimes which are either specific to or concentrated primarily within the working class" (Platt and Takagi, 1977). In this respect, Jeffery is no different: the "crime problem" is synonymous with "street" crime. In his article for *Criminology* and in his address to the ASC, Jeffery simply ignores other kinds of crime. "Environmental engineering," "biosocial criminology," cybernetics, psychopharmacology, etc., are reserved exclusively for working class criminals.

Lumping together "crimes involving morality, political corruption, and financial violations," Jeffery (1971: 221) argues that they are basically different from ordinary criminality because they do not primarily involve harm against individuals. Consequently, "the control of crime in these categories is not possible through the traditional techniques... or through science, technology, and urban design" (Ibid.). While Jeffery believes that some "victimless crimes, especially those involving alcohol and other drugs can be controlled by biochemical or conditioning therapy" (Ibid.: 229), he is not sure that business crime is a legitimate concern of criminology. "Perhaps organized and white-collar crime should be regarded not as problems in criminology but as problems of politics and economics" (Ibid.: 231).

In other words, "street" crime is a behavioral problem which can be disassociated from the political economy, whereas business crime is primarily a political-economic problem which can

not be controlled behaviorally; "street" crime is committed against individuals, whereas business crime is committed against the "general public"; "street" criminals can be controlled by penal sanctions before and after they commit crimes, whereas the "criminal sanction is not the proper one for organized and white-collar crime"; and "street" crime can be controlled by a "merging of biology, psychology, and sociology" (Jeffery, 1978a), but not history, economics and political science. Such is the word magic and definitional gymnastics which Jeffery employs to explain, for example, why corporate criminals should be exempt from biochemical and genetic therapies. In the same way that there is one law (civil) for the bourgeoisie and another (criminal) for the working class, Jeffery similarly organizes his scientific frame of reference on the basis of class distinctions.

There are several different levels at which Jeffery's work can be criticized. We could, for example, hold his version of sociobiology up to close scrutiny and demonstrate his inaccurate understanding of genetics, biology and social psychology. Like other scientists who have ventured outside their fields of expertise to develop a theory of behavior or society, Jeffery demonstrates that a little knowledge can be irresponsible as well as dangerous.

But even if Jeffery had a profound and sophisticated grasp of, for example, genetics, we would find his explanation of criminality no more scientific and no less reactionary. The problem lies not so much in his shoddy scholarship as in the scientific and ideological premises which motivate his scholarship. The theoretical underpinnings of Jeffery's proposals are to be found in his address to the ASC (1978). Here, Jeffery brings to bear an impressive inventory of research findings from biology, psychology, biochemistry and genetics to argue why punishment, as currently practiced, is not a deterrent to crime. Jeffery argues that a theory of punishment must be based upon behavioral genetics and psychobiology.

Jeffery's psychobiology as well as the debate surrounding Edward O. Wilson's sociobiology (1975) deserve close reading and critical analysis. Their concept of a *biosocial man* in a theory of human behavior needs to be assessed on scientific grounds. It would be a serious error to dismiss psychobiology as simply a revival of Lombrosian criminology.

In the specific area of Jeffery's concern, we are told that "each individual is different in terms of brain structure, past experience, genetic inheritance, and present environmental conditions." This is a way of saying that individuals have certain fixed propensities and if we can develop a *formula* which captures these elements, then we can determine that "punishment works under certain conditions for certain individuals" (Jeffery, 1978b: 18). Jeffery suggests that we should look into his big black box to discover the formula.

His empiricist-positivist paradigm takes individuals as the basic units of analysis and abstracts human beings from their social conditions of existence and their dynamic potential for change and development. He paradoxically ignores what we have learned from the physical and biological sciences: the atom, once thought to be eternal and indivisible, has been dissolved and even its constituent particles are not fundamental in any absolute sense. Science teaches us that they too come into being, undergo several transformations, and pass away. Similarly, people are not things, units, or fixed entities, nor can they be summed up in a mechanistic formula and isolated from ongoing social processes.

Jeffery's psychobiology, despite its scientific trappings, is metaphysics. He hypothesizes some *ultimate* constituent in human behavior, be it the gene structure or the brain code. For example, he identifies intelligence as an emerging issue in criminology—as in the proposed link between low intelligence and delinquency, or education and class mediated by intelligence, or between protein intake and brain development. Jeffery, however, fails to recognize that IQ is not an observable *thing*. Intelligence, as measured by paper and pencil tests, is a reification, a mechanistic construct which assumes that cognitive ability is a fixed attribute. Even after everything has been learned about genes and the structure of the brain, bourgeois science will surely fantasize some other mechanism to explain human behavior.

Central to Jeffery's and others' positivist philosophy is a view of science as antithetical to ideology and scientists as non-participants in politics. While many positivists readily concede that this is not a reality, they nevertheless claim that it is both desirable and possible. Like many "traditional" intellectuals, to use Gramsci's term, Jeffery professes to be an independent, value-free criminologist. In fact, one of the issues which motivates his crusading urgency is his concern that criminology has become too politicized in recent years, too tied to governmental interests, and too practically oriented. Criminology, he says, "must shift from a service orientation to a scientifically based *research* orientation."

Jeffery is very much opposed to the government giving millions of dollars to government agencies. This collusion, he says, between government and agencies corrupts effective crime control. Instead, "we would do better granting the money to three or four research centers which would be responsible for a five-to-ten-year research program in crime and criminal justice. The centers would be attached to universities, independent of any governmental agency, and the research emphasis would be determined by the scientists, not by the governmental bureaucracy" (Ibid: 273–74). Aside from the self-serving aspect of this recommendation, why does Jeffery believe that intellectuals would be any less corruptible or contaminated than criminal justice professionals? How could these research centers be "independent" if they are funded by the state at taxpayers' expense?

The theme of intellectual neutrality appears again and again in the writings of the new "realists." It is certainly not monopolized by Jeffery. Donald Cressey, another leading criminologist, criticizes both the "realists" and radicals for allowing ideology and emotion to overwhelm rationality. Cressey (Cressey, 1978) argues that "criminologists should not abandon science to become policy advisers.... Neither should they retreat into broad intellectualizing, accompanied by political proselytizing."

As a model for what criminologists should be doing Cressey refers us to *The New Criminology*, written by Max Schlapp and Edward Smith in 1928. Subtitled *A Consideration of the Chemical Causation of Abnormal Behavior*, this book is representative of the "scientific racism" genre of the 1920's. Schlapp, a professor of neuropathology at the New York Graduate Medical School, and Smith, a mystery writer, proposed that crime is caused by glandular disturbances which result from chemical imbalances in the

blood and lymph of the criminal's mother during pregnancy (Schlapp and Smith, 1928: 103—15).

Schlapp and Smith's policy recommendations include compulsory treatment for defectives, euthanasia, registration of delinquents, sterilization, and forced labor (Ibid.: 271–81). They argue for the inferiority of women and against social equality: "In spite of the howls of the demons, mankind probably must go back to some sort of caste system founded on productiveness, upon ability, upon service to the state" (Ibid: 287).

While Cressey makes it clear that he rejects Schlapp and Smith's glandular theory of criminality, he defends their "new criminology" for being "based on the scientific principle that crime control should depend on knowledge rather than on defense and terror." He admires their "empirical criminology" and their efforts to develop "positive, constructive programs." He urges contemporary criminologists to follow their exemplary scientific methodology and ideological neutrality (Cressey, 1978: 188).

CONCLUSION

The strenuous revival and defense of bourgeois positivism, which characterizes so much of the recent criminological literature, can perhaps be understood as a part of the counter-offensive against radical social science in general and interest in Marxism in particular. It is not by accident that Jeffery's call for an interdisciplinary criminology exempts only those disciplines which are at the heart of Marxism—history, politics and economics. The writings of the "realists," Jeffery's bioscial criminology, and the right-wing tendency among criminologists are not only an indication of the crisis and bankruptcy of liberalism, they also reveal a conscious unwillingness to even consider the scientific merits of Marxism. Whatever the petty internal squabbles among the old boys' club which dominates the American Society of Criminology, they are united in their hostility to historical materialism.

Jeffery's biosocial criminology and the "realists" quest for scientific neutrality are examples of the confusion and utopianism of petty bourgeois intellectuals. Stripped of a veneer of scientific rhetoric, it becomes clear that the "realists" and their allies are not more "independent" than the corporate foundations, government agencies, and boards of trustees who finance and regulate their work. Jeffery and the other leaders of the American Society of Criminology may genuinely believe that they are still sitting on the fence, but we have no doubt that objectively their ideas and practice locate them squarely in right field.

REFERENCES

Ann Arbor Science for the People Collective, 1977. Biology as a Social Weapon. Minneapolis: Burgess Publishing Co.

Bravermann, Harry, 1974. Labor and Monopoly Capital. New York: Monthly Review Press.

Cressey, Donald R., 1978. "Criminological Theory, Social Science, and the Repression of Crime." Criminology 16 (August): 171–91.

Criminology, 1979. Volume 16 (February).

Engels, Frederick, 1972. The Origin of the Family, Private Property and the State. New York: International Publishers.

Fink, Arthur E., 1962. Causes of Crime: Biological Theories in the United States, 1800–1915. New York: A. S. Barnes.

Galliher, John F., 1978. "The Life and Death of Liberal Criminology," Contemporary Crises 2 (July): 245–63.

Harris, Marvin, 1968. The Rise of Anthropological Theory. New York: Thomas Crowell.

Jeffery, C. Ray, 1971. Crime Prevention Through Environmental Design. Beverly Hills: Sage Publications.

1978a "Criminology as an Interdisciplinary Behavioral Science." Criminology 16 (August): 149–69.

1978b "Punishment and Deterrence: A Psychobiological Statement." Unpublished paper presented to annual meeting of American Society of Criminology in Dallas (November).

Mednick, Sarnoff and Karl O. Christiansen, 1977. Biosocial Bases of Criminal Behavior. New York: Gardner Press.

Moran, Richard, 1978. "Biomedical Research and the Politics of Crime Control: A Historical Perspective." Contemporary Crises 2 (July): 335–57.

Platt, Tony and Paul Takagi, 1977. "Intellectuals for Law and Order: A Critique of the New 'Realists.'" Crime and Social Justice 8 (Fall-Winter): 1–16.

Quadagno, Jill S., 1979. "Paradigms in Evolutionary Theory: The Sociobiological Model of Natural Selection." American Sociological Review 44 (February): 100–09.

Rhodes, Robert P., 1977. The Insoluble Problems of Crime. New York: John Wiley.

Sahlins, Marshall, 1977. The Use and Abuse of Biology: An Anthropological Critique of Sociobiology. Ann Arbor: University of Michigan Press.

Schlapp, Max G. and Edward H. Smith, 1928. The New Criminology: A Consideration of the Chemical Causation of Abnormal Behavior. New York: Boni and Liveright.

Schwendinger, Herman and Julia R. Schwendinger, 1974. The Sociologists of the Chair: A Radical Analysis of the Formative Years of North American Sociology (1883–1922). New York: Basic Books.

Society, 1978. Volume 15 (September-October).

The Criminologist, 1979. Volume 3 (January).

Washburn, S. L., 1978. "Animal Behavior and Social Anthropology." Society 15 (September-October).

Wilson, E. O., 1975. Sociobiology: The New Synthesis. Cambridge, Belknap.

Wilson, James Q., 1977. Thinking About Crime. New York: Vintage.

POSTSCRIPT

Is Criminal Behavior Biologically Determined?

One of the most important contributions from a structural/sociological perspective reflected generally in sociology, anthropology, and psychology is that crime is largely *learned* behavior that results from both the cultural environment and individual interactions. Social scientists have dismissed the rough biological explanations of late-nineteenth-century criminologists as they have consistently found that sociocultural factors, such as the values of a particular group, socialization patterns, poverty levels, and population density, are all much better predictors of crime rates than race, ethnicity, and even family membership per se.

Sociobiological criminology is a very emotional issue—one in which remaining neutral is difficult. Thus far, the literature seems conclusive that there are chemical and other physiological differences among individuals and that some crimes of violence are caused by chemical imbalances. In spite of the conclusions found in books such as *Born to Crime: The Genetic Causes of Criminal Behavior* by Lawrence Taylor (Greenwood Press, 1984), there are few feasible policy changes thus far to be made from insights provided by this approach to crime.

By far, the most controversial work in the 1990s pertaining to biology and behavior is R. Herrnstein and C. Murray's *The Bell Curve* (Free Press, 1994). In it, the authors link low IQ with social handicaps resulting in poverty and high crime rates. *The Bell Curve* has touched a raw nerve; hundreds of articles have been written about it, some damning it and some defending the analysis. See a representation of the controversy in *The Bell Curve Debate* edited by R. Jacoby and N. Glauberman (Random House, 1995). Many criminologists dismiss Herrnstein and Murray's arguments by pointing out that (a) their theory says nothing about white-collar crime, only street crime; (b) a genetic approach to crime explanation does not hold up when it is observed that rates within and between groups change dramatically within a generation, hardly reflecting a "genetic shift" in propensity to commit crimes of any type; and (c) the data they based their conclusions on is either inappropriate or false. Regardless, others feel it is functional to get these kinds of issues out in the open.

Recent articles dealing with the general topic of crime and biology include "Biomedical Factors in Crime," by P. Brennan et al., and R. Herrnstein, "Criminogenic Traits," both in *Crime* edited by J. Q. Wilson and J. Petersilia (ICS Press, 1995). Also see T. Regulus, "Race, Class and Sociobiological Perspectives on Crime," in *Ethnicity, Race, and Crime* edited by D. Hawkins (State University of New York Press, 1995).

ISSUE 3

Does Rap Music Contribute to Violent Crime?

YES: Dennis R. Martin, from "The Music of Murder," *ACJS Today* (November/December 1993)

NO: Mark S. Hamm and Jeff Ferrell, from "Rap, Cops, and Crime: Clarifying the 'Cop Killer' Controversy," *ACJS Today* (May/June 1994)

ISSUE SUMMARY

YES: Dennis R. Martin, president of the National Association of Chiefs of Police, theorizes that since "music has the power both to 'soothe the savage beast' and to stir violent emotions," then rising racial tensions and violence can be attributed to rock music's promotion of "vile, deviant, and sociopathic behaviors."

NO: Criminologists Mark S. Hamm and Jeff Ferrell reject Martin's analysis of the relationship between music and violence, charging that the theory is based on racism and ignorance of both music and broader cultural forces.

Traditionally, science has been about ascertaining causal relations between two or more variables. The producing, contributing, influencing, forcing, or cause variable is known as the *independent variable*, symbolized as X. The result, effect, outcome, produced, or caused variable is known as the *dependent variable*, or Y. In the social sciences, independent variables were generally traced to specific social factors (e.g., gender, wealth, education, neighborhood, family, race, religion, age, and so on). Such objective factors predicted or explained individuals' and groups' attitudes and behaviors.

Throughout the twentieth century, however, many philosophers of science have questioned the value and validity of causal analysis. This is especially true in the social sciences, including criminology. Drawing from the sixteenth-century philosopher David Hume, questions are asked about how we can ever "know" causes. Frequently, cause cannot be seen. In addition, in human behavior one must often take into account subjective attitudes, feelings, motivations, and such. There are no isomorphic relationships in criminology as there are in the physical sciences. That is, there are no one-to-one relationships, such as that at sea level, water will freeze at temperatures below 32 degrees or that what goes up on the planet Earth must come down. Instead, there are only contingencies or probabilities, such as that living in an impoverished area and having a parent and several siblings in prison will probably result in a younger brother becoming a criminal as well. In such a situation there may be a *high probability*, but there is hardly a certain link between environment and behavior. Likewise, the child of a college professor will probably become a college student, but not necessarily.

Not only is there no inevitable relation between background factors and outcomes (such as crime), but usually the behavior of people has multiple causes: positive or negative parental role models, area of residency, types of and relations with peers, and so on. Sometimes influencing factors on subsequent behaviors lie dormant or gradually accumulate. Poverty, for instance, can demoralize individuals; coupled with racism, it can lead to low self-esteem and self-destructive behaviors such as alcoholism, partially resulting in medical problems, preventing working when jobs become available, which can lead to reinforcing prejudiced people's negative stereotyping that "poor people do not want to work anyway."

Due to these and other reasons, some social scientists eschew searching for causal relations. Instead, they search for correlations. For instance, when there is a poverty, racism, declining jobs, and so on, there is usually more crime. All of the identified variables would be examined to determine if they correlate with crime and, if so, what type.

Ascertaining the causes of most things, especially human behavior, is remarkably difficult, and many view such a search as a waste of time. When there are widespread perceptions that serious problems are upon us and that things are "out of control" (such as the current views toward violent crime), people demand immediate solutions. Often the entire scientific process and even reason itself are shortcircuited because powerful figures—or those wanting to become powerful—formulate "self-evident" explanations of the problem.

Although scholars trained in scientific methodology can see the fallacies and dangers of glib explanations (and concomitant glib solutions), for others it makes sense to blame some misunderstood phenomenon or even categories of people for societal problems. In its extreme version, this is scapegoating.

But how do we know that blaming something for some undesirable outcome (e.g., crime, violence, and hatred) is empirically inaccurate when causal relations are often so complicated? Could attitudes and actions that appear unfair to some be realistic to others?

In the following selections, Dennis R. Martin provides many examples through history of how music has been linked with violence. He also discusses the marketing of some gangsta rap albums, which, because of their lyrics and strident sounds, generate hostilities toward police officers and others. Mark S. Hamm and Jeff Ferrell dismiss Martin's linking of rap music and violence as bad sociology, bad history, and worse criminology. They attack Martin's historical analysis of current music as being racist because he does not mention the contributions of black musicians. They also maintain that rap musicians do little more than "tell it like it is" in inner cities.

YES

THE MUSIC OF MURDER

In my career in law enforcement I have weathered the rough seas of society, first as a patrol officer, then as a director of police training, shift commander, police chief, and now as the President of the National Association of Chiefs of Police. As tumultuous as contemporary society is, it could not exist without the foundation of law. We Americans are fortunate to live under a government of laws, not of men.

The United States Constitution is a remarkable and unique compact between the government and its people. The First Amendment, in particular, states a once revolutionary concept with great power and simplicity: "Congress shall make no law ... abridging the freedom of speech". In our three-branched system of government, the will of the people is expressed through duly elected legislators in Congress and enforced by an elected executive; the Constitution finds its voice in the judicial branch. What are the people to do when the laws that are meant to ensure their freedom are abused in a manner that erodes the very foundation of law?

Early First Amendment cases sanctioned restrictions on speech where its free exercise created a clear, existing danger, or where a serious evil would result. In two centuries, First Amendment law has evolved to the point where practically the only prohibited speech involves the mention of God in public assemblies.

The misuse of the First Amendment is graphically illustrated in Time-Warner's attempt to insert into the mainstream culture the vile and dangerous lyrics of the Ice-T song entitled *Cop Killer*. The *Body Count* album containing *Cop Killer* was shipped throughout the United States in miniature body bags. Only days before distribution of the album was voluntarily suspended, Time-Warner flooded the record market with a half million copies. The *Cop Killer* song has been implicated in at least two shooting incidents and has inflamed racial tensions in cities across the country. Those who work closely with the families and friends of slain officers, as I do, volunteering for the American Police Hall of Fame and Museum, are outraged by the message of *Cop Killer*. It is an affront to the officers—144 in 1992 alone—who have been killed in

From Dennis R. Martin, "The Music of Murder," *ACJS Today* (November/December 1993). Copyright © 1993, 1996 by The National Association of Chiefs of Police, Inc. Reprinted by permission. All rights reserved.

the line of duty while upholding the laws of our society and protecting all its citizens.

Is it fair to blame a musical composition for the increase in racial tensions and the shooting incidents? Music has the power both to "soothe the savage beast" and to stir violent emotions in man. Music can create an ambiance for gentle romance, or unleash brutal sensuality. It can transcend the material world and make our hearts soar to a realm of spiritual beauty. Yet the trend in American rock music for the last decade has been to promote ever more vile, deviant, and sociopathic behaviors. Recognition, leading to fame and fortune far exceeding merit, propels performers and the industry to attack every shared value that has bound our society together for more than two centuries.

The power that music works on the human mind can be seen throughout history; it has existed in every known society. The Bible contains numerous references to music. Music is found in the ancient tales of China, as well as in the traditions of Native Americans. In the beginning of human history, music stood at the center of life, acting as an intermediary between the natural and supernatural. It was both handmaiden to religion and the cornerstone of education. While there may be music without culture, culture without music is unthinkable.

The earliest music consisted of a vocal melody with rhythmic, regular beats kept by the hands and feet. In time, the pattern of beats evolved into more complicated rhythms. Formal music found its roots in China, beginning around 2000 BC. Ritualistic music emerged around 1900 BC among the Israelites during the reign of the Canaanites. By setting stories and teachings to music, preliterate Hebrew leaders were able to memorize and recite long passages, and to entertain and instruct their audience with greater impact than words alone could convey. One generation handed down to the next Hebrew laws, traditions, and important historic events in song, often accompanied by a simple harp.

Folk music is the basis for formal music. The march, for example, dates from the Roman Empire. Its insistent rhythm, powerful major chords, and strong simple melody were designed to ignite courage in the hearts of those preparing for battle (and, possibly, fear in the enemies' camp).

Led by St. Benedict, the early Christian Church developed the art of choral singing. Over the centuries, sacred choral music has provided us with a view of the world to come. A branch of choral music evolved into opera, a form of music more than once credited with inciting riots. In 1830, the Brussels premiere of *La Muette de Portici* by Daniel Esprit Auber ignited the Belgian independence movement against the Dutch. In 1842, Giuseppe Verdi achieved overnight fame after the debut of his third opera, *Nabucca*, which inspired rioting in Milan. One of the choruses, *Va Pensilero*, so touched the Italian soldiers that it was adopted as the Italian anthem.

Perhaps the greatest composition combining choral and symphonic modes is the *Ninth Symphony* of Beethoven. An utterly revolutionary work, both musically and politically, it proclaims that all men will be brothers when the power of joy resides in their hearts, binding together the fabric of society torn asunder by different cultural mores. This was not a popular sentiment to express in Vienna, the seat of power of the reactionary Austrian Empire.

The twentieth century brought new sounds to America: atonal classical music, the big band era, jazz, and country and western, among others. History recorded two world wars in which Germanic leaders preyed upon human society; the American musical response, spearheaded by George M. Cohan, was proudly defiant, full of valor and resolve. Across the Atlantic, German composer Paul Hindemith was charged with a war crime because his compositions reflected spiritual ideas and themes of renewal. He was barred from performing music.

The 1950s and '60s ushered in a new era for music in which elements of jazz, bluegrass, and country music combined to create early rock and roll. Bill Haley, of Bill Haley and the Comets, holds the distinction of being the country's first composer of rock and roll, in 1955. With the rise of "the King of Rock and Roll," Elvis Presley, rock and roll forever changed the world. For the first time, contemporary music did not reflect the values of society but glamorized rebelliousness and adolescent sexuality.

Later, lyrics of the 1960s and '70s espoused drug abuse. Heavy metal bands of the '70s, '80s, and even into the '90s with bands such as Guns 'N' Roses, promote a panoply of anti-social behaviors and attitudes. The common denominator of their music is that self-gratification and self-expression excuse aggressively violent and sexual behavior inflicted on others.

The new kid on the popular music scene has stretched the fabric of our First Amendment like none before. Rap music is a culmination of the course charted by Elvis Presley. Put his rebellion, swagger, and sexuality into the pressurized cauldron of a black ghetto and the resulting music explodes with rage. It is primitive music—stripped of melodic line and original chord progressions. The beat alone propels the street smart rhyming verse lyrics through topics of deprivation, rebellion, poverty, sex, guns, drug abuse, and AIDS.

Since the Rodney King incident* and the subsequent riots in Los Angeles, the media has contributed to a climate wherein police bashing is socially and politically correct. Ignored is the role police play in safe-guarding the lives and liberties of all law-abiding citizens. The ingrained hatred of police authority, already prevalent in poor urban "hoods" is easily mobilized by the suggestive lyrics of rap.

The framers of the Constitution lived in a world far different from our own. Could they have imagined a day when music would become a tool to destabilize a democratic society by provoking civil unrest, violence, and murder? Yet, the lyrics of rapper Ice-T's *Cop Killer* do precisely that by describing steps to kill a cop. Time-Warner's recording company not only defended the "instructional" song, but marketed the album by shipping it in miniature body bags, complete with a three by four foot poster graphically depicting a cop killer. The company flooded the United States market with an additional half-million copies just prior to Ice-T's announcement that distribution would be suspended voluntarily.

While on patrol in July 1992, two Las Vegas police officers were ambushed

*[This refers to the severe beating of black motorist Rodney King by four white Los Angeles police officers in 1991, which was captured on videotape by a bystander and broadcast on national television. The later acquittal of the officers sparked public outrage and touched off the 1992 Los Angeles riots. —Ed.]

and shot by four juvenile delinquents who boasted that Ice-T's *Cop Killer* gave them a sense of duty and purpose, to get even with "a f—king pig". The juveniles continued to sing its lyrics when apprehended.

Notwithstanding the predictability of police being ambushed after such a rousing call-to-arms, Time-Warner continues to defend the song. In a letter addressed to Chief Gerald S. Arenberg, Executive Director of the National Association of Chiefs of Police, Time-Warner Vice Chairman Martin D. Payson gave his rationale for Warner Bros recording and mass-marketing *Cop Killer*:

> Ice-T is attempting to express the rage and frustration a young black person feels in the face of official brutality and systematic racism. Though the incidents of brutality may be perpetrated by a small number of police, the impact on the black community is intense and widespread. The anger that exists is neither an invention of Ice-T's nor a figment of the creative imagination. It is real and growing. Our job as a society is to address the causes of this anger, not suppress its articulation.

This last sentence is disingenuous at best. Is Time-Warner addressing the causes of black anger, or is it magnifying isolated instances of anger into a fashionable popular sentiment and reaping handsome profits in the process? Would Thomas Jefferson have advocated using the First Amendment as a shield to publish a step-by-step guide on how to ambush and murder the police? The *Body Count* album also contains *Smoked Pork*, a song describing how Ice-T murders two police officers, with dialogue so graphic the lyrics were not printed with the album. Freedom of speech ought to end short of advocating violent physical harm to fellow members of society. If Ice-T had, instead, produced a song describing how to sexually abuse and torture young children, perhaps there would be an appropriate public outcry. A full measure of consideration ought to be given to the lives and welfare of our nation's police officers and their families.

Safety and order in any community requires a partnership of a type that can exist only in a functioning democracy. Public attitudes toward the police may play a part in the frightening rise in crime rates. Disrespect for the law enforcement officer breeds disrespect for the law. A child who is raised to laugh at cops is not likely to grow up with any great respect for the laws that the police enforce. Youthful experimenters, confused by adolescent anxiety, look up to Ice-T as a powerful role model who supports hatred, racism, sexual abuse, and vile crimes that he depicts through dialogue in his lyrics.

Decades of misrepresentation and abuse of law enforcement in entertainment and education have left their mark. Society is now finding that it cannot ridicule the enforcers of the law on one hand and build respect for the law on the other. You cannot separate the two, any more than you can separate education from teachers, justice from judges, and religion from the ministry.

It is a sad irony that, in our society, scandal breeds financial gain. Sales of *Cop Killer*, and the *Body Count* album on which it appears, have soared since law enforcement officers from around the country rallied behind police organizations like the National Association of Chiefs of Police, CLEAT (Combined Law Enforcement Officers of Texas), and the American Federation of Police.

Ice-T is but one rapper encouraging violent reaction to the presence of law enforcement. Rap group Almighty RSO defiantly sings *One in the Chamber*, referring to the bullet they would use to kill a cop. Kool G-Rap and DJ Polo's song *Live and Let Die* describes how G-Rap brutally murders two undercover police officers as he tries to complete a drug deal.

Tragically, this violent message is too often followed by its young audience. On April 11, 1992, Trooper Bill Davidson, formerly with the Texas Department of Public Safety, was killed in cold blood as he approached the driver of a vehicle he had stopped for a defective headlight. The trooper's widow, Linda Davidson, described to me an account of the events surrounding the killing and the impact of this tragedy on the Davidson Family. The teen-age killer, Ronald Howard, explained to law enforcement authorities that he felt hypnotized by the lyrics of six songs by the rap group 2 Pac, from their album 2 *Pacalyypse Now,* which urge the killing of police officers. Howard claims that the lyrical instructions devoured him like an animal, taking control over his subconscious mind and compelling him to kill Trooper Davidson as he approached Howard's vehicle. The rap's influence, however, apparently continues to affect Howard's judgment. Two psy-chiatrists found that the music still affects his psycho-social behavior. In a meeting with Linda Davidson, Howard expressed his desire to completely carry out the rap's instruction by putting away a pig's wife and dusting his family. Howard's reaction has left Linda dumfounded, confused, bewildered, and most of all, angry.

The Davidson's anger is aimed not solely at Howard, but has also expressed itself in a civil lawsuit against Time-Warner, the company that promotes 2 Pac. Again, Time-Warner claims the First Amendment protects its right to promote songs that advocate the killing of police. In preparation for trial, the corporation's lawyers are closely observing the criminal trial of Ron Howard. Given the current state of American law, one can only hope that Time-Warner will tire of the expense of defending state court actions prompted by such lyrics and attacks on police.

With growing lawlessness and violence in our society, every American is at risk of losing his property and his life to criminals. Police officers risk their lives daily to preserve peace and property rights for all Americans. The officers deserve protection from abusive speech when that abuse imperils not only their ability to protect citizens, but also their ability to protect their very lives.

NO

**Mark S. Hamm and
Jeff Ferrell**

RAP, COPS, AND CRIME: CLARIFYING THE "COP KILLER" CONTROVERSY

Perhaps the most enduring feature of the ACJS [Academy of Criminal Justice Sciences] is that it routinely brings practitioners and researchers together in a public forum where they can debate the current state of criminal justice. In this spirit, we offer a counterpoint to the attacks made by Dennis R. Martin, President of the National Association of Chiefs of Police, on rapper Ice-T's song "Cop Killer" and its alleged relationship to violent acts ("The Music of Murder," *ACJS Today*, Nov/Dec 1993).

"COP KILLER" IN CULTURAL CONTEXT

As a starting point, Martin offers a truncated and distorted description of rap's gestation that largely misses the music's social and cultural meanings. To suggest, as does Martin, that rap is "a culmination of the course charted by Elvis Presley" is to commit a double fallacy. First, Martin's characterization of Elvis Presley as the founder of rock 'n' roll, and Bill Haley as "the country's first composer of rock and roll," constitutes a racist and revisionist rock history which curiously excludes Louis Jordan, Chuck Berry, Bo Diddley, and a host of other black musicians and musical traditions which established the essentials of rock 'n' roll. (This sort of myopic ethnic insensitivity echoes in Martin's subsequent claim that rap is "primitive" (!) music.)

Second, Martin compounds these sorts of mistakes by tracing rap's lineage to rock 'n' roll—or, apparently, white Southern rockabilly. Rap artists have in fact explicitly denied this lineage. Early rappers, for example, sang "no more rock 'n' roll," and rappers Public Enemy have attacked Elvis Presley, and his racist attitudes, specifically. To draw a parallel between white Southern rockabilly of the mid-1950's and today's black urban rap is therefore analogous to comparing Joshua's trumpets at the battle of Jericho with the Wagnerian operas of Nazi storm troopers, or to equating the horn-calls which led Caesar's troops into England with the thrash metal of Slaughter and Megadeth absorbed by US Air Force pilots prior to bombing raids during the Persian Gulf War. Other than to say that militaries have routinely used music to lead soldiers into battle, the analogies have little heuristic value. What Martin's analysis lacks is the crucial historical specificity and sociological contextualization, the framework of conceptual clarity and appreciation necessary to explain the complex relationship between particular forms of music, popular culture dynamics, and incidents of violence.

Most commentators, in fact, locate the beginnings of rap (or, more broadly, hip-hop) in the funkadelic period of the mid–late 1970s, a la George Clinton, Parliament, P-Funk, Kurtis Blow, and Grandmaster Flash and the Furious Five. Evolving from this musical base, rap gained its popular appeal in the grim ghettos of New York City—first in the Bronx, and then in Harlem and Brooklyn. Rap caught the sounds of the city, capturing the aggressive boasts and stylized threats of street-tough black males. By the mid-1980s, rap was injected into the American mainstream via Run-D.M.C.'s version of Aerosmith's "Walk this Way" and other cross-over hits. MC Hammer, Tone Loc, Public Enemy, Ice-T, NWA (Niggers with Attitude), De La Soul, and a legion of others soon followed, infusing rap with R and B, jazz, and other influences, and introducing rap to world-wide audiences of all ethnicities.

In ignoring this rich history, Martin misunderstands both the aesthetics and the politics of rap. Martin, for example, leaps to the extraordinary conclusion that rap is a "vile and dangerous" form of cultural expression, a "primitive music" that attacks "every shared value that has bound our society together for more than two-hundred years." From within this sort of uncritical, consensus model of contemporary society, Martin then locates this portentous social threat in a wider cultural crisis. "[T]he trend in American rock music for the last decade," he argues, "has been to promote ever more vile, deviant, and sociopathic behaviors." And if this trend is not reversed, Martin concludes, "every American is at risk of losing his [sic] property and his life to criminals." A careful analysis of rock's lyrical diversity and social effects would, of course, undermine these sorts of hysterical generalizations. A careful analysis of rap music's lyrical content and cultural context likewise reveals a very different social dynamic.

"Message Rap" (or "Gangster Rap," the focus of the remainder of this essay) deals head-on with universal themes of injustice and oppression—themes which have both bound and divided US society from its inception. But at the same time, gangster rap is proudly localized as "ghetto music," thematizing its commitment to the black urban experience. (This is also, by the way, part of what constitutes rap's appeal for millions of middle-class white kids who have never been inside a black ghetto.) In fact, rap focuses on aspects of ghetto life that most adult whites, middle-class blacks, and self-protective police officers and politicians would rather ignore. Rappers record the everyday experiences of pimping, prostitution, child abandonment, AIDS, and drugs (as in Ice-T's *anti*-drug song, "I'm Your Pusher"). Other rappers deal with deeper institutionalized problems such as poverty, racial conflict, revisionist history books, the demand for trivial consumer goods, the exploitation of disenfranchised blacks through military service, and black dislocation from Africa. And still other rap songs lay bare the desperate and often violent nature of ghetto life, as played out in individual and collective fear, sadly misogynistic and homophobic fantasies, street killings, and, significantly, oppressive harassment by police patrols.

These themes are packed in the aesthetic of black ghetto life, an aesthetic which features verbal virtuosity as a powerful symbol in the negotiation of social status. Rap is developed from US and Jamaican verbal street games like "signifying," "the dozens," and "toasting." Rap in turn encases this verbal jousting in the funky beat of rhythms reworked through the formal musical devices which give birth to the rap sound: "sampling," "scratch mixing," and "punch phrasing" (hardly the "primitive" or "stripped" music which Martin describes). The result of this complex artistic process is a sensual, bad-assed gangster who "won't be happy till the dancers are wet, out of control" and wildly "possessed" by the rapper's divine right to rhyme the ironies, ambiguities, and fears of urban ghetto life (Ice-T, "Hit the Deck"). Musically, rap certainly emerges more from studio funk and street poetry than the blues; but like Sonny Boy Williamson, Muddy Waters, Willie Dixon and a host of other great postwar US bluesmen, Ice-T and other rappers twist and shout from within a world of crippling adversity.

"COP KILLER" ON TRIAL

Because he misses this cultural context, it is no surprise that Martin attempts to "kill the messenger" by attacking rap music as itself a social problem. His choicest blows are saved for Ice-T, whose album *Body Count* integrates rap and "metal" styling, and includes a trilogy of protest sirens on police brutality written "for every pig who ever beat a brother down": "Smoked Pork," "Out in the Parking Lot," and "Cop Killer." Martin argues that one of these, "Cop Killer," is a "misuse of the First Amendment" because it has been "implicated in at least two shooting incidents and has inflamed racial tensions in cities across the country."

Here, though, is the available evidence on "Cop Killer": Since its release in early 1992, an unknown number of persons have heard the song. Martin claims that Time-Warner shipped 500,000 copies of *Body Count* upon its *initial* release. This number is important because subsequent pressings of *Body Count* did not contain "Cop Killer." It was pulled by Time-Warner after US Vice-President Dan Quayle, Parents' Music Resource Center spokeswoman and future Vice-Presidential associate Tipper Gore, and a host of influential media personalities and "moral entrepreneurs" leveled a highly organized and well-publicized campaign of "moral panic" against the song (see Becker, 1963; Cohen, 1972).

But our repeated inquiries to Time-Warner revealed that no such sales figures are available. We were told that Ice-T has since left Time-Warner and is now under contract with Profile records. Yet Profile cannot document sales figures for the first *Body Count* album either, claiming that these figures are known only to Ice-T himself—who, despite our attempts to reach him, remains unavailable for comment. We simply don't know—and neither does Martin—how many young Americans have heard "Cop Killer."

Setting all this aside, let's assume that the President of the National Association of Chiefs of Police is correct: some 500,000 persons have heard "Cop Killer" via the music recording industry. Because popular music is a highly contagious commodity (especially among the young), we may cautiously estimate that three times that number have listened to this song (each buyer sharing the song with just two others). From this very conservative estimate, then, it is not unreasonable to conclude that at least 1.5 million young Americans have heard "Cop Killer."

According to Martin, 144 US police officers were killed in the line of duty during 1992. This is indeed a tragic fact, the seriousness of which we do not wish in any way to diminish. But the fact also remains that there is no evidence to show that the perpetrators of these 144 homicides were influenced by "Cop Killer." Martin bases his argument on a brief review of four juveniles arrested in Las Vegas (NV) for wounding two police officers with firearms, allegedly behind the emotional impetus of "Cop Killer." Put another way, while some 1.5 million persons may have listened to this song, only four may have acted on its message. Thankfully, none were successful.

In summary, Martin claims that "Ice-T's Cop Killer [sic] gave [the Las Vegas youths] a sense of duty and purpose, to get even with a f—king pig." If so, we should expect this same "sense of duty and purpose" to influence the behavior of some of the other 1.5 million listeners. Martin, in fact, describes popular music as "a tool to destabilize a democratic society by provoking civil unrest, violence, and murder," and argues that "the lyrics of rapper Ice-T's 'Cop Killer' do precisely that...". He further notes the "predictability of police being ambushed after such a rousing call-to-arms...". But we cannot, in fact, find another "predictable" case. The relationship between listening to "Cop Killer"

and committing subsequent acts of violence appears to more closely resemble a statistical accident than a causal equation. (The probability of attacking a police officer with a loaded firearm after listening to "Cop Killer" is, according to Martin's count, less than 1 in 375,000). Treating this relationship as one of cause and effect therefore not only misrepresents the issues; it intentionally engineers self-serving moral panic around rap music, and obstructs solutions to the sorts of problems which rap portrays.

"COP KILLER," CULTURE, AND CRIME

Ice-T is not the first artist to embed a "cop killer" theme in United States popular culture. This theme has been the subject of countless cinematic and literary works, and has appeared many times before in popular music. During the Great Depression, for example, musicians celebrated Pretty Boy Floyd and his exploits, which included the murder of law enforcement personnel. Similarly, the highly respected fiddler Tommy Jarrell wrote and sang "Policeman," which begins, "Policeman come and I didn't want to go this morning, so I shot him in the head with my 44." But perhaps the best-known case is Eric Clapton's cover version of Bob Marley and the Wailers' "I Shot the Sheriff," which reached the top of the US music charts in the mid-1970s (a feat not approached by Ice-T). "I Shot the Sheriff," though, never suffered the sort of moral and political condemnation leveled at "Cop Killer." How do we account for this difference?

First, "I Shot the Sheriff" was released by a white artist, and in an era when the availability and allure of firearms and ammunition had not reached the saturation point we see today. Clapton's white bread portrayal of an armed and heroic Jamaican "rudeboy" was therefore comfortably abstract and romantic. In contrast, Ice-T's shotgun-toting black US gangster is all too concrete, stripped of romantic pretense and lodged uncomfortably in everyday life. Firearms and ammunition are now prevalent in the black community, and are the leading cause of death among young black males. Within the context of gangster rap, artists like Ice-T portray, with chilling clarity, this tragic obsession with lethal weapons.

Second, the social aesthetic of rap music creates a key cultural and political difference. Because rap constitutes a strident form of cultural combat and critique, it generates in response organized censorship, blacklisting, arrests, and the police-enforced cancellation of concerts. Rap's cultural roots and primary audience are among the impoverished, minority residents of US inner cities. While many of these citizens are unable or unwilling to speak out—for lack of access to cultural channels, for fear of reprisal—rappers invoke a militant black pride, and portray and confront social injustice in ways that threaten the complacent status quo of mainstream society. And as part of this critique, rappers lay bare the daily reality of police violence against minority populations, and remind us how many Rodney Kings haven't made it onto videotape.

For these reasons, Dennis Martin and other defenders of the status quo are loath to acknowledge or appreciate rap on any level—as innovative music, verbal virtuosity, or cultural critique. In fact, their discomfort with rap's politics intertwines with their displeasure over its style and sound. Gangster rap is frequently raunchy, sometimes violent, and often played loud, with a heavy emphasis on the staccato, thumping back beat. By artistic design, it is meant to be "in your face" and threatening. This, in combination with the evocative power of rap's imagery, generates loud and urgent condemnations of rap from those who benefit, directly and indirectly, from contemporary social arrangements. For them, personal offense becomes a measure of political superiority.

Finally, the remarkable attention given to "Cop Killer" reflects a growing concern, among both criminologists and the general public, over the intersections of popular culture and crime. Our own studies in this area have led us to conclude that contemporary music can in some cases be significantly linked to criminality—but only when particular forms of music take on meaning within the dynamics of specific subcultures like neo-Nazi skinheads (Hamm, 1993) or hip-hop graffiti artists (Ferrell, 1993). And in this regard, we end by commending Martin for an important discovery. The fact that four youths may have in fact used the cultural material of "Cop Killer" as an epistemic and aesthetic framework for attacking two police officers is cause for serious criminological concern. And to demonstrate *how* this song may have changed the social and political consciousness of these would-be cop killers, within the dynamics of their own subcultural arrangements, is of paramount importance for understanding the situated social meanings of gangster rap.

But this sort of research requires something more than Martin offers in his essay. It demands an attention to ethnographic particulars, in place of Martin's wide generalizations and blanket condemnations. It calls for a sort of criminological *verstehen*, a willingness to pay careful attention to the lyrics of gangster rap and to the lives of those who listen to it, in place of Martin's dismissive disregard. Ultimately, it requires that criminologists confront and critique the kinds of social injustices which rap exposes, rather than participating, as does Martin, in their perpetuation.

POSTSCRIPT

Does Rap Music Contribute to Violent Crime?

Neither Martin nor Hamm and Ferrell mention that in many ways the twentieth century is relatively unique in that much of the popular music sharply divides generations. In the past, it was rare to think about "old people's music," "teenagers' music," and so on. Today's popular music often functions to divide generations as well as regions, races, and ethnic groups (although within generations, popular music frequently unites younger listeners).

Both sides of this issue are highly selective in their sensitivities. Martin is offended because police are treated with contempt in some rap albums. Hamm and Ferrell are indignant that racism and poverty are a fact of life. Neither side of the controversy considers the fact that rates of violence and homicide committed by young blacks against other blacks is skyrocketing. Might teenagers in inner cities listening to messages of violence turn heightened hostilities on each other instead of the police or whites? The alleged criminal acts of performers such as Snoop Doggy Dogg, Tupack Shakur, Dr. Dre, and others involved black, not white, victims (see M. Dyson, "Gansta Rappers Speak for a Generation," *Baltimore Sun*, June 23, 1995).

Many black religious and political leaders, writers, and columnists would be amused at criminologists' characterizing rappers as Robin Hoods, romantic messengers, voices of the oppressed, and such. Hamm and Ferrell's discrediting of Martin for characterizing gansta rap as primitive might bring belly laughs to blacks who in their speeches and columns refer to such music as trash or worse. Some blacks resent what they see as whites' justifying rap lyrics because they allegedly speak for poor (or any) blacks.

For a follow-up of this debate, see L. Crzycki, "It's Not That Simple!" *ACJS Today* (September/October 1994) and W. Hall, "We Should Not Tolerate Lyrics That Insult Women," *Baltimore Sun* (May 18, 1995). For some balanced accounts of rap music, see F. Krohn, "Contemporary Urban Music: Controversial Messages in Rap Music and Hip Hop," *ETC* (Summer 1995); E. Blair, "Commercialization of the Rap Music Youth Subculture," *Journal of Popular Culture* (Winter 1993); and T. Dodge, "From Spirituals to Gospel Rap," *Serials Review* (vol. 20, no. 4, 1994). For a broader perspective on changing music, see *Hole in Our Soul: The Loss of Meaning in American Popular Music* by M. Bayles (Free Press, 1994). Also see the technical discussion *Spectacular Vernaculars: Hip-Hop and the Politics of Postmodernism* by R. Porter (State University of New York Press, 1995). For a contrast between two recent hit songs, listen to Adina Howard's "Freak Like Me" and "Why We Sing" by Kirk Franklin and the Family.

ISSUE 4

Is Street Crime More Serious than White-Collar Crime?

YES: James Q. Wilson and Richard J. Herrnstein, from *Crime and Human Nature* (Simon & Schuster, 1985)

NO: Jeffrey Reiman, from *The Rich Get Richer and the Poor Get Prison: Ideology, Class, and Criminal Justice,* 4th ed. (Allyn & Bacon, 1995)

ISSUE SUMMARY

YES: Professor of management and public policy James Q. Wilson and psychologist Richard J. Herrnstein argue that the focus of crime study ought to be on persons who "hit, rape, murder, steal, and threaten."

NO: Professor of philosophy Jeffrey Reiman contends that a focus on street crimes is little more than a cover-up for more serious crimes such as pollution, medical malpractice, and dangerous working conditions that go uncorrected.

By now, from your course and the readings in this volume, it is probably clear to you that scholars and the general public differ intellectually, ideologically, and politically in their definitions of crime as well as with regard to why it exists. Liberal, conservative, or radical ideologies are likely to generate different definitions and explanations of crime.

One aspect of American society is its extremely heavy emphasis on economic success. Apparently, for many who desire the material benefits that "the haves" take for granted but who are thwarted by lack of training or skills or by discrimination, one recourse is to engage in predatory street crimes. Others are able to succeed financially because they are taught how to and are fully allowed to participate: they can attend good schools, join a solid corporation, and work their way up the ladder. Probably very few business executive types would dream of holding up someone, breaking into a house, or attacking someone in a rage.

Yet in certain companies, the pressure to succeed, to keep corporate profits up, and to fulfill the expectations of managers and administrators drives many to commit white-collar crimes. No one knows for sure how many street crimes occur each day (many are not reported). Nor do we know how many white-collar crimes occur each day. The latter are much more likely to be carefully hidden and their consequences delayed for months or even years. Moreover, white-collar crimes are far more likely to be dismissed as "just another shrewd business practice by an ambitious executive in order to keep ahead of competitors." Most of us never directly see the results of white-collar crimes, nor do we know many people who are visibly harmed by them. By contrast, many of us have been victims of street crimes or know such victims. The results of a direct physical assault or the fear of discovering a burglarized home or a stolen car are relatively easy to observe in a victim of these crimes.

But how should we view those who shiver in the cold because their utility bills were hiked illegally, forcing them to keep their thermostats under 60 degrees? Or those robbed of health because of lung infections contracted while they worked in unsafe mines or around unsafe chemicals? Are they usually thought of as the victims of criminals? Are people who are killed in traffic accidents because their automobiles left the factory in unsafe condition —with the factory's full knowledge and approval—thought of as murder victims?

Frequently, both the general public and criminologists concentrate on street crimes, their perpetrators and victims, while ignoring white-collar crimes. But beginning with the seminal work of Edwin Sutherland, *White Collar Crime*, some criminologists have demonstrated concern with this form of violation.

In spite of the fact that, in general, white-collar crime receives less attention and less serious attention than street crime, several white-collar criminals have in recent years been the focus of extensive media coverage. Yet in almost each case, the criminals have been viewed as isolated deviants who just happened to engage in wrongdoing. Neither the organizations for which they worked nor the broader corporate system and the values it promotes came under much scrutiny by the public. Among the more widely known corporate criminals of the past few years are Ivan Boesky and Michael Milken (now out of prison after serving 22 months for a variety of securities law violations).

White-collar crimes are currently being investigated at the top levels of government. For example, part of the investigation into the Whitewater Development Company, an Arkansas company linked to a failed savings and loan institution with which President Bill Clinton and Hillary Clinton were involved (when he was still governor of Arkansas), has resulted in the imprisonment of some close friends of the Clintons. A congressional committee is now looking into possible wrongdoing on the part of Hillary Clinton herself, as well as the Arkansas law firm she was a part of. In spite of this and other sensational cases and allegations of corruption, corporate misdealings, and white-collar crime, the focus in the general public's perception and the media remains on street criminals. Is this fair?

As you study the position of James Q. Wilson and Richard J. Herrnstein and that of Jeffrey Reiman, notice that it remains problematic as to not only what crime is and what its most adequate scientific explanations are but also which crimes are the most harmful and dangerous to members of society.

YES

James Q. Wilson and
Richard J. Herrnstein

CRIME AND HUMAN NATURE

CRIME AND ITS EXPLANATION

Predatory street crimes are most commonly committed by young males. Violent crimes are more common in big cities than in small ones. High rates of criminality tend to run in families. The persons who frequently commit the most serious crimes typically begin their criminal careers at a quite young age. Persons who turn out to be criminals usually do not do very well in school. Young men who drive recklessly and have many accidents tend to be similar to those who commit crimes. Programs designed to rehabilitate high-rate offenders have not been shown to have much success, and those programs that do manage to reduce criminality among certain kinds of offenders often increase it among others.

These facts about crime—some well known, some not so well known—are not merely statements about traits that happen occasionally, or in some places but not others, to describe criminals. They are statements that, insofar as we can tell, are pretty much true everywhere. They are statements, in short, about human nature as much as about crime.

All serious political and moral philosophy, and thus any serious social inquiry, must begin with an understanding of human nature. Though society and its institutions shape man, man's nature sets limits on the kinds of societies we can have. Cicero said that the nature of law must be founded on the nature of man (*a natura hominis discenda est natura juris*).... We could have chosen to understand human nature by studying work, or sexuality, or political activity; we chose instead to approach it through the study of crime, in part out of curiosity and in part because crime, more dramatically than other forms of behavior, exposes the connection between individual dispositions and the social order.

The problem of social order is fundamental: How can mankind live together in reasonable order? Every society has, by definition, solved that problem to some degree, but not all have done so with equal success or without paying a high cost in other things—such as liberty—that we also value. If we believe

From James Q. Wilson and Richard J. Herrnstein, *Crime and Human Nature* (Simon & Schuster, 1985). Copyright © 1985 by James Q. Wilson and Richard J. Herrnstein. Reprinted by permission of Simon & Schuster, Inc.

that man is naturally good, we will expect that the problem of order can be rather easily managed; if we believe him to be naturally wicked, we will expect the provision of order to require extraordinary measures; if we believe his nature to be infinitely plastic, we will think the problem of order can be solved entirely by plan and that we may pick and choose freely among all possible plans. Since every known society has experienced crime, no society has ever entirely solved the problem of order. The fact that crime is universal may suggest that man's nature is not infinitely malleable, though some people never cease searching for an anvil and hammer sufficient to bend it to their will.

Some societies seem better able than others to sustain order without making unacceptable sacrifices in personal freedom, and in every society the level of order is greater at some times than at others. These systematic and oft-remarked differences in the level of crime across time and place suggest that there is something worth explaining. But to find that explanation, one cannot begin with the society as a whole or its historical context, for what needs explanation is not the behavior of "society" but the behavior of individuals making up a society. Our intention is to offer as comprehensive an explanation as we can manage of why some individuals are more likely than others to commit crimes.

THE PROBLEM OF EXPLANATION

That intention is not easily realized, for at least three reasons. First, crime is neither easily observed nor readily measured. . . . [T]here is no way of knowing the true crime rate of a society or even of a given individual. Any explanation of why individuals differ in their law-abidingness may well founder on measurement errors. If we show that Tom, who we think has committed a crime, differs in certain interesting ways from Dick, who we think has not, when in fact both Tom and Dick have committed a crime, then the "explanation" is meaningless.

Second, crime is very common, especially among males. Using interviews and questionnaires, scholars have discovered that the majority of all young males have broken the law at least once by a relatively early age. By examining the police records of boys of a given age living in one place, criminologists have learned that a surprisingly large fraction of all males will be arrested at least once in their lives for something more serious than a traffic infraction. Marvin Wolfgang found that 35 percent of all the males born in Philadelphia in 1945 and living there between the ages of ten and eighteen had been arrested at least once by their eighteenth birthday.[1] Nor is this a peculiarly American phenomenon. Various surveys have found that the proportion of British males who had been convicted in court before their twenty-first birthday ranged from 15 percent in the nation as a whole to 31 percent for a group of boys raised in London. David Farrington estimates that 44 percent of all the males in "law-abiding" Britain will be arrested sometime in their lives.[2] If committing a crime at least once is so commonplace, then it is quite likely that there will be few, if any, large differences between those who never break the law and those who break it at least once—even if we had certain knowledge of which was which. Chance events as much as or more than individual predispositions will determine who commits a crime.

Third, the word "crime" can be applied to such varied behavior that it is not clear that it is a meaningful category of analysis. Stealing a comic book, punching a friend, cheating on a tax return, murdering a wife, robbing a bank, bribing a politician, hijacking an airplane—these and countless other acts are all crimes. Crime is as broad a category as disease, and perhaps as useless. To explain why one person has ever committed a crime and another has not may be as pointless as explaining why one person has ever gotten sick and another has not. We are not convinced that "crime" is so broad a category as to be absolutely meaningless—surely it is not irrelevant that crime is that form of behavior that is against the law—but we do acknowledge that it is difficult to provide a true and interesting explanation for actions that differ so much in their legal and subjective meanings.

To deal with these three difficulties, we propose to confine ourselves, for the most part, to explaining why some persons commit serious crimes at a high rate and others do not. By looking mainly at serious crimes, we escape the problem of comparing persons who park by a fire hydrant to persons who rob banks. By focusing on high-rate offenders, we do not need to distinguish between those who never break the law and those who (for perhaps chance reasons) break it only once or twice. And if we assume (as we do) that our criminal statistics are usually good enough to identify persons who commit a lot of crimes even if these data are poor at identifying accurately those who commit only one or two, then we can be less concerned with measurement errors.

THE MEANING OF CRIME

A crime is any act committed in violation of a law that prohibits it and authorizes punishment for its commission. If we propose to confine our attention chiefly to persons who commit serious crimes at high rates, then we must specify what we mean by "serious." The arguments we shall make and the evidence we shall cite ... will chiefly refer to aggressive, violent, or larcenous behavior; they will be, for the most part, about persons who hit, rape, murder, steal, and threaten.

In part, this limited focus is an unfortunate accident: We report only what others have studied, and by and large they have studied the causes of what we call predatory street crime. We would like to draw on research into a wider variety of law-violating behavior—embezzlement, sexual deviance, bribery, extortion, fraud—but very little such research exists.

But there is an advantage to this emphasis on predatory crime. Such behavior, except when justified by particular, well-understood circumstances (such as war), is condemned, in all societies and in all historical periods, by ancient tradition, moral sentiments, and formal law. Graeme Newman ... interviewed people in six nations (India, Indonesia, Iran, Italy, the United States, and Yugoslavia) about their attitudes toward a variety of behaviors and concluded that there is a high—indeed, virtually universal—agreement that certain of these behaviors were wrong and should be prohibited by law.[3] Robbery, stealing, incest, and factory pollution were condemned by overwhelming majorities in every society; by contrast, abortion and homosexuality, among other acts, were thought to be crimes in some places but not in others. Interestingly, the characteristics of the individual respondents in these countries —their age, sex, education, social class— did not make much difference in what they thought should be treated as crimes. Newman's finding merely reinforces a fact long understood by anthropologists: Certain acts are regarded as wrong by every society, preliterate as well as literate; that among these "universal crimes" are murder, theft, robbery, and incest.[4]

Moreover, people in different societies rate the seriousness of offenses, especially the universal crimes, in about the same way. Thorsten Sellin and Marvin E. Wolfgang developed a scale to measure the relative gravity of 141 separate offenses. This scale has been found to be remarkably stable, producing similar rankings among both American citizens and prison inmates,[5] as well as among Canadians,[6] Puerto Ricans,[7] Taiwanese,[8] and Belgian Congolese.[9]

By drawing on empirical studies of behaviors that are universally regarded as wrong and similarly ranked as to gravity, we can be confident that we are in fact theorizing about *crime* and human nature and not about actions that people may or may not think are wrong. If the studies to which we refer were to include commercial price-fixing, political corruption, or industrial monopolization, we would have to deal with the fact that in many countries these actions are not regarded as criminal at all. If an American business executive were to bring all of the nation's chemical industries under his control, he would be indicted for having formed a monopoly; a British business executive who did the same thing might be elevated to the peerage for having created a valuable industrial empire. Similarly, by omitting studies of sexual deviance (except forcible rape), we avoid modifying our theory to take into account changing social standards as to the wrongness of these acts and the legal culpability of their perpetrators. In short, we seek... to explain why some persons are more likely than others to do things that all societies condemn and punish.

To state the same thing a bit differently, we will be concerned more with criminality than with crime. Travis Hirschi and Michael Gottfredson have explained this important distinction as follows. *Crimes* are short-term, circumscribed events that result from the (perhaps fortuitous) coming together of an individual having certain characteristics and an opportunity having certain (immediate and deferred) costs and benefits.... *Criminality* refers to "stable differences across individuals in the propensity to commit criminal (or equivalent) acts."[10] The "equivalent" acts will be those that satisfy, perhaps in entirely legal ways, the same traits and predispositions that lead, in other circumstances, to crime. For example, a male who is very impulsive and so cannot resist temptation may, depending on circumstances, take toys from his playmates, money from his mother, billfolds from strangers, stamps from the office, liquor in the morning, extra chocolate cake at dinner time, and a nap whenever he feels like it. Some of these actions break the law, some do not.

THE CATEGORIES OF EXPLANATION

Because we state that we intend to emphasize individual differences in behavior or predisposition, some readers may feel that we are shaping the argument in an improper manner. These critics believe that one can explain crime only by beginning with the society in which it is found. Emile Durkheim wrote: "We must, then, seek the explanation of social life in the nature of society itself."[11] Or, put another way, the whole is more than the sum of its parts. We do not deny that social arrangements and institutions, and the ancient customs that result from living and working together, affect behavior, often profoundly. But no explanation of social life explains anything until it explains individual behavior. Whatever significance we attach to ethnicity, social class, national character, the opinions of peers, or the messages of the mass media, the only test of their explanatory power is their ability to account for differences in how individuals, or groups of individuals, behave.

Explaining individual differences is an enterprise much resisted by some scholars. To them, this activity implies reducing everything to psychology, often referred to as "mere psychology." David J. Bordua, a sociologist, has pointed out the bias that can result from an excessive preference for social explanations over psychological ones.[12] Many criminologists, he comments, will observe a boy who becomes delinquent after being humiliated by his teacher or fired by his employer, and will conclude that his delinquency is explained by his "social class." But if the boy becomes delinquent after having been humiliated by his father or spurned by his girl friend, these scholars will deny that these events are explanations because they are "psychological." Teachers and employers are agents of the class structure, fathers and girl friends are not; therefore, the behavior of teachers and employers must be more important.

We believe that one can supply an explanation of criminality—and more important, of law-abidingness—that begins with the individual in, or even before, infancy and that takes into account the impact on him of subsequent experiences in the family, the school, the neighborhood, the labor market, the criminal justice system, and society at large. Yet even readers who accept this plan of inquiry as reasonable may still doubt its importance. To some, explaining crime is unnecessary because they think the explanation is already known; to others, it is impossible, since they think it unknowable.

Having taught a course on the causes of crime, and having spoken to many friends about our research, we have become acutely aware that there is scarcely any topic—except, perhaps, what is wrong with the Boston Red Sox or the Chicago Cubs—on which people have more confident opinions. Crime is caused, we are told, by the baby boom, permissive parents, brutal parents, incompetent schools, racial discrimination, lenient judges, the decline of organized religion, televised violence, drug addiction, ghetto unemployment, or the capitalist system. We note certain patterns in the proffered explanations. Our tough-minded friends blame crime on the failings of the criminal justice system; our tender-minded ones blame it on the failings of society.

We have no *a priori* quarrel with any of these explanations, but we wonder whether all can be true, or true to the same degree. The baby boom may help explain why crime rose in the 1960s and 1970s, but it cannot explain why some members of that boom became criminals and others did not. It is hard to imagine that both permissive and brutal parents produce the same kind of criminals, though it is conceivable that each may contribute to a different kind of criminality. Many children may attend bad schools, but only a small minority become serious criminals. And in any case, there is no agreement as to what constitutes an incompetent school. Is it an overly strict one that "labels" mischievous children as delinquents, or is it an overly lax one that allows normal mischief to degenerate into true delinquency? Does broadcast violence include a football or hockey game, or only a detective story in which somebody shoots somebody else? Economic conditions may affect crime, but since crime rates were lower in the Great Depression than during the prosperous years of the 1960s, the effect is, at best, not obvious or simple. The sentences given by judges may affect the crime rate, but we are struck by the fact that the most serious criminals begin offending at a very early age, long before they encounter, or probably even hear of, judges, whereas those who do not commit their first crime until they are adults (when, presumably, they have some knowledge of law and the courts) are the least likely to have a long or active criminal career. Racism and capitalism may contribute to crime, but the connection must be rather complicated, since crime has risen in the United States (and other nations) most rapidly during recent times, when we have surely become less racist and (given the growth of governmental controls on business) less capitalist. In any event, high crime rates can be found in socialist as well as capitalist nations, and some capitalist nations, such as Japan and Switzerland, have very little crime. In view of all this, some sorting out of these explanations might be useful.

But when we discuss our aims with scholars who study crime, we hear something quite different. There is no well-accepted theory of the causes of crime, we are told, and it is unlikely that one can be constructed. Many explanations have been advanced, but all have been criticized. What is most needed is more research, not better theories. Any theory specific enough to be testable will not explain very much, whereas any theory broad enough to explain a great deal will not be testable. It is only because they are friends that some of our colleagues refrain from muttering about fools rushing in where wise men, if not angels, fear to tread. . . .

But there is one version of the claim that explaining crime is impossible to which we wish to take immediate exception. That is the view, heard most frequently from those involved with criminals on a case-by-case basis (probation officers and therapists, for example), that the causes of crime are unique to the individual criminal. Thus, one cannot generalize about crime because each criminal is different. Now, in one sense that argument is true—no two offenders are exactly alike. But we are struck by the fact that there are certain obvious patterns to criminality, suggesting that something more than random individual differences is at work. We think these obvious patterns, if nothing else, can be explained.

PATTERNS IN CRIMINALITY

Crime is an activity disproportionately carried out by young men living in large cities. There are old criminals, and female ones, and rural and small-town ones, but, to a much greater degree than would be expected by chance, criminals are young urban males. This is true, insofar as we can tell, in every society that keeps any reasonable criminal statistics.[13] These facts are obvious to all, but sometimes their significance is overlooked. Much time and effort may be expended in trying to discover whether children from broken homes are more likely to be criminals than those from intact ones, or whether children who watch television a lot are more likely to be aggressive than those who watch it less. These are interesting questions, and we shall have something to say about them, but even if they are answered satisfactorily, we will have explained rather little about the major differences in criminality. Most children raised in broken homes do not become serious offenders; roughly half of such children are girls, and... females are often only one-tenth as likely as males to commit crimes. Crime existed abundantly long before the advent of television and would continue long after any hint of violence was expunged from TV programs. Any worthwhile explanation of crime must account for the major, persistent differences in criminality.

The fact that these regularities exist suggests that it is not impossible, in principle, to provide a coherent explanation of crime. It is not like trying to explain why some people prefer vanilla ice cream and others chocolate. And as we shall see... there are other regularities in criminality beyond those associated with age, sex, and place. There is mounting evidence that, on the average, offenders differ from nonoffenders in physique, intelligence, and personality. Some of these differences may not themselves be a cause of crime but only a visible indicator of some other factor that does contribute to crime.... [W]e shall suggest that a certain physique is related to criminality, not because it causes people to break the law, but because a particular body type is associated with temperamental traits that predispose people to offending. Other individual differences, such as in personality, may directly contribute to criminality.

There are two apparent patterns in criminality that we have yet to mention, though they are no doubt uppermost in the minds of many readers—class and race. To many people, it is obvious that differences in social class, however defined, are strongly associated with lawbreaking. The poor, the unemployed, or the "underclass" are more likely than the well-to-do, the employed, or the "respectable poor" to commit certain kinds of crimes. We are reluctant, however, at least at the outset, to use class as a major category of explanations of differences in criminality for two reasons.

First, scholars who readily agree on the importance of age, sex, and place as factors related to crime disagree vigorously as to whether social class, however defined, is associated with crime. Their dispute may strike readers who have worked hard to move out of slums and into middle-class suburbs as rather bizarre; can anyone seriously doubt that better-off neighborhoods are safer than poorer ones? As John Braithwaite has remarked, "It is hardly plausible that one can totally explain away the higher risks of being mugged and raped in lower class areas as a consequence of the activities of middle class people who come into the area to perpetrate such acts."[14]

We have much sympathy with his view, but we must recognize that there are arguments against it. When Charles R. Tittle, Wayne J. Villemez, and Douglas A. Smith reviewed thirty-five studies of the relationship between crime rates and social class, they found only a slight association between the two variables.[15] When crime was measured using official (e.g., police) reports, the connection with social class was stronger than when it was measured using self-reports (the crimes admitted to by individuals filling out a questionnaire or responding to an interview). This conclusion has been challenged by other scholars who find, on the basis of more extensive self-report data than any previously used, that crime, especially serious crime, is much more prevalent among lower-class youth.[16] Michael J. Hindelang, Travis Hirschi, and Joseph G. Weis have shown that self-report studies tend to measure the prevalence of trivial offenses, including many things that would not be considered a crime at all (e.g., skipping school, defying parents, or having unmarried sex).[17] Even when true crimes are reported, they are often so minor (e.g., shoplifting a pack of gum) that it is a mistake—but, alas, a frequently made mistake—to lump such behavior together with burglary and robbery as measures of criminality. We agree with Hindelang et al., as well as with many others,[18] who argue that when crime is properly measured, the relationship between it and social class is strong—lower-class persons are much more likely to have committed a serious "street" crime than upper-status ones. But we recognize that this argument continues to be controversial, and so it seems inappropriate to begin an explanation of criminality by assuming that it is based on class.

Our second reason for not starting with class as a major social factor is, to us, more important. Unlike sex, age, and place, class is an ambiguous concept. A "lower-class" person can be one who has a low income, but that definition lumps together graduate students, old-age pensioners, welfare mothers, and unemployed steelworkers—individuals who would appear to have, as far as

crime is concerned, little in common. Many self-report studies of crime use class categories so broad as to obscure whatever connection may exist between class and criminality.[19] And studies of delinquency typically describe a boy as belonging to the class of his father, even if the boy in his own right, in school or in the labor force, is doing much better or much worse than his father.[20] By lower class one could also mean having a low-prestige occupation, but it is not clear to us why the prestige ranking of one's occupation should have any influence on one's criminality.

Class may, of course, be defined in terms of wealth or income, but using the concept in this way to explain crime, without further clarification, is ambiguous as to cause and effect. One's wealth, income, status, or relationship to the means of production could cause certain behavior (e.g., "poor people must steal to eat"), or they could themselves be caused by other factors (impulsive persons with low verbal skills tend to be poor and to steal). By contrast, one's criminality cannot be the cause of, say, one's age or sex....

Race is also a controversial and ambiguous concept in criminological research. Every study of crime using official data shows that blacks are heavily overrepresented among persons arrested, convicted, and imprisoned.[21] Some people, however, suspect that official reports are contaminated by the racial bias of those who compile them. Self-report studies, by contrast, tend to show fewer racial differences in criminality, but these studies have the same defect with respect to race as they do with regard to class— they overcount trivial offenses, in which the races do not differ, and undercount the more serious offenses, in which they do differ.[22] Moreover, surveys of the victims of crimes reveal that of the offenders whose racial identity could be discerned by their victims, about half were black; for the most serious offenses, two-thirds were black.[23] Though there may well be some racial bias in arrests, prosecutions, and sentences, there is no evidence... that it is so great as to account for the disproportionate involvement of blacks in serious crime, as revealed by both police and victimization data and by interviews with prison inmates.[24]

Our reason for not regarding, at least at the outset, race as a source of individual differences in criminality is not that we doubt that blacks are overrepresented in crime. Rather, there are two other considerations. First, racial differences exist in some societies and not others, yet all societies have crime. Though racial factors may affect the crime rate, the fundamental explanation for individual differences in criminality ought to be based—indeed, must be based, if it is to be a general explanation—on factors that are common to all societies.

Second, we find the concept of race to be ambiguous, but in a different way from the ambiguity of class. There is no reason to believe that the genes determining one's skin pigmentation also affect criminality. At one time in this nation's history, persons of Irish descent were heavily overrepresented among those who had committed some crime, but it would have been foolish then to postulate a trait called "Irishness" as an explanation. If racial or ethnic identity affects the likelihood of committing a crime, it must be because that identity co-varies with other characteristics and experiences that affect criminality. The proper line of inquiry, then, is first to examine those other characteristics and experiences to see how

and to what extent they predispose an individual toward crime, and then to consider what, if anything, is left unexplained in the observed connection between crime and racial identity. After examining constitutional, familial, educational, economic, neighborhood, and historical factors, there may or may not be anything left to say on the subject of race....

ARE THERE TYPES OF CRIMINALS?

We are concerned mainly with explaining criminality—why some people are more likely than others to commit, at a high rate, one or more of the universal crimes. But even if the behaviors with which we are concerned are alike in being universally regarded as serious crimes, are not the *motives* for these crimes so various that they cannot all be explained by one theory? Possibly. But this objection assumes that what we want to know are the motives of lawbreakers. It is by no means clear that the most interesting or useful way to look at crime is by trying to discover the motives of individual criminals—why some offenders like to steal cash, others like stolen cash plus a chance to beat up on its owner, and still others like violent sex—any more than it is obvious that the best way to understand the economy is by discovering why some persons keep their money in the bank, others use it to buy tickets to boxing matches, and still others use it to buy the favors of a prostitute. The motives of criminal (and of human) behavior are as varied as the behavior itself; we come to an understanding of the general processes shaping crime only when we abstract from particular motives and circumstances to examine the factors that lead people to run greater or lesser risks in choosing a course of action.

To us, offenders differ not so much in what kind of crimes they commit, but in the rate as which they commit them. In this sense, the one-time wife murderer is different from the persistent burglar or the organized drug trafficker—the first man breaks the law but once, the latter two do it every week or every day.... [T]he evidence suggests that persons who frequently break universal laws do not, in fact, specialize very much. A high-rate offender is likely to commit a burglary today and a robbery tomorrow, and sell drugs in between.

Explaining why some persons have a very high rate and others a low one is preferable, we think, to the major alternative to this approach: trying to sort offenders and offenses into certain categories or types. Creating—and arguing about—typologies is a major preoccupation of many students of crime because, having decided that motives are what count and having discovered that there are almost as many motives as there are people, the only way to bring any order to this variety is by reducing all the motives to a few categories, often described as personality types.

For example, a common distinction in criminology is between the "subcultural" offender and the "unsocialized" or "psychopathic" one. The first is a normal person who finds crime rewarding (perhaps because he has learned to commit crimes from friends he admires) and who discounts heavily the risks of being punished. The second is abnormal: He commits crimes because he has a weak conscience and cares little about the opinions of friends. Now, as even the authors of such distinctions acknowledge, these categories overlap (some sub-cultural thieves, for example, may also take pleasure in beating up on their victims), and not all offenders fit into either category. But to us, the chief difficulty with such typologies is that they direct attention away from individual differences and toward idealized—and abstract—categories.

Crime is correlated, as we have seen, with age, sex, and place of residence, and it is associated ... with other stable characteristics of individuals. Understanding those associations is the first task of criminological theory. Our approach is not to ask which persons belong to what category of delinquents but rather to ask whether differences in the frequency with which persons break the law are associated with differences in the rewards of crime, the risks of being punished for a crime, the strength of internalized inhibitions against crime, and the willingness to defer gratifications, and then to ask what biological, developmental, situational, and adaptive processes give rise to these individual characteristics.

NOTES

1. Wolfgang, 1973.
2. Farrington, 1979c, 9$_{25}$, 1981.
3. Newman, G., 1976.
4. Hoebel, 1954.
5. Sellin and Wolfgang, 1964; Figlio, 1972.
6. Akman and Normandeau, 1968.
7. Valez-Diaz and Megargee, 1971.
8. Hsu, cited in Wellford, 1975.
9. DeBoeck and Houschou, cited in Wellford, 1975.
10. Hirschi and Gottfredson, 1984.
11. Durkheim, 1964, p. 102.
12. Bordua, 1962.
13. Radzinowicz and King, 1977; Archer, Gartner, Akert, and Lockwood, 1978.
14. Braithwaite, 1981.
15. Tittle, Villemez, and Smith, 1978.
16. Elliott and Ageton, 1980; Elliott and Huizinga, 1983.

17. Hindelang, Hirschi, and Weis, 1979, 1981.
18. For example, Kleck, 1982.
19. Johnson, R. E., 1979.
20. Braithwaite, 1981.
21. For example, Wolfgang, Figlio, and Sellin, 1972.

22. Hindelang, Hirschi, and Weis, 1979, 1981; Berger and Simon, 1982.
23. Hindelang, Hirschi, and Weis, 1979, p. 1002; Hindelang, 1978.
24. Blumstein, 1982; Petersilia, 1983.

NO

Jeffrey Reiman

A CRIME BY ANY OTHER NAME...

If one individual inflicts a bodily injury upon another which leads to the death of the person attacked we call it manslaughter; on the other hand, if the attacker knows beforehand that the blow will be fatal we call it murder. Murder has also been committed if society places hundreds of workers in such a position that they inevitably come to premature and unnatural ends. Their death is as violent as if they had been stabbed or shot. . . . Murder has been committed if society knows perfectly well that thousands of workers cannot avoid being sacrificed so long as these conditions are allowed to continue. Murder of this sort is just as culpable as the murder committed by an individual.

—Frederick Engels
The Condition of the Working Class in England

WHAT'S IN A NAME?

If it takes you an hour to read this chapter, by the time you reach the last page, three of your fellow citizens will have been murdered. *During that same time, at least four Americans will die as a result of unhealthy or unsafe conditions in the workplace!* Although these work-related deaths could have been prevented, they are not called murders. Why not? Doesn't a crime by any other name still cause misery and suffering? What's in a name?

The fact is that the label "crime" is not used in America to name all or the worst of the actions that cause misery and suffering to Americans. It is primarily reserved for the dangerous actions of the poor.

In the February 21, 1993, edition of the *New York Times*, an article appears with the headline: "Company in Mine Deaths Set to Pay Big Fine." It describes an agreement by the owners of a Kentucky mine to pay a fine for safety misconduct that may have led to "the worst American mining accident in nearly a decade." Ten workers died in a methane explosion, and the company pleaded guilty to "a pattern of safety misconduct" that included falsifying reports of methane levels and requiring miners to work under unsupported roofs. The company was fined $3.75 million. The acting foreman at the mine was the only individual charged by the federal government, and for his

From Jeffrey Reiman, *The Rich Get Richer and the Poor Get Prison: Ideology, Class, and Criminal Justice*, 4th ed. (Allyn & Bacon, 1995). Copyright © 1979, 1984, 1990, 1995 by Jeffrey Reiman. Reprinted by permission of Allyn & Bacon. Notes omitted.

cooperation with the investigation, prosecutors were recommending that he receive the minimum sentence: probation to six months in prison. The company's president expressed regret for the tragedy that occurred. And the U.S. attorney said he hoped the case "sent a clear message that violations of Federal safety and health regulations that endanger the lives of our citizens will not be tolerated."

Compare this with the story of Colin Ferguson, who prompted an editorial in the *New York Times* of December 10, 1993, with the headline: "Mass Murder on the 5:33." A few days earlier, Colin had boarded a commuter train in Garden City, Long Island, and methodically shot passengers with a 9-millimeter pistol, killing 5 and wounding 18. Colin Ferguson was surely a murderer, maybe a mass murderer. My question is, Why wasn't the death of the miners also murder? Why weren't those responsible for subjecting ten miners to deadly conditions also "mass murderers"?

Why do ten dead miners amount to an "accident," a "tragedy," and five dead commuters a "mass murder"? "Murder" suggests a murderer, whereas "accident" and "tragedy" suggest the work of impersonal forces. But the charge against the company that owned the mine said that they "repeatedly exposed the mine's work crews to danger and that such conditions were frequently concealed from Federal inspectors responsible for enforcing the mine safety act." And the acting foreman admitted to falsifying records of methane levels only two months before the fatal blast. Someone was responsible for the conditions that led to the death of ten miners. Is that person not a murderer, perhaps even a *mass murderer?*

These questions are at this point rhetorical. My aim is not to discuss this case but rather to point to the blinders we wear when we look at such an "accident." There was an investigation. One person, the acting foreman, was held responsible for falsifying records. He is to be sentenced to six months in prison (at most). The company was fined. But no one will be tried for *murder.* No one will be thought of as a murderer. *Why not? ...*

Didn't those miners have a right to protection from the violence that took their lives? *And if not, why not?*

Once we are ready to ask this question seriously, we are in a position to see that the reality of crime—that is, the acts we label crime, the acts we think of as crime, the actors and actions we treat as criminal—is *created:* It is an image shaped by decisions as to *what* will be called crime and *who* will be treated as a criminal.

THE CARNIVAL MIRROR

It is sometimes coyly observed that the quickest and cheapest way to eliminate crime would be to throw out all the criminal laws. There is a sliver of truth to this view. Without criminal laws, there would indeed be no "crimes." There would, however, still be dangerous acts. This is why we cannot really solve our crime problem quite so simply. The criminal law *labels* some acts "crimes." In doing this, it identifies those acts as so dangerous that we must use the extreme methods of criminal justice to protect ourselves against them. This does not mean the criminal law *creates* crime—it simply "mirrors" real dangers that threaten us. What is true of the criminal law is true of the whole justice system. If police did not arrest or prosecutors charge or juries convict, there would be no "criminals." This does not mean that police or prosecutors or juries create criminals any more than legislators do. They *react* to real dangers in society. The criminal justice system—from lawmakers to law enforcers—is just a mirror of the real dangers that lurk in our midst. *Or so we are told.*

How accurate is this mirror? We need to answer this in order to know whether or how well the criminal justice system is protecting us against the real threats to our well-being. The more accurate a mirror is, the more the image it shows is created by the reality it reflects. The more misshapen a mirror is, the more the distorted image it shows is created by the mirror, not by the reality reflected. It is in this sense that I will argue that the image of crime is created: The American criminal justice system is a mirror that shows a distorted image of the dangers that threaten us—an image created more by the shape of the mirror than by the reality reflected. What do we see when we look in the criminal justice mirror?

On the morning of September 16, 1975, the *Washington Post* carried an article in its local news section headlined "Arrest Data Reveal Profile of a Suspect." The article reported the results of a study of crime in Prince George's County, a suburb of Washington, D.C. It read in part as follows:

> The typical suspect in serious crime in Prince George's County is a black male, aged 14 to 19....

This report is hardly a surprise. The portrait it paints of "the typical suspect in serious crime" is probably a pretty good rendering of the image lurking in the back of the minds of most people who fear crime.... [T]he portrait generally fits the national picture presented in the FBI's *Uniform Crime Reports* for the same year, 1974. In Prince George's County, "youths between the ages of 15 and 19 were accused of committing nearly half [45.5 percent] of all 1974 crimes....

That was 1974. But little has changed since. In his 1993 book, *How to Stop Crime*, retired police chief Anthony Bouza writes: "Street crime is mostly a black and poor young man's game." And listen to the sad words of the Reverend Jesse Jackson: "There is nothing more painful to me at this stage of my life than to walk down the street and hear footsteps and start thinking about robbery—and then look around and see someone white and feel relieved."

This, then, is the Typical Criminal, the one whose portrait President Reagan described as "that of a stark, staring face, a face that belongs to a frightening reality of our time—the face of a human predator, the face of the habitual criminal. Nothing in nature is more cruel and more dangerous." This is the face that Ronald Reagan saw in the criminal justice mirror, more than a decade ago. Let us look more closely at the face in today's criminal justice mirror, and we shall see much the same Typical Criminal:

He is, first of all, a *he*. Out of 2,012,906 persons arrested for FBI Index crimes [which are criminal homicide, forcible rape, robbery, aggravated assault, burglary, larceny, and motor vehicle theft] in 1991, 1,572,591, or 78 percent, were males. Second, he is a *youth*.... Third, he is predominantly *urban*.... Fourth, he is disproportionately *black*—blacks are arrested for Index crimes at a rate three times that of their percentage in the national population.... Finally, he is *poor*: Among state prisoners in 1991, 33 percent were unemployed prior to being arrested

—a rate nearly four times that of males in the general population....

This is the Typical Criminal feared by most law-abiding Americans. Poor, young, urban, (disproportionately) black males make up the core of the enemy forces in the war against crime. They are the heart of a vicious, unorganized guerrilla army, threatening the lives, limbs, and possessions of the law-abiding members of society—necessitating recourse to the ultimate weapons of force and detention in our common defense.

But how do we know who the criminals are who so seriously endanger us that we must stop them with force and lock them in prisons?

... "Arrest records" reflect decisions about which crimes to investigate and which suspects to take into custody. All these decisions rest on the most fundamental of all *decisions:* the decisions of legislators as to which acts shall be labeled "crimes" in the first place.

The reality of crime as the target of our criminal justice system and as perceived by the general populace is not a simple objective threat to which the system reacts: *It is a reality that takes shape as it is filtered through a series of human decisions running the full gamut of the criminal justice system*—from the lawmakers who determine what behavior shall be in the province of criminal justice to the law enforcers who decide which individuals will be brought within that province.

Note that by emphasizing the role of "human decisions," I do not mean to suggest that the reality of crime is voluntarily and intentionally "created" by individual "decision makers." Their decisions are themselves shaped by the social system, much as a child's decision to become an engineer rather than a samurai warrior is shaped by the social system in which he or she grows up. Thus, to have a full explanation of how the reality of crime is created, we have to understand how our society is structured in a way that leads people to make the decisions they do. In other words, these decisions are part of the social phenomena to be explained—they are not the explanation.

... Where the reality of crime does not correspond to the real dangers, we can say that it is a reality *created* by those decisions. And then we can investigate the role played by the social system in encouraging, reinforcing, and otherwise shaping those decisions.

It is to capture this way of looking at the relation between the reality of crime and the real dangers "out there" in society that I refer to the criminal justice system as a "mirror." Whom and what we see in this mirror is a function of the decisions about who and what are criminal, and so on. Our poor, young, urban, black male, who is so well represented in arrest records and prison populations, appears not simply because of the undeniable threat he poses to the rest of society. As dangerous as he may be, he would not appear in the criminal justice mirror *if* it had not been decided that the acts he performs should be labeled "crimes," *if* it had not been decided that he should be arrested for those crimes, *if* he had access to a lawyer who could persuade a jury to acquit him and perhaps a judge to expunge his arrest record, and *if* it had not been decided that he is the type of individual and his the type of crime that warrants imprisonment. *The shape of the reality we see in the criminal justice mirror is created by all these decisions.* We want to know how accurately the reality we see in this mirror reflects the real dangers that threaten us in society.

... The acts of the Typical Criminal are not the only acts that endanger us, nor are they the acts that endanger us the most. As I shall show ..., we have as great or sometimes even a greater chance of being killed or disabled by an occupational injury or disease, by unnecessary surgery, or by shoddy emergency medical services than by aggravated assault or even homicide! Yet even though these threats to our well-being are graver than those posed by our poor young criminals, they do not show up in the FBI's Index of serious crimes. The individuals responsible for them do not turn up in arrest records or prison statistics. *They never become part of the reality reflected in the criminal justice mirror, although the danger they pose is at least as great and often greater than the danger posed by those who do!*

Similarly, the general public loses more money *by far* ... from price-fixing and monopolistic practices and from consumer deception and embezzlement than from all the property crimes in the FBI's Index combined. Yet these far more costly acts are either not criminal, or if technically criminal, not prosecuted, or if prosecuted, not punished, or if punished, only mildly.... *Their faces rarely appear in the criminal justice mirror, although the danger they pose is at least as great and often greater than that of those who do....*

The criminal justice system is like a mirror in which society can see the face of the evil in its midst. Because the system deals with some evil and not with others, because it treats some evils as the gravest and treats some of the gravest evils as minor, the image it throws back is distorted like the image in a carnival mirror. Thus, the image cast back is false not because it is invented out of thin air but because the proportions of the real are distorted....

If criminal justice really gives us a carnival-mirror of "crime," we are doubly deceived. First, we are led to believe that the criminal justice system is protecting us against the gravest threats to our well-being when, in fact, the system is protecting us against only some threats and not necessarily the gravest ones. We are deceived about how much protection we are receiving and thus left vulnerable. The second deception is just the other side of this one. If people believe that the carnival mirror is a true mirror—that is, if they believe the criminal justice system simply *reacts* to the gravest threats to their well-being—they come to believe that whatever is the target of the criminal justice system must be the greatest threat to their well-being....

A CRIME BY ANY OTHER NAME...

Think of a crime, any crime. Picture the first "crime" that comes into your mind. What do you see? The odds are you are not imagining a mining company executive sitting at his desk, calculating the costs of proper safety precautions and deciding not to invest in them. Probably what you do see with your mind's eye is one person physically attacking another or robbing something from another via the threat of physical attack. Look more closely. What does the attacker look like? It's a safe bet he (and it is a *he*, of course) is not wearing a suit and tie. In fact, my hunch is that you—like me, like almost anyone else in America—picture a young, tough lower-class male when the thought of crime first pops into your head. You (we) picture someone like the Typical Criminal described above. The crime itself is one in which the Typical Criminal sets out to attack or rob some specific person.

This last point is important. It indicates that we have a mental image not only of the Typical Criminal but also of the Typical Crime. If the Typical Criminal is a young, lower-class male, the Typical Crime is *one-on-one harm*—where harm means either physical injury or loss of something valuable or both. If you have any doubts that this is the Typical Crime, look at any random sample of police or private eye shows on television. How often do you see the cops on "NYPD Blue" investigate consumer fraud or failure to remove occupational hazards? And when Jessica Fletcher (on "Murder, She Wrote") tracks down well-heeled criminals, it is almost always for garden-variety violent crimes like murder.... [C]riminals portrayed on television are on the average both older and wealthier than the real criminals who figure in the FBI *Uniform Crime Reports*, "TV crimes are almost 12 times as likely to be violent as crimes committed in the real world." TV crime shows broadcast the double-edged message that the one-on-one crimes of the poor are the typical crimes of all and thus not uniquely caused by the pressures of poverty; *and* that the criminal justice system pursues rich and poor alike—thus, when the criminal justice system happens mainly to pounce on the poor in real life, it is not out of any class bias.

In addition to the steady diet of fictionalized TV violence and crime, there has been an increase in the graphic display of crime on many TV news programs. Crimes reported on TV news are also far more frequently violent than real crimes are.... [A] new breed of nonfictional "tabloid" TV show has appeared in which viewers are shown films of actual violent crimes—blood, screams, and all—or reenactments of actual violent crimes, sometimes using the actual victims playing themselves! Among these are "COPS," "Real Stories of the Highway Patrol," "America's Most Wanted," and "Unsolved Mysteries." Here, too, the focus is on crimes of one-on-one violence, rather than, say, corporate pollution. The *Wall Street Journal*, reporting on the phenomenon of tabloid TV, informs us that "Television has gone tabloid. The seamy underside of life is being bared in a new rash of true-crime series and contrived-confrontation talk shows." Is there any surprise that a survey by *McCall's* indicates that its readers have grown more afraid of crime in the mid-1980s—even though victimization studies show a stable level of crime for most of this period?

It is important to identify this model of the Typical Crime because it functions like a set of blinders. It keeps us from calling a mine disaster a mass murder even if ten men are killed, even if someone is responsible for the unsafe conditions in which they worked and died. I contend that this particular piece of mental furniture so blocks our view that it keeps us from using the criminal justice system to protect ourselves from the greatest threats to our persons and possessions.

What keeps a mine disaster from being a mass murder in our eyes is that it is not a one-on-one harm. What is important in one-on-one harm is not the numbers but the *desire of someone (or ones) to harm someone (or ones) else*. An attack by a gang on one or more persons or an attack by one individual on several fits the model of one-on-one harm; that is, for each person harmed there is at least one individual who wanted to harm that person. Once he selects his victim, the rapist, the mugger, the murderer all want this person they have selected to suffer. A mine executive, on the other hand, does not want his employees to be harmed. He would truly prefer that there be no accident, no injured or dead miners. What he does want is something legitimate. It is what he has been hired to get: maximum profits at minimum costs. If he cuts corners to save a buck, he is just doing his job. If ten men die because he cut corners on safety, we may think him crude or callous but not a murderer. He is, at most, responsible for an *indirect harm*, not a one-on-one harm. For this, he may even be criminally indictable for violating safety regulations —but not for murder. The ten men are dead as an unwanted consequence of his (perhaps overzealous or undercautious) pursuit of a legitimate goal. So, unlike the Typical Criminal, he has not committed the Typical Crime—or so we generally believe. As a result, ten men are dead who might be alive now if cutting corners of the kind that leads to loss of life, whether suffering is specifically aimed at or not, were treated as murder.

This is my point. Because we accept the belief... that the model for crime is one person specifically trying to harm another, we accept a legal system that leaves us unprotected against much greater dangers to our lives and well-being than those threatened by the Typical Criminal....

According to the FBI's *Uniform Crime Reports*, in 1991, there were 24,703 murders and nonnegligent manslaughters, and 1,092,739 aggravated assaults. In 1992, there were 23,760 murders and nonnegligent manslaughters, and 1,126,970 aggravated assaults.... Thus, as a measure of the physical harm done by crime in the beginning of the 1990s, we can say that reported crimes lead to roughly 24,000 deaths and 1,000,000 instances of serious bodily injury short of death a year. As a measure of monetary loss due to

property crime, we can use $15.1 billion —the total estimated dollar losses due to property crime in 1992 according to the UCR. Whatever the shortcomings of these reported crime statistics, they are the statistics upon which public policy has traditionally been based. Thus, I will consider any actions that lead to loss of life, physical harm, and property loss comparable to the figures in the UCR as actions that pose grave dangers to the community comparable to the threats posed by crimes....

Work May Be Dangerous to Your Health

Since the publication of *The President's Report on Occupational Safety and Health* in 1972, numerous studies have documented the astounding incidence of disease, injury, and death due to hazards in the workplace *and* the fact that much or most of this carnage is the consequence of the refusal of management to pay for safety measures and of government to enforce safety standards—and sometimes of willful defiance of existing law.

In that 1972 report, the government estimated the number of job-related illnesses at 390,000 per year and the number of annual deaths from industrial disease at 100,000. For 1990, the Bureau of Labor Statistics (BLS) of the U.S. Department of Labor estimates 330,800 job-related illnesses and 2,900 work-related deaths. Note that the latter figure applies only to private-sector work environments with 11 or more employees. And it is not limited to death from occupational disease but includes all work-related deaths, including those resulting from accidents on the job.

Before we celebrate what appears to be a dramatic drop in work-related mortality, we should point out that the BLS itself "believes that the annual survey significantly understates the number of work-related fatalities." And there is wide agreement that occupational diseases are seriously underreported....

For these reasons, plus the fact that BLS's figures on work-related deaths are only for private workplaces with 11 or more employees, we must supplement the BLS figures with other estimates. In 1982, then U.S. Secretary of Health and Human Services Richard Schweiker stated that "current estimates for overall workplace-associated cancer mortality vary within a range of five to fifteen percent. With annual cancer deaths currently running at about 500,000, that translates into about 25,000 to 75,000 job-related cancer deaths per year. More recently, Edward Sondik, of the National Cancer Institute, states that the best estimate of cancer deaths attributable to occupational exposure is 4 percent of the total, with the range of acceptable estimates running between 2 and 8 percent. That translates into a best estimate of 20,000 job-related cancer deaths a year, within a range of acceptable estimates between 10,000 and 40,000.

Death from cancer is only part of the picture of death-dealing occupational disease. In testimony before the Senate Committee on Labor and Human Resources, Dr. Philip Landrigan, director of the Division of Environmental and Occupational Medicine at the Mount Sinai School of Medicine in New York City, stated that

> Recent data indicate that occupationally related exposures are responsible each year in New York State for 5,000 to 7,000 deaths and for 35,000 new cases of illness (not including work-related injuries). These deaths due to occupational disease include 3,700 deaths from cancer....

> [I]t may be calculated that occupational disease is responsible each year in the United States for 50,000 to 70,000 deaths, and for approximately 350,000 new cases of illness.

... The BLS estimate of 330,000 job-related illnesses for 1990 roughly matches Dr. Landrigan's estimates. For 1991, BLS estimates 368,000 job-related illnesses. These illnesses are of varying severity.... Because I want to compare these occupational harms with those resulting from aggravated assault, I shall stay on the conservative side here too, as with deaths from occupational diseases, and say that there are annually in the United States approximately 150,000 job-related serious illnesses. Taken together with 25,000 deaths from occupational diseases, how does this compare with the threat posed by crime?

Before jumping to any conclusions, note that the risk of occupational disease and death falls only on members of the labor force, whereas the risk of crime falls on the whole population, from infants to the elderly. Because the labor force is about half the total population (124,810,000 in 1990, out of a total population of 249,900,000), to get a true picture of the *relative* threat posed by occupational diseases compared with that posed by crimes, we should *halve* the crime statistics when comparing them with the figures for industrial disease and death. Using the crime figures for the first years of the 1990s,... we note that the *comparable* figures would be

	Occupational Disease	Crime (halved)
Death	25,000	12,000
Other physical harm	150,000	500,000

... Note... that the estimates in the last chart are *only* for occupational *diseases* and deaths from those diseases. They do not include death and disability from work-related injuries. Here, too, the statistics are gruesome. The National Safety Council reported that in 1991, work-related accidents caused 9,600 deaths and 1.7 million disabling work injuries, a total cost to the economy of $63.3 billion. This brings the number of occupation-related deaths to 34,600 a year and other physical harms to 1,850,000. If, on the basis of these additional figures, we recalculated our chart comparing occupational harms from both disease and accident with criminal harms, it would look like this:

	Occupational Hazard	Crime (halved)
Death	34,600	12,000
Other physical harm	1,850,000	500,000

Can there be any doubt that workers are more likely to stay alive and healthy in the face of the danger from the underworld than in the work-world? If any doubt lingers, consider this: Lest we falter in the struggle against crime, the FBI includes in its annual *Uniform Crime Reports* a table of "crime clocks," which graphically illustrates the extent of the criminal menace. For 1992, the crime clock shows a murder occurring every 22 minutes. If a similar clock were constructed for occupational deaths—using the conservative estimate of 34,600 cited above and remembering that this clock ticks only for that half of the population that is in the labor force—this clock would show an occupational death about every 15 minutes! In other words, in the time it takes for three murders on the crime clock, four workers have died *just from trying to make a living.*

To say that some of these workers died from accidents due to their own carelessness is about as helpful as saying that some of those who died at the hands of murderers asked for it. It overlooks the fact that where workers are careless, it is not because they love to live dangerously. They have production quotas to meet, quotas that they themselves do not set. If quotas were set with an eye to keeping work at a safe pace rather than to keeping the production-to-wages ratio as high as possible, it might be more reasonable to expect workers to take the time to be careful. Beyond this, we should bear in mind that the vast majority of occupational deaths result from disease, not accident, and disease is generally a function of conditions outside a worker's control. Examples of such conditions are the level of coal dust in the air ("260,000 miners receive benefits for [black lung] disease, and perhaps as many as 4,000 retired miners die from the illness or its complications each year"; about 10,000 currently working miners "have X-ray evidence of the beginnings of the crippling and often fatal disease") or textile dust... or asbestos fibers... or coal tars...; (coke oven workers develop cancer of the scrotum at a rate five times that of the general population). Also, some 800,000 people suffer from occupationally related skin disease each year....

To blame the workers for occupational disease and deaths is to ignore the history of governmental attempts to compel industrial firms to meet safety standards that would keep dangers (such as chemicals or fibers or dust particles in the air) that are outside the worker's control down to a safe level. This has been a continual struggle, with firms using everything from their own "independent" research institutes to more direct and often questionable forms of political pressure to influence government in the direction of loose standards and lax enforcement. So far, industry has been winning because OSHA [Occupational Safety and Health Administration] has been given neither the personnel nor the mandate to fulfill its purpose. It is so understaffed that, in 1973, when 1,500 federal sky marshals guarded the nation's airplanes from hijackers, only 500 OSHA inspectors toured the nation's workplaces. By 1980, OSHA employed 1,581 compliance safety and health officers, but this still enabled inspection of only roughly 2 percent of the 2.5 million establishments covered by OSHA. The *New York Times* reports that in 1987 the number of OSHA inspectors was down to 1,044. As might be expected, the agency performs fewer inspections that it did a dozen years ago....

According to a report issued by the AFL-CIO [American Federation of Labor and Congress of Industrial Organizations] in 1992, "The median penalty paid by an employer during the years 1972–1990 following an incident resulting in death or serious injury of a worker was just $480." The same report claims that the federal government spends $1.1 billion a year to protect fish and wildlife and only $300 million a year to protect workers from health and safety hazards on the job....

Is a person who kills another in a bar brawl a greater threat to society than a business executive who refuses to cut into his profits to make his plant a safe place to work? By any measure of death and suffering the latter is by far a greater danger than the former.

Because he wishes his workers no harm, because he is only indirectly responsible for death and disability while pursuing legitimate economic goals, his acts are not called "crimes." Once we free our imagination from the blinders of the one-on-one model of crime, can there be any doubt that the criminal justice system does *not* protect us from the gravest threats to life and limb? It seeks to protect us when danger comes from a young, lower-class male in the inner city. When a threat comes from an upper-class business executive in an office, the criminal justice system looks the other way. This is in the face of growing evidence that for every three American citizens murdered by thugs, at least four American workers are killed by the recklessness of their bosses and the indifference of their government.

Health Care May Be Dangerous to Your Health

... On July 15, 1975, Dr. Sidney Wolfe of Ralph Nader's Public Interest Health Research Group testified before the House Commerce Oversight and Investigations Subcommittee that there "were 3.2 million cases of unnecessary surgery performed each year in the United States." These unneeded operations, Wolfe added, "cost close to $5 billion a year and kill as many as 16,000 Americans." ...

In an article on an experimental program by Blue Cross and Blue Shield aimed at curbing unnecessary surgery, *Newsweek* reports that

a Congressional committee earlier this year [1976] estimated that more than 2 million of the elective operations performed in 1974 were not only unnecessary—but also killed about 12,000 patients and cost nearly $4 billion.

Because the number of surgical operations performed in the United States rose from 16.7 million in 1975 to 22.4 million in 1991, there is reason to believe that at least somewhere between... 12,000 and... 16,000 people a year still die from unnecessary surgery. In 1991, the FBI reported that 3,405 murders were committed by a "cutting or stabbing instrument." Obviously, the FBI does not include the scalpel as a cutting or stabbing instrument. If they did, they would have had to report that between 15,405 and 19,405 persons were killed by "cutting or stabbing" in 1991.... No matter how you slice it, the scalpel may be more dangerous than the switchblade....

Waging Chemical Warfare Against America

One in 4 Americans can expect to contract cancer during their lifetimes. The American Cancer Society estimated that 420,000 Americans would die of cancer in 1981. The National Cancer Institute's estimate for 1993 is 526,000 deaths from cancer. "A 1978 report issued by the President's Council on Environmental Quality (CEQ) unequivocally states that 'most researchers agree that 70 to 90 percent of cancers are caused by environmental influences and are hence theoretically preventable.'" This means that a concerted national effort could result in saving 350,000 or more lives a year and reducing each individual's chances of getting cancer in his or her lifetime from 1 in 4 to 1 in 12 or fewer. If you think this would require a massive effort in terms of money and personnel, you are right. How much of an effort, though, would the nation make to stop a foreign invader who was killing a thousand people and bent on capturing one-quarter of the present population?

In face of this "invasion" that is already under way, the U.S. government has allocated $1.9 billion to the National Cancer Institute (NCI) for fiscal year 1992, and NCI has allocated $219 million to the study of the physical and chemical (i.e., environmental) causes of cancer. Compare this with the (at least) $45 billion spent to fight the Persian Gulf War. The simple truth is that the government that strove so mightily to protect the borders of a small, undemocratic nation 7,000 miles away is doing next to nothing to protect us against the chemical war in our midst. This war is being waged against us on three fronts:

- Pollution
- Cigarette smoking
- Food additives

... The evidence linking *air pollution* and cancer, as well as other serious and often fatal diseases, has been rapidly accumulating in recent years. In 1993, the *Journal of the American Medical Association* reported on research that found " 'robust' associations between premature mortality and air pollution levels." They estimate that pollutants cause about 2 percent of all cancer deaths (at least 10,000 a year)....

A ... recent study ... concluded that air pollution at 1988 levels was responsible for 60,000 deaths a year. The Natural Resources Defense Council sued the EPA [Environmental Protection Agency] for its foot-dragging in implementation of the Clean Air Act, charging that "One hundred million people live in areas of unhealthy air."

This chemical war is not limited to the air. The National Cancer Institute has identified as carcinogens or suspected carcinogens 23 of the chemicals commonly found in our drinking water.

Moreover, according to one observer, we are now facing a "new plague—toxic exposure." ...

The evidence linking *cigarette smoking* and cancer is overwhelming and need not be repeated here. The Centers for Disease Control estimates that cigarettes cause 87 percent of lung cancers—approximately 146,000 in 1992. Tobacco continues to kill an estimated 400,000 Americans a year. Cigarettes are widely estimated to cause 30 percent of all cancer deaths. ...

This is enough to expose the hypocrisy of running a full-scale war against heroin (which produces no degenerative disease) while allowing cigarette sales and advertising to flourish. It also should be enough to underscore the point that once again there are threats to our lives much greater than criminal homicide. The legal order does not protect us against them. Indeed, not only does our government fail to protect us against this threat, it promotes it! ...

If you think that tobacco harms only people who knowingly decide to take the risk, consider the following: Documents recently made public suggest that, by the mid-1950's, Liggett & Myers, the makers of Chesterfield and L&M cigarettes, had evidence that smoking is addictive and cancer-causing, and that they were virtually certain of it by 1963—but they never told the public and "actively misled" the U.S. surgeon general. Moreover, the cigarette industry intentionally targets young people—who are not always capable of assessing the consequences of their choices—with its ads, and it is successful. Some 2.6 million youngsters between the ages of 12 and 18 are smokers.

In addition, the Environmental Protection Agency has released data on the dangers of "secondhand" tobacco smoke (which nonsmokers breathe when smoking is going on around them). They report that each year secondhand smoke causes 3,000 lung-cancer deaths, contributes to 150,000 to 300,000 respiratory infections in babies, exacerbates the asthmatic symptoms of 400,000 to 1,000,000 children with the disease, and triggers 8,000 to 26,000 new cases of asthma in children who don't yet have the disease. A 1993 issue of the *Journal of the American Medical Association* reports that tobacco contributes to 10 percent of infant deaths.

The average American consumes *one pound* of chemical *food additives* per year. ... A hard look at the chemicals we eat and at the federal agency empowered to protect us against eating dangerous chemicals reveals the recklessness with which we are being "medicated against our will." ...

Based on the knowledge we have, there can be no doubt that air pollution, tobacco, and food additives amount to a chemical war that makes the crime wave look like a football scrimmage. Even with the most conservative estimates, it is clear that *the death toll in this war is far higher than the number of people killed by criminal homicide!*

Poverty Kills

... We are prone to think that the consequences of poverty are fairly straightfoward: less money means fewer things. So poor people have fewer clothes or cars or appliances, go to the theater less often, and live in smaller homes with less or cheaper furniture. This is true and sad, but perhaps not intolerable. However, in addition, one of the things poor people have less of is *good health*. Less money means less nutritious food, less heat in winter, less fresh air in summer, less distance from other sick people or from unhealthy work or dumping sites, less knowledge about illness or medicine, fewer doctor visits, fewer dental visits, less preventive health care, and (in the United States at least) less first-quality medical attention when all these other deprivations take their toll and a poor person finds himself or herself seriously ill. The result is that the poor suffer more from poor health and die earlier than do those who are well off. Poverty robs them of their days while they are alive and kills them before their time. A prosperous society that allows poverty in its midst is a party to murder.

A review of more than 30 historical and contemporary studies of the relationship of economic class and life expectancy affirms the obvious conclusion that "class influences one's chances of staying alive. Almost without exception, the evidence shows that classes differ on mortality rates." An article in the November 10, 1993 issue of the *Journal of the American Medical Association* confirms the continued existence of this cost of poverty:

> People who are poor have higher mortality rates for heart disease, diabetes mellitus, high blood pressure, lung cancer, neural tube defects, injuries, and low birth weight, as well as lower survival rates from breast cancer and heart attacks.

... In short, *poverty hurts, injures, and kills—just like crime.* A society that could remedy its poverty but does not is an accomplice in crime.

SUMMARY

Once again, our investigations lead to the same result. The criminal justice system does not protect us against the gravest threats to life, limb, or possessions. Its definitions of crime are not simply a reflection of the objective dangers that threaten us. The workplace, the medical profession, the air we breathe, and the poverty we refuse to rectify lead to far more human suffering, far more death and disability, and take far more dollars from our pockets than the murders, aggravated assaults, and thefts reported annually by the FBI. What is more, this human suffering is preventable. A government really intent on protecting our well-being could enforce work safety regulations, police the medical profession, require that clean air standards be met, and funnel sufficient money to the poor to alleviate the major disabilities of poverty—but it does not. Instead we hear a lot of cant about law and order and a lot of rant about crime in the streets. It is as if our leaders were not only refusing to protect us from the major threats to our well-being but trying to cover up this refusal by diverting our attention to crime—as if this were the only real threat.

As we have seen, the criminal justice system is a carnival mirror that presents a distorted image of what threatens us. The distortions do not end with the definitions of crime.... All the mechanisms by which the criminal justice system comes down more frequently and more harshly on the poor criminal than on the well-off criminal take place *after* most of the dangerous acts of the well-to-do have been excluded from the definition of crime itself. The bias against the poor within the criminal justice system is all the more striking when we recognize that the door to that system is shaped in a way that excludes in advance the most dangerous acts of the well-to-do.

POSTSCRIPT

Is Street Crime More Serious than White-Collar Crime?

American society is currently in the throes of disdain, if not out-and-out hate, for street crimes and the people who commit them. Yet, according to Reiman and others, street thugs are not nearly as dangerous or harmful to life and limb as are corporate criminals. Ironically, many political candidates have made a partial career out of attacking street criminals while at the same time generously borrowing some of their verbal mannerisms. For instance, on more than one occasion, President Ronald Reagan challenged drug dealers and the like to give him the opportunity to "stomp them" or, in his inimitable vernacular, to "make my day."

Similarly to Wilson and Herrnstein, Paul Tappan, in "Who Is the Criminal?" *American Sociological Review* (February 1947), insists that white-collar criminals and the like are not really the concerns of criminologists—at least not until laws are passed prohibiting certain acts. Otherwise, to attack corporations simply because we may disagree with their standards or efforts to make a profit is to dilute our definition of crime. Mainstream criminology probably rejects this perspective. See J. Albanese, ed., *Contemporary Issues in Organized Crime* (Criminal Justice Press, 1995); K. Jamieson, *Organization of Corporate Crime* (Sage Publications, 1994); *White Collar Crime* edited by D. Nelken (Dartmouth, 1995); and M. Tonry and A. Reiss, eds., *Beyond the Law: Crime in Complex Organizations* (University of Chicago Press, 1993).

For a provocative view of crimes of criminal justice agencies, see J. Henderson and D. Simon's *Crimes of the Criminal Justice System* (Andersen, 1994). For four outstanding articles looking at organized crime in Europe and the United States, see *Journal of Contemporary Criminal Justice* (December 1994). A good introduction to the issue that parallels Reiman's views is *Corporate Crime, Corporate Violence: A Primer* by M. Lynch and N. Frank (Harrow & Hester, 1994).

Two books that argue that corporate crimes are more dangerous than street crimes are the highly controversial *Poisoning for Profit: The Mafia and Toxic Waste in America* by A. A. Block and F. R. Scarpitti (William Morrow, 1985) and Marshall B. Clinard's *Corporate Corruption* (Praeger, 1990). A good discussion of the important and controversial issue of legal control of organized crime is the symposium "Reforming RICO," *Vanderbilt Law Review* (April 1990). Also, the *Corporate Crime Reporter*, published weekly since 1987 and edited by Russell Mokhiber, is an invaluable source.

An interesting cultural analysis, which reflects Reiman's perspective, is S. Scheingold's *Politics of Street Crime* (Temple University Press, 1991). Empirical research that partially gets at this issue is "Are White-Collar and Common Offenders the Same?" by M. Benson and E. Moore, *Crime and Delinquency* (August 1992). Suggestions for controlling corporate crime can be found in "Deterring Corporate Crime," by S. Simpson and C. Koper, *Criminology* (August 1992). Two books of interest are *Occupational Crime* by G. Green (Nelson-Hall, 1990) and M. Ermann and R. Lundman's *Corporate and Government Deviance*, 4th ed. (Oxford University Press, 1992).

ISSUE 5

Are General Theories of Crime Useful?

YES: Charles R. Tittle, from "The Assumption That General Theories Are Not Possible," in Robert F. Meier, ed., *Theoretical Methods in Criminology* (Sage Publications, 1985)

NO: Michael J. Lynch and W. Byron Groves, from "In Defense of Comparative Criminology: A Critique of General Theory and the Rational Man," in Freda Adler and W. S. Laufer, eds., *The Legacy of Anomie Theory* (Transaction, 1993)

ISSUE SUMMARY

YES: Criminologist Charles R. Tittle links the advancement of science with general theory building and insists that criminology will remain stagnant if it continues to neglect general theory.

NO: Professors Michael J. Lynch and W. Byron Groves argue that building general theories is unproductive. They insist that it is better to develop specific, grounded theories and to engage in careful comparative criminology.

For several years within the social sciences, including criminology but especially in sociology, students and professors debated furiously over what was more important: theory or research methods. Others argued over what was "better" theory: microstructural or macrostructural theory. That is, should criminologists attempt to explain and study only small slices of reality, such as child molestation or burglary, or should they develop large, comprehensive theories? In the debate that follows, Charles R. Tittle links scientific advancement with the development of a comprehensive, or general, theory of criminology. Tittle says that we need a good general theory of crime, however difficult formulating such a theory might be.

By contrast, Michael J. Lynch and W. Byron Groves reject this ambitious call to arms. To begin with, they assert, no theory can explain *all* types of crime, even within the same society or historical period. They attack Tittle's idea and argue that if such a general theory were developed, it would force different kinds of crime into one false mold.

As a point of interest, the debate over what is more important, theory or research methods, has largely been resolved. Criminologists now realize that both are equally important: one is blind without good theory to guide research, and theory that does not generate hypotheses for testing is scientifically worthless. Moreover, many of the pioneering American criminological theorists, such as Sellin, Sutherland, and Cressey, as well as distinguished current criminologists, such as Hagan, Hirschi, Gottfredson, and Wilson, to mention a few, are also well known as researchers. They are theoreticians who also do important criminological research.

But the debate over theory continues, and, to a certain extent, it boils down to a debate between a "nomothetic" position and an "idiographic" one. During the early development of the various social science disciplines, most social scientists maintained that their work was involved with abstract, general, or universal statements. They were *not* interested in simply describing a single event or thing, such as a revolution, a crime (or even a type of crime), or a specific government. Instead, as scientists, they were interested in searching for uniform patterns and in coming up with explanations in terms of laws or principles or generalized statements. Their work was *nomothetic.* Instead of discussing Revolution-1, R-2, R-3, and so on, or Crime-1, C-2, C-3, etc., their task would be to develop a *theory* of revolutions or crime and then to study each revolution or crime as a particular empirical case.

In contrast to early efforts by some social scientists to develop general explanations, others (for example, some historians and anthropologists) tended to emphasize the unique or particular nature of social events. This is referred to as an *idiographic* approach. Historians often attempted to gather as much data or facts as possible on some unique historical event, such as a particular revolution or a particular president. The goal was to *describe* as fully as possible the unique event, not to try to form abstract theories or generalizations. Many anthropologists also tended to zero in on one culture or society, or even to select elements within specific societies (for example, dating customs, technology, or religious rites), at specific historical periods.

As you read Tittle and form your own opinions, think about his many interesting ideas in terms of whether or not they apply to criminological realities as you understand them. Could you consider creating a general theory of crime that would enable us to better understand crime?

As you read Lynch and Groves, do you agree with their understanding of theory? In what ways are they highly selective in their criticisms of Tittle? Whose *style of understanding* of crime (and other types of behavior) are you most comfortable with as a student of criminology: the particularistic approach of Lynch and Groves or the abstract theorizing called for by Tittle?

YES

Charles R. Tittle

THE ASSUMPTION THAT GENERAL
THEORIES ARE NOT POSSIBLE

THE PROBLEM

There is evidence that the majority of criminologists at least pay lip service to the goal of developing general theory. Yet considerable ambivalence is obvious. There are strong and influential undercurrents declaring that theory is impossible, undesirable, or of only ancillary import. Some of these dyspeptic views stem from conviction that science is inappropriate for studying social phenomena, others flow from faulty perceptions of the scientific process, and a few reflect frustration at slow progress toward general theory. Yet they all share a common assumption: Pursuit of general theory is a fool's errand because of inherent features of criminological phenomena.

I contend that this is an erroneous assumption and that general theory is quite possible....

Complexity

To most criminologists, the best known and probably most discouraging barrier to general theory is the supposed fact that social phenomena are too complex, involving a multitude of causes, to permit one explanatory scheme. This belief rests on two assumptions: (1) Any theory can conceivably explain only those phenomena that are essentially alike, and (2) a single theory implies a single cause or process....

This pessimistic axiom, however, seriously underestimates the potentialities of theory, and its assumptions are mistaken. First, it is incorrect to assume that all phenomena to be explained by a single theory must be empirically alike. Phenomena have only to be subsumable within a similar causative process. The object of theory building is to rise above the confines of everyday categorization and causal assumptions to grasp the ways in which phenomena are abstractly connected. The first step in that process is conceptualization that captures theoretical commonality in the fact of empirical dissimilarity. For example, theft, burglary, rape, homicide, and voyeurism seem quite unalike, each a product of different causal factors, when viewed with the cognitive tools provided by the cultures in which they occur. But on an abstract level all may be perceived as instances of the same act—intrusion into private domains. In most Western societies, at least, individuals are entrusted with control of the properties they use every day, their residential domains, and their lives, and with decisions as to who may observe their performance of bodily functions. Burglary, rape, and other crimes intrude into one of these private domains and are therefore theoretically alike, although not essentially alike in an empirical, culturally defined sense.

Second, all of these intrusions may be encompassed within a similar causal theory that provides explanation for intrusive as well as other behaviors. Such a theory necessarily also rests upon integration of divergent causative variables within unifying conceptual categories. For instance, broken homes, personality disorders, and peer pressures have all been implicated as relevant but desultory and fundamentally different causes, or factors, in various empirically distinct behaviors that are here regarded as conceptually similar instances of intrusion. But they may all reflect a single underlying construct that might be theoretically labeled as *interpersonal insecurity*. This generic concept varies independently of whether a child resides with both parents, although it might have some general association with family intactness; it subsumes many psychological variables often thought to express personality disorders; and it reflects an antecedent condition allowing peer influences to prevail. Thus what appear to be different causes may really be expressions of a common causal dimension.

Further, a general theory spelling out the causal intricacies of interpersonal insecurity and intrusive behavior as well as other causal dimensions and other abstract patterns of behavior, all of which would be included in the same domain of individual conduct, is logically conceivable. At the risk of being accused of setting forth yet another incomplete and faulty theory, I will continue with a hypothetical example to illustrate the form such a theory might take. Suppose a theorist begins with a general statement that all behavior (deviant or otherwise) involves five variables: (1) motivation (impulse, instigation, utility, desire, drive), (2) competing motivations, (3) constraint (cost, inhibition, restraint, control), (4) opportunity to commit the act, and (5) ability to perform the behavior. The theory then postulates that *any specific behavior* will result whenever there is X amount of opportunity to commit that behavior, the actor has Y degrees of ability to act, the strength of motivation to do it exceeds, by Z degrees, the motivation to do something else, and, by Q degrees, the strength of restraint. Borrowing from others, the theorist contends that one variable in the equation—the degree of *motivation* to do anything—is a product of (1) past differential association with social definitions favorable to doing it, (2) the relationship between culturally defined goals and means, (3) various biological conditions, (4) previous reinforcements for similar behavior, and (5) interpersonal insecurity. Under various conditions, these factors are postulated to contribute different amounts to motivation. For one condition, intrusive behavior, the theory suggests that interpersonal insecurity will account for 60 percent of the motivation to intrude, past association will account for 25 percent and so on. Continuing, the theorist maintains that another variable in the equation—the degree of *constraint* for any individual contemplating intrusive behavior—is a product of (1) social bonds to conforming other, (2) perceived chances of being sanctioned by the law, (3) level of moral feelings against particular types of acts, (4) certain biological conditions, and (5) a particular kind of bodily chemical imbalance. The theory postulates that these factors contribute variously to constraint under different conditions and that in the case of intrusive behavior, social bonds contribute 50 percent to the level of constraint, perceived chances of being sanctioned by the law, 30 percent and so on. Similarly, the processes and variables affecting the other variables in the equation—*competing motives, opportunity, and ability*—are spelled out.

Furthermore, the theory provides an intellectual rationale for all its internal linkages and postulates, continually attempting to answer the question of why at all steps along the way. For instance, in this hypothetical example interpersonal insecurity is theorized to be the primary determinant of motivation to intrude into the private domains of others. The theorist might maintain that this is because interpersonal insecurity causes anxiety about personal autonomy in regulating one's own privacy, making the individual feel relatively disadvantaged in the social arena, where others are perceived as having more complete control of their domains. Since feelings of disadvantage are discomforting, the individual attempts to reduce them by intruding into the privacy of others to equalize autonomy.

In like manner, and calling often upon other theory fragments, the scheme provides explanatory rationales for every proposed interconnection that will in the aggregate specify the conditions under which each element of the main causal statement takes various values. Moreover, the theory goes on to show how the inputs to that main causal process are themselves influenced by other causal processes. Thus the degrees of interpersonal insecurity, differential association, social bonds, and so on must themselves be explained by designation of the variables or processes influencing them to various degrees under given conditions and by provision of theoretical rationales for these effects.

The result of all this would be a pyramidlike edifice of general theory. The most abstract statement would be at the apex because it applies to all instances. Other abstract statements would be at a lower level in the pyramid because each applies only to specific parts of the more abstract statement at the top and each is expressed in conditional terms. And still less abstract, more conditional, statements will fit at a still lower level toward the base of the pyramid. In this way all supposed causal variables and processes having a systematic influence are part of one theory, linked together in a hierarchical network to feed one causal process at the top. Any degree of complexity and any number of causal factors could thereby be accommodated, and the explanatory process could extend as far down as anybody wanted to take it.

Failure

... A sense of theoretical failure has also been fostered by a malfunctioning interplay between theory and research. Theory grows as initial formulations are modified in light of empirical evidence. But criminologists rarely modify their theories through research reciprocation.

Like all social scientists, they repeatedly test original statements, conclude they are wrong, and let it go at that. For instance, anomie theory is much the same today as it was when first formulated, despite decades of empirical research, and it is regarded as just one of many failed general theories. Had anomie theory been expanded, altered, conditionalized, refined, and restructured by various scholars as the results of research and logical critique were fed back into it, it would now be quite different, having a cosmopolitan texture, and producing better explanations that would be more congruent with empirical facts. And had this same process been followed for each of the various theories in the criminological repertoire at the same time that they were being merged into one general theory along the lines suggested before, judgments about the failure of general theory would probably now be muted.

The tendency to preserve theories in their original infantile state while condemning them as failures is also the result of misapplied criteria of success. If A causes B, it does so under particular conditions, including specific degrees of A and other variables such as C, D, ... Z, and it produces specific degrees of B. The ultimate job of theory is to detail those conditions, tell why the process works as it does, and portray the circumstances under which A, C, D, ... Z will assume particular values. But this full conditional specification cannot emerge full blown from the minds of individual thinkers. To achieve it, one must continuously pump research information back into the theoretical structure and elaborate the theory to accommodate that information. This means that scholars must treat universal-appearing assertions, such as "A causes B," that might be derived from infan-

tile theories as actually only tentative, incomplete starting points. When such hypotheses are regarded as actual truth claims to be accepted or refuted whole, theories are killed before they can grow. Rigid testing of hypotheses strictly for judging the merits of a theory is appropriate only for the ad vanced stages of theoretical development, when mature schemes are comprehensively structured and deductively organized. Judging infant theories by adult standards is self-defeating and leads to unwarranted pessimism.

In light of all this, it cannot be said that efforts to construct general theories in criminology have failed or must necessarily fail; it is more appropriate to say that such efforts have never really been put forth. We have no idea what might be accomplished because criminologists have never seriously engaged in a collective movement to *build* general theory.

DISCIPLINARY OBSTRUCTIONS

Characteristics of the subject matter of criminology such as ambiguity, uniqueness, apparent indeterminacy, and complexity do not preclude general theory, nor does the relative weakness of the current product. They do, however, mandate careful attention to strategy. The tactics necessary for building general theory include (1) abstractive categorization and generalization; (2) integrative, hierarchical, conditional structuring of diverse causal processes; and (3) flexible reciprocation between theory and research. Yet it is precisely these strategic tactics that have been suppressed by academic subcultural and organizational norms and processes.

The first of these obstructions is the inability of the criminological community to mobilize enough scientifically oriented scholars to do the job. Theory building is a collective endeavor that requires a lot of people to add their contributions within a similar framework. But, despite ostensible commitment to science, criminology is actually so fragmented in its work philosophy that concerted efforts are difficult. Many criminologists literally have no consistent sense of what they are doing or how to do it. Scientific scholarship oriented from beginning to end toward theory is not a clear enough priority, and even those who claim to appreciate the theoretical task often misunderstand what it is. . . .

Second, employment of the necessary tactics for building general theory has been impeded by a collective adversarial approach to theoretical work. It seems that the social scientific community is more united in trying to prove the impossibility of general theory than it is in trying to construct one. New ideas or attempts to advance the theoretical enterprise are typically greeted with a barrage of attacks designed to refute those ideas rather than evaluate and use them. Innovators feel compelled to defend their offerings as if they were the whole truth, resisting modifications; and the collectivity refuses to rest until it has convinced itself of the utter worthlessness of a given theoretical effort. Thus the academic community polarizes itself into opposing camps, with critics bent on making would-be theorists admit they are wrong (as well as naive for ever having thought they might make a contribution to theory), while innovators and their defenders feel forced to prove they are right. The result is little cooperative movement toward achieving a common goal and, in addition, thinkers are made reluctant to

introduce bold, clear statements for fear of being mauled. . . .

Third, scholarly training has failed to convey the crucial difference between empirical variables and theoretical constructs, thereby hampering abstract formulation and research-theory reciprocation. Inability to understand and act on this fundamental duality has caused much grief. Among other things, it allows some to think they can measure aspects of empirical reality without theoretical guidance; that is, that important features inhere in phenomena themselves. And it leads others into despair because empirical observations per se refuse to yield to theoretical expression. . . . This two-way street mandates imagination on one hand and empirical discipline on the other. Unfortunately, students are sometimes persuaded that imagination is enough, although this is a rare fault. More often they are misled into believing that empirical discipline will suffice, particularly as this is embodied in routinized methodological procedures. Learning standard methods for data collection and analysis often diverts students from the ultimate goal, encouraging the belief that data contain within themselves knowledge that can be ferreted out mechanically. Tools in the hands of a skilled carpenter with a plan can lead to wonderful things, but their use without a plan will rarely produce anything worthwhile. . . .

Fourth, the criminological community has rendered theoretical progress difficult by promoting status criteria that emphasize individualized achievement rather than collective benefit. Social scientists are taught to be loners, self-possessed and defensive. Theories are assumed to belong to individuals and are not be to tampered with except by the inventors. This means that they cannot easily be adjusted to empirical results or merged into a larger scheme. But it is totally unrealistic to imagine that any one person can invent an adequate general theory. Such a theory must grow through the cooperative efforts of many scholars, as they add their small contributions. Criminology will be on the right track when its practitioners stop talking about so-and-so's theory and begin to speak of the theory of socially disapproved behavior, the theory of law (or social disapproval), or the theory of managerial organization (as it bears on management of socially disapproved behavior), signifying by these designations integrated products with many subparts. Then theory will rightfully be regarded as every scholar's responsibility.

Finally, criminologists have handicapped theoretical work by tolerating confusing, tautological, amphibolic writing. Theories must contain clear, unequivocal ideas, propositions, and implications, so that they can be understood and manipulated, and made to yield genuine predictions for empirical test. Otherwise there can be no meaningful feedback and no progress... Since communication is never completely successful, even under the best of conditions, it is mandatory that any scholarly endeavor strive for clarity, particularly in its theoretical work. But the criminological community has been so tolerant of meaningless language that many empty, disappointing schemes have provoked serious attention because it took so long to figure out what they were saying.

CONCLUSION

Although general theory is the preeminent goal of scientific criminology, not all agree that it is possible or desirable. Examination of aspects of criminological phenomena that have been alleged to prevent general theory suggests that critics are mistaken. Cultural and organizational features of the community of scholars have, however, thwarted the theoretical enterprise, and will continue to do so unless corrected. Nevertheless, there are hopeful signs that the theoretical enterprise is healthier than many realize.

NO

Michael J. Lynch and W. Byron Groves

IN DEFENSE OF COMPARATIVE CRIMINOLOGY: A CRITIQUE OF GENERAL THEORY AND THE RATIONAL MAN

This [essay] offers a defense of criminological research and theory that is both historically and culturally grounded, in light of a growing literature arguing in favor of general theory (e.g., Hirschi and Gottfredson 1986, 1987a, b, 1988, 1989; Gottfredson and Hirschi 1989, 1990; Tittle 1985). We offer this defense because we believe that general theory speaks against comparative theory; that it does so without providing an adequate critique of a comparative perspective; that it fails to pay heed to comparative research findings, especially those that demonstrate that "irregularities" require explanation (Kohn 1987); and because general theory fails to pay adequate attention to history and culture as important explanatory variables (Mills 1959/1977). Further, general theories are thought to be the end process of "science"; they result when enough particular problems have been solved, and enough evidence is amassed to allow the construction of general explanations from existing evidence (see Turner 1976; Aubert 1952: 263). We do not believe that criminology has reached such a stage.

We offer no specific comparative theory of crime..., since to do so would be at odds with our stated goal: criticizing general theory. Our goal is to defend historically informed comparative approaches by pointing out how and why general theories fail as explanations of crime.

...In our opinion, historically specific, culturally informed, and empirically valid theory is needed if criminology is to free itself from universal claims that exhibit ethnocentric biases and a retreat to the realm of metaphysical explanation....

GENERAL THEORY AND COMPARATIVE CRIMINOLOGY

My purpose in all this is to help grand theorists get down from their useless heights.

—C. Wright Mills,
The Sociological Imagination

The claim that comparative criminology should seek out universal causes of crime can be found in numerous works (e.g., Glueck 1964; Rokkan 1964; Cavan and Cavan 1968; Newman 1976; Clinard and Abbot 1973; Slomczynski, Miller, and Kohn 1981; Shelley 1981; Tittle 1985; Hirschi and Gottfredson 1987a, 1987b; Kohn 1987). As the name implies, advocates of universal (general) theory wish to ensure that causal regularities are not "mere particularities, the product of some limited set of historical or cultural or political circumstances" (Kohn 1987: 13). Thus, whatever the cause, the general theorist's concern is that it apply to all persons, cultures, and historical periods without exception.

In attempting to accomplish this goal, general theories differ with regard to the universal cause(s) of crime they specify. Sometimes the cause is found in human nature (e.g., crime is caused by the unbridled pursuit of pleasure), sometimes in drawn-out historical processes (e.g., crime is caused by modernization or industrialization) that are decontextualized or made abstract by the claim that the same process occurs everywhere, and sometimes in abstract principles (e.g., crime is behavior that promotes interpersonal insecurity). Regardless of the specific assumptions concerning crime, general theories favor interpretations that are "quintessentially transhistorical" (Kohn 1987: 729), lacking culturally grounded or historically specific qualifiers.

In addition to this transhistorical preference, general theory is ambitious in another regard. The flavor of that ambition is captured by Hirschi and Gottfredson's (1987a: 958) claim that their theory "is designed to account for the distribution of *all forms* of criminal behavior" (emphasis ours). This ambition is also evident in the work of Charles Tittle (1985: 101), who believes that all crime—acts as diverse as homicide and failure to stop at a traffic light—can be subsumed under one general theory. But, general theories of crime go much further than this when they claim that there is no need to explain different forms of crime with different forms of explanation (Hirschi and Gottfredson 1987a: 950), or even to address whether the same form of crime committed in different cultures or historical eras is caused by a different set of factors. The assumption has been made that the causes are the same, everywhere and always—seemingly without respect to the empirical evidence (e.g., see Katz 1988)....

Logical Style of General Theories

... Advocates of general theory tend to employ a similar logical style in constructing cross-cultural theories of crime. This style is drawn from a deductive model (Fay 1980: 30–36) which assumes that particular events (e.g., a crime) can be deduced from general assertions concerning those events (e.g., a general theory). Sutherland's theory of differential association, long thought to have cross-cultural applicability, is one example of this type of deductive reasoning (Friday 1974). In Sutherland's theory, the general assertion is that criminal behavior is learned, while the deductions entailed specification of the conditions and content of learned behavior (e.g., criminal behavior is learned from other persons in intimate groups, while the content of this learned behavior includes definitions favorable to law violation, techniques for committing crime, etc.; see Vold and Bernard 1985: 211). Tittle (1985: 112) highlights the top-to-bottom flavor of the deductive style as follows:

> The results of all this would be a pyramid-like edifice of general theory. The most abstract statement would be at the apex because it applies to all instances. Other abstract statements would be at a lower level in the pyramid.... And still less abstract, more conditional statements will fit at a still lower level toward the base of the pyramid. In this way all the supposed causal variables and processes having systematic influences are part of one theory..., and the explanatory process could extend as far down as anybody wanted to take it.

The problem with this approach, in our view, is not only with how far down this process is taken, but how far up (how general or universal) the argument is extended—or with how abstract the general theory becomes. The deductive style, in short, not only leads to reductionist arguments that can be extended down to the smallest unit (e.g., molecules, atoms, etc.; see Turner 1976: 253–57 and discussion below), but to abstractions that become meaningless because they lack a tangible connection to the lives of real individuals living in real, concrete social circumstances (Mills 1959/1977)....

Levels of Abstraction

... The following discussion provides a brief summation of [C. Wright] Mills' objections to general theory.

First, Grand Theorists tend to work with Concepts, thus excluding an examination of structural arrangements basic to an understanding of social life (Mills 1959/1977: 35). In short, the theorists who construct grand theory play a "conceptual game" devoted to defining concepts they believe necessary to an understanding of social order. In reality, these concepts fail to be meaningful since, in the construction of these concepts, the theorist omits a critical examination of how real-life structures, not theoretical concepts, affect life processes. In short, contextual theoretical development is sacrificed to conceptual development and clarification.

Second, Grand Theorists tend to begin with a priori assumptions (e.g., concerning human nature, the nature of social interactions, the nature of social order, etc.) that serve as nonempirical anchoring points for subsequent arguments (Mills 1959/1977: 39–42). Thus, the Grand Theorist's arguments are not only abstract because the discussion is confined to conceptual definitions, but also because theoretical assumptions and concepts are not grounded in the empirical realities generated by social structure.

Third, because Grand Theorists believe that their conceptions are of general or universal import, they are inclined to ignore historically specific empirical problems (Mills 1959/1977: 49; see also Kohn 1987). In effect, certain types of empirical evidence are ignored in general theory construction and concept building. As a result, historically specific instances that contradict the logic of the theory are ignored and treated as deviations from the norm that require no special explanation (see Kohn 1987 for further criticisms of this approach).

Finally, the fetishized concepts of grand theorists serve ideological and legitimation purposes (Mills 1959/1977: 48–49). General theory is not, as is commonly assumed, a neutral or objective framework through which social processes can be examined. Rather, general theory supports a particular (usually unstated) value position (see Myrdal 1969 for discussion of the problem of objectivity). Thus, the theory's structure mirrors and incorporates values that reflect idealistic versions of social processes. The purpose of such theory is to reinforce and legitimize values and interests that support the theory—values and interests that cannot be empirically grounded....

HIRSCHI AND GOTTFREDSON: A GENERAL THEORY OF CRIME

Under the heading "A General Theory of Crime," Hirschi and Gottfredson (1987b: 15; see also 1990, 1989, 1987a for similar arguments) propose the following program for comparative research:

> We ... *assume* ... that *cultural variability is not important* in the causation of crime, that we should look for constancy rather than variability in the definition and causes of crime, and that a single theory of crime can encompass the reality of cross-cultural differences in crime rates. From all this it follows that a general theory of crime is possible. (Emphasis ours)

Consistent with their view that partisans of universal theory should look for constancy in the definition and causes of crime, Hirschi and Gottfredson (1987b: 15–16) argue that the concept of crime must not build culture into its definition, and must not be defined in a strictly legalistic manner. Were crime defined in a legalistic way (as it has in fact been defined in a variety of cultures), then the general theorist would have to contend with the slew of objections concerning cultural (as well as historical) variations in the definitions of illegal behaviors (see Beirne 1983a: 383, 1983b for review of objections to this position). To avoid this problem, the authors sidestep empirical referents (cultural and historical variation in the definition of crime) and derive their definition of crime from a transhistorical conception of human nature. According to Hirschi and Gottfredson, "the conception of human nature that satisfies these requirements is found in the classical assumption that human behavior is motivated by pleasure and the avoidance of pain. Crimes, then, are events in which force or fraud are used to satisfy self-interest...." (1987b: 16, see also 1987a: 959, 1989: 360, 362). Grafting an individualistic emphasis onto this assumption, these authors argue that criminals are people who pursue short-term personal gratification without regard to long-term social interests (1987a: 959–60; 1989: 360). And finally, with reference to the issue of why persons might be inclined to seek immediate gratification, the authors state that "individual differences in the tendency to commit criminal acts are established early in life (in preadolescence) and are relatively stable thereafter" (Hirschi and Gottfredson 1987b: 19).

In the following sections we outline several objections to this style of theorizing. Some of these objections are external to the theory (i.e., they concern issues or assumptions not directly addressed by the authors but which nevertheless underlie the general assertion); while others concern internal components of the theory (i.e., the use of terms, assumptions, and deductions specified in the model).

External Objections

First, there is no reference to the considerable literature rejecting or sharply qualifying Hirschi and Gottfredson's assumptions concerning human nature; they do not attempt to account for the widely held view that human nature is historically variable or socially constructed (e.g., Allport 1955; Rogers 1961; Becker 1971; Henry 1963; Mills 1959/1977; Maslow 1982; Grose and Groves 1988)....

Second, there is no attempt to account for the sociological premise that motives are social rather than personal (Mills 1974; Becker 1964; Goffman 1959); nor is there reference to concrete historical circumstances and structures that guide motivations and intentions (Gerth and Mills 1964; Mills 1974); nor is there reference to the historically contingent relationship between opportunities and crime (Cohen and Felson 1979; Cohen, Felson, and Land 1980; Groves and Frank 1987). To give a brief example of an argument that links motivations to historically and culturally specific structures, we refer to the work of Jules Henry. Henry (1963: 20) notes that industrialized cultures have a market-driven mandate to create desire and stimulate consumption that required a mass psychological reorientation of society. Part of the psychic reorganization required in industrial cultures was the unleashing of impulse controls prevalent in Hebrew, Indo-European, and Islamic societies. Our point: There are clear and major theoretical differences between Henry's and Hirschi and Gottfredson's attempts to understand behavior. Henry, using a broad historically and culturally informed approach, situates drives for immediate gratification in an empirical, historical, and cultural context, while Hirschi and Gottfredson root drives in ahistorical/universal drives (for similar criticism of Homans' exchange theory see Turner 1976: 258–60). Henry's approach allows us to understand the behavior in different cultures on their own terms; Hirschi and Gottfredson's model forces the behavior of diverse cultures into an a priori theoretical framework, destroying any variation that existed in the object of study.

Third, there is no reference to literature in developmental psychology, or the existential tradition that challenges the claim that personality is fixed in preadolescence. Speaking directly to the claim that criminal predispositions are set in childhood, Harry Stack Sullivan (1953: 252) argued that "the notion that preadolescence readily constitutes a criminal, antisocial career is the most shocking kind of nonsense...." (see also Erikson 1959; Allport 1955; and Sartre 1962).

Fourth, there is no reference to literature linking personality to social relationships, social relationships to productive relationships, and productive relationships to specific historical context (Colvin and Pauly 1983; Turner 1976: 259)....

Fifth, there is no reference to literature in the philosophy of science that questions the applicability of this logical (deductive) style to the study of human behavior (Habermas 1971; Von Wright 1971; Bernstein 1971; Fay 1980; MacIntyre 1984; Otto-Apel 1984)....

Sixth, the deductive style of logic employed in Hirschi and Gottfredson's argument is reductionist....

And finally, there is no attempt to treat history as a variable of sociological relevance. History, in other words, is viewed as a description of factual relationships rather than a social record of processes reflecting cultural power relations....

Internal Objections

First, Hirschi and Gottfredson's use of the term *fraud* threatens their argument with circularity. On one hand, fraud is a legal category, and hence it is tautological to argue that criminals fraudulently pursue self-interest. On the other hand, if fraud is meant to be used in a broader, nonlegalistic sense, as these authors argue, then a variety of legally acceptable behaviors could be classified as fraud (i.e., criminal). The use of the term *force* poses similar problems. If force includes rapes, assaults, and robberies, we again face the tautological issue. If force is used in a broader sense, then a vast range of noncriminal behaviors might fall under this definition of criminality.

Second, Hirschi and Gottfredson's use of the terms *force* and *fraud* are not clearly defined. For example, we are instructed that "crimes are events in which force or fraud are used to satisfy self-interest" (1987a: 959), yet many noncriminal events involve the use of "force" and "fraud" to achieve the individual's desired goal. For instance, university professors often compel (force) their students to perform reading assignments by threatening to administer nonexistent quizzes (fraud) or in order to insure that classroom discussions run smoothly (the professor's self-interest). Here we have Hirschi and Gottfredson's three components of crime, yet no crime, as legally recognized, has occurred.

Third, the use of pleasure and pain and the relationship between pleasure and pain is caricatured.... Motivations, in other words, are far more complex than a simple pleasure/pain dichotomy suggests....

Fourth, there is no discussion of ways in which social structural arrangements central to any sociologically sound explanation define the contents of pleasure and pain, or determine those behaviors that will be responded to as force or fraud within a given cultural or historical era. In market economies, for example, the acquisition of commodities is "pleasurable."... In short, what counts as pleasure cannot be discussed apart from cultural definitions of the "good life."

Fifth, there is no discussion of ways in which social-structural arrangements condition the relative availability of, as well as access to, culturally defined pleasures and pains (Cloward and Ohlin 1960; Merton 1938)....

THE ROLE OF HISTORY AND CULTURE IN CRIMINOLOGICAL THEORY

...First and foremost, history is important insofar as it allows us to explain cross-cultural *differences* in rates of crime or the meaning of crime within a particular culture (Kohn 1987). For example, in order to make sense of the discrepant crime rates and approaches to crime in the United States and Japan, an extended analysis would have be performed that would incorporate the following historical materials: (1) A review of geographic and demographic differences, including relative population density, ethnic homogeneity/heterogeneity; (2) the relatively short history of the United States compared with the 1400-year written history of Japan, which has considerable impact on the importance of tradition in each culture; (3) the difference between Japan's historically situated aristocratic hierarchy and the United States's short history of nominal democracy and equality and how these traditions affect attitudes toward and respect for authority; (4) the differences between a recently emergent industrial/technological society in the United States, and a slowly evolving "rice economy" that requires cooperative efforts and centralized leadership for survival in Japan; and (5) the ways in which all of the above culminate in different cultural emphasis (i.e., on group relatedness, respect for authority, and work in Japan, and on individualism and competition in the United States; see Westerman and Burfeind 1986; Fishman and Dinitz 1989).... [B]y neglecting history and culture and their impact, general theory may well be producing claims that depend upon spurious relationships, and certainly upon relations and explanations abstracted from their social, historical, and cultural context....

THE RATIONAL "MAN"

The construct of the rational man is part of all theoretical structures that owe a dept to the utilitarian tradition. Hirschi and Gottfredson's approach is no exception.

The idea behind this approach can be boiled down to the claim that rational or calculating individuals assess the costs and rewards of their behavior before acting, pursuing self-interest and pleasure while avoiding pain. There is an undeniable link between this position and the approach adopted by economists who defended capitalist social relations as an outgrowth of human nature (cf. Smith 1776/1982; Turner 1976: 2ll). This construct, rather than being a description of real, human behavior, is a description of what "ought" to be, at least under

a capitalist system of production (Smith 1776/1982). In short, the premises of the utilitarian approach are historically specific constructs that fit societies, like capitalism, in which self-interest and the pursuit of pleasure are paramount concerns. Thus, such principles cannot apply to all situations, nor can they explain behaviors that are undertaken outside the context of market economies (Henry 1963)....

The Limits of Rational Man Models as Explanations for Crime

It is now well accepted within criminology that a theory of crime must explain at least three things in order to be complete and efficient: (1) motivation/cause; (2) opportunity structure; and (3) law enforcement activity and the structure of laws to be enforced, or reactive variables (Cohen, Felson, and Land 1980; Cohen and Felson 1979; Gibbs 1987: 831–33). A general theory that relies upon a rational man or pleasure/pain argument may successfully (though we do not believe it does) explain motivation, but it fails to address the other major elements that make up crime (e.g., opportunity structure, enforcement/reactions). Thus, even if we grant, for the moment, that Hirschi and Gottfredson are correct and that all people in all cultures and historical time periods act according to pleasure/pain determinations, it is still impossible to say anything of importance about crime, given that (1) rationality is a constant, meaning that it cannot explain cross-cultural or interpersonal variations in crime rates, and (2) that both opportunity and enforcement must be considered in order to explain variations in crime (Cohen and Felson 1979; Cohen, Felson, and Land 1980). For example, before there were laws expressly forbidding theft (see

Hall 1952), an individual who took some-thing that did not belong to him or her was not committing a crime, since in that culture and at that time, taking was not a crime. Likewise, hijacking of planes was impossible before the advent of the plane; the invention of the plane and its uses in modern society, coupled with political goals and motivations, create the oppor-tunity for this type of behavior....

CONCLUSIONS

In sum, we have argued that a general theory of crime—a theory that attempts to explain crime in all cultural and histor-ical milieus without reference to history or culture, but with reference to static, immutable forces—is impossible. There is too much variation in human behavior, criminal motives, cultures, economic con-ditions and circumstances, and historical contexts to expect *one* theory to be ap-plicable in all cultures and eras, or even in the majority of circumstances. General theory, in other words, is too broad to provide enough specific detail to explain crime.

What we argue in favor of is theory that is culturally and historically specific (see also Laufer and Adler 1989), and speaks directly to the context in which crime is committed, reacted to and constructed (e.g., Quinney 1970). According to this view, an adequate theory of crime must (1) address multiple levels of cau-sation; (2) demonstrate a connection between structural and subjective factors (Groves and Lynch 1990); (3) include a discussion of opportunity structure as an important (but not the only) dimension of understanding crime; (4) discuss the effects of enforcement policy, the content and construction of law as these elements bear upon the social construction of crime; (5) build theory from the bottom up (from the concrete), keeping in mind the cultural and historical limits of explanation (Mills 1959/1977; Kohn 1987); and (6) construct explanations for crime that are grounded in empirical realities while avoiding the pitfalls of brute empiricism (Groves 1985; Lynch 1987; Beirne 1979)....

In conclusion, we would also like to note that the history of criminology is replete with attempts to construct and apply general or universal theories of crime. Such an approach has yielded few answers to the problem of crime. Thus, it may be time to tear down the walls built by general theory and reconstruct a criminology that is sensitive to culture and history.

POSTSCRIPT

Are General Theories of Crime Useful?

Lynch and Groves reject the goal of eventually developing general theory. They contend that such a theory of crime would be no theory at all, since a general theory is both an empirical and logical impossibility. In this sense, it would seem that Lynch and Groves part company with many social scientists.

Tittle provides several reasons why he feels criminologists are so defeatist about general theory. He suggests that general theory has not failed, it simply has not yet been tried!

Within his discussion, Tittle advances a "mini-theory" of the forces, the organizational constraints, that have worked against the development of a general theory. He omits discussion, though, of several additional cultural factors equally inhibiting of general theory. These include the many research-funding organizations that are more interested in financing fairly narrow crime control studies, not broad, abstract theory building.

The current political situation is also one in which both politicians and the public tend to desire studies of how to more efficiently arrest, process, manage, and punish criminals. Theories, general or otherwise, about why people commit crimes are not particularly in vogue among policymakers. Moreover, a criminal justice administration mentality is far more appealing even to many criminologists. Traditionally, criminal justice has been an atheoretical, applied science interested in policy solutions to managing criminals. Although more progressive criminal justice programs are changing so that theory is being discussed more frequently, the political and financial situation seeks a very different kind of scholarly agenda than theory building.

Yet it can be argued that as rates of incarceration rapidly increase, and as the fear of crime and the perception of violent crime escalate, perhaps we are more in need of scientific explanations of crime than ever before. Many scholars would agree with Tittle's argument that general theory is a requirement for science. Efforts to incarcerate ever more citizens as a response to political and/or public hysteria border on the absurd, if not the dangerous. If crime is truly a problem, then what is needed is good theory to explain what is happening and to provide knowledgeable, logical, empirically based social responses. Tittle insists that general criminological theory can provide that knowledge.

Unfortunately, it is possible that this issue is so completely removed from the arena of academic organizations and discussions that the Tittle and Lynch-Groves debate matters little. Ironically, it seems that some people want the perception of a "quick fix" crime solution, such as increasing incarceration and/or executions, not theory (general or otherwise).

Are solutions possible without scientific explanations? Are explanations possible without theory? What is your favorite theory?

A mere 15 years ago there were almost no books on theoretical criminology or criminal justice as such. Now there are dozens of articles and texts. Among the more accessible undergraduate works are *Theoretical Methods in Criminology* edited by R. F. Meier (Sage Publications, 1985); G. B. Vold and T. J. Bernard's *Theoretical Criminology* (Oxford University Press, 1986); and *A General Theory of Crime* by M. Gottfredson and T. Hirschi (Stanford University Press, 1991). For several studies involving the building of general theories, see T. Hirschi and M. Gottfredson, eds., *The Generality of Deviance* (Transaction Publishers, 1994). J. Holman and J. Quinn's *Criminology: Applying Theory* (West, 1992) is one of the clearest statements of applied criminological theory. Also see J. R. Lilly et al., *Criminological Theory: Context and Consequences*, 2d ed. (Sage Publications, 1995). Two excellent criminological theory primers are R. Acker's *Criminological Theories* (Roxbury, 1994) and D. Gibbons's *Talking About Crime and Criminals* (Prentice Hall, 1994). Two good philosophy of science of criminology primers are B. DiCristina's *Methods in Criminology* (Harrow & Heston, 1995) and W. Einstadter and S. Henry's *Criminological Theory* (Harcourt Brace, 1995). Works that look at criminological theorists and ideas of the past include *Criminological Thought: Past and Present* by R. Martin et al. (MacMillan, 1990) and *Criminological Theory: Selected Classic Readings* edited by F. Williams and N. McShane (Anderson, 1992). Among the few books dealing with theory within criminal justice are M. Davis's *To Make the Punishment Fit the Crime: Essays in the Theory of Criminal Justice* (Westview, 1992) and R. D. Ellis and C. S. Ellis's *Theories of Criminal Justice: A Critical Reappraisal* (Hollowbrook, 1989).

Articles that examine criminological and/or criminal justice theories include T. Bernard and R. Ritti, "The Role of Theory in Scientific Research," in *Measurement Issues in Criminology* edited by K. L. Kempft (Springer-Verlag, 1990) and D. Garland, "Criminological Knowledge and Its Relation to Power," *British Journal of Criminology* (Autumn 1992).

One of the clearest statements as to what theory is that is still useful is R. Merton's *Social Theory and Social Structure* (Free Press, 1968). For a discussion of comparative criminology, see D. Nelken, "Whom Can You Trust? The Future of Comparative Criminology," in D. Nelken, ed., *The Futures of Criminology* (Sage Publications, 1994). An interesting analysis of feminist orientations within criminology that parallels Lynch and Groves's selection is S. Caulfield and N. Wonders, "Gender and Justice: Feminist Contributions to Criminology," in G. Barak, ed., *Varieties of Criminology* (Praeger, 1994). Finally, for a seminal delineation of the development of general theories within the social sciences, see E. Tiryakian's "Hegemonic Schools and the Development of Sociology," in R. Monk, ed., *Structures of Knowing* (University Press of America, 1986).

PART 2

Race, Gender, and the Criminal Justice System

Defining and explaining crime are only part of the problem. Sometimes the acts of investigating, arresting, and incarcerating criminals seem to have as much to do with maintaining societal inequities as with achieving justice. The criminal justice system has been accused of ignoring crimes and injustices committed against specific groups of people, such as women and minorities. Some say that a war on black criminals is being waged in the United States. A related contention is that the death penalty discriminates against blacks and other minorities. Are blacks unfairly persecuted by the U.S. criminal justice system, or do they simply represent the bulk of criminal offenders? Also examined in this section is whether pornography is a reinforcement of the unfair status that many feel women have in America or a constitutionally recognized exercise of free speech.

- Is the War on Black Criminals Misguided?

- Is the Death Penalty Racially Discriminatory?

- Should Pornography Be Banned as a
  Threat to Women?

ISSUE 6

Is the War on Black Criminals Misguided?

YES: Jeremy Seabrook, from "Crime and the Paradoxes of Consumerism," *Toward Freedom* (March 1995)

NO: Ed Koch, from "Blacks, Jews, Liberals, and Crime," *National Review* (May 16, 1994)

ISSUE SUMMARY

YES: Journalist Jeremy Seabrook, reflecting a radical perspective, argues that capitalism and increasing economic expansion based on greed leads to alienation, violence, and crime in many countries, including the United States.

NO: Former New York City mayor Ed Koch, joining a rapidly growing chorus of ex-liberals and traditional conservatives, both black and white, dismisses the view that a racist system is to blame for violent crime as apologetic nonsense.

A few years ago, when prominent black leader Jesse Jackson remarked that when he heard footsteps behind him he would feel relieved after looking around to see somebody white, he perhaps unwittingly reframed both public and academic dialogue about race and crime. Although since the 1980s there have been serious challenges to the common assumption that the criminal justice system is racist, very few mainstream politicians or criminologists would publicly characterize the war on crime as a needed war on black criminals.

The closest statement to this effect by respected scholars might have been James Q. Wilson and Richard J. Herrnstein's efforts to link "predatory" or "street" crime to young males in *Crime and Human Nature* (Simon & Schuster, 1985). Many were horrified by their analysis, claiming it was little more than antiseptic blaming of crime on black males. The posthumous publication of Herrnstein's coauthored book *The Bell Curve: Intelligence and Class Structure in American Life* in 1994, which claims that blacks have on average lower IQs than whites, causing them to be more criminogenic, served to confirm this view. Although the majority of the respondents to *The Bell Curve* bitterly attacked it, there are many who defend it and many prominent criminologists who have remained silent on the issue or who have indirectly supported Herrnstein's thesis. In addition, a growing number of conservative scholars, who may reject the alleged genetic link between race and crime, nonetheless feel that the solution to America's crime problem is largely a matter of catching and incarcerating more black criminals. Princeton University professor John J. DiIulio, Jr., in two recent issues of *Public Interest*, openly embraces this perspective. This is also the approach supported by Ed Koch in his selection.

The point is that 5 or 10 years ago such a simplistic approach to crime explanation and solutions (young, inner-city males running amuck, harming both blacks and whites) would have been unthinkable. Poverty, unemployment, deteriorating families, racism, discrimination, lack of training and opportunities—these were the explanations for crimes, not the criminals or some category of criminals themselves. The concomitant treatment modalities would consist of remedying the societal causes, not increasing incarceration rates and sentence lengths.

Theoretically, science (including criminology) strives to remain objective. Its causal analyses of phenomena are supposed to remain detached from momentary political constructions of explanations and solutions for problems, both cognitive and practical. Yet, as we move into increasingly conservative times accompanied by increased rates of violence and apparent escalating uncertainty, many political figures (including Koch) and some criminologists seem to openly eschew a search for causal explanations of crime.

Jeremy Seabrook scorns such blaming of blacks for crime. He acknowledges that there exists a crime problem, especially one of violence. He also feels that most existing programs to combat crime have failed. However, unlike Koch, he looks at social problems from a global perspective and theorizes that "solutions" are not intended to work. He argues that some industries make a great deal of money from crime problems, so the real causes of crime, such as consumerism and unfair competition, are kept hidden from the public. Crime is thus perpetuated and exploited for profit.

Notice that Seabrook's discussion of economies of the South pertain to Third World nations, not southern U.S. states. Does he cast his net too far in looking at the crime problem from a global perspective? Assuming that his causal analysis is correct, can any workable solutions be derived from his thinking?

Koch notes that most victims of street violence are poor blacks. What solutions does he specifically recommend? Do you think they are workable? Are his criticisms of some black leaders fair? Are they relevant to his discussion of black criminals?

In what ways might the "war on black criminals" be part of an alleged war on black Americans (e.g., reversals of affirmative action, open attacks on black leaders and achievements, and the denigration of black intelligence)? Is Seabrook correct in thinking that the war on black criminals is not only misguided but silly and racist? Is Koch correct in asserting that we need to step up the war to save the black communities from being destroyed by black criminals?

YES   Jeremy Seabrook

CRIME AND THE PARADOXES
OF CONSUMERISM

In a recent study of South Side Chicago, 47 percent of high school students reported having seen a stabbing, almost two-thirds had witnessed a shooting, and almost half had seen someone get killed. Shocking as they are, such statistics are part of the tireless accounting system of Western economics.

For example, 67 million handguns are owned by US private citizens, yet Smith and Wesson notes that sales of its Lady Smith line of rosewood-grip guns doubled [in 1994]. "We must teach our citizens that guns are dangerous consumer products," Health and Human Services Secretary Donna Shalala has declared in response.

Crime has reached the top of the American political agenda. The public is angry at the failure of previous efforts to solve the problem; nothing seems to stem the tide, not massive spending on social programs, or more prison-building, or mandatory minimum sentences. The problem is that the war against crime is a metaphor and a screen for the war against the poor.

What is occurring in rich societies—in increasingly beleaguered neighborhoods where lives are circumscribed by fear and insecurity—is reflected on the global scale; *mafiosi*, drug lords and criminal networks have come to play a role that equals or exceeds that of government in countries intent upon implementing the Western developmental model. In other words, the fates of Russia, Brazil, Colombia and the US are converging. Perhaps more than anything else, this is the effect of "global integration," the product of an overarching ideology that now pervades the entire world; the promise—or is it the illusion?—of Western consumerism.

FEAR AS A GROWTH INDUSTRY

More people are murdered in the US every year than are killed in many conventional wars. Meanwhile, the population inside American jails has increased over the last two decades from 218,000 to almost one million. Since it is hard to believe that human wickedness has increased fourfold since the mid-1970s, it's time to look more radically at the society which produces so much disorder.

Two elements in the graph of rising crime in the West stand out. One is the reality of the increase itself; the other, in some ways more significant, is the fear of crime and the ideological ends served by this psychosis. Fear imprisons the envied well-to-do in their gilded cells almost as effectively as the US penal system incarcerates its own malefactors in what has been called the American gulag.

Children increasingly must talk to friends via telephone and computer, or else lose themselves in the endless autism of video-games and cable TV— that window on a world which they may not enter unaccompanied. More and more women dare not go out, especially after nightfall. Old people refuse to open the door to callers. In many cities, parks and gardens have become no-go areas. It is a curious freedom that inhibits people from going out, a strange mutation in a mobile society which immobilizes so many, and a bizarre form of choice that leaves people with no option but to carry guns for self-defense against their fellow human beings.

Fed by dramatic media coverage, urged on by TV programs which must increase their ratings or perish, and whipped up by news media threatened with extinction if they don't provide ever greater levels of sensation, fear has become a powerful servant of a society which sees people only as individuals. And as if to prove it, society separates, isolates and atomizes its citizens so that they scarcely trust even their nearest and dearest, let alone some stranger on the street. Today, one in three US households consists of a single person, a fragmentation reflected in heightened economic ac-

tivity. People learn to defend themselves and take the offered consolations in the privacy of their own spaces. Thus, monstrous social evils are transformed into an economic good.

It is no wonder that the West is reluctant to examine the true relationship between crime, fear of crime, and society. Social dislocations have become business opportunities for the security industry, with its apparatus of protection; the firearms industry; the health-care industry, which must deal with the human wreckage; employees of the penal system; the builders of prisons; the judges and bureaucrats who administer the justice and corrections systems; and the healers of psychological trauma and social breakdown.

HUMAN NATURE AND CRUMBLING CULTURE

There has been considerable research into the origins of violence. In one study, published by the American Academy of Child and Adolescent Psychiatry, Dorothy Otnow Lewis found that 12 out of 14 juveniles on death row had long histories of severe beatings and sexual abuse, sometimes by drug-addicted parents. To some extent, all of them were re-enacting childhood traumas. But, as is often the case, the analysis stops here, severed from its social context.

Western Europe and North America face a strange paradox: the same societies that promote themselves as models of social peace and progress must accommodate themselves to escalating crime. What they nevertheless find hard to examine is the social patterns that produce deranged or damaged individuals. Some claim that poverty and unemployment are largely responsible, an assertion vigorously repudiated by the Right. There is rarely a whisper that other social pathologies might be involved. Yet if we hope to understand the meaning of crime figures, this is the place to look.

Britain, for example, recently faced a scare that occurred somewhat earlier in the more "advanced" US: abduction of children, kidnappings and sexual abuse. A curious fervor gripped the public imagination when social workers announced that they had uncovered widespread "satanic abuse" of children—sexual molestation in conjunction with devil-worship. Children from poor families all over the country were seized by the authorities and placed out of harm's way. However, an inquiry revealed that the allegations were unfounded.

The hysteria over satanic abuse demonstrated that some constituency is always ready to appropriate and professionalize the management of any social evil. It also showed that any new discovery about the depravity of human beings will find acceptance among credulous "realists" who claim to know human nature. Virtually every revelation further disgraces and diminishes human beings. Every week brings some fresh atrocity, reconfirming the popular perception that people are not to be trusted. This in turn furthers the spread of a lonely, fearful culture.

Such revelations also serve a deeper ideology, based on the concept of an unregenerate and unchanging human nature, and assist those who adamantly declare—despite convincing evidence to the contrary—that you cannot change the world. This argument is at the heart of the conservative project. But it is actually not so much human nature that is resistant to change, but rather the conformist requirements of a rigid socio-economic system.

Abuse of children, whether physical or sexual, is both a real problem and a resonant metaphor in Western countries. In one sense, abuse is part of their upbringing. Mysterious economic enticements reach them through the electronic media, turning them into apprentice consumers from infancy. Selling things to children—from toys and sweets to experiences—is a major industry that consistently interferes with their growth and development. They are sabotaged and subverted at every turn by amoral, restless economic forces whose goal is perpetual expansion, without regard for social or moral consequences. As a result, children cannot wait to grow up, to imitate the adults who they come to see as conspirators keeping them from consumerism's holy trinity—money, fun and sex.

Meanwhile, adults remain in perpetual childhood, infantilized by the rewards, treats and prizes offered by consumerism. Look at any American quiz show: the excessive whoops of joy and noisy ecstacies of a screaming audience in response to trivial amusements do not suggest a mature citizenry. In the West, humanity has been diminished by its appearance principally as customers, clients and consumers. In this context, it becomes easy for adults to neglect the protection of children and view them instead as rivals.

Such a way of life, which systematically urges people to abandon control of their needs and desires, to give in to temptation and indulge themselves, is bound to uncover some fairly unsavory tastes and predilections.

PARADOXES OF DESIRE

Giving people what they want has become the highest imperative of consumer society. "Few articles in the economist's creed outrage non-economists more than the pure, imperturbable belief that human wants are insatiable," writes Stanley Lebergott in his book, *Pursuing Happiness*. While it is true that humans have always yearned to be more beautiful and intelligent, and to free themselves from loss, decline and death, these have never before been seen as legitimate arenas for economic exploitation.

The consumer society falsifies unrealizable fantasies; indeed, it feeds longings for eternal youth and immortality —things that cannot be achieved—while remaining resolutely impotent in the face of poverty and exploitation, about which something can be done. This is a curious reversal, a cruel paradox: Magic remedies are offered for incurable maladies of our existence, but readily curable ills are perceived as part of the unalterable laws of nature. A system which so effectively estranges people from their own humanity is bound to have fateful consequences.

The awakening of ever fresh wants emanates from a social and economic structure that requires continuous growth and expansion. Human needs and the necessities of capitalism occasionally coincide, but more often they are far apart. Moreover, the arousal of desires—and the offering of often bogus satisfiers—has deep repercussions. You can't create a need for some new commodity through tantalizing TV ads and not expect other, less acceptable wants to be kindled at the same time. Along with a newly discovered need for, let's say, cordless electric scissors, a pivoted swing golf-tee, "Living with Divorce" videos and an electronic thesaurus, other strange wants are stimulated—perhaps a desire for sexual relations with children, a murderous hatred of women, an uncontrollable urge for power, or a reluctance to be thwarted by anyone standing in your way. In 1992, for example, an American teenager in Florida shot three people and stabbed another in a fast-food restaurant because, "I had a boring day."

The iconography of consumerism is derived from an aristocratic model of imperious desire and whim that has been elevated into mass marketing. Such a process inevitably breaks down other inhibitions and restraints. Those who bemoan "loss of discipline" are actually deploring the very basis on which their culture rests. The infinity of human desire is an invention of industrial economics, as revolutionary in its way as the discovery of steam power. The analogy is not far-fetched: The immense pressure of desire is what drives the economic motors of the Western system, just as steam once drove mills, ships and locomotives.

The swelling of this system to the point that no one can see an alternative is truly tragic. In the process, human resources are laid waste at the same time as the earth itself is ravaged and gutted. Getting money becomes the primordial human need, superceding all others. In answering this need, resources are used up, and we are used up with them. Quantities of waste are produced, including those people who live on the debris of consumerism—mostly in the South.*

Another paradox is that freedom of choice both drives people into these excesses and actually abridges choice by

*[Seabrook refers to nations in the Southern Hemisphere, i.e., Third World countries.—Ed.]

extinguishing biodiversity. The imagery of effortless luxury spreads a true mono-culture in which pluralism, tolerance and diversity are increasingly difficult to dis-cern. Consider this unexpressed caveat in Western concepts of freedom: You are free to buy anything you can afford, but you aren't free to set up other ways of an-swering human needs. Crime—and the debate about it—cannot be truly under-stood outside this context.

AN ABSENCE OF ALTERNATIVES

Those who promote global capitalism as the supreme achievement of world civilization are swift to absolve society from responsibility for the increase in crime. Not all the disadvantaged or un-employed become criminals, they say. Most of the poor are law-abiding. There-fore, poverty and unemployment play no part in the growth of wrongdoing.

But the orgiastic nature of the mar-ket economy is itself a source of pro-found disorder—and not only for those excluded from its questionable benefits. The buy-in culture, far from rendering life more satisfying, actually robs human be-ings of the ability to provide goods and services for themselves and each other. It leads them to dependency on distant and unknown providers, many of them transnational entities whose deepest pur-poses are scarcely commitment to the public good.

In the West, human identity is pared down to its most irreducible character-istics—black or white, male or female, young or old, gay or straight. We are then offered the "freedom" to buy what we want, to be whom we choose, to forge an identity out of the hypermarket that is culture. Traditions and customs are swept away. It is no accident that the image of

the melting pot emerged in the US—a meltdown of local, regional and rooted cultural traditions and its replacement by the human being as consumer.

For those seeking to understand crime, there are at least two consequences to consider. First, anyone without the money to create a commerciogenic iden-tity is truly an outcast. Second, people's power and energy must be directed to a single end: getting money to acquire the extensive necessities of life in this bare, denuded culture. But only the very rich can keep pace, the poor are left stranded, and the rate of consumption continu-ously increases.

There are other important effects on structures of human feeling. The public rituals and celebrations that once acted as a communal purge of emotion have fallen into profitless extinction. The juvenile killer says he turned a gun on his class-mates because he was bored. Of course he was bored. There's nothing for him to do but want and desire, and he will never have enough money to satisfy them.

In destroying neighborhoods, ruining kinship networks, breaking down com-munity and family, outlawing solidarity and undermining trade unions, society has produced its own cancellation. In-dividuals have been left alone to make their own private accommodation with the market. In the richest societies, the ba-sic needs of a whole generation have been neglected—and not merely adequate nu-trition and shelter, but also the need for meaning and social purpose. The ni-hilism and detachment that flourish in the absence of significant purpose are the consequences of a malignant ideology of extreme individualism.

Extremism. It is something the West professes to abhor. Yet what could be more extreme than a society which uses up vast quantities of the earth's substance, robbing the poor of the space to breath, and yet also fails to satisfy its own population? This is development, Western-style.

Crime flourishes in the absence of alternatives. In the West, it has become a form of unofficial private enterprise, through which people who have given up hope in social or economic change take the remedy for their dispossession into their own hands. Having no other form of expression, they become destructive and violent. This provides a clear advantage for society's leaders. Crime is, of course, more manageable than popular organization for change. It is also both a caricature and reflection of the values of enterprise, the buccaneering which the Right so admires.

To the impoverished countries of the South, the sacrifice of human well-being on the altar of economic growth may seem like a small price to pay. But the social costs should be clearly understood. Although the West has resisted counting them, they are being forced onto the political agenda. Therefore, countries which are busily applying prescriptions for success offered by the West ought to reflect on the frightful costs their people may someday have to pay. If the connections are made, governments of the South may yet avoid some of the social dislocation and violence. But if they don't, at least they won't be able to say, "Nobody ever told us that the dream of Western wealth spelled such human desolation."

NO

Ed Koch

BLACKS, JEWS, LIBERALS, AND CRIME

In 1964, I, along with thousands of other young men and women, went to Mississippi and elsewhere in the South to assist in the program initiated by black organizations to register black voters. The group was mostly white and preponderantly Jewish.

I spent a week in Mississippi, and the only place I felt comfortable was in the black community, either in the church where we met to plan strategy, or in the homes of black citizens where I spent each night. Everywhere else, in Jackson and in Laurel, the city where I actually tried cases and was subject to mob threats, I was very frightened—not of blacks, but of whites.

This was an historic moment for me personally and for the nation. In the church every night we sang "We Shall Overcome" with great feeling.

Today, most whites, myself included, would feel very uncomfortable in a totally black neighborhood, particularly at night. What has happened in the last thirty years? Well, Jesse Jackson summed up the reasonableness of white fear in black neighborhoods when he recently said, "There is nothing more painful to me at this stage in my life than to walk down the street and hear footsteps and start thinking about robbery—then look around and see somebody white and feel relieved."

So the fear is not irrational. To finish the story, however, when Jackson was later condemned for telling what is clearly the truth, he gave a ludicrous explanation. He said, in effect, what I really meant was that if I saw a white face I would know that whites were moving into the neighborhood and that there would therefore be more cops around. Poor man. Plain fear of his colleagues caused him to so demean himself. But, as his earlier and more honest remarks had conceded, fear of black crime is not irrational or rooted in prejudice.

In New York City, 57 per cent of those in prison are black and 35 per cent Hispanic. According to Department of Justice statistics, 45 per cent of violent crimes are committed by black males, who are only 6 per cent of the population. And black males aged 15 to 24, who are 1 per cent of the population, are responsible for at least 19 per cent of the murders.

BLACK VICTIMS, WHITE FEAR

It is true that large numbers of these crimes are committed black on black; but what difference does that make? If a person is brutalized, it makes no difference to whites if the victim is black, not white. Whites are still frightened by the violence, as are the overwhelming majority of blacks who are law-abiding. Several years ago, if I had cited these violent-crime figures, I would have been attacked as a racist even though they are accurate. I take some credit for having been willing to cite them in a quest for truth and in order to call attention to the cancer of crime, realizing that unless the cancer is identified you cannot treat and remove it.

It has now become acceptable to discuss black crime. Two years ago Bill Bradley stepped onto the Senate floor and said, "In politics for the last 25 years, silence or distortion has shaped the issue of race and urban America... there are two phenomena here. There is white fear, and there is the appearance of black emboldening... you snatch a purse, you crash a concert, break a telephone box, and no one, white or black, says stop. You rob a store, rape a jogger, shoot a tourist, and when they catch you, if they catch you, you cry racism. And nobody, white or black, says stop."

And President Clinton himself last November called for an end to the violence in a speech to black ministers at the Memphis church where the Reverend Martin Luther King Jr. delivered his last sermon. Said Mr. Clinton: "I tell you, unless we do something about crime and violence and drugs that is ravaging the community, we will not be able to repair this country."

He went on: "If he [Martin Luther King] were to reappear at my side today and give us a report card on the last 25 years, what would he say? 'You did a good job,' he would say—voting and electing people who formerly were not electable because of the color of their skin.... He would say, '[You] did a good job creating a black middle class of people who really are doing well, and the middle class is growing more among African-Americans than among non-African-Americans.'... But he would say, 'I did not live and die to see the American family destroyed. I did not live and die to see 13-year-old boys get automatic weapons and gun down 9-year-olds just for the kick of it... I fought to stop white people from being so filled with hate that they would wreak violence on black people. I did not fight for the right of black people to murder other black people with reckless abandonment.'"

It is interesting to note that the *New York Times*, commenting on this speech, remained true to its traditional role of denigrating jail time for criminals and always seeking to identify the "root causes" of crime. It sought in this case to link minority crime not so much to personal responsibility, as the President did, but rather to vicissitudes with which the individual could not cope. The *Times* wrote, "As inspiring as it was, Mr. Clinton's sermon was only a prologue to an urban policy. Big-city mayors will surely want to hear more of how he intends to stimulate investment in cities... What of gun control?... What of welfare reform?"

I must say that when I hear the words "root causes," I want to got to the nearest window, as Peter Finch did in *Network*, and yell, "I'm mad as hell and I'm not going to take it any more." When we find those root causes, and when we find what it is that will prevent people from engaging in crime, we should put it all in a pill and force-feed those miscreants. But until then, punishment and incarceration are the only answers we have available. Those who in effect urge designer ankle bracelets for home monitoring instead of jail—so that we will know where the criminals are so we can send them their Social Security checks—generally live in Connecticut and summer in the Hamptons. They do not have to live with the consequences of their sentimentality. When their hearts bleed for criminals the rest of us can expect to find other parts of our bodies bleeding in due course. We can no longer afford the "decency" of the *New York Times* because it is decency at other people's expense.

I agree wholeheartedly with what Prime Minister John Major said concerning... two ten-year-olds accused of kidnapping and murdering a toddler: "I feel strongly that society needs to condemn a little more and understand a little less."

Unless we deal with the disaffiliated in our cities—who are overwhelmingly, but not exclusively, black and Hispanic —we will not overcome the enormous racial division in our society. In addition to the proposals in the crime bill now being debated in Congress, I have two modest suggestions on how that can be done. One of the few votes I regret casting while I was a congressman was ending the military draft without creating a mandatory National Service Corps. We should now institute such a corps, requiring all dropouts and new high-school graduates to serve for two years. Unlike the military, it should not exclude drug addicts or those with criminal records. Indeed, the key is to remove those who are disaffiliated from their current environment and instill some self-discipline and decent values in them.

The National Service Program I propose goes much further than President Clinton's, which I fear will only end up assisting those who would make it anyway. The larger program I am proposing would be expensive, but it would be more than worth it if it helps get potential criminals back on track.

In addition, we should institute a system whereby any person who has a criminal record but who completes service in the corps would be eligible for an executive pardon, allowing him to start fresh in return for clear evidence of self-reformation. To be eligible, a person would have to have gotten his GED, been off drugs for three years with weekly testing, and not been convicted of a crime in that period. With such a pardon, when he applies for a job and is asked, "Have you ever been convicted of a crime," he will be able to answer, "No." That will give him an opportunity for a new start. Of course, there are some crimes for which such pardons can never be available: murder, rape, pedophilia, to name the most obvious.

RACIST STATISTICS?

Let me now address those who reject the crime statistics I have cited, alleging that racism causes these arrests. It must be noted that in the last thirty years, black mayors have been or are in charge of Chicago, Detroit, Los Angeles, New York, Philadelphia, and hundreds of other cities. Currently, blacks have elected forty members to Congress, many holding positions in the leadership, and a senator, Carol Moseley Braun, from Illinois, a state that has a black population of only 12 per cent. And the highest position in our armed forces was held until recently by Colin Powell, a black man who would be a popular candidate for President if he were to run in '96.

Yet in Washington, D.C., with a black mayor, a black city council, and many black judges, 42 per cent of black males aged 18 to 35 were awaiting trial, in jail, or on probation in 1991. Across the river in Baltimore, also with a black mayor, etc., the figure was 56 per cent. Yes, racism does exist, but it cannot be blamed for the deplorable state of the black underclass. Indeed, the claim that it can is an important influence making crime worse and law enforcement more feeble.

Pulitzer Prize–winning columnist William Raspberry wrote in January 1993, "For them [young African-Americans] the culprit isn't lack of money but racial disadvantage, and the 'cure' is not a lucky lottery ticket but the defeat of racism.

" 'If it weren't for racism, [they say] I'd have better grades and I'd be able to get into the graduate school of my choice—and also have the money to pay the tuition there. If it weren't for racism, I would have had my promotion by now. I wouldn't have been stopped for speeding, and if I had I certainly wouldn't have been given that big a ticket. You think that cop would have arrested me for what I said if I'd been white?'

"I hear the recitals—the excuses—and I find them as fanciful as my dreams of winning the lottery and getting in shape. Most of the things complained of would be considerably eased by some combination of exertion, self-discipline, and mouth control. Racism serves as a sort of generalized rationalization for not trying."

The Farrakhan phenomenon is directly related to this problem. In a recent poll

of blacks conducted for *Time* magazine, Farrakhan was the second most popular black leader with 9 per cent. Number one was Jesse Jackson, who now has embraced Farrakhan, with 34 per cent. In addition, in a survey conducted by a University of Chicago professor, 62 per cent of the African-Americans polled said Louis Farrakhan represents "a positive view within the black community."

What is it that makes Farrakhan acceptable to mainstream black leaders and organizations? It is their failure to deal with black crime, the drug culture, and the pathology of illegitimacy, where 66 per cent of black children are born out of wedlock (in Harlem, it's more than 80 per cent). These leaders are throwing up their hands and looking to Farrakhan, who, with his demagogic anti-Semitism and racism, has done for blacks what Hitler did for a dispirited German population. The Führer told Germans their condition wasn't their fault, it was everybody else's fault, particularly the fault of the Jews, and that is exactly what Farrakhan is saying to blacks.

Farrakhan tells his people, You are better than white people—not just equal to white people, but better. And, as reported in a March 5 *New York Times* article, "According to the Nation [of Islam], whites were created by Yakub, the mad scientist, as a test for the superior black race, who are the chosen people, and also as a curse on it." This has been going on for years.

Yet we witnessed a shocking spectacle [in] September [1994] when the Congressional Black Caucus, the NAACP, and Jesse Jackson's Rainbow Coalition announced, at a panel discussion I saw on C-SPAN, that they were joining in a "Sacred Covenant" with Farrakhan. Farrakhan was one of five panel members addressing the all-black audience, which cheered his every statement. His co-panelists were Jesse Jackson; NAACP director Ben Chavis; Representative Kweisi Mfume, the head of the Congressional Black Caucus; and Representative Maxine Waters, cheerleader for the L.A. rioters.

And when the House of Representatives overwhelmingly adopted a resolution denouncing the hate-mongering speech of Khalid Muhammad, 20 members of the Black Caucus voted in favor, but 11 voted against it, 4—including Mfume—voted present (i.e., abstained), and 3 didn't vote at all. Can you imagine the outcry if, on a House resolution condemning David Duke, a comparable percentage of the 32 Jewish members of the House had voted "no" or "present," or not voted at all?

Some extraordinary leaders in the black community, like Congressman John Lewis of Georgia, have shown enormous courage by standing up and separating themselves from their colleagues in the Black Caucus. On the House floor during the debate on the Muhammad resolution, Lewis said, "I deeply feel we have a moral obligation and a mandate and a mission to speak out against the remarks made by Khalid Abdul Muhammad at Kean College. Mr. Muhammad delivered a poisonous and a hateful speech. Any time such hateful expression rears its ugly head, it should not go unchallenged."

Black leaders correctly say to white America, "You cannot tell us who our leaders should be." I agree, but I say to them you cannot expect decent white people, whether they be Christians or Jews, to embrace organizations that have embraced Farrakhan and his ilk.

At this point we should say to black organizations with which—whether Khalid Muhammad wants to believe it or not—we have fought side by side in the civil-rights battle, that we can no longer accept their explanations that they are only supporting Farrakhan's positive anti-crime and anti-drug messages. It would be just as unacceptable if someone sought to separate David Duke's concern for the white underclass in Louisiana and its standard of living from his anti-black, anti-Semitic rhetoric. You cannot segregate the good from the bad in a racist demagogue.

Missing in discussions of "black rage" is its mirror image, "white rage." There is discrimination in this country, but whites fail to see how lingering discrimination can be used as an excuse for black violence.

Each year we see further advancement of minorities toward equality. But equality implies two sides. It means a single standard whether you are white or black. It means working together, not segregation. There was a time when white racists like David Duke predominated. Regrettably, we see a replay of that prejudice, but this time in the hands of some blacks like Louis Farrakhan.

There will come a time when the vast majority of blacks—tired of being the target of crimes by other blacks, tired of the false leaders who use the racism of some whites to excuse the ills in their community—will turn away from these demagogues. Until that day arrives we have to be willing to tell the truth.

POSTSCRIPT

Is the War on Black Criminals Misguided?

In 1905 the preeminent black social scientist W. E. B. Du Bois observed that the problem of the twentieth century would be the problem of the color line. His comments, uncanny in their accuracy, remain true today. This is especially so for criminology. In 1944, in his book *American Dilemma*, Swedish social scientist Gunnar Myrdal said that America indeed has a problem with race: it is the problem of how white people treat blacks. Is the war on black criminals (and by extension the creation and perpetuation of the idea that crime in America is really crimes committed by a disproportionate number of young, black males) rational? Or is this simply another example of the color line being resurrected or of powerful whites and their scholarly allies misrepresenting the nature of the crime problem, mistreating blacks in the process?

Does the media's and politicians' concentration on street crime deflect attention away from white-collar crime to crimes of the poor and minorities, as Seabrook contends? Although Koch makes no genetic claims for a black propensity toward deviancy, is he misguided in his ignoring of corporate crimes and those of the government? Koch waxes nostalgic for the "good old days," when both whites and blacks were "safe" in black communities. Should we ask *why* many folks, including blacks, apparently no longer feel safe? Seabrook would answer that greed and a rapidly developing economy dislocate many young people, generating alienation and crime. But might the answer lie somewhere in between Koch's sweeping attack on blacks and Seabrook's blanket condemnation of the system?

For several early discussions of the issue, see W. E. B. Du Bois's *Philadelphia Negro* (Benjamin Blom, 1899) and *Some Notes on Negro Crime* (Atlanta University Press, 1904). A more recent work on blacks and crime is Shaun L. Gabbidon, "Blackaphobia: What Is It, and Who Are Its Victims?" in P. Kedia, ed., *Black on Black Crime* (Wyndham Hall Press, 1994). For a challenge to Koch's views, see C. Mann, "The Contribution of Institutionalized Racism to Minority Crime," in D. Hawkins, ed., *Ethnicity, Race, and Crime* (State University of New York Press, 1994). An outstanding analysis of the effects of residential segregation is *American Apartheid: Segregation and the Making of the Underclass* by D. Massey and N. Denton (Harvard University Press, 1993).

A stimulating work that many love to hate is W. Wilbank's *Myth of a Racist Criminal Justice System* (Brooks/Cole, 1987). Important challenges to Seabrook's position are in J. DiIulio, Jr., "The Question of Black Crime," *Public Interest* (Fall 1994), which includes several pointed responses.

ISSUE 7

Is the Death Penalty Racially Discriminatory?

YES: Adalberto Aguirre, Jr., and David V. Baker, from "Empirical Research on Racial Discrimination in the Imposition of the Death Penalty," *Criminal Justice Abstracts* (March 1990)

NO: Stanley Rothman and Stephen Powers, from "Execution by Quota?" *The Public Interest* (Summer 1994)

ISSUE SUMMARY

YES: Sociology professors Adalberto Aguirre, Jr., and David V. Baker contend that with regard to the most severe penalty for committing a crime possible —the death penalty—racial discrimination remains a fact of life in America.

NO: Social scientists Stanley Rothman and Stephen Powers adamantly reject the common view that race is a factor in the imposition of the death penalty. When researchers control for type of crime, they find that capital punishment is not at all discriminatory.

Until recently, discrimination against black Americans by the criminal justice system has been universal. Blacks, almost all studies of the past show, were more likely than whites to be harassed by police, arrested, brought to trial, given prison sentences rather than probation, given longer prison sentences, be denied parole, and have more severe guidelines for parole when it was granted. Within courtrooms in the South and occasionally other regions, judges sometimes allowed different forms of address for blacks. For instance, as late as 1968 in Alabama, both prosecuting and defense attorneys had the right to refer to black female defendants (or witnesses) as "Auntie" or "Missy," regardless of their social achievements or professional titles. Black males were likely to be called "Boy" or "Uncle." Such demeaning labels served to minimize the credibility of black witnesses and defendants.

Even in northern and western states, blacks were almost never judges, prosecutors, legislators, police administrators, or wardens. Blacks were also systematically excluded from jury duty in many counties, especially in major cases. Thus, black defendants were often denied the right to a trial by their peers.

Historically, the greatest injury and miscarriage of justice were executions. It is well documented that prior to the U.S. Civil War (1861–1865), slaves and even "free" blacks were subject to capital sentences for many crimes that would have entailed a relatively short prison term if committed by whites. In addition, for blacks, executions, even legal ones (i.e., nonlynchings), were sometimes quite brutal. These included burning, beheading, drowning, being beaten to death, and being dragged behind horses. For blacks who were lynched, the mutilations and tortures were sometimes even worse (3,446 known lynchings occurred between 1882 and 1968). Symbolically, lynchings, which were at least indirectly sanctioned by the legal system (no lynchers were prosecuted), are the most extreme form of racism.

Since 1930 almost 4,100 persons have been executed in the United States, either by electrocution, lethal injection, the gas chamber, firing squad, or hanging (lethal injection is becoming the method of choice). Currently, 38 states have capital crimes. Until the Supreme Court ruled that execution for rape is unconstitutional, some 455 persons were executed for this crime, mainly in the South (where almost 90 percent of all executed rapists were black). Of all people executed since 1930, almost 55 percent were black or members of other minority groups. Currently, blacks compose 12.4 percent of the U.S. population. Of the 3,000-plus now on death row, 40 percent are black males. Of the three dozen women awaiting execution, one-third are black females.

In the following selections, Adalberto Aguirre, Jr., and David V. Baker argue that these statistics are proof that the death penalty remains discriminatory. Stanley Rothman and Stephen Powers counter that sociologists and others who make the discrimination case rely only on extralegal variables (e.g., race) in analyzing the number sentenced to die. What should be taken into account, Rothman and Powers insist, is the circumstances surrounding the crimes. These clearly meet the Supreme Court guidelines for execution in that they always involve a heinous murder of one or more persons. Blacks, they say, are statistically more likely to commit extremely violent acts and are therefore more likely to be sentenced to death. Indeed, they maintain, when type of crime and circumstances are controlled for, whites are actually more likely to be sentenced to death and executed than blacks. Moreover, they suggest, this has been true historically. A racially discriminatory criminal justice system has been and remains a myth contrived by sociologists and criminologists who know little about legal research.

As you read this debate, remember that the stakes are high. Thousands of men and women have been executed, and many are currently on death row. Statistically, a disportionate number are blacks and other minority group members. Does this indicate that discrimination is occurring?

YES

Adalberto Aguirre, Jr.,
and David V. Baker

EMPIRICAL RESEARCH ON RACIAL DISCRIMINATION IN THE IMPOSITION OF THE DEATH PENALTY

The U.S. Bureau of Justice Statistics (1985) reports that between 1930 and 1984 there were 3,891 prisoners executed under civil authority in the United States. Of these figures, 2,067 (53.1%) were black, 1,773 (45.5%) were white and 42 (1.0%) were of other races. There were 1,640 (48.7%) blacks and 1,686 (50.8%) whites executed for murder. Racial disparity in imposing the death penalty becomes even more clearly defined among executions for rape. Of the 455 executions for rape during this period, 89% (405) were of blacks and 10.5% (48) were of whites. The South executed 98.3% (398) of all blacks executed for rape. While the north central region of the country executed the remaining seven blacks executed for rape, the western and northwestern sections have never executed a black for rape. The District of Columbia, Virginia, West Virginia, Mississippi, Louisiana and Oklahoma have never executed a white for the crime of rape.

Given that blacks have consistently represented about 11% of the total American population since 1930, these statistics overwhelmingly indicate that the death penalty has been disproportionately applied to blacks. Blacks have been executed for murder at over five times the rate of executions for whites, and blacks have been executed for rape at about nine times the execution rate than whites. These statistics alone do not show that racial discrimination has characterized the imposition of the death penalty to blacks. But a number of empirical studies have shown that in the case of blacks, disproportionality in the application of the death penalty amounts to racial discrimination. The purpose of this paper, then, is to review the empirical studies that have established rather pervasive evidence that the death penalty has not only been disproportionately applied to blacks convicted of rape and murder, but that the death penalty has been imposed on black prisoners in a discretionary and discriminatory manner. This review will clearly illustrate that racial discrimination has become so well entrenched and routinized

From Adalberto Aguirre, Jr., and David V. Baker, "Empirical Research on Racial Discrimination in the Imposition of the Death Penalty," *Criminal Justice Abstracts*, vol. 22, no. 1 (March 1990). Copyright © 1990 by Willow Tree Press, P.O. Box 249, Monsey, NY 10952. Reprinted and condensed by permission of *Criminal Justice Abstracts*.

in imposing the penalty of death on blacks that it has developed into a "systematic pattern of differential treatment" of blacks.

Many studies have documented evidence of racial discrimination in the imposition of the death penalty on blacks. These studies will be reviewed in relation to whether they were conducted before, during the interim, or after the United States Supreme Court decisions in *Furman v. Georgia* (1972) and *Gregg v. Georgia* (1976). The *Furman* decision basically held that all death penalty statutes in the United States were unconstitutional because they permitted capital punishment to be applied in a discretionary and discriminatory manner amounting to "cruel and unusual punishment" in violation of the Eighth Amendment of the U.S. federal Constitution. The *Furman* decision did not abolish capital punishment in the United States; the court argued that the death penalty "in and of itself" does not constitute cruel and unusual punishment, but, the capricious manner in which the penalty had been applied in the cases before the court at the time of *Furman* was held unconstitutional. In the *Gregg* decision, the court attempted to curb the extent to which the death penalty was applied to blacks in a discretionary and discriminatory manner by providing for guided discretion in capital sentencing. The court affirmed the death sentences of the cases under review in *Gregg* because the states from which the cases had originated, in their capital statutes, had directed attention to the circumstances of the crimes and provided for consideration of mitigating factors designed to protect against arbitrary imposition of the death penalty.

PRE-*FURMAN* STUDIES

The earliest study of black-white differentials in the administration of justice was completed by Brearley in 1930. Brearley found that among 407 homicide cases in South Carolina between 1920 and 1926, 52% of the accusations resulted in guilty verdicts. Of these convictions, 64% involved black defendants and 32% involved whites. Brearley ... attributes this finding to "such factors as race prejudice by white jurors and court officials and the Negro's low economic status, which prevents him from securing 'good' criminal lawyers for his defense" ...

As early as 1933, Myrdal reported that in ten southern states: "The Negro constitutes less than thirty percent of the population in these states, but has more than twice as many death sentences imposed. Actual executions make the racial differential still greater, for 60.9% of the Negro death sentences were carried out as compared with 48.7% of the white" ...

In 1940, Mangum studied racial disparities in imposing the death penalty in several southern states. In his book *The Legal Status of the Negro*, Mangum reports that for the years 1920 to 1938, 74% of the blacks and 50% of the whites sentenced to death were executed....

Allredge (1942) reported that conviction rates for criminal homicide dramatically differed for blacks and whites in several regions of the South from 1940 to 1941. Allredge found that 89% of the blacks accused of murdering whites were convicted; 67% of the blacks accused of killing blacks were convicted; 64% of the whites accused of murdering whites were convicted; and only 43% of the whites accused of murdering blacks were convicted....

Johnson (1957) studied rape cases resulting in the application of the death penalty in North Carolina between 1909 and 1954. He found that 56% of all persons executed during this period were black, and 43% were white. Johnson's study concluded that blacks were far more likely to suffer the death penalty for rape than whites convicted of rape.

The Florida Civil Liberties Union reported similar findings from a study conducted in that state in 1964. In Florida between 1940 and 1964, 54% (45) of the black males who raped white women, but none of the eight white males convicted of raping a black female, received the death penalty....

Kleck (1981), who has critically evaluated the studies on racial discrimination in the use of the death penalty conducted prior to the *Furman* decision, makes two observations about these various studies. First, he argues that while there are conclusive patterns of racial discrimination against blacks in the use of the death penalty, these patterns are mostly restricted to the imposition of the death penalty in southern states. On this point, however, Kleck is incorrect. While racial disparities in imposing the penalty of death are more pronounced in the South, studies by the Ohio Legislative Service Commission (1961), Wolfgang et al. (1972), Zimring et al. (1976), Carter and Smith (1969), Kalven (1969), Bowers and Pierce (1980), Bedau (1964, 1965), and Gross and Mauro (1984, 1989) have shown that patterns of racial discrimination in presentencing, sentencing, and postsentencing decisions are not simply restricted to southern jurisdictions.... Gross and Mauro (1984), in fact, have commented on Kleck's conclusion. They note that "(t)o say there is no racial discrimination in capital sentencing, except

in the South, is a bit like saying that there is no housing discrimination in a metropolitan area, except in the major residential district."...

The second observation made by Kleck is that black defendants who murder black victims are the least likely defendant-victim category associated with the death penalty outside of the South. This observation has substantial merit, as noted above. In attempting to explain the apparently lenient treatment of black defendants convicted of murdering a black victim, Kleck suggests that "interracial crimes... are considered by [the] predominantly white social-control agents to be less serious offenses, representing less loss or threat to the community than crimes with white victims."...

Review of pre-*Furman* studies on capital punishment demonstrates that the death penalty was systematically applied to black defendants in a discretionary and discriminatory manner. We have seen that this practice has not simply been relegated to the South, but that racial discrimination in the use of the death penalty has been a national characteristic. Moreover, these various studies illustrate the extent to which racism has permeated the criminal justice institution in the United States....

THE INTERIM PERIOD (POST-*FURMAN*, PRE-*GREGG*)

Several studies have been conducted on racial discrimination during the interim period after *Furman* was decided by the U.S. Supreme Court in 1972, but before the court handed down its decision in *Gregg* in 1976. One of the most important studies conducted during this period compared the racial composition of offenders under the sentence of death in December 1971 (pursuant to pre-*Furman* capital statutes) with offenders under the sentence of death as of December 1975 (pursuant to mandatory and discretionary post-*Furman* capital statutes). Riedel (1976) not only found that the racial disparities affecting death row inmates in the pre-*Furman* era remained unchanged in the post-*Furman* period, but also that black defendants-white victims was the racial category with the highest rate of death sentences imposed. Riedel reported that 53% of the death row inmates in December 1971 were nonwhite, and that this figure rose to 62% in December 1975. While the racial disparity of death row populations in the South had declined from 67% to 63% during this period, the western region of the United States increased its degree of racial disparity of black/white death row inmates from 26% to 52%. From these figures, Riedel concluded that the statutes enacted before and after the *Furman* decision produced the same degree of racial disproportion in death sentences.

Riedel also found that 87% of the death sentences were for white-victim murders, and 45% were for the murder of white victims by black defendants. The degree of racial disparity in death sentences is even more pronounced in this period (1971–1975), and the white victim-black defendant category comprised the smallest proportion of the total number of murder cases.

In a study of first-degree murder prosecutions in Dade County, Florida, from 1973 to 1976, Arkin (1980) reported that black defendants who murdered whites were more likely to be sentenced to death than white defendants. Arkin's data reveal that black offenders who killed whites were convicted of first-degree murder about four times more often than blacks who killed blacks. While the black offender/white victim category of criminal offense comprised only 21% of the 350 murder cases prosecuted, 50% of the cases resulting in death penalty sentences came from that category of offender....

In sum, these studies show that the *Furman* decision had little or no diminishing effect on the extent to which black capital offenders were subjected to racial discrimination in imposition of the death penalty. As noted, the *Furman* decision ruled that discrimination in applying the death penalty is blatantly unconstitutional. These studies show, however, that the death penalty was still used as a mechanism by which to protect a specific class of individuals—namely whites—from criminal victimization. Black defendants whose victims were white were overwhelmingly convicted and sentenced to death when compared to other racial categories of defendant-victim. *Furman* had no demonstrable effect on the manner in which the death penalty was being applied in this country.

POST-*GREGG* STUDIES

In *Gregg*, the U.S. Supreme Court upheld the constitutionality of the death penalty for murder. The court affirmed the convictions because the states from which the capital cases originated had provided for: bifurcated trials (one trial to establish the guilt of the defendant, and another trial to determine an appropriate sentence); consideration of mitigating circumstances of the defendant and the crime; and appellate review of capital sentences. These guidelines were affirmed by the court because they were specifically designed to prevent arbitrary and discriminatory imposition of the death penalty....

Within the past few years, empirical analyses have revealed that the guidelines established in *Gregg* have failed to eliminate racial disparities in capital cases. One of the most extensive studies analyzing data collected after the *Gregg* decision was conducted by Bowers and Pierce (1980). Bowers and Pierce examined patterns of death sentencing in Florida, Texas, Ohio, and Georgia from 1972 to 1977.... Basically, Bowers and Pierce found that the decision to execute in these states reflects the same arbitrariness and discrimination that has characterized the imposition of the death penalty in the past (before the *Furman* and *Gregg* decisions). In each of these states, Bowers and Pierce found that killers of whites were more likely to be sentenced to death than killers of blacks, and that black defendants with white victims were more likely to receive the death penalty than white defendants with black victims. In Florida, black defendants with white victims were found to have a 22% chance of being sentenced to death; white defendants with white victims had a 20% chance; and black defendants with black victims had a .6% chance. It should be noted that in Florida, no white was sentenced to death for the killing of a black. Georgia and Texas had somewhat lower rates of death sentences according to defendant-victim categories, but the pattern of racial discrimination in imposing the death penalty in particular defendant-victim racial combinations still prevailed.... More specifically, black defendants with white victims were eight times more likely to be sentenced to death than black defendants with black victims. In addition, Florida prosecutors overcharged non-felony homicide cases involving black killers of white victims as felony homicides. Bowers and Pierce have pointed out that the data on felony homicides suggests that "in black offender/white victim cases, prosecutors may have alleged felony circumstances to enhance their plea bargaining positions or as a demonstration of concern for the kinds of crimes the community finds most shocking."... Likewise, in Florida and Georgia, appellate review of capital sentences did not correct for patterns of racial discrimination in imposing death to blacks. Thus, the guidelines established in *Gregg* have "become the instruments of arbitrariness and discrimination, not their cure."...

Radelet (1981) examined whether race remains a significant factor in the processing and outcome of post-*Furman* homicide cases in 20 Florida counties in 1976 and 1977. He discovered that blacks accused of murdering whites were more likely to be sentenced to death than blacks accused of murdering blacks. This trend is explained by Radelet as due primarily to higher probabilities that blacks accused of murdering whites would be indicted for first-degree murder.... Thus, Radelet's study tends to indicate that racial discrimination is alive and well in Florida's criminal justice system to the extent that a lower value is placed on the lives of blacks than on the lives of whites....

Using data on 1,400 homicide cases in some 32 Florida counties between 1973 and 1977, Radelet and Pierce (1985) examined disparities between police reports and court records on "felony," "possible felony" and "non-felony" homicides. Among racial combinations of defendant-victim, black defendants who killed white victims were considerably more likely to have their cases upgraded to a felony charge and least likely to have their cases downgraded to a lesser charge as they moved through the judicial process....

In South Carolina, Paternoster (1983) found that when the race of the offender and of the victim are considered together a clear pattern of racial disparity in prosecutors' decisions to seek the death penalty is evidenced.... The race of the victim appears to be a more important consideration of public prosecutors than is the race of the offender, concludes Paternoster. Hence, post-*Furman* capital punishment statutes fail to remedy the problem of racial discrimination influencing imposition of the death penalty in capital cases....

Gross and Mauro... conducted a very extensive study of sentencing under post-*Furman* death penalty laws in Arkansas, Florida, Georgia, Illinois, Mississippi, North Carolina, Oklahoma and Virginia.... While the data permitted separate analyses for Georgia, Florida and Illinois, death sentences for the states of Arkansas, Mississippi, North Carolina, Oklahoma and Virginia were analyzed collectively. In Georgia, Florida and Illinois, Gross and Mauro... found that while blacks and other racial minorities comprised a larger percentage of homicide victims than whites, the risk of a death sentence was far lower for suspects charged with killing blacks than for defendants charged with killing whites. For the state of Georgia, defendants who killed whites were almost ten times more likely to be sentenced to death than defendants whose victims were blacks; in Florida, the killers of whites were eight times more likely to be sentenced to death; and in Illinois, killers of whites were about six times more likely to be sentenced to death.

When controlling for the race of the victim, Gross and Mauro found that blacks who killed whites were far more likely to be sentenced to death than whites who killed whites....

McCLESKY v. KEMP (1987)

In 1978, Warren McClesky, a black man, was convicted in Fulton County, Georgia of murdering a white police officer during an armed robbery of a furniture store. The conviction was in keeping with the Georgia statute, under which a jury cannot sentence a defendant to death for murder without a finding that the crime was aggravated by at least one of ten particular circumstances. McClesky failed to present any mitigating evidence to the jury and was subsequently sentenced to death.

On appeal to the U.S. Supreme Court, McClesky claimed that the Georgia capital sentencing process is administered in a racially discriminatory manner in violation of the eighth amendment protection against "cruel and unusual punishment," and that the discriminatory system violates the fourteenth amendment guarantee to the "equal protection of the law." McClesky proffered the results of the Baldus et al.... study in support of his claim. In 2,484 murder and non-negligent manslaughter cases in Georgia between 1973 and 1979, defendants who killed whites were sentenced to death in 11% of the cases, while defendants who killed blacks were sentenced to death in only 1% of the cases. Baldus et al. discovered that the death penalty was imposed in 22% of the cases where the defendant was convicted of murdering a white, 8% of the cases with white defendants and white victims, 3% of the cases with white defendants and black victim, and only 1% of the cases involving black defendants and black victims. Baldus et al. controlled for some 230 non-racial variables and found that none could account for the racial disparities in capital sentences among the different racial combinations of defendant-victim. Killers of whites were 4.3 times more likely to be sentenced to death than killers of blacks, and black defendants were 1.1 times more likely to be sentenced to death than other defendants.

McClesky claimed that race had, therefore, infected the administration of capital punishment in Georgia in two distinct ways. First, "prisoners who murder whites are more likely to be sentenced to death than prisoners who murder blacks," and, secondly, "black murderers are more likely to be sentenced to death than white murderers" (*McClesky*, 1987:9). McClesky held that he was discriminated against by the Georgia system of imposing the death penalty because he is a black man who killed a white.

On April 22, 1987, the U.S. Supreme Court handed down its decision.... The question before the court in *McClesky* was "whether a complex statistical study that indicates a risk that racial consideration enters into capital sentencing determinations ... is unconstitutional under the Eighth and Fourteenth Amendments" (*McClesky*, 1987:1).

Writing for the majority, Justice Powell held that the Baldus study does not prove that the administration of the Georgia capital punishment system violates the equal protection clause of the fourteenth amendment or the eighth amendment's protection against cruel and unusual punishment. The court held that "a defendant who alleges an equal protection violation has the burden of proving 'the existence of purposeful discrimination,'" and that the "purposeful discrimination had a discriminatory effect on him." That is, McClesky must prove that the jury in his particular case acted with a discriminatory purpose; to establish only that a "pattern" of racial discrimination in imposing the death penalty to a select group of defendants is not sufficient to support a claim of constitutional violation of equal protection of the law. The court further held that McClesky's claim of cruel and unusual punishment also fails because McClesky "cannot prove a constitutional violation by demonstrating that other defendants who may be similarly situated did not receive the death penalty." The Georgia sentencing procedures were found by the court to be sufficient to focus discretion "on the particularized nature of the crime and the particularized characteristics of the individual defendant," and that it cannot, therefore, be presumed that McClesky's death sentence was "wantonly and freakishly" imposed.

The essence of the court's holding in *McClesky* is that there are acceptable standards of risk of racial discrimination in imposing the death penalty. The court held that the Baldus study simply shows that a discrepancy appears to correlate with race in imposing death sentences, but the "statistics do not prove that race enters into any capital sentencing decisions or that race was a factor in petitioners' cases." The court was also concerned that a finding for the defendant in this case would open other claims that "could be extended to other types of penalties and to claims based on unexplained discrepancies correlating to membership in other minority groups and even to gender."

To Justices Brennan, Marshall, Black-mun, and Stevens, "McClesky has clearly demonstrated that his death sentence was imposed in violation of the Eighth and Fourteenth Amendments," and that "(n)othing could convey more power-fully the intractable reality of the death penalty: 'that the effort of eliminate ar-bitrariness in the infliction of that ulti-mate sanction is so plainly doomed to failure that it—and the death penalty—must be abandoned all together" .... The dissenters argued that whether McClesky can prove racial discrimination in his par-ticular case is totally irrelevant in evaluat-ing his claim of a constitutional violation because the court has long recognized that to establish that a "pattern" of sub-stantial risk of arbitrary and capricious capital sentencing suffices for a claim of unconstitutionality.

The dissenting justices also called into question the effectiveness of the statutory safeguards designed to curb discretionary use of the death penalty. Justice Brennan specifically argued that "(w)hile we may hope that a model of procedural fairness [as that established in *Gregg*] will curb the influence of race on sentencing, 'we cannot simply assume that the model works as intended; we must critique its performance in terms of its results" ....

CONCLUSIONS

This review has examined several of the more important studies that have been conducted on the extent to which arbi-trariness and discrimination characterize the imposition of capital punishment in the United States. Two substantive con-clusions emerged. First despite the at-tempts by the U.S. Supreme Court in *Fur-man v. Georgia (1972)* and *Gregg v. Georgia*

(1976) to thwart racial discrimination in the use of capital punishment, the death penalty continues to be imposed against blacks in a "wanton" and "freakish" man-ner. Second, the specific finding by many of the studies that blacks who victim-ize whites consistently have the high-est probability of receiving a capital sen-tence tends to substantiate the claim that capital punishment serves the extralegal function of majority group protection; namely, the death penalty acts to safe-guard (through deterrence) that class of individuals (whites) who are least likely to be victimized.

The review has shown that the death penalty continues to be imposed to blacks in a capricious manner. That is, the ev-idence tends to confirm the hypothesis that arbitrariness is an inherent charac-teristic of the use of the death penalty. Studies by Riedel (1976) and Arkin (1980) show that the same degree of racial disparity present in pre-*Furman* cases is also prevalent in post-*Furman* cases. Several other studies have also shown that the safeguards for guided discre-tion in the use of the death penalty have failed to correct for the racial dispari-ties. Specific analyses have shown that as long as individual prosecutors con-tinue to have broad-based discretion to select which cases they will try as capi-tal cases, racial discrimination in applica-tion of the death penalty will undoubt-edly continue. Racial discrimination in the use of the death penalty has also been found to be perpetuated through appel-late review of capital cases. The irony here is that the appellate courts were highly touted in *Gregg* as the foremost safeguard against unguided discretion in the appli-cation of the death penalty.

Various studies reviewed in this paper have shown that black defendants with white victims have been overwhelmingly convicted and sentenced to death when compared to other defendant-victim racial categories. . . . These findings clearly show that when whites are the victims of heinous crimes perpetrated by blacks, punishment is much more harsh. The review clearly illustrates that racism has become so well entrenched and routinized in the imposition of the death penalty that it has developed into a systematic pattern of differential treatment of blacks that is specifically designed to protect members of the dominant white group. While a preponderance of contemporary authors and jurists writing on theories of crime and punishment readily cite retribution and deterrence as foremost rationales for imposing the death penalty on those who commit heinous crimes, this review of empirical studies shows that the death penalty serves the extralegal function of protecting whites.

As we have seen in reviewing post-*Gregg* studies, the wrongs of racial prejudice, racial inequality, and caprice in the imposition of the death penalty have not been abolished by the procedural safeguards established in *Gregg*. Capital punishment continues to be imposed in a wanton and freakish and discriminatory manner against black criminal defendants. As Goodman has explained, "the sentencer's choice between life and death increasingly appears inchoate and uncontrollable, a decision more visceral than cerebral." . . . Empirically-based evidence that racial discrimination continues to influence the imposition of the death penalty has literally been ignored by the court in *McClesky*. The proposed safeguards that surround the application of the death penalty amount to no safeguards at all. The only substantive conclusion that can be drawn from this re-

view is that the court has moved from a position of formally recognizing that imposition of the death penalty is imbued with racial prejudice (*Furman*), to a position of sanctioning racial prejudice as a cost of imposing the penalty (*McClesky*). It appears from the cases handed down from the court that racism is a legitimate penological doctrine. For the advocates of racial and ethnic equality, the death penalty cannot be morally justified on the premise that racial oppression, subjugation, and social subservience are legitimate liabilities of maintaining social order. Social order under these circumstances amounts to social order predicated upon racism.

REFERENCES

Allredge, E. (1942). "Why the South Leads the Nation in Murder and Manslaughter." *The Quarterly Review* 2:123.

Arkin, Steven (1980). "Discrimination and Arbitrariness in Capital Punishment: An Analysis of Post-*Furman* Murder Cases in Dade County, Florida, 1973–1976." *Stanford Law Review* 33:75–101.

Baldus, David C., Charles Pulaski and George Woodworth (1983). "Comparative Review of Death Sentences: An Empirical Study of the Georgia Experience." *Journal of Criminal Law and Criminology* 74(3):661–770.

―― (1985). "Monitoring and Evaluating Contemporary Death Sentencing Systems: Lessons from Georgia," *University of California, Davis Law Review* 18(4):1375–1407.

Bowers, William J. (1974). *Executions in America*, Lexington, MA: D.C. Heath and Company.

―― (1983). "The Pervasiveness of Arbitrariness and Discrimination Under Post-*Furman* Capital Statutes." *Journal of Criminal Law and Criminology* 74(3):1067–1100.

―― and Glenn L. Pierce (1980). "Arbitrariness and Discrimination Under Post-*Furman* Capital Statutes." *Crime & Delinquency* 26(4):563–635.

Brearley, H. (1930). "The Negro and Homicides." *Social Forces* 9(2):247–253.

Carter, Robert M. and LaMont A. Smith (1969). "The Death Penalty in California: A Statistical Composite Portrait." *Crime & Delinquency* 15(1):63–76.

Furman v. Georgia (1976). 408 U.S. 238.

Johnson, Elmer (1957). "Selective Factors in Capital Punishment." *Social Forces* 35(2):165–169.

Kalven, Harry, Jr. (1969). "A Study of the California Penalty Jury in First-Degree Murder Cases. [Preface.]" *Stanford Law Review* 21:1297–1301.

Kleck, Gary (1981). "Racial Discrimination in Criminal Sentencing: A Critical Evaluation of the Evidence with Additional Evidence on the Death Penalty." *American Sociological Review* 46:783–804.

McClesky v. Kemp (1987), Slip Opinion #84–6811.

Paternoster, Raymond (1983). "Race of Victim and Location of Crime: The Decision to Seek the Death Penalty in South Carolina." *Journal of Criminal Law and Criminology* 74(3):754–785.

___ (1984). "Prosecutorial Discretion in Requesting the Death Penalty: A Case of Victim-Based Racial Discrimination." *Law & Society Review* 18(3):437–478.

Radelet, Michael (1981). "Racial Characteristics and the Imposition of the Death Penalty." *American Sociological Review* 46:918–927.

___ and Glenn Pierce (1985). "Race and Prosecutorial Discretion in Homicide Cases." *Law & Society Review* 19:587–621.

___ and Margaret Vandiver (1983). "The Florida Supreme Court and Death Penalty Appeals."

Journal of Criminal Law and Criminology 73:913–926.

Riedel, Marc (1976) "Discrimination in the Imposition of the Death Penalty: A Comparison of the Characteristics of Offenders Sentenced pre-*Furman* and post-*Furman*." *Temple Law Quarterly* 49:261–287.

Wolfgang, Marvin E. (1974). "Racial Discrimination in the Death Sentence for Rape." In: William J. Bowers ed., *Executions in America*. Lexington, MA: D.C. Heath and Company, 109–120.

___ and Marc Riedel (1973). "Racial Discrimination and the Death Penalty." *Annals of the American Academy of Political and Social Science* 407:119–133.

___ and Marc Riedel (1975). "Rape, Race, and the Death Penalty in Georgia." *American Journal of Orthopsychiatry* 45:658–668.

___, Arlene Kelley and Hans C. Nolde (1962). "Comparison of the Executed and the Commuted Among Admissions to Death Row." *Journal of Criminal Law, Criminology, and Police Science* 53(3):301–311.

Zimring, Franklin, Sheila O'Malley and Joel Eigen (1976). "The Going Price of Criminal Homicide in Philadelphia." *University of Chicago Law Review* 43:227–252.

NO

Stanley Rothman and Stephen Powers

EXECUTION BY QUOTA?

On March 17, 1994, the House Judiciary Committee voted to incorporate the Racial Justice Act into this year's Omnibus Crime Control Bill. The Act essentially would create quotas for the administration of the death penalty, under the assumption that the penalty is applied in a manner discriminatory to black Americans. While the legislation has been opposed by House Republicans, one should not, given the temper of the times and the mood of Congress, discount the possibility that it eventually will become law.

The Racial Justice Act would prohibit "the imposition or execution of the death penalty in a racially discriminatory pattern." Further, the Act provides that to establish a prima facie showing of discrimination:

> it shall suffice that death sentences are being imposed or executed ... upon persons of one race with a frequency that is disproportionate to their representation among the numbers of persons arrested for, charged with, or convicted of, death-eligible crimes....

THE CONTROVERSY

The employment of the death penalty as the ultimate criminal sanction has been the subject of enormous debate. Execution has been challenged not only on moral and religious grounds, but more recently on constitutional grounds—as a violation of the Eighth Amendment's protection against cruel and unusual punishment. Opponents of the death penalty contend that it is employed so arbitrarily as to amount to a game of state-sponsored Russian roulette. While the Supreme Court has not ruled capital punishment to be unconstitutional, in 1972 it held that the death penalty was unconstitutional as then practiced, finding evidence of arbitrariness sufficient to require that states overhaul death sentencing procedures.

One of the most controversial aspects of the arbitrariness claim is the charge—leveled by numerous activists and social scientists—that the death penalty has been applied in a manner unfair to blacks. In *Furman vs. Georgia* (1972), several members of the Court observed that racial discrimination had

From Stanley Rothman and Stephen Powers, "Execution by Quota?" *The Public Interest* (Summer 1994). Copyright © 1994 by National Affairs, Inc. Reprinted by permission. References omitted.

produced different patterns of sentencing and rates of execution for blacks and whites. Indeed, numerous studies of the late 1800s and early 1900s have found that blacks were executed in disproportionate numbers, particularly when the victims of their crimes were white.

The apparently discriminatory impact of capital punishment has not gone unnoticed in Congress. In fact, one aim of the Racial Justice Act is to circumvent prior federal court decisions which have held that statistical research does not provide sufficient evidence of "discriminatory intent" to trigger Fourteenth Amendment protection. The Act states that "it shall not be necessary to show discriminatory motive, intent, or purpose on the part of any individual or institution."

If the Racial Justice Act becomes law, state and federal authorities will have to demonstrate that any racial disparities in sentencing are "clearly and convincingly" explained by non-racial factors. Given the high cost of litigation and likely delays, as well as the difficulty of proving non-discrimination when sentencing is based partly on factors not easily subjected to statistical analysis (how does one quantify the "heinousness" of a crime?), states could be forced to abandon death sentences against some black defendants, irrespective of the merits of the cases. If this occurred, sooner or later it might also be an easy matter for white defendants to show discriminatory sentencing under the same law. The death penalty would be effectively eliminated.

But is death sentencing truly discriminatory? The truth is complicated by a number of factors that opponents of the death penalty have tended to discount or ignore. There appear to be legitimate reasons for racially disparate sentencing. In-

deed, a number of social scientists have argued that racial prejudice is not a significant determinant of execution rates. These social scientists have demonstrated that when a number of legal factors are taken into account, the relationship between a defendant's race and the likelihood of execution tends to disappear. Why, we must ask, in spite of the questionable validity of the discrimination thesis, does the death penalty continue to be assailed as one of the most repugnant manifestations of American racism?

PAST STUDIES

Before the Supreme Court's decision in *Furman,* a majority of death penalty studies had reported that discrimination against black defendants was substantial, particularly in cases of rape and in the South. Certainly there was ample historical precedent. By law, black slaves were subject to the death penalty for numerous crimes for which whites received much more lenient sentences. In 1848, for example, Virginia enacted a statute which required that blacks be executed for any crime for which whites might receive three years' imprisonment (Dike, 1981). The evidence for discriminatory death sentencing through the nineteenth and early twentieth centuries, particularly in the South, seems incontrovertible.

Even when discriminatory sentencing was not actually prescribed by law, statistical studies show that before the 1950s black offenders were much more likely than whites to be executed for murder. In 1930, H. C. Brearley reported that in South Carolina, from 1920 to 1926, blacks accused of murder were twice as likely as whites to be convicted. And during the period from 1915 to 1927, blacks were more than three times as likely as whites to be executed. Numerous researchers reported similar findings from the 1930s through the late 1960s.

Nevertheless, by the mid-1970s studies were uncovering methodological problems with some of the earlier research. In 1974, John Hagan reanalyzed a number of studies involving capital sentencing and found that most of the studies had confused correlation and causation. When Hagan controlled for prior record and type of offense, he found that the influence of race dropped dramatically. He concluded that:

> knowing the race of the offender... increases the accuracy of predicting judicial disposition by 1.5 percent. The causal importance of even this minimum relationship, however, is called into doubt by the single study controlling simultaneously for charge, and related "third" variables.

In a similar vein, a 1981 study by Gary Kleck found that between 1929 and 1966 the rate of execution for blacks (9.7 per 1,000 murders) was slightly lower than that for whites (10.4 per 1,000 murders). Indeed, Kleck made another important observation: "in the recent past, outside of the South, white execution risk has been substantially higher than the nonwhite risk, a fact which apparently has gone unnoticed in the literature."

In the past, Kleck suggested, black criminals may have been treated relatively leniently because their crimes against other blacks were not taken seriously, or perhaps because of white paternalism (blacks frequently were viewed as less culpable for their actions). In more recent times, Kleck suggested, the relatively lenient treatment of blacks may be due to the attempts of judges to compensate for what they perceive as institutional racism, or to make up for their own unconscious racism. Kleck also noted that his own figures do not take into account prior sentencing records and that, since in other studies this factor has tended to suppress racial disparities, his own findings probably understate the higher execution risk for whites. Overall, although Kleck found evidence of discrimination in certain historical periods (especially in the South), and for particular classes of crime such as rape, he found no evidence of system-wide discrimination in the imposition of the death penalty beyond the 1950s.

Since the publication of Kleck's study, many other studies have appeared that also find white defendants to be at greater risk in murder cases than black defendants, even in the South, though one or two of the studies have attempted to explain the findings away in a manner described below (Baldus et. al., 1990; Ekland-Olsen, 1988; Gross, 1985; Katz, 1989; Nakel and Hardy, 1987; Pesternoster, 1984; and Radelet, 1981).

With some research indicating that discriminatory sentencing of black offenders was confined to the South and probably had ended by the 1950s, sociologists began to search for more subtle evidence of discrimination. As far back as the 1930s, a handful of studies had reported that blacks who killed whites were more likely to receive the death penalty than blacks who killed other blacks, or than whites who killed members of either race. One of the first of these studies hypothesized that, as a subjugated race, blacks were "treated with undue severity" (Johnson, 1941). The author of the study found that in a sample drawn from parts of three southern states, black offenders were significantly more likely to be executed when their victims were white than black. Only 64 percent of blacks sentenced to death for killing other blacks were executed, whereas 81 percent of blacks who killed whites were put to death.

The researcher argued that blacks who killed other blacks were treated leniently because they were viewed by authorities as childish and not fully culpable for their actions. Yet when blacks killed members of the dominant racial caste, they were punished especially severely, to keep them in their place. Without considering the influence of factors other than race, the author concluded that the data "point toward a partial confirmation of our hypothesis." This failure to consider alternative explanations is characteristic of the research prior to the 1960s.

However, some later and better-constructed studies have reached similar conclusions. One study, published in 1983, found that the offender-victim racial combination was at least as significant as predictive factor in death sentencing as any other legal variable (e.g., contemporaneous felony, multiple victims).

A number of studies have attributed this seeming racism to prosecutorial discretion. A recent study in Kentucky, for example, suggested that prosecutors tend to view cases in which blacks kill whites as more serious than other types of cases. The researchers were cautious in attempting to explain why this might be, and pointed out that factors beyond the scope of their analysis might have been influential. Nevertheless, their study clearly implies that race continues to be a significant and obviously illegitimate factor in death sentencing (Keil and Vito, 1991).

Still other studies have found that social class is an important factor. A few notable studies have shown that once one controls for the offender's social class, race becomes an insignificant predictor. For example, a 1969 study by Charles Judson and others found that race was not a statistically significant determinant of death sentencing. If anything, Judson's statistics suggest that whites were more likely to receive death sentences than blacks (48 percent of whites received death sentences, and 40 percent of blacks). But when Judson and his colleagues controlled for various crime-related variables, the influence of race disappeared. The socio-economic status of the offender, however, did seem to be important. Of course the substitution of one extra-legal variable for another does not justify differential sentencing, but it does suggest that our knowledge of the factors involved in sentencing is very limited. Indeed, the number of variables that can be shown to influence sentencing seems sometimes to be limited only by the ingenuity of the researchers involved.

A 1983 report of the Panel on Sentencing Research, commissioned by the prestigious National Research Council (NRC), concluded that even among the more sophisticated studies which found discrimination in cases with black offenders and white victims, race was a relatively weak predictive variable. The NRC panel cautioned that the "validity of statistical inferences about the determinants of sentences depends crucially on the methodological rigor with which the effects were estimated.... [and] the findings presented here are weighed in light of potentially serious methodological flaws in research" (Blumstein et al., 1983).

Other critics point out that key legal variables, such as prior record and seriousness of offense, have been difficult for researchers to document and even more difficult to quantify. Other legally relevant factors, such as degree of criminal intent, frequently have been overlooked. The fundamental problem with studies of the relationship between race and the death penalty is that they fail to establish convincing causal explanations. In fact, most studies demonstrate that numerous variables influence capital sentencing. For all we know, many other influential variables may be as yet untested. Some may be unquantifiable. On the basis of the available research, one simply cannot conclude that racial discrepancies are a function of racism.

Reviewing the history of research on race and sentencing generally, William Wilbanks found at least seven different "models of method and interpretation" in the literature (Wilbanks, 1987). Despite the wide variation, he contends that some general observations on race and sentencing are possible. Among them, he includes the following:

> Racial discrimination in sentencing has declined over time.... The black/white variation in sentences is generally reduced to near zero when several legal variables are introduced as controls.... The race effect, even before controls, is not substantially significant, in that the predictive power of race is quite low.... Most sentencing studies have a large residual variation, suggesting that the models used did not fit the actual decision making of judges....

These observations have proved to be especially applicable to research on discrimination and the death penalty.

WHO KILLS WHOM AND WHY

The vast majority of murderers who receive the death penalty are involved in intra-racial offenses—that is, in cases of whites killing whites or blacks killing blacks. Most analysts agree that between 92 and 97 percent of homicides are intra-racial. In the much smaller number of cases in which blacks kill whites, the circumstances surrounding the crimes appear to be substantially different. (The number of cases in which whites kill blacks is usually too small to be factored into analyses.)

Black on black homicides are most likely to occur during altercations between persons who know one another. On the other hand, black on white homicides (and to a somewhat lesser extent, white on white) are often committed during the course of a felony or by a multiple offender. In fact, these are examples of aggravating conditions that the Supreme Court has held to be valid criteria in determining sentence severity. Yet while judges and juries take these factors into account, sociological studies often do not. Lest one think the motivation of judges and juries is racism, these factors are given consideration in societies all over the world, whatever their racial composition. They are seen universally as both fair and conducive to public order.

The key issue, then, is whether blacks convicted of killing whites are more likely to be executed because of the racial identity of their victims or because of qualitative differences in the nature of their crimes. In fact, the latter is clearly the case and would appear to explain much of the racial disparity in death sentencing.

THE McCLESKEY CASE

One of the most effective challenges to the claim of racial discrimination actually arose in a court case that supporters of the discrimination thesis had hoped would prove their point. In the 1980s, the National Association for the Advancement of Colored People (NAACP) funded a major study of the effect of race on criminal sentencing. The study, directed by university professors David Baldus, Charles Pulaski, and C. George Woodworth, gained notoriety when it was used in the defense of Warren McCleskey, a black man sentenced to death for the shooting of a white police officer in Georgia. Defense attorneys relied on the Baldus study to substantiate their claim of systemic discrimination against black defendants. The study showed that in cases of mid-range aggravation, blacks who killed whites were more likely to receive the death penalty than whites who killed whites. (In cases of low and high aggravation, the study found race to be an insignificant factor.) The authors of the study argued that racial bias occurred because prosecutors and juries were prejudiced.

The attorneys prosecuting McCleskey countered by hiring an expert methodologist, Joseph Katz, who analyzed the NAACP study and found a number of conceptual and methodological problems. For one, it turned out that police reports often did not include some of the case circumstances that were supposed to have been weighted in the study. In these instances, the researchers recorded that the circumstances were not present, when, in fact, that was not possible to determine. Katz also pointed out that the researchers had not accounted satisfactorily for the fact that black offender-white victim homicides were often quite different from intra-racial homicides. Katz showed that black on white murders tended to be the most aggravated of all, and frequently were combined with armed robbery, as McCleskey's was. Katz

also testified that by Baldus's own measures, McCleskey's was not a mid-range case but a highly aggravated one, and that in such cases the death penalty was as likely to be applied to whites as blacks.

The Supreme Court ended up rejecting the McCleskey defense, and ruled that statistical models alone do not provide sufficient evidence of discrimination. Later, Katz testified before the Senate Judiciary Committee, and offered further evidence of the differences between homicides in which blacks kill blacks and blacks kill whites. Katz reported that the reason why 11 percent of blacks who killed whites in Georgia received the death penalty—as opposed to only 1 percent of blacks who killed blacks—was that the killings of whites more often involved armed robbery (67 percent of the black on white cases, compared with only 7 percent of the black on black cases). In addition, black on white murders more frequently involved kidnapping and rape, mutilations, execution-style murders, tortures, and beatings. These are all aggravating circumstances that increase the likelihood of a death sentence.

By contrast, 73 percent of the black victim homicides were precipitated by a dispute or fight, circumstances viewed by the courts as mitigating. Katz also observed that 95 percent of black victim homicides were committed by black offenders, and that there were so few white on black cases that no distinctive homicide pattern could even be ascertained. Among the fewer than thirty Georgia cases identified by Katz as white on black, mitigating circumstances seemed to outweigh aggravating. These crimes rarely involved a contemporaneous felony and often were precipitated by a fight. This pattern may or may not hold outside of Georgia, but to date there has been no detailed national study of white on black crime. (Research has also shown that death sentences are especially likely in cases in which police officers are killed in the line of duty, and that 85 percent of police officers killed are white.)

As pointed out earlier, some findings suggest that blacks may actually be treated more leniently than whites. Analysts at the Bureau of Justice Statistics have pointed out that the percentage of inmates on death row who are black (42 percent) is lower than the percentage of criminals charged with murder or non-negligent manslaughter who are black (48 percent). If the legal system still discriminates against blacks, why do they make up a higher percentage of those charged with murder than those executed for murder?

Some critics reply that the police may be more likely to arrest and charge blacks than whites. Yet we have found few data that support this assertion. In fact, Patrick Langan, a senior statistician at the Bureau of Justice Statistics, investigated the possibility of such discrimination and found little evidence of it. Langan based his research on victims' reports of the race of offenders, and found that blacks were sentenced at rates similar to those who would expect given the reports of victims (Langan, 1985). Obviously, this kind of research could not be conducted for murder cases (because the victims are dead) but the research suggests that the discriminatory arrest argument is highly problematic.

In the federal courts, the discrimination argument has found little support. In a number of cases, judges have concluded that the evidence of systemic bias is extremely weak. Rather than order an overhaul of the legal system on the basis of highly problematic and conflicting social science research, judges have preferred to adjudicate discriminatory sentencing claims on a case by case basis. The preferred corrective has been procedural reforms. A number of states have adopted clearer sentencing standards, various provisions to remove extra-legal influences, and the judicial review of death sentences.

IDEOLOGY PREVAILS

Why, then, have some researchers continued to find evidence of racial discrimination? One possible explanation is that while the sociologists who design death penalty studies are most interested in and competent to measure such variables as the demographic characteristics of groups, these sociologists are ill-equipped to assess the importance of the legal variables that influence the operation of the criminal justice system. In the past, researchers did not bother to control for even the most obvious of legal variables.

Yet despite the crudeness of their methods, sociologists have concluded confidently that racism in the legal system is rampant. Mindful of the history of racial discrimination in capital cases, sociologists perhaps are predisposed to conclude that discrimination persists today. It seems obvious.

An additional difficulty with many of the sociologists is that their assumptions concerning discrimination are often overly idealistic—for example, the belief that extra-legal variables must be entirely absent from the criminal justice system for it to be legitimate, and the assumption that complete objectivity is even possible. Taken to their logical extremes, these kinds of utopian beliefs would require us to condemn virtually every legal system in the history of the world. At best, legal systems are imperfect institutions, reflecting community standards of fairness and objectivity. The jury system and judicial discretion are indispensable instruments of social justice, which permit broad principles to be tailored to the particulars of each case. Without these instruments, and the attendant margin of error or abuse that all free exercises of judgment hazard, the legal system would be doomed either to excessive punishments or to a forbearance that placed innocent individuals at great risk.

While there is justification for the claim that discriminatory capital sentencing and execution occurred in the past, the charge that they persist today lacks support. The best available evidence indicates that disproportionate numbers of blacks commit murder, and that in those cases in which the victims are white the crimes generally are aggravated. That is why blacks are overrepresented on death row.

POLITICS AND THE DEATH PENALTY

Clearly there are reasons other than statistical analysis for the continued belief that the legal system discriminates against black defendants. Those who oppose the death penalty on principle, for example, tend to incorporate the discrimination argument into their litany of protest. These critics perceive capital punishment as a vestige of an outmoded, barbaric, and irrational penal code. Black elites, meanwhile, often perceive discrimination in places others do not. They are joined by members of the white cultural establishment, who are quick to sympathize with those who allege racial unfairness.

This may sound like a harsh indictment, but how else are we to explain the facts? For decades, those who argued that the death penalty was administered in a biased manner maintained that the fact that more blacks were executed than whites revealed a lack of concern for black lives. When this argument became untenable—when it became clear that white murderers were actually more likely to be executed than black murderers—these same critics turned to other, equally unsatisfactory arguments. Now, however, they reject the implication of their previous view—that the execution of a larger percentage of whites than blacks must reveal a lack of concern for white lives. The only issue now is the race of the criminal's victim. These critics rationalize their position, but, we submit, their stance can be explained only by a need to find racism everywhere. One is reminded of the world in Aesop's fable. The wolf insisted that the lamb was injuring him, and was quick to change his story each time the lamb pointed out the factual errors in his claims. Finally, the wolf killed and ate the lamb anyway, proving that desire can overcome the failure of rationalization.

AND SO

If the controversy over racial discrimination and the death penalty turned on the merits of the research, politicians would have to concede that death penalty discrimination has been virtually eliminated. Alas, the news media have done little to clarify matters. Most reporting on the issue is inaccurate. An article that appeared in the *New York Times* on April 21,

1994, is typical. The article concluded as follows:

> That some bias occurs is not much at issue. Many studies show that juries mete out the death penalty to black and other minority defendants in a disproportionate number of murder cases, particularly when the victims are white and especially in states and counties that have a history of racial problems.

In fact, as we have shown, these comments are patently false.

Of course, many key questions remain. Is the death penalty arbitrary, given that only a fraction of those eligible are ever executed? Is it barbaric? Is it ineffective as a deterrent? If the answers to these questions are affirmative, two remedies are available: the death penalty can be abolished or subjected to further reform. But whatever society decides, such a decision should not be based on unsubstantiated charges of racial discrimination.

In researching this controversy, we have examined more than sixty of the leading articles in the field, as well as eight books. If you would like a complete list of references, please write us at the Center for the Study of Social and Political Change, Smith College, Northampton, Massachusetts, 01063.

POSTSCRIPT

Is the Death Penalty Racially Discriminatory?

At the beginning of their selection, Rothman and Powers discuss the Racial Justice Act of the Omnibus Crime Control Bill, which would establish quotas for the administration of the death penalty to prevent discrimination in its use. This act, however, was defeated by the U.S. Senate. The White House maintains an "aggressively neutral" stance on the issue.

In the 1958 Supreme Court case *Trop v. Dulles*, Chief Justice Earl Warren predicted that "evolving standards of decency" would eventually result in the elimination of capital punishment. In 1972 *Furman v. Georgia* effectively halted executions in the United States. As a result, many were convinced that capital punishment had finally ended in America for both blacks and whites. However, many states worked hard to put together specific guidelines for carrying out the death penalty in a consistent and fair manner. Reflecting this effort, *Gregg v. Georgia* (1976)—which tested a new Georgia statute that would reduce the incidence of discrimination in applying the death penalty —resulted in the Court's approval. Opponents of executions then contended in *McCleskey v. Kemp* (1987) that statistical analysis proved that blacks were discriminated against. The Supreme Court rejected this, saying there was no proof that others who "may be similarly situated did not receive the death penalty."

Defenders of the Court, such as Rothman and Powers, say that it may be true that blacks who kill whites are more likely to be sentenced to death than whites who kill blacks (only a few have been executed since 1976) or blacks who kill other blacks. This, however, has little to do with discrimination. Instead, interracial killing is likely to be more heinous than intraracial because the latter usually involves a previous relationship between the murderer and the victim. An intraracial crime is often one of anger (e.g., domestic assault) that does not entail other felonies, such as robbery, or premeditation.

Recent articles on the death penalty include "Should Capital Punishment Be Abolished?" *Jet* (February 13, 1995) and J. Barnes, "Capital Punishment Gridlock?" *Investor's Business Daily* (April 11, 1995). For a more comprehensive treatment of the issue of race and capital punishment, see C. Mann's *Unequal Justice* (Indiana University Press, 1993). One of the most recent studies of lynchings is *A Festival of Violence: An Analysis of Southern Lynchings* by S. Tolnay and E. Beck (University of Illinois Press, 1995). A very different kind of study is reported by S. Burgins in "Jurors Ignore, Misunderstand Instructions: The Result . . . Is a Bias in Favor of the Death Penalty," *ABA Journal* (May 1995).

ISSUE 8

Should Pornography Be Banned as a Threat to Women?

YES: Alice Leuchtag, from "The Culture of Pornography," *The Humanist* (May/June 1995)

NO: Nadine Strossen, from "The Perils of Pornophobia," *The Humanist* (May/June 1995)

ISSUE SUMMARY

YES: Freelance writer Alice Leuchtag condemns pornography and prostitution as crude, primordial, lingering vestiges of patriarchy that continue to degrade and define women. Both should be banned as threats to women and humanity.

NO: Professor of law Nadine Strossen argues that campus "political correctness" movements and misguided feminist assaults on pornography have resulted in censorship that ranges from the silly to the barbaric.

> *I have sworn upon the altar of God, eternal hostility against every form of tyranny over the mind of man.*
>
> —Thomas Jefferson

> *Congress shall make no law respecting an establishment of religion, or prohibiting the free exercise thereof; or abridging the freedom of speech, or of the press.*
>
> —First Amendment of the U.S. Constitution

In spite of these valiant declarations, there have always been restraints on speech and writing with both practical and legal supports. Not that the issue of freedom of expression (including speaking, writing, publishing, painting, photography, and, more recently, Internet communications) has ever been close to a settled one. To the literati and the cultural elite, the very idea of outside constraints on expression is unacceptable. To the religious right and a variety of special interest groups, society simply could not function if there were no regulations on communication that might threaten decency.

Chief Justice Oliver Wendell Holmes ruled over 70 years ago that the First Amendment does not allow someone the right to shout "Fire!" in a crowded theatre because of the harm that such an act could cause. This ruling, though frequently ignored in current debates, supports antipornography feminists such as law professor Catherine MacKinnon and author Andrea Dworkin, who contend that words and images can be physically harmful and hence should be illegal. These feminists call for banning not only "traditional" pornography but also publications, acts, and verbalizations that can be construed as offensive or demeaning to women.

Liberals, writers, reporters, civil libertarians, and intellectuals of the post–World War II era often view the current attacks on speech as eroding the core of Western civilization. Radical antipornography factions, as well as many advocates of political correctness, counter that Western civilization is based on little more than the racist, sexist, elitist canon that they feel should be discarded. To some extent paralleling Herbert Marcuse's *One Dimensional Man* (Beacon Press, 1966), critics claim that freedom of speech has always been the freedom of the dominant group to either demean oppressed minorities or to give them the illusion that they could really do something about their exploitation. Women's complaints against and writing about sexist jokes, pornography, and verbal harassment had no effect. It was not until women gained political power and the ability to alter pornography laws that changes began to occur.

The courts have yet to take a strong stand on the pornography issue. In the past 20 years, U.S. Supreme Court rulings have tended to allow local communities to decide if specific cultural productions violated community standards of decency. Meanwhile, a conservative Congress has passed laws criminalizing child pornography. Efforts are also being made to eliminate the National Endowment for the Arts and the National Endowment for the Humanities, partially, many insist, because they have funded works of art that are seen as offensive to family values.

To depict the pornography battle as one of females against males would be misleading. It is more complicated and interesting than that (as well as potentially even more divisive). To some extent, it reflects a generational schism between older people (both liberals and conservatives) and younger intellectuals who have matured since the 1960s. Within the feminist movements themselves, the conflict reflects a division between women who see the gender issue as boiling down to an effort to gain greater political and economic equality for women and those who apparently do not trust men. Others claim that the war on pornography is really an example of elitist white females worrying about themselves and their "sensitivities" while ignoring the very real physical violence that inner-city residents face daily.

As you read the following selections by Alice Leuchtag and Nadine Strossen, try to develop a classificatory scheme of pornography and decide which, if any, you would censor. For instance, should "soft-core" displays (depictions of nudity) be treated the same as "hard-core" productions (graphic sexual depictions)? The latter could include books, films, and photos of sexual intercourse, bondage, beastiality and so on. What about live strippers at bars or parties? Suggestive advertisements? Telephone porn?

YES
Alice Leuchtag

THE CULTURE OF PORNOGRAPHY

Despite many gains in the latter part of this century, women as a group are still clearly inferior to men in status, power, knowledge, and wealth. As a result, many unresolved ethical issues still exist in the relationship between the sexes. Two of the thorniest of these are prostitution and pornography.

Many great feminists of the past considered the institution of prostitution as central to an understanding of the socially subordinate position of women. These individuals include essayist and historian Mary Wollstonecraft, poet and novelist Olive Schreiner, political activist and anarchist Emma Goldman, writer and suffragist Charlotte Perkins Gilman, and economist and sociologist Victoria Woodhull—to mention only a few of the most notable.

This concern about a very old institution has carried over into the present day, both in the work of feminist scholars and in the debates that are taking place within the women's liberation movement. Even though there is a minority of women who defend prostitution and other work in the sex industry as a legitimate career choice, many women—even some who would not label themselves as feminist—feel that the sex industry in general, and the institution of prostitution in particular, diminishes the lives of the women who work in it, as well as diminishing the general status of all women. Yet there are differences as to what changes can and should be made within the constraints posed by our constitutional system.

Activist scholar, teacher, and writer Jane Anthony, in her article "Prostitution As 'Choice'" (*Ms.*, January/February 1992), points out that, traditionally, prostitution has been considered a necessary evil that helps to preserve the institution of marriage by providing a readily available outlet for men's sexual desires. To illustrate this attitude, Anthony quotes from Thomas Aquinas, who wrote that "prostitution is like a sewer system, despicable but necessary." As Anthony points out, Aquinas' view overlooks the fact that there are casualties in the system brought about by the fact that "one class of women is granted status as wives or girlfriends at the expense of another class, whores, who are reduced to sperm receptacles for numerous men."

Some recent literature, written by women who consider themselves feminists, has presented a pro-prostitution stance in which prostitution is

From Alice Leuchtag, "The Culture of Pornography," *The Humanist*, vol. 55, no. 3 (May/June 1995), pp. 4–6. Copyright © 1995 by The American Humanist Association. Reprinted by permission.

portrayed as a "career choice." Anthony maintains that pro-prostitution ideology, often considered sexual liberalism, reflects a dualism in which nineteenth-century views of prostitutes as victims are set off against current views of prostitutes as women who make active decisions to become whores. According to Anthony, only if commercial sex is decontextualized from the social and cultural forces that constrict women's choices—such as job discrimination, gender inequality in the courts, and a "sexism so pervasive it is often invisible"—can prostitution be seen as a choice. Thus, says Anthony, "in decontextualizing women's choices, pro-prostitution ideology inadvertently trivializes prostitution."

Anthony also calls into question those who see prostitution as a form of empowerment for women. She maintains that this may be true temporarily for those women who have been sexually abused prior to becoming prostitutes (and these constitute a large percentage of prostitutes, according to Anthony) and for whom a sense of empowerment exists relative to their previous abuse. Still, under conditions of prostitution, a sense of empowerment is transitory and illusory, Anthony maintains. She states that she speaks from personal experience, having worked as a prostitute for several years. She also quotes Evelina Giobbe of Women Hurt in Systems of Prostitution Engaged in Revolt (WHISPER), who says: "Dismantling the institution of prostitution is the most formidable task facing contemporary feminism."

In a more academic vein is philosopher Laurie Shrage, who contributed an article to the anthology *Feminism and Political Theory* entitled "Should Feminists Oppose Prostitution?" Declaring that "prostitution raises difficult issues

for feminists," Shrage asks whether or not persons opposed to the social subordination of women should seek to discourage commercial sex. Her answer is emphatically yes. Shrage focuses her arguments on what must be done to subvert widely held beliefs that legitimize prostitution in our society, because once these beliefs are undermined, "nothing closely resembling prostitution, as we currently know it, will exist."

Shrage, like Anthony, considers prostitution within its cultural context. She declares that "it epitomizes and perpetuates pernicious patriarchal beliefs and values, and, therefore, is both damaging to the women who sell sex and, as an organized social practice, to all women in our society." She also argues that it reinforces certain cultural assumptions which give legitimacy to women's social subordination, including the belief that men are naturally suited for dominant social roles and the belief that a person's sexual practice defines him or her as a particular kind of person (for example, a "homosexual," a "whore," a "virgin," or a "pervert").

In Shrage's view, the principles that organize and sustain the sex industry are the same ones that underlie many other pernicious and oppressive gender asymmetries in our social institutions. She concludes:

> I am unable to imagine nonpernicious principles which would legitimate the commercial provision of sex and which would not substantially alter or eliminate the industry as it now exists. Since commercial sex, unlike marriage, is not reformable, feminists should seek to undermine the beliefs and values which underlie our acceptance of it. Indeed, one way to do this is to outwardly oppose prostitution itself.... In this respect, a

consumer boycott of the sex industry is especially appropriate.

* * *

There is a close historical connection between pornography and prostitution. (The word *pornography* itself means, quite literally, "writing about prostitutes.") Along with the concern and debate over prostitution, then, an even fiercer debate is raging in the current women's movement over pornography.

The name most prominently associated with the abolitionist view regarding pornography is Catharine A. MacKinnon, professor of law at the University of Michigan Law School. In her own contribution to *Feminism and Political Theory*, entitled "Sexuality, Pornography, and Method: Pleasure Under Patriarchy," MacKinnon focuses on the processes by which the social subordination of women to men is accomplished and maintained under patriarchy—processes in which, she claims, the learning and practice of a sexuality of dominance and submission play a crucial role. To MacKinnon, pornography is one of the ways in which the system of dominance and submission is maintained, a system whose underlying dynamic depends on the sexual objectification of women. MacKinnon places the dehumanization of women along a continuum of female submission—from visual appropriation of the female in pornography, to physical appropriation in prostituted sex, to forced sex in rape, to sexual murder.

MacKinnon cites many recent feminist studies on rape, battery, sexual harassment, sexual abuse of children, prostitution, and pornography that point out specific mechanisms of sexual objectification. According to MacKinnon, when pornography is seen as part of a totality of mutually reinforcing sex practices, it both symbolizes and actualizes the distinctive social power that men as a class have over women as a class in patriarchal society. To quote MacKinnon:

> In feminist terms, the fact that male power has power means that the interests of male sexuality construct what sexuality as such means in life, including the standard way it is allowed and recognized to be felt and expressed and experienced. A theory of sexuality becomes feminist to the extent that it treats sexuality as a social construct of male power: defined by men, forced on women, and constitutive in the meaning of gender. Existing theories, until they grasp this, will not only misattribute what they call female sexuality to women as such, as if it is not imposed on women daily, they will participate in enforcing the hegemony of the social construct "desire," hence its product, "sexuality," hence its construct "woman," on the world. The gender issue thus becomes the issue of what is taken to be "sexuality": what sex means and what is meant by sex, when, how, and with whom and with what consequences to whom.
>
> Such questions are almost never systematically confronted, even in discourses that purport feminist awareness. Feminist theory becomes, then, a project of analyzing that situation in order to face it for what it is, in order to change it.

Thus, MacKinnon sees pornography as one of the primary means by which women are made into sexual objects: "First in the world, then in the head, first in visual appropriation, then in forced sex, finally in sexual murder...." It is partly through the means of pornography itself, claims MacKinnon, that the gender qualities we know culturally as "male" and "female" are socially created and enforced in everyday life.

Like Anthony and Shrage, MacKinnon sees human sexuality not as a given of nature but as a construct of a specific culture, conditioned in both women and men by the ubiquitous existence of gender inequality in a patriarchal culture. To MacKinnon, being a thing for sexual use is fundamental to the content of sexuality for women under patriarchy:

Specifically, "woman" is defined by what male desire requires for arousal and satisfaction and is socially tautologous with "female sexuality" and "the female sex."... To be clear: what is sexual is what gives a man an erection. Whatever it takes to make a penis shudder and stiffen with the experience of its potency is what sexuality means culturally.

To the question, "What do men want?" MacKinnon notes:

Pornography provides an answer.... From the testimony of the pornography, what men want is: women bound, women battered, women tortured, women humiliated, women degraded and defiled, women killed, or, to be fair to the soft core, women sexually accessible, have-able, there for them, wanting to be taken and used, with perhaps just a little light bondage.

To buttress this point, MacKinnon cites experimental data on pornography which, she claims, substantiates the connection between gender inequality, pornography, and male sexuality. When "normal" men in a laboratory setting view pornography over time, they become more aroused by scenes of rape than by scenes of explicit (but not expressly violent) sex, even if the woman is shown as hating it. Apparently, sustained perceptual exposure to pornography inures subjects to the violent component in overtly violent sexual material, while in-creasing the arousal value of such material. Experimental studies also show that viewing sexual material containing explicit aggression against women makes normal men more willing to aggress against women, as well as more likely to see a woman rape victim as less human and more blameworthy. Even so-called nonviolent material in which women are verbally abused, dominated, or treated as sexual toys makes men more likely to see women as less than human, good only for sex, blameworthy when raped, and unequal to men.

MacKinnon, Shrage, and Anthony, as representative modern feminist scholars, agree that specific forces in our patriarchal culture create and maintain a hierarchy of gender in which the social institutions of prostitution and pornography can flourish. None of the three believes there is an innate human sexuality as such, unconditioned by specific cultures, although at times MacKinnon seems to forget her basic premise and writes about male sexuality as if it is a natural, unconditioned given, outside of culture.

These three writers also agree that feminists cannot ignore these issues, difficult as they are with their many legal, political, and social ramifications. They take to task those people who defend prostitution or the pornography industry as legitimate career choices for women. They maintain that, overall, women who work in these areas are exploited and demeaned, that their civil rights are frequently trampled upon, and that they face severe physical and psychological risks. While not blaming the victim for being a victim, all three are searching, both theoretically and practically, for ways in which these institutions can be altered or abolished. To accomplish such formidable tasks within the constitutional framework of law is seen by these writers and by many other feminists as primary among the compelling ethical, legal, and political challenges facing the women's movement in the twenty-first century.

* * *

What should the humanist position be on those questions? I think this depends on which aspect of the humanist movement one considers most important: the free-thought, skeptical, liberal current of humanism, or the (in my opinion) far deeper current that humanism shares with certain other philosophical traditions—namely, concern for the welfare and betterment of humanity. If concern for humanity's welfare is considered as foremost in humanism, then attitudes of skepticism and liberality are viewed as a means to an end rather than as ends in themselves. They are employed where useful (for example, to critique religious dogma) but not revered on general principles. Skepticism and liberalism need not hobble us in the face of pernicious social institutions. If one stresses humanity's welfare, prostitution and pornography would have to be viewed as giant-sized stumbling blocks to human progress, inasmuch as they demean one class of humans by converting them into commercial objects.

NO

Nadine Strossen

THE PERILS OF PORNOPHOBIA

In 1992, in response to a complaint, officials at Pennsylvania State University unceremoniously removed Francisco de Goya's masterpiece, *The Nude Maja*, from a classroom wall. The complaint had not been lodged by Jesse Helms or some irate member of the Christian Coalition. Instead, the complainant was a feminist English professor who protested that the eighteenth-century painting of a recumbent nude woman made her and her female students "uncomfortable."

This was not an isolated incident. At the University of Arizona at Tucson, feminist students physically attacked a graduate student's exhibit of photographic self-portraits. Why? The artist had photographed *herself* in her *underwear*. And at the University of Michigan Law School, feminist students who had organized a conference on "Prostitution: From Academia to Activism" removed a feminist-curated art exhibition held in conjunction with the conference. Their reason? Conference speakers had complained that a composite videotape containing interviews of working prostitutes was "pornographic" and therefore unacceptable.

What is wrong with this picture? Where have they come from—these feminists who behave like religious conservatives, who censor works of art because they deal with sexual themes? Have not feminists long known that censorship is a dangerous weapon which, if permitted, would inevitably be turned against them? Certainly that was the irrefutable lesson of the early women's rights movement, when Margaret Sanger, Mary Ware Dennett, and other activists were arrested, charged with "obscenity," and prosecuted for distributing educational pamphlets about sex and birth control. Theirs was a struggle for freedom of sexual expression and full gender equality, which they understood to be mutually reinforcing.

Theirs was also a lesson well understood by the second wave of feminism in the 1970s, when writers such as Germaine Greer, Betty Friedan, and Betty Dodson boldly asserted that women had the right to be free from discrimination not only in the workplace and in the classroom but in the

From Nadine Strossen, "The Perils of Pornophobia," *The Humanist*, vol. 55, no. 3 (May/June 1995), pp. 7–9. Copyright © 1995 by The American Humanist Association. Reprinted by permission.

bedroom as well. Freedom from limiting, conventional stereotypes concerning female sexuality was an essential aspect of what we then called "women's liberation." Women should not be seen as victims in their sexual relations with men but as equally assertive partners, just as capable of experiencing sexual pleasure.

But it is a lesson that, alas, many feminists have now forgotten. Today, an increasingly influential feminist pro-censorship movement threatens to impair the very women's rights movement it professes to serve. Led by law professor Catharine MacKinnon and writer Andrea Dworkin, this faction of the feminist movement maintains that sexually oriented *expression*—not sex-segregated labor markets, sexist concepts of marriage and family, or pent-up rage—is the preeminent cause of discrimination and violence against women. Their solution is seemingly simple: suppress all "pornography."

Censorship, however, is never a simple matter. First, the offense must be described. And how does one define something so infinitely variable, so deeply personal, so uniquely individualized as the image, the word, and the fantasy that cause sexual arousal? For decades, the U.S. Supreme Court has engaged in a Sisyphean struggle to craft a definition of *obscenity* that the lower courts can apply with some fairness and consistency. Their dilemma was best summed up in former Justice Potter Stewart's now famous statement: "I shall not today attempt further to define [obscenity]: and perhaps I could never succeed in intelligibly doing so. But I know it when I see it."

The censorious feminists are not so modest as Justice Stewart. They have fashioned an elaborate definition of *por-nography* that encompasses vastly more material than does the currently recognized law of *obscenity*. As set out in their model law (which has been considered in more than a dozen jurisdictions in the United States and overseas, and which has been substantially adopted in Canada), pornography is "the sexually explicit subordination of women through pictures and/or words." The model law lists eight different criteria that attempt to illustrate their concept of "subordination," such as depictions in which "women are presented in postures or positions of sexual submission, servility, or display" or "women are presented in scenarios of degradation, humiliation, injury, torture... in a context that makes these conditions sexual." This linguistic driftnet can ensnare anything from religious imagery and documentary footage about the mass rapes in the Balkans to self-help books about women's health. Indeed, the Boston Women's Health Book Collective, publisher of the now-classic book on women's health and sexuality, *Our Bodies, Ourselves*, actively campaigned against the MacKinnon-Dworkin model law when it was proposed in Cambridge, Massachusetts, in 1985, recognizing that the book's explicit text and pictures could be targeted as pornographic under the law.

Although the "MacDworkinite" approach to pornography has an intuitive appeal to many feminists, it is *itself* based on subordinating and demeaning stereotypes about women. Central to the pornophobic feminists—and to many traditional conservatives and right-wing fundamentalists, as well—is the notion that *sex* is inherently degrading to women (although not to men). Not just sexual expression but sex itself—even consensual, nonviolent sex—is an evil from which women, like children, must be protected.

MacKinnon puts it this way: "Compare victims' reports of rape with women's reports of sex. They look a lot alike.... The major distinction between intercourse (normal) and rape (abnormal) is that the normal happens so often that one cannot get anyone to see anything wrong with it." And from Dworkin: "Intercourse remains a means or the means of physiologically making a woman inferior." Given society's pervasive sexism, she believes, women cannot freely consent to sexual relations with men; those who do consent are, in Dworkin's words, "collaborators... experiencing pleasure in their own inferiority."

These ideas are hardly radical. Rather, they are a reincarnation of disempowering puritanical, Victorian notions that feminists have long tried to consign to the dustbin of history: woman as sexual victim; man as voracious satyr. The MacDworkinite approach to sexual expression is a throwback to the archaic stereotypes that formed the basis for nineteenth-century laws which prohibited "vulgar" or sexually suggestive language from being used in the presence of women and girls.

In those days, women were barred from practicing law and serving as jurors lest they be exposed to such language. Such "protective" laws have historically functioned to bar women from full legal equality. Paternalism always leads to exclusion, discrimination, and the loss of freedom and autonomy. And in its most extreme form, it leads to purdah, in which women are completely shrouded from public view.

* * *

The pro-censorship feminists are not fighting alone. Although they try to distance themselves from such traditional "family-values" conservatives as Jesse Helms, Phyllis Schlafly, and Donald Wildmon, who are less interested in protecting women than in preserving male dominance, a common hatred of sexual expression and fondness for censorship unite the two camps. For example, the Indianapolis City Council adopted the MacKinnon-Dworkin model law in 1984 thanks to the hard work of former council member Beulah Coughenour, a leader of the Indiana Stop ERA movement. (Federal courts later declared the law unconstitutional.) And when Phyllis Schlafly's Eagle Forum and Beverly LaHaye's Concerned Women for America launched their "Enough Is Enough" anti-pornography campaign, they trumpeted the words of Andrea Dworkin in promotional materials.

This mutually reinforcing relationship does a serious disservice to the fight for women's equality. It lends credibility to and strengthens the right wing and its anti-feminist, anti-choice, homophobic agenda. This is particularly damaging in light of the growing influence of the religious right in the Republican Party and the recent Republican sweep of both Congress and many state governments. If anyone doubts that the newly empowered GOP intends to forge ahead with anti-woman agendas, they need only read the party's "Contract with America" which, among other things, reintroduces the recently repealed "gag rule" forbidding government-funded family-planning clinics from even discussing abortion with their patients.

The pro-censorship feminists base their efforts on the largely unexamined assumption that ridding society of pornography would reduce sexism and violence against women. If there were any evidence that this were true, anti-censorship feminists—myself included—would be compelled at least to reexamine our opposition to censorship. But there is no such evidence to be found.

A causal connection between exposure to pornography and the commission of sexual violence has never been established. The National Research Council's Panel on Understanding and Preventing Violence concluded in a 1993 survey of laboratory studies that "demonstrated empirical links between pornography and sex crimes in general are weak or absent." Even according to another research literature survey that former U.S. Surgeon General C. Everett Koop conducted at the behest of the staunchly anti-pornography Meese Commission, only two reliable generalizations could be made about the impact of "degrading" sexual material on its viewers: it caused them to think that a variety of sexual practices was more common than they had previously believed, and to more accurately estimate the prevalence of varied sexual practices.

Correlational studies are similarly unsupportive of the pro-censorship cause. There are no consistent correlations between the availability of pornography in various communities, states and countries and their rates of sexual offenses. If anything, studies suggest an inverse relationship: a greater availability of sexually explicit material seems to correlate not with higher rates of sexual violence but, rather, with higher indices of gender equality. For example, Singapore, with its tight restrictions on pornography, has experienced a much greater increase in rape rates than has Sweden, with its liberalized obscenity laws.

There *is* mounting evidence, however, that MacDworkinite-type laws will be used against the very people they are supposed to protect—namely, women. In 1992, for example, the Canadian Supreme Court incorporated the MacKinnon-Dworkin concept of pornography into Canadian obscenity law. Since that ruling, in *Butler v. The Queen*—which MacKinnon enthusiastically hailed as "a stunning victory for women"—well over half of all feminist bookstores in Canada have had materials confiscated or detained by customs. According to the *Feminist Bookstore News*, a Canadian publication, "The *Butler* decision has been used ... only to seize lesbian, gay, and feminist material."

Ironically but predictably, one of the victims of Canada's new law is Andrea Dworkin herself. Two of her books, *Pornography: Men Possessing Women* and *Women Hating*, were seized, custom officials said, because they "illegally eroticized pain and bondage." Like the MacKinnon-Dworkin model law, the *Butler* decision makes no exceptions for material that is part of a feminist critique of pornography or other feminist presentation. And this inevitably overbroad sweep is precisely why censorship is antithetical to the fight for women's rights.

The pornophobia that grips MacKinnon, Dworkin, and their followers has had further counterproductive impacts on the fight for women's rights. Censorship factionalism within the feminist movement has led to an enormously wasteful diversion of energy from the real cause of and solutions to the ongoing problems of discrimination and violence against women. Moreover, the "porn-made-me-do-it" defense, whereby convicted rapists cite MacKinnon and Dworkin in seeking to reduce their sentences, actually impedes the aggressive enforcement of criminal laws against sexual violence.

A return to the basic principles of women's liberation would put the feminist movement back on course. We women are entitled to freedom of expression—to read, think, speak, sing, write, paint, dance, photograph, film, and fantasize as we wish. We are also entitled to our dignity, autonomy, and equality. Fortunately, we can—and will—have both.

POSTSCRIPT

Should Pornography Be Banned as a Threat to Women?

The issue of pornography and its potential harms, especially in reinforcing the subjugation and humiliation of females, is a perplexing one. It is also an important component of the ongoing cultural wars. Both Leuchtag and Strossen make salient points, but neither one discusses elements of their debate within a broader historical framework. Efforts to censor speech and writing are a continuous part of the American landscape. Also, both libertarian and liberal critics of bans on pornography sometimes link the issue with "political correctness," or the effort to eliminate speech and practices that may be offensive to specific groups of people. Ironically, extreme conservatives who never wanted pornography to be allowed often use the debate to attack feminists. The conservative argument is that extreme leftists are trying to censor people's behavior, reading and writing, and attitudes in terms of their own criteria of political correctness and of what is "offensive." Regardless of the accuracy of these charges, there have always been organized groups attempting to control speech and actions.

George Bernard Shaw once called America a puritan society, defining *puritan* as someone who wakes up in the night with a haunting fear that someone somewhere just might be having a good time! The most shameful example of thought control in U.S. society occurred in the early 1950s, when Senator Joseph McCarthy and various congressional committees investigated people accused of being communists and "comsympths" (those who sympathized with communists, or who felt that integration was desirable, that the Soviet Union and the United States could peacefully coexist, and so on). Speaking before a Senate committee in the 1950s, government official Owen Lattimore (1900–1987), who was accused of being a traitor, made a statement that sounds uncannily similar to charges that are being made in the current fight over suppression: "You cannot, you must not permit a psychology of fear to paralyze the scholars and writers of this nation.... Attacks of this sort, which have the effect of intimidating scholars and researchers, are bound to affect the quality of their work."

Leuchtag and Strossen split on their interpretations of research on possibly harmful or threatening aspects of pornography. Leuchtag sees the data as proving a threat, while Strossen feels that it shows nothing of the sort. You might wish to look up existing studies or specific references. Do you find pornography to be a threat to women? If so, what kinds of pornography? Should it be banned from college courses? Bookstores? Adult shops? The Internet?

The list of readings on pornography is voluminous. A current reader with stimulating articles is *Women: A Feminist Perspective* edited by Jo Freeman (Mayfield, 1995). A reader that presents debates on the causes of violence against women is *Violence Against Women* edited by K. Swisher et al. (Greenhaven Press, 1994). Two works that look at changing views of the issue are *Soft Core: Moral Crusades Against Pornography in Britain and America* by W. Thompson (Cassell, 1994) and S. Tisdale's *Talk Dirty to Me: An Intimate Philosophy of Sex* (Doubleday, 1994). Two works that address conceptual problems include S. Easton's *The Problem of Pornography: Regulation and the Right to Free Speech* (Routledge, 1994) and J. Stoltenberg's *What Makes Pornography "Sexy"?* (Milkweed Editions, 1994).

An article that sides with Strossen is "Porn Is a Yawn," by M. Harris, *The Spectator* (December 10, 1994). Among the many technical discussions are "Discrepancies Between the Legal Code and Community Standards: An Empirical Challenge to Traditional Assumptions in Obscenity Law," by D. Linz et al., *Law and Society Review* (vol. 29, no. 1, 1995). In that same issue see L. Douglas, "The Force of Words: Fish, Matsuda, MacKinnon and the Theory of Discursive Violence."

For several blunt attacks on censorship in general and perceived extremes of misguided social movements, see " The Will to Power Rangers," by M. Gallagher, *National Review* (March 10, 1995); *Professing Feminism: Cautionary Tales from the Strange World of Women's Studies* by D. Patai and N. Koertge (Basic Books, 1995); Christina Hoff Sommers, "Figuring Out Feminism," *National Review* (June 27, 1994); and Sommers's book *Who Stole Feminism?* (Simon & Schuster, 1994). Patai, Koertge, and Sommers often sound remarkably like Owen Lattimore, only the insidious "thought police" are not the 1950s McCarthyites but the 1990s "politically correct."

For interesting articles by supporters of the procensorship movement, see the interview with Andrea Dworkin by M. Moorcock, "Fighting Talk," *New Statesman and Society* (April 21, 1995); C. MacKinnon, "Pornography Left and Right," *Harvard Civil Rights–Civil Liberties Law Review* (Winter 1995); and C. MacKinnon, "Vindication and Resistance: A Response to the Carnegie Mellon Study of Porn in Cyberspace," *Georgetown Law Review* (June 1, 1995). A vigorous attack on MacKinnon's earlier works is V. Kesic's "A Response to Catharine MacKinnon's Article 'Turning Rape into Porn,'" *Hastings Women Law Journal* (Summer 1994). Other attacks are in Strossen's book *Defending Pornography: Free Speech, Sex, and the Fight for Women's Rights* (Schrier, 1994).

PART 3

Criminological Research and Public Policy

Among the most important criminological research findings of the past 25 years is that a relatively small core of criminals commit a disproportionate amount of crime. These include juveniles who commit violent offenses. Yet how helpful are such findings? Does criminological research tell us why some people seem to choose crime as a career or why violent crimes occur? Equally important is how research is applied by members of the public and by policymakers to create new programs for juveniles, sentencing policies, and capital punishment policies. In a rapidly changing world, how often do detected patterns of crime become dated, making policy formulations even more tenuous? Perhaps researching crime and then deciding how to use the results is one of criminology's biggest problems.

- Is Research on Criminal Careers Helpful?

- Can Traditional Criminology Make Sense Out of Domestic Violence?

- Is Waiver to Adult Courts a Solution to Juvenile Crime?

- Are Violent Criminals and Delinquents Treated Too Leniently?

- Is Capital Punishment Bad Policy?

ISSUE 9

Is Research on Criminal Careers Helpful?

YES: Alfred Blumstein and Jacqueline Cohen, from "Characterizing Criminal Careers," *Science* (August 1987)

NO: Michael Gottfredson and Travis Hirschi, from "Science, Public Policy, and the Career Paradigm," *Criminology* (February 1988)

ISSUE SUMMARY

YES: Professors Alfred Blumstein and Jacqueline Cohen declare that traditional criminological knowledge of the correlates of crime, such as low income and race, is not helpful. Based on Blumstein's extensive research over the past 15 years, they conclude that criminal career studies are far more helpful.

NO: Professor of management and policy Michael Gottfredson and professor of sociology Travis Hirschi, continuing their running debate with Blumstein and his followers, charge that research on criminal careers is pretentious, ignores counterevidence, is conceptually and methodologically unsound, and will lead "public policy ... in the wrong direction."

"When giants fight the earth trembles," the ancients observed, and we could use this saying to characterize what happens in this debate. The debate over the meaning and value of research on criminal careers has pitted criminological and criminal justice heavyweights against one another for over 50 years, and continues to make waves throughout the discipline. The debate first heated up in the 1930s when Eleanor and Sheldon Glueck of Harvard University published to wide acclaim their studies of career criminals, but the preeminent criminological scholar Edwin Sutherland of Indiana University attacked their work as being atheoretical and misguided.

In the selections here, we have the current, contemporary version of the debate. Alfred Blumstein and Jacqueline Cohen have picked up the Gluecks' sword, and Michael Gottfredson and Travis Hirschi are walking in Sutherland's boots. The stakes are high. The direction criminological theory takes and the accompanying thrust of public policies, and how public monies are spent, as regards crime and crime control are partially dependent upon the resolution of this issue.

What is this all about? Blumstein and Cohen, writing in the prestigious journal *Science*, contend that the usual explanations of crime based on analyzing crime rates against such variables as the socioeconomic status (SES), racial composition, and population density of a community are misleading. This is so because the correlates are based on cross-sectional research, which can be static. Yes, they concede, race, low socioeconomic status, and so on, do correlate with crime rates. However, correlation is not causation; a correlation does not a cause make. In order to both understand differences in crime rates and make intelligent policy recommendations, Blumstein and Cohen insist, you must analyze individuals' rates of crime commission.

Blumstein and Cohen argue that existing criminological theory is intellectually impoverished. To get criminology out of this impasse, which many criminologists are apparently unaware of, they propose recasting how the discipline conceptualizes crime, and they recommend a focus on the notion of criminal careers. *Career* implies time and process: a beginning, middle, and end. They argue that the careers of certain criminals can be followed longitudinally (over different points of time). They conclude that examining individual criminal careers provides opportunities for new insights not otherwise available and that these insights would have the potential to make various crime control strategies more effective.

Do you feel they succeed in making their case? Notice from reading Blumstein and Cohen that their findings include the fact that while *participation* in crime is indeed much higher for the usual categories (the poor, minorities), the *frequency* of criminal acts (which they symbolize as lambda, λ) is about the same for all groups. When this is taken into account, they point out, existing criminological understandings are reduced to superstition and nonsense.

You have got to be kidding! Gottfredson and Hirschi shout in a major criminological journal. Blumstein and Cohen, according to Gottfredson and Hirschi, suffer from bad criminology, bad science, and worse policy recommendations. They chastise Blumstein and Cohen for abandoning criminological theory. They contend that looking at different time periods when individual criminals are charged with crimes is hardly experimental research because there is no control group. They also complain about the use of criminal careers as a meaningful construct, among other things.

As you read this issue, keep in mind the possible policy implications of Blumstein and Cohen's position. Note Gottfredson and Hirschi's reason for dismissing their opponents' well-known distinction between crime participation and crime frequency (λ). How much of the debate hinges on this distinction, would you say?

YES

Alfred Blumstein and
Jacqueline Cohen

CHARACTERIZING CRIMINAL CAREERS

Even though the subjects of crime and crime control have been major issues of public debate, and despite their regular appearance as one of the nation's most serious problems, significant advances in empirical research related to these issues are relatively recent. This partly reflects the strong value component in the policy choices. It is also due to the considerable difficulty of observing directly individual crimes or tracking carefully the patterns of offending by individual criminals in order to collect reliable data.

The policy choice at the center of most public debate involves the use of imprisonment, primarily the choice of who should go to prison and for how long. This policy choice involves a sequence of dichotomies (Fig. 1). The objectives of imprisonment involve some combination of retribution—punishment for its own sake—and crime control. Crime control is obtained in macro terms through general deterrence, by communicating symbolically to the public at large that they risk punishment if they commit crimes. At the micro level—involving individual offenders—one can try to incapacitate them, typically through imprisonment, and thereby block their access to potential victims in the community during the period of confinement. Alternatively, one can try to improve their behavior subsequent to some treatment that may focus on punishment (working through individual deterrence) or on enhancing individual skills in legitimate activities (sometimes indicated as rehabilitation).

Information on criminal careers—the longitudinal sequence of offenses committed by individual offenders—is potentially an important element for informing the choices made at the various decision points. Knowledge about criminal careers is most directly useful for assessing the effects on crime through incapacitation. The magnitude of the incapacitative effect of incarceration depends fundamentally on the nature of criminal careers: the more frequently an individual offender engages in crime, the more benefit that would accrue by removing him from the street and thereby eliminating his opportunity to commit crimes in the community. The dynamics of criminal careers, especially their potential for change, are also relevant for assessing likely rehabilitation or individual deterrent effects. An important question when assessing general deterrence is distinguishing between the impact of deterrent threats in curtailing the careers of already active offenders and in inhibiting initiation of criminal careers among nonoffenders.

Empirical knowledge about criminal careers may even be of value in imposing prison terms for retributive purposes. It is a fundamental principle of U.S. criminal law that individuals should be punished only for crimes that they have committed. In accordance with this principle, the candidates for punishment are limited to those who have been convicted of a current offense. In choosing how much punishment to impose, however, an offender's prior criminal career might reasonably be viewed as a legitimate element—reflecting the offender's blameworthiness—in setting the punishment for that offense.

Although there had been some important classic statistical work examining crime in the 19th century by Quetelet and criminal careers beginning in the 1930s by the Gluecks (1), it is only in recent years that we have seen significant new estimates of characteristics of criminal careers and new insights for policy relating to those careers. These are covered in some detail in a recent report by the Panel on Research on Criminal Careers of the National Research Council (2).

A significant factor inhibiting the growth of knowledge about criminal careers has been that traditional research focuses on developing correlates of crime, typically derived from cross-sectional studies of states or cities, looking for community characteristics that tend to be associated with high crime rates. Not surprisingly, many indicators of social deprivation are associated with crime, among them low income, high population density, and high minority racial composition. Knowing of such associations, however, is not very helpful. The strong mutual association among these correlates provides little guidance on their relative individual contributions to crime, and such partitioning is crucial in order to isolate and identify useful social investments to address these presumed causes. The traditional approach is also deficient because crime is dealt with as a unitary phenomenon without distinguishing the diverse ways in which causal factors might affect individual offenders. The criminal career paradigm partitions these effects into those that contribute to participation in crime and others that affect frequency of offending or that affect termination of a criminal career.

Figure 1

Key Decision Points in Policy Choices on Uses of Imprisonment

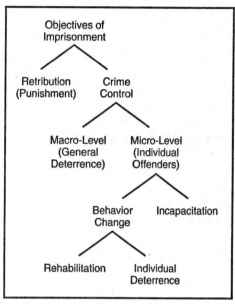

Research on criminal careers involves the characterization of the longitudinal pattern of crime events for offenders and assessment of the factors that affect that pattern. Use of the concept of a "career" is not meant to imply that crime need be the primary economic activity from which an offender derives a substantial part of his livelihood; it is merely a metaphor for the longitudinal process. It is also important to distinguish the concept of criminal careers from the policy-oriented reversal of that phrase, the "career criminal," which refers to offenders whose criminal careers are of such serious dimension that they represent prime targets for the criminal justice system.

BASIC STRUCTURE OF A CRIMINAL CAREER

Examining the basic structure of criminal careers within any population involves first assessing the fraction that participates in crime and then, for that subset, developing information on the statistical properties of the parameters that characterize their criminal careers. "Participation" represents a primary filter between the general population and the subset who are criminally active. If crime is defined very broadly to include many minor infractions, participation in crime is virtually universal. However, as interest is focused more narrowly on serious offenses, participation becomes an important filter in distinguishing active offenders from nonoffenders. The intensity of criminal activity may vary considerably across these participants. "Frequency" refers to these individual crime rates, or the number of crimes per year committed by those who are active.

The basic identity linking the aggregate population crime rate, C, to the fraction participating, P, and their individual crime frequency, λ, is $C = P\lambda$ when crime types and offender subgroups are treated homogeneously. In this identity, the crimes per year per capita (C) is partitioned between participation, P (in terms of active criminals per capita), and frequency, λ (in terms of crimes per year per active criminal). This basic partition provides the opportunity to distinguish those factors that affect participation, which in general may be quite different from those that influence frequency by active offenders.

Among active offenders, three fundamental parameters represent the simplest characterization of a career structure: (i) age of initiation, A_0; (ii) age at termination, A_N; and (iii) mean number of crimes committed per year while active, λ. An important parameter of the criminal career is thus the career length represented by the interval $T = A_N - A_0$. Also at any point in the career, A_t, we are interested in the residual career length, $T_R = A_N - A_t$.

A simple configuration of a criminal career that invokes these basic parameters is shown in Fig. 2. Here the career begins at age A_0 and the individual crime frequency rises immediate to λ, stays constant at that value for the duration of the career, and drops instantaneously to 0 at age A_N when the career is terminated. Obviously, variations on this basic structure are possible. There could be a finite rise time or termination period between the maximum crime frequency, λ, and 0. Over the course of an individual's career, λ could fluctuate stochastically around his true underlying rate; in addition, there could well be variation in the true underlying λ including the possibility of dropping to 0 for intermittent periods, and many other variations. All

Figure 2
An Individual Criminal Career (2)

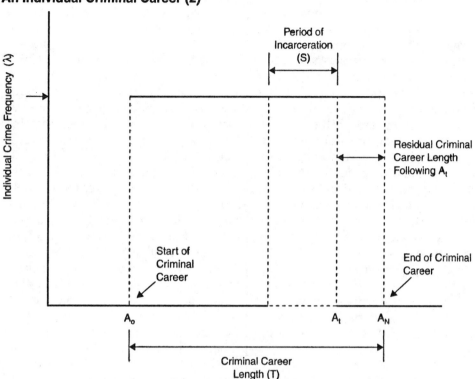

of these involve greater complexity and would require more elaborate assumptions.

ESTIMATION OF CRIMINAL CAREER PARAMETERS

Estimation of criminal career parameters is particularly difficult because of the general invisibility of most crimes to any observer. An ideal observation method would involve a random sample of the population who would maintain a regular log of their criminal activities. The obvious fancifulness of such an approach requires a diversity of indirect approaches, relying on multiple data sources to develop estimates of the parameters.

A long-standing data source, which has now been available for over 40 years in the United States, is the Uniform Crime Reports (UCR). Published annually by the Federal Bureau of Investigation, the UCR is a compilation of monthly reports submitted to the FBI by individual police departments of the numbers of crimes reported to the police and the numbers of arrests, categorized by size of city and by demographic attributes (age, race, and sex) of the arrestees. The potential for bias in crime counts is clear, since fewer than half of the crimes experienced by victims are ever reported by them to the police, and this report percentage could well vary across jurisdictions. In addition, there could be variations across police departments in the criteria used to define a crime, or in efforts to manipulate the amount of crime reported to the FBI.

The UCR arrest data are particularly valuable because they provide some basic descriptive information about the offenders, and thus serve as a basis for distinguishing among them. Arrest statistics, however, are also subject to biases. In addition to reporting errors like those found in crime counts, arrest counts may be distorted by differential vulnerability to arrest (for example, more careful or more experienced offenders may be less likely to be arrested), or from differences in police discretion in issuing a warning as opposed to recording an arrest. Indeed, considerable criminological research energy has gone into a variety of efforts to demonstrate the possibility of these various biases in arrest data.

Participation rates. Most cross-sectional research on the correlates of crime reflects participation in crime. There are not many surprises among the variables associated with participation: low measured IQ, parental criminality, disruptive family situation, lower social class, low income, high unemployment, drug abuse, and others. One problem with this array of factors is the difficulty of identifying means of intervening in any of them in a significant and influential way. Even if one could influence one of these variables with regard to any particular individual, it is not clear how that would affect that individual's propensity to become a participant in crime. Since the research relies primarily on cross-sectional data, it has not been adequately demonstrated that a change in the associated variable will necessarily change the consequences for an individual.

Participation rates, P, as well as rates of recidivism (rates of recurrence of crime by offenders), can be estimated from a feedback model with first-time offenders as an exogenous forcing-function and with recidivists making up the feedback loop. The probability that an American male would be arrested some time in his life for a nontraffic offense has been estimated as 50 to 60%, a level of participation in crime that is probably an order of magnitude higher than most people would guess. In Great Britain, the lifetime conviction probability for males is estimated to be in the same range—44%.

These surprisingly high estimates might be dismissed because they include arrests for any kind of offense (other than traffic), and many people may be vulnerable to arrest for minor offenses like disorderly conduct. Subsequent estimates have focused more narrowly on only the FBI "index" offenses (murder, forcible rape, aggravated assault, robbery, burglary, larceny, and auto theft) that comprise the usual reports on "serious" crime published periodically by the FBI. [Arson is the eighth UCR Index crime.—Ed.] Examining these data for the 55 largest cities (with populations over 250,000), the lifetime chance of an index arrest for a male in these cities was estimated to be 25%, with important differences between the races in their participation rates—the chances were 14% for whites and 50% for blacks. Further, excluding larceny arrests—relatively minor offenses (including shoplifting and theft of auto parts and bicycles) that account for 50% of all index arrests—does not significantly affect participation rates. The adjustment eliminates those individuals who were arrested only for larceny, and these are only a small fraction of those ever arrested for index offenses.

In sharp contrast to the large race difference in participation rates, the recidivism rates for serious crimes were about the same for blacks and for whites, about an 85 to 90% chance of rearrest for both groups. This highlighted an important substantive insight: whereas there appears to be an important difference in the degree to which individuals from the two groups became offenders, those who did become offenders in the two race groups appear much more similar in their offending patterns.

Of course, the policy implications of this are also very important: since the criminal justice system deals with people only after they have passed through the "participation filter," that system has no direct interest in the factors that affect participation. Rather, their primary professional concern is with the factors that distinguish among those who do penetrate the "filter"—namely, the factors associated with active criminal careers. If race is not one of those factors, then racial discrimination by the criminal justice system, aside from being ethically wrong, is also empirically incorrect.

In research terms, the most important implication of these different results regarding race demonstrates the necessity to separate the determinants of participation from those of the criminal career for those who are active as offenders. In terms of the previous identity, we can now claim that $C(x,y) = P(x)\lambda(y)$, and the determinants of P and λ in variable sets x and y, respectively, could well be quite different. This thus motivates a search for the isolated set y that is of greatest interest to the criminal justice system.

Crime frequency by active offenders. Knowledge about the magnitude of λ in various populations is of particular interest in developing crime-control policies. The mean λ indicates the troublesomeness of any group of offenders, whereas the distribution over the group indicates the variation across individual offenders. For any fixed total crime rate, if the mean λ is high, then the total crime rate is attributable to a reasonably small number of offenders, and perhaps the crime problem might be significantly alleviated by isolating them. On the other hand, if the mean frequency is low with the same total crime rate, then the number of offenders is large and may well exceed the capacity of the criminal justice system, and it would be well to focus on the other crime-control strategies, including strategies directed at reducing participation in offending.

Some rather surprising results have emerged in studies of λ. Considerable diversity was found in estimates of λ based on inmates' self-reports of the crimes they committed during the period just before the arrest leading to their current incarceration. Figure 3 highlights the highly skewed distribution of λ found among the inmates. For those who ever committed a robbery during the measurement period, half reported committing fewer than 4 robberies per year while they were free on the street, but 10% reported committing more than 70 robberies per year while free. Similarly for burglary, the median rate was 5 per year, but the 90th percentile claimed a rate of over 195 per year.

Estimates from official records are not likely to display such considerable diversity, largely because no offender is likely to experience a very large number of arrests. If we define $\mu = \lambda q$, where μ

Figure 3
Distribution of Robbery Frequency Among Incoming Inmates in California, Michigan, and Texas (2)

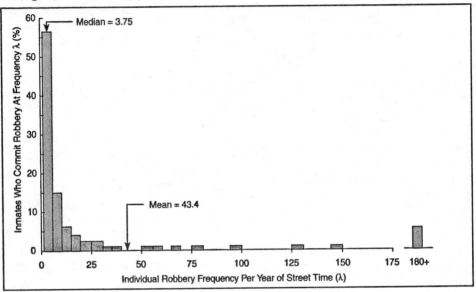

is the individual arrest frequency (arrests per year while free for active offenders), and q is the probability of an arrest conditional on committing a crime, then an individual with a limited number of arrests can display a large value of λ only if he is extremely skillful or very lucky in evading arrest (so that q is very low). Official arrest records, however, do have some compensating virtues. They are reasonably complete, they provide detailed information on dates of arrest, and they do not suffer from the biases of nonresponse or intentional misrepresentation associated with self-reports. They can thus also be used to develop alternative estimates of λ for different populations.

With data drawn from computerized criminal history files maintained by the FBI, longitudinal arrest histories were obtained for all adults arrested for mur-der, rape, robbery, aggravated assault, burglary, or auto theft in Washington, D.C., during 1973, or in the Detroit Standard Metropolitan Statistical Area (SMSA) during the period 1974 to 1977. The arrest histories included information on any arrests as adults occurring before or during the sampling years for sampled individuals, as well as dispositions in court and dates of admission or release from correctional institutions.

Adult arrestees for serious offenses were almost exclusively male ($\geq 90\%$) in both sites. The two populations differed markedly with respect to race. The Washington, D.C., arrestees, who reflected the racial composition of that city in the early 1970s (71% black in the 1970 census), included 92% nonwhites. The arrestees from the Detroit SMSA, which included the suburban counties surrounding Detroit, included 43% nonwhites, a figure that much more closely resembles the racial composition found nationally (45% nonwhite) among urban arrestees for serious offenses.

The arrestee populations in both study sites numbered several thousand—5,338 in Washington, D.C.; 10,588 whites and 8,022 blacks in the Detroit SMSA. The analyses of frequencies, λ, however, focused on selected cohorts of about 150 arrestees active in a crime type within these annual cross sections. Cohort subsamples permit analysis of changes in λ over time for the same arrestees. Examination of changes in λ with age in the histories of the full sampling cross section, for example, includes different subsets of arrestees at different ages. Estimates at age 20 are based on a broad cross section of offenders, some who were age 20 many years ago but most of whom were near age 20 at the time of sampling because most arrestees are young (see Fig. 4). In contrast, λ estimates at older ages, say 35, are based on individuals who are 35 or older at the time of sampling; arrestees who were younger at the time of sampling cannot be observed at these older ages. Thus the estimates at older ages are dominated by individuals who grew up at an earlier time and also who persisted in their criminal careers for a long time. Analyses of age differences in cross-sectional data—even longitudinal data for the cross-section sample—thus result in different sample compositions at each age, thereby confounding changes over age with possible cohort effects and historical period changes.

Cohorts included those arrestees who reached age 18 in the same year and whose first arrest as adults occurred at ages 18 to 20, thereby ensuring that they were active in criminal careers as adults before age 21. The resulting λ estimates

Figure 4

U.S. Age-Specific Arrest Rates (Arrests Per 100,000 Population of Each Age) For 1983

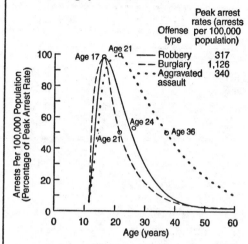

Note: The curve for each offense type is displayed as a percentage of the peak arrest rate. The curves show the age at which the peak occurs (at 100%) and the age at which the peak falls to 50% of the peak rate(2)

were thus based on the arrest experiences of offenders who had at least two arrests, one in the sampling year and another earlier in their careers at age 18, 19, or 20. This restriction, combined with the further requirement that the arrest in the sampling year be for a serious offense, limits the analysis to frequency rates for reasonably serious adult arrestees who were presumably criminally active throughout the estimation interval.

Individual annual arrest frequencies, μ, were estimated for the cohorts in Washington, D.C., and in the Detroit SMSA. The required arrests at either end of the estimation period were excluded, and time spent incarcerated was excluded from the time at risk of arrest in the estimation period. The mean frequencies estimated for adult arrestees who were

Table 1

Mean Individual Arrest Frequencies (μ) from Official Arrest Histories, Probabilities of Arrest Per Crime (q), and Associated Estimates of Mean Individual Crime Frequencies (λ), 1966–1973

Offense type	Washington, D.C.			Detroit SMSA		
	μ	q	λ	μ	q	λ
Robbery	0.23	0.069	3.3	0.20	0.043	4.7
Aggravated assault	0.19	0.111	1.7	0.18	0.062	2.9
Burglary	0.26	0.049	5.3	0.20	0.038	5.3
Larceny	0.27	0.026	10.4	0.22	0.030	7.3
Auto theft	0.14	0.047	3.0	0.14	0.015	9.3

in their 20s between 1966 and 1973 are reported for the jurisdictions in Table 1. When not incarcerated, arrestees active in robbery, burglary, or larceny are arrested about once every 4 years for these crime types; mean interarrest intervals are longer for aggravated assault (5 years) and auto theft (7 years).

These μ estimates can be used to develop estimates of λ that include the many more crimes committed that do not result in arrest. If the q is independent of λ, then $\mu = \lambda q$. The ratio of police statistics on reported arrests, A, divided by reported crimes, R, represents a starting point for estimating the offense-specific probability of arrest per crime. This simple ratio is adjusted by the offense-specific rate at which victims report crimes to the police, r, to account for unreported crimes among total crimes committed. Another offense-specific adjustment is made to account for the average number of multiple offenders arrested for the same crime incidence, O.

From the relationship $q = (A/O)/(R/r)$, for each crime type, an average probability of arrest per crime for the different offenses is reported in Table 1. These estimates are generally under 0.05. The somewhat higher value for aggravated assault probably reflects the direct confrontation between offender and victim, and the high proportion of offenders who are known to victims, 36.5% in 1980. These estimates of q based on aggregate published data are similar to other estimates of q based on self-reports of arrests and crimes by prison inmates.

Within any crime type and jurisdiction, the average λ in Table 1 is estimated from μ/q, applying q uniformly to all active arrestees. Subsequent analyses of variations in q among offenders suggest a negative relation between q and λ, particularly with the highest frequency offenders subject to lower arrest risks per crime. This relation implies that the estimates of λ in Table 1 are understated. The analysis of q for individuals, however, did not find systematic variations in q with other factors examined—jurisdiction, age, race, or prior arrests—and so patterns of differences in λ with these factors are not likely to be distorted.

Mean λ estimates in the two sites were generally similar in magnitude for most offense types. Individual frequencies were lowest for offenses involving actual or threatened violence. Arrestees active in aggravated assault were estimated to commit an average of two to three of these

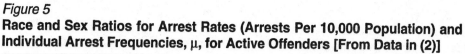

Figure 5

Race and Sex Ratios for Arrest Rates (Arrests Per 10,000 Population) and Individual Arrest Frequencies, μ, for Active Offenders [From Data in (2)]

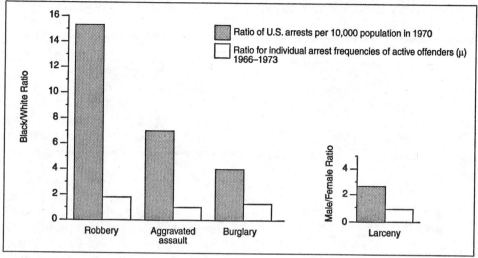

crimes annually, and offenders active in robbery were estimated to commit an average of three to five robberies per year while free. Individual frequencies for property crimes were generally higher, at more than five per year. The largest difference in λ was found for auto theft; λ, on average, was three auto thefts per year in Washington, D.C., compared to nine in the Detroit SMSA, perhaps attributable to differences between the jurisdictions in the availability of crime targets.

It is particularly interesting to compare estimates of the race-specific arrest rates (on a per-capita basis in the general population) with the corresponding values of μ for active offenders only, as in Table 2 and Fig. 5. We see here that, even though the ratios of black-to-white arrest rates in the general population are high (15 for robbery, 7 for aggravated assault, and 4 for burglary), the ratio of the values of μ are much closer to unity. A similar situation is shown in Table 3 and Fig. 5 when sex-specific rates for larceny are compared: male-to-female ratios of 2.5 in aggregate arrest rates are associated with μ ratios that are again close to unity.

The relationship of μ with age is also surprising when the effects of μ are separated from those of P. The typical information suggesting very sharp age differences in involvement in crime is given by age-specific arrest rates in the general population (where the age effect on crime is inferred from the ages of arrestees), as shown in Fig. 4. Many presume that this pattern of a rapid rise to a peak in the late teens, followed by a steady decline at older ages, must also apply to the age-specific pattern of μ. Empirically, however, μ's for individual crime types are much less sensitive to age: when average μ's are compared, none of the expected large declines with age are observed for cohorts of arrestees during their 20s.

Arrest frequencies for active offenders are thus found to be much more simi-

Table 2

Race-Specific Population Arrest Rates and Mean Individual Arrest Frequencies (μ) for Active Offenders (2)

Race	Race-specific rates		
	Robbery	Aggravated assault	Burglary
U.S. arrests per 10,000 population			
Whites			
1970	1.84	4.55	12.93
1980	3.09	8.84	18.33
Blacks			
1970	28.22	31.51	53.37
1980	31.74	37.49	56.00
μ, Detroit SMSA 1974–1977			
Whites	0.13	0.18	0.18
Blacks	0.23	0.18	0.22

Table 3

Sex-Specific Population Arrest Rates and Mean Individual Arrest Frequencies (μ) for Active Offenders (2)

Year	Males	Females
U.S. arrests for larceny per 10,000 population		
1970	54.30	19.88
1980	76.91	29.60
μ for larceny in Albany and Erie counties, New York		
1972–1976	0.16	0.18

lar across different demographic groups than are aggregate arrest rates. This suggests, of course, that the considerable variability in population arrest rates with demographic variables is attributable predominantly to differences in P with these variables. This reflects higher participation in crime by males and by blacks, and a rapid buildup of participation in the early teen years, followed by steady termination of criminal careers in the later teen years and early 20s. For those offenders who remain active, however, the value of μ seems to be fairly constant over age and across race and sex.

It is striking how few variables have yet been identified as significantly influencing λ. One of the important ones is the frequency and intensity of drug use. During periods of heavy drug use offenders commit crimes at frequencies six times as high as nonusing offenders.

Duration of criminal careers. Aside from the frequencies, the second most important parameter describing the criminal career is career length, and particularly the related residual career length. These are difficult to observe directly, partly because of the difficulty of determining just when the career is actually terminated. We have addressed this issue by using methods similar to those in life-table analysis.

In this approach, if there are significantly fewer 30-year-olds than 25-year-olds among active offenders, then one explanation for that decline is career termination between ages 25 and 30. Obviously, other competing explanations include differences in the sizes of the age cohorts in the general population, different rates of recruitment into criminal activity across the different cohorts, differential imprisonment with age, and decreases in λ with age. Controlling for these alternative explanations, Blumstein and Cohen develop estimates of termination rates and of their reciprocal, the mean residual career length, as a function of age. These estimates are shown in Fig. 6 for offenders whose adult careers began before age 21.

Figure 6
Variation in Mean Residual Career Length (T_R) With Time Already in a Career for 18- to 20-Year-Old Starters

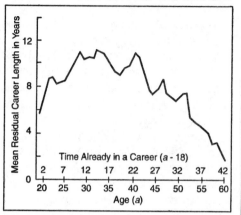

Conventional wisdom about criminal career termination is unduly influenced by examination of Fig. 4. In that figure, it is apparent that by age 30 there is a sharp decline in the number of active offenders. Thus, common belief suggests that offenders are about to terminate their criminal careers by age 30, so that long sentences for such offenders would be particularly wasteful of prison resources. From Fig. 6, however, it becomes clear that among those offenders who do remain active, mean residual career length actually rises until about age 30, is fairly flat through the 30s, and then begins to decline rapidly in the early 40s.

This process is similar to many other lifetime phenomena that are characterized by high failure early in life (infant mortality, break-in failures of machines), maximum expected lifetime in the middle, and high failure again at the end (aging, wear-out failures in machines). Because a large number of offenders do terminate their careers quickly during the early break-in period, adult careers are reasonably short, averaging under 6 years for serious offenses. Relatively few offenders survive these early high termination rates and remain active in criminal careers into their 30s, but they are the ones with the most enduring careers. Termination rates do begin to increase at older ages, but that does not occur until after age 40.

It is interesting to speculate on those factors that might be contributing to the high termination rates in the later years. They could be attributable to increased mortality, but the career termination rates, in the order of 15% per year, are a factor of more than 10 higher than ordinary mortality rates for males of under 1.5% at ages 45 to 54. Of course, the population of individuals who are still active offenders in their 40s may be subject to higher death rates than those of the general population. Indeed, death rates among parolees are two to three times as high as general population rates. This difference in mortality rates, however, is not sufficient to fully explain the higher termination rates that are observed. Another possible explanation could be associated with the kind of physiological effects one sees in many other facets of young male activity (for example, athletics) with peaking in the early ages followed by a gradual decline and then a rapid decline at later ages.

POLICY IMPLICATIONS OF EMERGING CRIMINAL-CAREER KNOWLEDGE

Although much of the research on criminal careers is still embryonic and not yet ready for significant policy application, some of the emerging insights represent important challenges to the prevailing conventional wisdom about crime and about means for dealing with crime.

Prevention. Obviously, the most attractive policy approach involves a search for means of preventing individuals' involvement in crime in the first place. Most of the available knowledge of factors associated with crime—including social class, family situation, age, employment, and drug use—are appropriate concerns here. Of course, the great majority of these represent various forms of social disability that should be addressed regardless of their role in fostering crime. These factors are sufficiently strongly intercorrelated with each other that isolating that effect of any one of them is extremely difficult both analytically and empirically. This makes it particularly difficult to assess the effect of manipulation of any single one of those variables. The strong interdependence of various social disabilities is no doubt a factor in the general failure to find evidence of demonstrable effects for programs directed at alleviating one or another of these disabilities.

Incapacitation. The mechanism of crime control which is most directly related to criminal careers is incapacitation. Incapacitation refers to the crimes averted in the community by removing an offender who would otherwise be active in a criminal career. Those crimes are averted only if the crimes "leave the street" with the offender's removal. To the extent that crimes derive from an economic market —as is the case with drug sales, for example—then removing a single supplier is not likely to affect the market in any significant way because a replacement supplier is likely to appear to meet the continuing demand. Even burglaries that

are carried out in the service of a fence, for example, could simply be continued by the fence finding new recruits to replace an imprisoned burglar. Continued offending by criminal groups after the incarceration of some group members also decrease incapacitation effects.

Crimes that are carried out without such obvious structural sources, but which are linked more to the personal circumstances of individual offenders, and particularly acts of personal violence, are much more likely to be averted through incapacitation. For such crimes, in the context of the simple criminal-career structure indicated in Fig. 2, a sentence of S years served between A_0 and A_N should avert λS crimes.

It is possible, however, that the sentence is imposed later in the criminal career so that the time served extends after the career would have been terminated anyway at A_N. In that case the period between the end of the career (A_N) and the end of the sentence is "wasted" in terms of incapacitative effects. Obviously, if the judge could anticipate when the career would be terminated, he could take account of that in his sentence. The stochastic quality of the termination process, however, limits his ability to make that prediction.

Rehabilitation. Incapacitation effects represent crime reduction that occurs while the individual is incarcerated. The incarceration experience, however, could also have longer term effects following release if it changes behavior, either through individual deterrence or through enhancing skills in functioning in legitimate activity. That effect might show itself through a reduction in λ or shortening of the residual criminal career. The effects of incarceration, however, could be criminogenic and work in the opposite direction by lengthening the criminal career or increasing λ. Research on rehabilitation suggests that the net effects for a variety of identified and evaluated treatment programs, both in and out of prison, are generally small. It is possible, then, that some offenders undergo rehabilitation, while others suffer a criminogenic effect of incarceration, but that in aggregate the two are roughly in balance. Distinguishing the features of criminal careers that are amendable to rehabilitative treatment from those that are not may provide a means of reducing crime through rehabilitation. Although the search is important, programs that are demonstrably effective in this regard have not yet been identified.

General deterrence. General deterrence is the crime reduction achieved through the symbolic threat communicated to others by the sanctions imposed on identified offenders. These effects have been widely explored but there are still no definitive estimates of the magnitudes of those effects. Research on deterrent effects most commonly relies on cross-sectional studies to determine the effect on aggregate population crime rates of sanction variations across jurisdictions. More fruitful results might be obtained by focusing deterrence research on the various aspects of criminal careers, and examining the separate deterrent effects of sanction threats on rates of initiation into criminal careers, on crime frequencies by active offenders, and on rates of termination.

SOME SUMMARY ISSUES

The issue of race. One of the important insights on crime that results from the research on criminal careers is the isolation of the role of the race variable. General population arrest rates are very different between blacks and whites, and especially so for violent crimes. This difference is due primarily to large race differences in participation, with very little difference between the races in the crime frequency of active offenders. Since the cases seen by the criminal justice system have already penetrated the participation filter, where race differences are large, this argues strongly that racial discrimination in arrest, sentencing, or parole decisions, which is unambiguously prohibited on normative grounds, is also empirically wrong as a basis for decisions about active offenders.

The role of drug use. The important influence of heavy drug use on λ is consistent with conventional wisdom, which suggests that drug users without other economic sources of support resort to other forms of crime to obtain the resources for their drug use. This has led some observers to argue that reduced enforcement, possibly even decriminalization, would lower the price and thereby diminish the need for crime to finance the purchase of drugs. Of course, this fails to account for any influence of higher price on inhibiting initiation or diminishing use by those who are current users.

Recognition of the relation between drug use and λ has also been used to argue for stricter enforcement against all drug offenses. Such a policy, however, fails to distinguish between drug users who engage primarily in drug offenses and those who engage in more threatening predatory crimes like robbery and burglary. To the extent that drug offenders are otherwise economically self-sufficient (for example, by earning considerable income from legitimate employment or by selling drugs to other users) a crackdown on their drug offenses will not affect predatory crimes directly. The strong association between drug use and λ for nondrug offenses, however, does suggest that, at least from the viewpoint of incapacitative effectiveness, the fact that a robber or other predatory offender uses drugs intensively should be viewed as an aggravating factor that would warrant a more certain sentence. Such a policy is contrary to the common practice of viewing drug involvement in the commission of a crime as a mitigating factor in establishing the sentence, largely because of concern over the diminished capacity—and the associated reduction in blameworthiness—of individuals under the influence of drugs.

Older criminals. The results here also suggest reconsideration of the conventional views about offenders who remain active in criminal careers into their 30s. After the teenage years, age certainly appears to be monotonically negatively related to P, that is, there is reasonably high termination and relatively little recruitment after about age 20, and so participation levels continue to decline. However, the common belief that offenders who remain in their criminal careers into their 30s will imminently terminate their careers is not empirically justified. On the contrary, those offenders who are still actively involved in crime at age 30 have survived the more typical early termination of criminal careers, and so are more likely to be the more persistent offenders. After their early 40s, however, their termination rates are quite high.

It is clear from the existing research that the microperspective of examining individual criminal careers does indeed provide the opportunity for significant new insights that are not otherwise available from examination of aggregate data regarding crime rates. It is also clear that the issues are quite complex and the causal connections are often elusive. Prospective longitudinal research on a large sample of individuals from multiple cohorts relying on official-record data and repeated self-reports of criminal activity and individual life events, would provide more precise indications of causal sequences. More effectively disentangling the apparent drug-crime nexus is of particular concern. The greatly enriched data on changes in life circumstances would also provide an expanded basis for identifying some of the factors most strongly associated with high and low crime frequencies and with early and late career terminations —aspects of criminal careers that bear directly on the effectiveness of various crime-control strategies.

NOTES

1. S. Glueck and E. T. Glueck, *500 Criminal Careers* (Knopf, New York, 1930); *One Thousand Juvenile Delinquents* (Harvard Univ. Press, Cambridge, MA, 1934); *Later Criminal Careers* (Commonwealth Fund, New York, 1937); *Juvenile Delinquents Grown Up* (Commonwealth Fund, New York, 1940; *Criminal Careers in Retrospect* (Commonwealth Fund, New York, 1943); *Unraveling Juvenile Delinquency* (Harvard Univ. Press, Cambridge, MA, 1950); *Delinquents and Nondelinquents in Perspective* (Harvard Univ. Press, Cambridge, MA, 1968).

2. A. Blumstein, J. Cohen, J. Roth, C. A. Visher, Eds., *Criminal Careers and "Career Criminals,"* National Research Council (National Academy Press, Washington, DC, 1986), vol. 1.

NO

Michael Gottfredson and Travis Hirschi

SCIENCE, PUBLIC POLICY, AND THE CAREER PARADIGM

The career model reappears with some consistency in the history of criminology. It consistently fails, however, to organize the facts about crime in a meaningful way. As a consequence, we predict that criminology will once again abandon career models in favor of theories of crime.

Research in the 1970's confirmed, for example, the existence of the career criminal. Following up on this important insight the Institute supported surveys to gauge the impact of the high-rate offender on crime and criminal justice operations. From this basic knowledge came the idea of focusing criminal justice resources selectively on the career criminals. Today, the concept of the career criminal is entrenched in criminal justice—a dramatic rethinking of policy and practice. Now research is examining ways to identify these offenders more accurately, moving toward the recommendation of one recent study that concluded that public safety would clearly benefit from incarcerating a larger proportion of high-risk probations and prisoners, and for longer periods of time. (James K. Stewart, director, National Institute of Justice, 1987: iii.)

Our paper, "The True Value of Lambda Would Appear to be Zero" (Gottfredson and Hirschi, 1986), sought to "introduce some small degree of tension into [an] otherwise complacent system" that had, we thought, "limited thinking about crime to the repetition of pretentious slogans," ignored research contrary to its assumptions, and proposed to lead public policy about crime in the wrong direction. We were concerned, too, that important theoretical traditions in criminology and even the social scientific approach to crime itself were being demeaned by the career paradigm. Our paper, "The Methodological Adequacy of Longitudinal Research on Crime" (Gottfredson and Hirschi, 1987a), argued that the popularity of the longitudinal study was not justified on methodological grounds and that it in fact reflected the narrow conceptual stance of the career paradigm. Our analysis of selective incapacitation, the policy often used to justify career research, likewise found this policy

From Michael Gottfredson and Travis Hirschi, "Science, Public Policy, and the Career Paradigm," *Criminology,* vol. 26, no. 1 (February 1988). Copyright © 1988 by The American Society of Criminology. Reprinted by permission. References and some notes omitted.

to be without empirical or considered theoretical support (Gottfredson and Hirschi, 1988).

The response by Alfred Blumstein, Jacqueline Cohen, and David Farrington... does little to reduce the concerns expressed in our papers. On the contrary, it pays little attention to the substance of our views, and it largely repeats the distinctions and even the figures and tables that have come to be associated with the career paradigm. Moreover, it continues the tradition of ignoring research whose conclusions argue against application of career terminology.

In this paper, we try to explain better why we believe that scientific criminology and sound public policy should reject the career approach to crime. Because we have dealt before with research design and policy issues, we consider here the conceptual foundation of the criminal careers paradigm and its implications for theory and analysis. In doing so, we try to avoid a blow-by-blow response to the details of Blumstein et al.'s defense of career research.

THE CAREER MODEL AND ITS PARAMETERS

Whether applied to dentistry, college teaching, or crime, the concept of a career implies several things. It suggests a beginning, as in "When did you become a teacher?" and an end, as in "When did you quit teaching?" Given a beginning and an end, the career concept also implies variable duration or length, as in "How long did you (or how much longer do you plan to) teach?" Once given, careers may be characterized along many dimensions, such as area of specialization (e.g., logic and the scientific method), amount of time and effort devoted to them (half time), level of accomplishment (professor), productivity (.19 articles a year), current direction (down), overall shape (peaked early), and time out for other activities (sabbatical, administration, jail). Once the decision to apply career terminology has been made, it is relatively straightforward to construct a career model and to outline the research necessary to estimate its "parameters" (see Blumstein and Cohen, 1987, Fig. 2; Blumstein et al, 1978, 1986: Fig. 1-1).

In our view, the concept of a *career* is not particularly problematic, and we have no quarrel with its application to dentists and professors. The question here is not whether career implies beginning, middle, end, and a minimum level of activity, it is whether the concept is applicable in some positive way to the study of crime. As far as we can see, Blumstein et al. do not bring to the career concept meanings derived from a conception of crime or a theory of criminality. Rather, they simply announce a decision to apply it to crime. The wisdom of this decision must be judged by its consequences.

When the Gluecks introduced career terminology, the idea appeared to have potential merit. In the 1930s it was reasonable to guess that individual offenders might engage in more serious crimes or at least in more specialized crimes as they grew older. In the 1930s it was reasonable to assume that concepts of onset, duration, and desistance might lead to better understanding of the crime problem. Not that the Gluecks had much choice in the matter. In the early days they were stuck with samples restricted to offenders. Following offenders over time and wondering about their "careers" was one way to escape the clearly unacceptable one-shot case study design implicit in their sampling procedure. (The absence of a control group continues to plague career methodology, and the solution adopted today is that adopted by the Gluecks— i.e., to produce variation in the dependent variable by following the same people over time.)

Fifty years later, it is not reasonable to wonder whether individual offenders engage in progressively more serious offenses as they grow older. Research on the topic shows that they do not(e.g., Glueck and Glueck, 1940, 1968). It is not now reasonable to assume that offenders tend to specialize in particular types of crime. Research shows that they do not (e.g., Blumstein and Cohen, 1979: 585; Hindelang et al., 1981; Wolfgang et al., 1972: 163). It is no longer possible to suggest that partitioning offenders into juveniles and adults makes fresh and meaningful the specialization question. It does not (Glueck and Glueck, 1968: Ch. 14). It is no longer possible to assert that these questions have been ignored. They have not.

So, the suggestion that criminology comes to these questions *de novo*, without benefit of prior experience, prepared only to absorb important breakthroughs soon to be made possible by the career paradigm, is no longer fresh. On the contrary, it ignores 50 years of research addressed precisely to the questions it raises. Put briefly, we see no *empirical* support for the view that the time has come to apply career terminology to the study of crime.

Conceptually, the situation is no better. Serious, direct efforts to apply career concepts to crime are, in our view, discouraging, to say the least (see, especially, Wootton, 1959: Ch. 5). Nonetheless, we have tried to understand the meaning of the large body of data gathered with

these concepts in mind (Hirschi and Gottfredson, 1983). Our conclusions from this effort have not been addressed by Blumstein and his colleagues. They have, however, been considered by others. For example, David Greenberg (1985: 1–2), in an article otherwise critical of our point of view, says this about our discussion of "onset":

> they provide a new interpretation of what the delinquency literature calls "early age of onset." Noting the existence of a strong negative correlation between age of first involvement in delinquency and the frequency and severity of delinquent acts in later years, several investigators have suggested that early onset leads to deeper, continuing involvement [citations omitted]. Hirschi and Gottfredson point out that if all groups share a common age distribution, young offenders will be disproportionately drawn from those groups whose level of involvement is high, as is true of older offenders. Thus no special explanation of age of onset is needed, beyond that of why some groups have higher levels of involvement in crime than others.

As Greenberg notes, our model accounts for "desistance" and "persistence" as well as "onset," and thus it accounts for all of the parameters of the career model. In doing so, it denies the validity of the career concept as applied to crime.

We have never considered the career parameter question conceptually simple.... But logical criticism of the career concept (see Hirschi, 1969: Ch. 4) is now coupled with a direct, parsimonious, and consistent alternative interpretation of the meaning of its parameters. Add to this research results inconsistent with expectations derived from the career model, and it seems to us that an especially heavy conceptual and empirical burden falls on those who would urge continued exploration of career parameters.

The substantive and statistical distinctions of the career model are not new. Nor do they appear to have been productive of insight in their earlier incarnations. (The Gluecks, given credit by Blumstein and his colleagues for introducing the career idea to criminology, made little use of career terminology in their later, better, and more influential works [Glueck and Glueck, 1950, 1968].) It appears that the ability to import a model and make distinctions (disaggregate, decompose) based on it should not be confused with evidence for the scientific value of the model in question. With this thought in mind, we will apply the career distinctions introduced by Blumstein and his colleagues to data and thereby illustrate their potential contribution to an understanding of the nature of crime.

THE EMPIRICAL STATUS OF THE PARTICIPATION-FREQUENCY DISTINCTION

The concept of a career leads to interest in factors affecting career choice or entry. Once entry has been addressed, attention shifts to differences among those within the career itself. As applied to crime, the career concept leads one to focus on the differences between those who commit at least one criminal act and those who do not (called "participation" by Blumstein et al.), and on differences in criminal activity among those active in crime during a particular period (called "lambda" or "frequency"). To justify this distinction, Blumstein et al. assert that the correlates of participation *may* be different from the correlates of lambda.

Before examining new data on the distinctions introduced by the career model, let us consider their logical status. Standard research determines the offensivity of people by counting the number of criminal acts they have committed in a specified period. The aim is to account for variation in the measure of offensivity. Ordinarily, researchers assume that the causes of one offense are the same as the causes of others, that is, that "crime" or "criminality" is a continuous variable. (They of course need not assume that the difference between 20 and 30 acts is 10 times greater than the difference between 2 acts and 3.) They also typically assume that the causal system producing offensivity is likely to remain stable over time unless acted upon by an outside force. Such assumptions have well-known statistical and theoretical advantages and are susceptible to direct, meaningful test. Researchers vary in where they draw the line between offenders and nonoffenders, and in how many levels of offenders they wish to acknowledge. The actual decisions on these issues are typically guided by inspection of the data and by previous research. Measurement decisions thus depend on the research question, the method of measurement, and the frequency of the offense in the population at issue. As a result they are made prior to examination of the data only with great risk. (Therefore, Blumstein et al.'s pronouncement of the *possibility* of a distinction among measures of crime is not proof of the utility of the distinction.)

The data we use are from the Richmond Youth Project (Hirschi, 1969), which collected police records and self-report data on 2,587 males and self-report data on females. The official data are counts of offenses recorded in police files, whatever the subsequent disposition of the case.

The large sample and the large number and seriousness of the offenses recorded and reported are sufficient to allow examination of the major parameters of the career model.

These data include the full range of offenders and nonoffenders typically of interest to criminologists, rather than a sample selected for its relevance to the career model. (In the data presented by Blumstein and Cohen,... there is reason to fear that sampling procedures are responsible for the results; see Gottfredson and Hirschi, 1986.) We can therefore use them to test the value of the distinctions advocated by Blumstein et al. to criminology as a whole.

These distinctions are illustrated with actual data in Table 1. Column 1 represents the number of offenses committed by males in the sample. This column, commonly called a "frequency distribution," is, in career terminology, "incidence" (I). Blumstein et al. would decompose this distribution on the grounds that it *may* be misleading. Following their logic, column 2 divides the sample into two groups, those who have and those who do not have a recorded offense. In career terms again, this distribution is called "participation" (P). Participation is said by Blumstein et al. to be of interest in prevention or in theories of deviance or trivial offending but to have little value in research focused on the effects of criminal justice policy.

Column 3 shows the distribution of offenses among those who have committed offenses—"frequency" (F) or lambda (λ). The central distinction of the career model can thus be represented by the formula: $F = I$, where $I \geq 1$, or $P \neq \phi$. The difference between the two measures is that one includes the value ϕ, nonoffenders, while the other does not. Where interest centers on the causes of the difference between ϕ's (nonoffenders) and any other number (offenders, however defined), lambda does not apply (as implied by the title of our paper critical of this measure).

At the bottom of column 3, we divided the number of offenses (3,067) by the number of offenders (957) to produce an oft-mentioned lambda, the average number of offenses per active offender, for the sample as a whole (3.2). Since lambda is advocated because it allows study of *individual* offenders, the frequent focus on this average lambda is puzzling. If the lambda of interest must vary from individual to individual, we compute such a lambda by counting the number of offenses committed by each offender during the reference period and dividing by 1. Since column 3 lists the number of offenses committed by offenders, it provides the requisite information. Those with scores of 2 have a lambda of 2, those with scores of 3 have a lambda of 3, and so on. The reader will note that individual lambdas are also found in column 1 when nonoffenders are removed.

Our procedure uses the number of offenses committed by an offender during a specific period to estimate the number of offenses he or she has committed during that period. Blumstein et al. appear to suggest that lambda is more esoteric or arcane than our procedure would imply. If, after all, lambda is nothing more than an offense count—even if calculated separately for crime "types"—it would hardly seem to justify its own research agenda, let alone radical restructuring of criminology. What, then, do Blumstein et al. have in mind?

Note that in their rejoinder, Blumstein et al. use *our* definition of lambda as an *average* number of criminal acts for all of-

Table 1

Measures of Incidence (I), Participation (P), and Frequency (λ) by Offense Type and Source of Data (Males Aged 13–18, Richmond, California)

| | Official Records | | | | | |
| | All Offenses | | | Serious Offenses[a] | | |
Number of Offenses	I	P	λ	I	P	λ
0	1,630	1,630	—	2,280	2,280	—
1	396	957	396	214	307	214
2	211	—	211	41	—	41
3	111	—	111	33	—	33
4	66	—	66	5	—	5
5	49	—	49	6	—	6
6 or more	124	—	124	8	—	8
Total Sample	2,587	2,587	957	2,587	2,587	307
Total Offenses/Offenders	3,067	957	3,067	509	307	509
Mean	1.19	.37	.320	.20	.12	1.66

| | Official Records Theft | | | Self-Reports[b] | | |
	I	P	λ	I	P	λ
0	2,220	2,220	—	724	724	—
1	232	367	232	643	1,757	643
2	73	—	73	482	—	482
3	23	—	23	343	—	343
4	18	—	18	171	—	171
5	6	—	6	79	—	79
6 or more	15	—	15	39	—	39
Total Sample	2,587	2,587	367	2,481	2,481	1,757
Total Offenses/Offenders	660	367	660	3,949	1,757	3,949
Mean	.26	.14	1.80	1.59	.71	2.25

[a]Robbery, burglary, assault (see Hirschi, 1969; 298–99).
[b]Six-item scale, with reference period "ever." Responses coded "yes" or "no" (see Hirschi, 1969: 54–62).

fenders during a specified time period. Note, too, that the lambdas accepted and calculated by Blumstein et al. are also averages that apply to all offenders in the sample at a particular age. In contrast, our lambdas in Table 1 are disaggregated, individual-level measures, the level of measurement said to justify lambda in the first place. It turns out that lambdas reported in the literature are group means that *ignore* individual variability (Blumstein and Cohen, 1979; Blumstein et al.,

1986). These lambdas are often a function of shifts in the definition of the sample ... or of artifactual methods of counting (see Gottfredson and Hirschi, 1986: note 5). Although constants describing groups may have theoretical and policy significance, we would not grant those created by sorting and sifting samples the status of scientifically discovered and generally applicable laws.

Another "career parameter" often mentioned by those endorsing the perspective is the seriousness of the crimes counted. Robbery, burglary, and assault are cited as being of particular interest to this perspective. Column 4 thus lists the count of these offenses for the sample as a whole. Obviously, this count, too, can be transformed without difficulty into its participation and lambda equivalents (columns 5 and 6).

Before subdividing further the distribution of crime, let us examine the consequences of the distinctions already introduced for the correlates of crime. Those familiar with the statistical implications of restricting the range of the dependent variable for correlation coefficients can predict the results of this exercise. They will be impressed if the career paradigm is sufficiently strong to shine through statistical tendencies to the contrary. They will also be impressed if the career paradigm successfully predicts *for no theoretical reason* results contrary to established statistical tendencies.

Table 2 depicts 7 common correlates[1] and their relation to 12 measures of crime based on distinctions used by Blumstein and his colleagues to justify the career paradigm. Crime is measured first with official records (columns 1–9) and then with self-reports (columns 10–12). The number of cases on which the correlations are based varies from measure to measure (the range of sample sizes is shown at the bottom of each column). (Sex is shown only for self-report data.) Pearson's r and gamma are reported for each comparison. (Unless otherwise noted, Pearson's correlations in the table are significant at the .05 level. The sample is described in Table 1.)

Inspection of the correlations in Table 2 yields two conclusions: First, they are substantively the same from one career measure to another. Contrary to Blum-

stein et al.'s predictions, and to the general thrust of the career model and its stated research agenda, the researcher could here focus on incidence, participation, or even on lambda in its various definitions without concern. We grant variation in the correlation coefficients in Table 2. We assert only that the direction, pattern, and relative magnitude of the correlations are much the same for all measures. In general, then, and decidedly contrary to the predictions of the career "paradigm," substantive conclusions about the causes and correlates of crime in Table 2 do not depend on career distinctions. Second, there is one important, easily predictable limitation to our conclusion: Generally, as one moves from participation to frequency to lambda to serious lambda, the correlations become smaller, eventually approaching insignificance as sample sizes also decline. Both problems are especially marked for "serious lambdas." The conclusion is inescapable: The career paradigm would have us pursue ever smaller correlations based on ever smaller sample sizes, with nothing but a statistical test to tell us whether the results are meaningful.

If we ask, "Would researchers studying *participation* measures be misled about the correlates of lambda?" the answer would be "no." In other words, to the extent this research is generalizable (and the findings of Table 2 are among the most heavily replicated in the field), findings based on standard measures are fully applicable to "active offenders," "serious offenders," "career criminals," and indeed to all of the categories and types of offenders said to be worthy of special study by advocates of the career model. Advocates of this model, thus, have no reason to question the relevance

Table 2

Correlations (Pearson's r and Gamma) Between Outside Variables and Incidence (I), Participation (P), and Frequency (λ) Measures of Crime (Richmond Youth Project Data)

Outside	Variable	Official Records					
		All Offenses			Serious Offenses		
		I	P	λ	I	P	λ
Race	r	.21	.25	.16	.17	.20	.10
	gamma	.46	.51	.24	.57	.58	.16
Smoke	r	.21	.25	.15	.14	.16	.06*
	gamma	.47	.52	.28	.47	.48	.21
Drink	r	.20	.23	.16	.14	.16	.09*
	gamma	.44	.48	.16	.46	.47	.26
Date	r	.14	.21	.07	.10	.11	.10*
	gamma	.38	.42	.10	.34	.34	.32
GPA	r	−.21	−.28	−.13	−.15	−.18	−.07*
	gamma	−.35	−.38	−.17	−.36	−.37	−.10
Friends	r	.21	.26	.14	.15	.16	.15
Picked Up	gamma	.37	.41	.21	.37	.38	.30
Number of Cases		1,858 – 2,587	1,858 – 2,587	699 – 957	1,858 – 2,587	1,858 – 2,587	206 – 307

		Official Records Theft			Self-Reports		
		I	P	λ	I	P	λ
Race	r	.24	.27	.19	.04	.02*	.04
	gamma	.67	.67	.42	.06	.03	.08
Smoke	r	.16	.15	.17	.35	.23	.30
	gamma	.42	.42	.27	.51	.58	.44
Drink	r	.16	.15	.15	.41	.26	.36
	gamma	.42	.43	.15	.60	.69	.51
Date	r	.11	.11	.12	.29	.22	.22
	gamma	.31	.31	.22	.40	.46	.34
GPA	r	−.13	−.14	−.11	−.15	−.10	−.13
	gamma	−.27	−.28	−.18	−.14	−.15	−.12
Friends	r	.16	.18	.10	.43	.29	.36
	gamma	.38	.39	.13	.46	.53	.39
Number of Cases		1,858 – 2,587	1,858 – 2,587	250 – 367	1,784 – 2,481	1,784 – 2,481	1,274 – 1,757
Sex	r				.28	.25	.21
	gamma				.48	.51	.43
Number of Cases					2,201	2,201	1,370

Note: The three measures of crime are defined and their distributions shown in Table 1.
*Correlation not significant at .05 level.

of prior research to questions of the utility and validity of their own "paradigm."

Prior research agrees with Table 2 that the correlates of crime are robust over method of measurement, crime types, crime seriousness, and even limitations of range. In fact, substantial consensus on the basic correlates of crime has developed in the face of considerable dispute about their theoretical meaning. This seems to us to place a heavy burden on those who argue that the correlates of crime depend on distinctions among incidence, prevalence, and frequency. Thus if Blumstein et al. (1986: 67–76) wish to argue that the correlations of race, sex, and age with *participation* differ from their correlations with *frequency*, it seems only reasonable to ask them to explain in some detail why their research appears contrary to the vast body of criminological research on these topics. We have attempted to show (in our 1986 paper) how particular artifacts of the Blumstein and Cohen design could lead to the conclusion that frequency (as they define it) has no correlates. (Clearly, if frequency is constructed as a constant for all members of the sample, it can have no correlates.) Similarly, we have offered theoretical reasons to expect the correlates of frequency and participation to be the same. In this respect, we are not alone. In our reading, virtually all theoretical traditions in criminology assume that "criminals" are subject to the same causal forces as "noncriminals." In our reading, the time has gone when criminology would look for features unique to the criminal to explain his or her behavior.

If we ask, "Would researchers who prefer self-report measures be misled by the comparisons in Table 2?" the answer would again be "no." We note that the data in Table 2 are also unkind to a "serious crime" emphasis; the table shows that all offenses are more predictable than the so-called serious offenses. Of course, the pattern of correlations is again much the same, which suggests that serious offenses are simply a subset of all offenses. (It may, for some purposes, sound better to engage in the study of serious offenders, but such purposes should not be confused with the purposes of science.)

We could continue making distinctions in the dependent variable, subdividing it by "crime type," for example. Ordinary research procedure would not, however, recommend further division, since the distinctions already in the table have proved to be inconsequential—with, if anything, a slight tendency to mislead about the correlates of "crime." (Note that the "theft" correlates behave identically to those already discussed.) We make this point to show that criminology is capable of disaggregation without the career model and that science is not necessarily on the side of disaggregation or of those who blame the field's *alleged* lack of knowledge on its failure to conduct "crime-type" analyses: "The traditional approach is also deficient because crime is dealt with as a unitary phenomenon without distinguishing the diverse ways in which causal factors might affect individual offenders" (Blumstein and Cohen, 1987: 985). Rather than castigating the field for failure to attend to individual offenders and offenses, it would be more constructive for Blumstein and Cohen to provide empirical examples of the advantages of their point of view....

AGE AND CRIME

Fundamental to our concern with the career paradigm and its implications is the relation between age and crime (Hirschi and Gottfredson, 1983). We earlier mentioned the logical implications of a relation between age and crime for the parameters of the paradigm, implications that do not depend on the validity of our invariance thesis. This point is obscured by defenders of the career paradigm... who apparently see in the invariance issue a device for deflecting attention from the implications for their work of the *current* age distribution of crime in the United States. It would be more constructive for them to attend to the logical and statistical problems introduced by this distribution than to the invariance thesis, a thesis that is not necessary to falsify the career hypothesis. However, since the invariance thesis has been raised by Blumstein et al., we are happy to defend it once again.

... Our point then and now is simply that criminology is better off when it stops pretending it has explained correlations it has not explained. The empirical challenge to our invariance thesis has come down to a search for statistical variation in the age distribution of crime with respect to such things as mode, level, or skew. As conducted by Blumstein et al. (and by Farrington, 1986), this search is unguided by theoretical purpose. As a result, it tends to lead to the improper conclusion that nonsubstantive and unexplained variations in the age distribution of crime bear on the invariance thesis....

[I]t is clear that Farrington (1986) and Blumstein et al. do not share our perceptions of similarity and difference (see also Table 2). We tend to see similarity where they see difference. We believe our bias can be justified by its consequences. For example, the conclusion that the age distribution of crime is substantially in-variant leads directly to several proportions about crime that can themselves be validated (see Hirschi and Gottfredson, 1983, 1986, 1987). The contrary conclusion of Farrington (1986), and now Blumstein et al., is that the age distribution of crime varies from year to year, place to place, crime type to crime type, and group to group. Observation of such statistical variation does not necessarily lead anywhere, and it does not require the scientific conclusion that trivial variation is more meaningful than the fundamental similarity in the distributions at issue. For example, three-quarters of a century ago, Goring (1913) found statistically significant differences in age distributions and concluded that such differences were scientifically trivial.... In our view, the question for criminology is whether the glass is 97 percent full or 3 percent empty, whether to pursue the important implications of a remarkably robust age effect or to continue to revel in the statistical noise generated by atheoretical research.

But the decline in crime with age is the fact directly relevant to the validity of the career paradigm. In our paper critical of this paradigm, we painted a picture of the criminal "career" we thought consistent with research. In this picture, the serious, predatory offenses said to be of interest to the career paradigm are in fact typically committed by young people, some of whom go on committing some of them for a while, but most of whom spend their declining years (late 20s) running afoul of the authorities over alcohol, drugs, and family squabbles. Our research is not the source of this picture. In perhaps their last word on the subject, after a lifetime of research on it, Glueck and Glueck (1968; 151–152) report among *delinquents* a "substantial reduction in criminalism, especially of the more serious kind" during the 25–31 age range, and they note that those offenders who do not during this period "achieve... maturity... tend to commit petty misdemeanors often associated with *disintegration* of organism and morale (emphasis in original)."

Blumstein et al. suggest that such *empirical* descriptions of criminal careers do not bear on the validity of the career construct because the features of the criminal career must be determined *empirically*! They then summarize earlier research of the Gluecks (Glueck and Glueck, 1940) showing essentially the same age pattern the Gluecks reported 28 years later. In the Blumstein et al. summary, however, the Gluecks' data "suggest distinct career paths for different crime types" and make it "possible to distinguish changes in frequency from changes in participation"—with the conclusion that frequency is not a function of age in the way participation is a function of age.

Since this conclusion contradicts our reading of research in the field and straightforward extrapolation from our Table 2, we must examine it further. How can it be said that in the Gluecks' data *participation* alone accounts for the decline in the rate of criminal activity with age? The Gluecks were apparently interested in the same kind of question for they computed several distinct "lambdas." One such lambda we might call a "serious-offense-participation lambda," since it divides the active offender population into two groups, those who commit serious offenses and those who do not. This lambda (the percentage of serious offenders among active offenders) takes the values 75.6, 77.4, 56.6, and 47.8 in the four periods identified in Blumstein et al.'s Table 1 (see also Glueck and Glueck, 1940: 317, Table 18). Such results led Glueck and Glueck (1940: 89) to report that "with the passing of years there was, among our... 1,000 delinquents, *both a decline in criminality and a decrease in the seriousness of the offenses of those who continued to commit crimes* (emphasis in original)." Those who defend lambda because of its connection to serious crime cannot dismiss as trivial a marked decline in serious crime with age among active offenders, especially when it occurs in data introduced by them....

Offenders in prison (presumably people of special interest to the criminal justice system) commit fewer "infractions" as they grow older, a clear "lambda" effect in a setting relatively free of the extraneous influences and ceiling effects of the outside world (Hirschi and Gottfredson, 1983: 561–562; see also Glueck and Glueck, 1940: 319). Research on offenders in the community also provides a large literature ignored by Blumstein et al. in their search for evidence that "lambda" remains constant with age for offenders. This literature repeatedly shows that offenders, even serious offenders, reduce the level of their criminal activity as they age. The parole follow-up literature, easily construed as research on serious offenders, has always found steep declines in offending as parolees age (see, e.g., Glaser, 1964: 474), so much so that age is typically included as a major predictor of success on parole. In fact, the Base Expectancy Measure (perhaps the most thoroughly validated prediction instrument in criminology) gives age one of the largest weights of the variables in the instrument (cited in Gottfredson and Gottfredson, 1980: 258; see also Gottfredson and Ballard, 1965). When a large sample of California parolees was followed for 8 years after release, and only those still free in the community considered, the violation rate for "major new offenses" declined precipitously with number of years since release (Gottfredson and Gottfredson, 1980: 265).

Perhaps the most thorough recent study specifically addressing the question of the stability of lambda over age is reported by Haapanen (1987). Haapanen collected 15-to-20-year follow-up data on a large sample of serious offenders in California. His conclusions (p. iii) are direct, to the point, and contrary to the claims of Blumstein et al.:

> Our longitudinal data allowed us to look not only at simple indices of involvement in crime but also at "career" characteristics, such as breadth of involvement and the extent of repetition for particular crime types. These analyses showed that for this large sample of serious offenders, both the kinds of crimes for which they were arrested and the rate of arrest clearly differed by race and clearly declined with age.

The Blumstein et al. position that crime does not decline with age among active offenders, or that crime *may* not decline with age among active offenders, is advanced in the face of much evidence to the contrary.

Is the distinction between criminal careers and career criminals really a distinction between science and policy? The search for a career criminal is as old as criminology. Whatever the details of the definition, it refers ultimately to some combination of criminal acts by individuals over time. Blumstein and Cohen (1987: 986) start with the idea of a criminal career, which, they say, is "merely a metaphor for the longitudinal process," and report no difficulty in deriving the career criminal from this concept: "It is... important to distinguish the concept of criminal careers from the policy-oriented reversal of that phrase, the 'career criminal,' which refers to offenders whose criminal careers are of such serious dimension that they represent prime targets for the criminal justice system." ...

Well, the criminal career "metaphor" is apparently hard to distinguish from a particular research design and a preference for focusing research attention on what Blumstein and Cohen themselves refer to as "the prime targets of the criminal justice system." We may be forgiven for thinking we saw policy interest in such statements when, we are now told, no such interest exists. However, we are not alone. The law enforcement community, criminal justice research agencies (see, the quote from Stewart, *supra*), and indeed members of the National Research Council's Panel on Research on Criminal Careers appear to believe that the goal of career research is to locate real, live career criminals (whatever they may be called) and to treat them accordingly:

> The National Academy of Sciences, in a lengthy project... supported by the National Institute of Justice, *Criminal Careers and Career Criminals,* has brought these data together.... It is one of the best and the most immediately practical emanations of social science research that's come to this field. For the first time from this there emerges the serious possibility of distinguishing the likely intensive repeaters from the likely desisters and adjusting our responses at the level of policing, prosecuting, and sentencing accordingly (Morris, 1987).

As this statement from a member of the criminal careers panel suggests, some would claim that knowledge sufficient to direct policy is already in hand ("one of... the most immediately practical emanations of social science"). We strongly disagree. If, however, such "knowledge" exists, we believe the time has come to share it with the academic community.

In our view, it is academically illegitimate to criticize a body of knowledge on the basis of its putative policy implications (see Gottfredson and Hirschi, 1987b). Unfortunately, this view has not tended to characterize the work of those pursuing the career paradigm:

> A significant factor inhibiting the growth of knowledge about criminal careers has been that traditional research focuses on developing correlates of crime.... Not surprisingly, many indicators of social deprivation are associated with crime, among them low income, high population density, and high minority racial composition. Knowing of such associations, however, is not very helpful. The strong mutual association among these correlates provides little guidance on their relative individual contributions to crime, and such partitioning is crucial in order to isolate and identify useful social investments to address these presumed causes (Blumstein and Cohen, 1987: 985).

Obviously, whatever the truth of the dubious assertion that traditional causes of crime have no policy implications, this purported lack of utility bears no connection to their status as causes of crime. We think career criminal public policies are without merit. As we hope is clear from this paper, however, we also believe that independent of its policy prescriptions, the career paradigm is of limited value to the scientific study of crime.

CONCLUSION

... Blumstein et al. seem to want it all ways. They want an important distinction between their "criminal career" approach and the policy-oriented hunt for the career criminal at the same time they justify the former by the latter. They want to suggest that their perspective is compatible with traditional criminology at the same time they declare traditional criminology fundamentally defective and misleading. They claim to be open to all research designs yet they develop a "model" whose "parameters" require longitudinal data. They claim to be open to a variety of prevention and intervention policies yet they develop a model so narrow that the criminal justice system alone can be the focus of public policy toward crime. They complain that their critics mock knowledge and obfuscate findings. We are all in favor of science, but believe the line between science and scientism is worthy of respect. In this regard, consider the presentation in *Science* of formulas for the computation of career length (Blumstein and Cohen, 1987: 986), the explanation of the value of scientific notation..., the extended discussions of elementary issues of research design, and the laborious statistical exercises that eventually produce smaller constants from larger ones, as though it mattered.... Finally, consider their Figure 6, which illustrates the relation between age and average years of schooling in the 1980 census. This figure is presented to show the dangers of cross-sectional data and the need for longitudinal data in inferring age effects. We believe it shows better the dangers of approaching criminology unaccompanied by substantive concepts. Even Martians with questions about the earthly relation between age and education would not conduct longitudinal research, nor would they take a cross-sectional census of the population of the United States. They would, instead, ask some *one* of the millions of people in the society likely to know the answer to their question, knowing full well that such "informant interviewing" is a perfectly adequate and incredibly efficient device for answering some questions. By the same token, in our view, those genuinely interested in the "parameters" of the career "model" would today conduct neither inefficient cross-sectional nor immensely inefficient longitudinal research. They would, instead, ask someone who knows. In our view, almost any "traditional" criminologist would do.

NOTES

1. The "outside variables" in table 2 are defined as follows: race (0 = white; 1 = black); smoke (0 = do not smoke; 1 = smoke); drink (0 = do not drink alcohol; 1 = drink); date (0 = do not date; 1 = date); GPA (decile scores of cumulative school-recorded grade point average in English); friends picked up (self-reported number of friends ever picked up by the police (don't know treated as "missing")—5 = four or more).

POSTSCRIPT

Is Research on Criminal Careers Helpful?

As the influential sociologist C. Wright Mills once observed, women and men of reason and good will frequently disagree with each other. The debate presented here is acrimonious at times, which is one indication that the stakes are high. Criminological methods and theory can be complex, but it is important that public policies regarding crime control be based on sound principles.

Unlike other issues in which there sometimes exists some room for compromise, the Blumstein and Cohen versus Gottfredson and Hirschi debate appears to be a straight win-or-lose situation. At least this seems to be what the protagonists think: one side is plain wrong. Is compromise possible?

Now that you have read the issue and thought about the controversy, what do you see as the policy implications of criminal career research? Do you feel that Gottfredson and Hirschi's charge that the criminal career approach is narrow and policy oriented is accurate? Would that necessarily be bad? Why, or why not?

For Blumstein and Cohen's reply to Gottfredson and Hirschi, see "Longitudinal and Criminal Career Research: Further Clarification," by Blumstein, Cohen, and D. Farrington, *Criminology* (February 1988). Also, in that same issue, see the excellent article by C. Tittle and the one by J. Hagan and A. Palloni. Both articles attempt to bridge the two sides.

For an outstanding review and discussion of the Gluecks-Sutherland debate, which is also a good example of a contextual analysis of criminological ideas, see John Laub and Robert Sampson's "The Sutherland-Glueck Debate: On the Sociology of Criminological Knowledge," *American Journal of Sociology* (May 1991). Also see Laub and Sampson's *Crime in the Making: Pathways and Turning Points Through Life* (Harvard University Press, 1993).

For research on this controversy, see D. Elliott, "Serious Violent Offenders: Onset, Developmental Course, and Termination," *Criminology* (February 1994) and D. Nagin, D. Farrington, and T. Moffit, "Life-Course Trajectories of Different Types of Offenders," *Criminology* (February 1995). For a critical discussion of the perceived neglect of criminal careers in textbooks, see R. Wright's "Stopped for Questioning but Not Booked: The Coverage of Career Criminals in Criminology Journals and Textbooks," *Journal of Criminal Justice Education* (1994). For an example of the criminal career approach in another country, see D. Farrington, "Criminal Career Research in the United Kingdom," *British Journal of Criminology* (Autumn 1992).

ISSUE 10

Can Traditional Criminology Make Sense Out of Domestic Violence?

YES: Lawrence W. Sherman, from "The Influence of Criminology on Criminal Law: Evaluating Arrests for Misdemeanor Domestic Violence," *The Journal of Criminal Law and Criminology* (vol. 83, no. 1, 1992)

NO: Cynthia Grant Bowman, from "The Arrest Experiments: A Feminist Critique," *The Journal of Criminal Law and Criminology* (vol. 83, no. 1, 1992)

ISSUE SUMMARY

YES: Lawrence W. Sherman, a professor of criminology and president of the Crime Control Institute, worries that political concerns may weaken experimental studies of domestic violence control. He insists that, if used judiciously, studies of arrests for misdemeanor domestic assault can be fundamental for understanding and reducing domestic violence.

NO: Law professor Cynthia Grant Bowman counters that traditional criminology has, until recently, ignored domestic violence. And current research is badly flawed since it is usually conducted from the perspective of the abuser, ignores feminist thinking, and does not address vital social factors.

Domestic violence. We do not know if spouse, lover, wife, or child abuse has actually increased significantly in the past several years or if such abuse has simply been discovered because the current political and social climate validates worrying about it, researching it, and demanding that something be done about it.

While there is little doubt that sexual, psychological, and physical assaults occur within all domestic arrangements regardless of race, socioeconomic status, religion, ethnic origin, and so on, solid information on the rate, intensity, and types of assault is not available. In the past, the received wisdom among police agencies was that cops should avoid intervening in domestic abuse cases. If intervention could not be avoided, however, then couples were to be counseled, but no arrests were to be made. But ways of thinking about and studying domestic violence changed dramatically in 1984 when Lawrence W. Sherman and Richard Berk published the results of their research on domestic violence in Minneapolis, Minnesota. They found that when the police arrested males involved in misdemeanor domestic assaults, the males the police arrested were less likely to assault in the future than those who were not arrested.

Sherman and Berk cautioned that their findings were tentative and that policies should *not* be based on a single study. Yet four months after the publication of their study, the U.S. Attorney General recommended that arrests be made in domestic assault cases. Within five years approximately 84 percent of urban police agencies had either preferred or mandatory arrest policies for misdemeanor domestic assault cases. As Sherman makes clear in his 1992 article that is reprinted here, the basic reversal of policy was largely a function of the presence of powerful vested interest groups, in addition to the fact that the time was ripe for a "get tough" approach toward men who assault their wives or girlfriends.

Meanwhile, at the same time that the political and legal fallout from Sherman and Berk's 1984 study was rapidly resulting in policies that advocated arresting assaulters, a number of frequently impressive studies, such as the one by Franklyn W. Dunford, David Huizinga, and Delbert S. Elliott on the Omaha police experiment, found that arrest did *not* deter domestic assault. In fact, the charge was made that in the case of poor black female victims, arresting the man only aggravated the situation.

Ironically, Sherman welcomes these refutations of his initial findings. He asserts that many of these studies have been following an experimental design (as did his) and hence are adding to our stock of knowledge about the issue. He also suggests that the seemingly inconsistent and contradictory findings can be explained when relevant factors are taken into account (e.g., background of assaulters, time between arrest and subsequent charges). These studies should continue, he believes. His main concern all along has been that policymakers should not prematurely utilize tentative research findings, because in their haste to take action, they might make matters worse.

Law professor Cynthia Grant Bowman directly responds to Sherman's points. She isolates and describes how criminological studies of domestic violence contain distortions. One of her concerns is that criminologists reduce the "subjects of the study to statistics and thus [lose] the important information which could be provided by the voices of the victims themselves." Bowman's lively attack raises issues that policymakers and researchers may benefit from considering.

As you read the two protagonists of this issue, try to recall what you have learned about research. If you conformed to Research 101 instructions and designed a study in which a control group and an experimental group were randomly selected, then performed a clear operation on the subjects in the experimental group, and finally carefully measured the results, how is it possible that your study, as suggested by Bowman, might still be invalid?

When did you first become aware of domestic violence? About how often, would you say, does it occur among your friends and/or relatives? In what form? As you read Sherman and Bowman, decide whose understanding of domestic assault is more accurate, and why.

YES

Lawrence W. Sherman

THE INFLUENCE OF CRIMINOLOGY ON CRIMINAL LAW: EVALUATING ARRESTS FOR MISDEMEANOR DOMESTIC VIOLENCE

On May 27, 1984, the U.S. National Institute of Justice announced the results of a randomized clinical trial of the use of arrest for misdemeanor domestic violence. The 314-case experiment, conducted with the Minneapolis Police Department, used a lottery method that assigned about one third of the probable cause suspects to be arrested, one third to be advised, and the rest to be sent away from the home on threat of arrest. Over a followup period lasting at least six months, about ten percent of the arrested suspects and about twenty percent of the suspects not arrested were officially detected to have committed one or more repeated domestic assaults. Citing these results, the Attorney General of the United States four months later issued a report recommending that arrest be made the standard treatment in cases of misdemeanor domestic assault. Within two years, "preferred" arrest became the most common urban police policy for those cases. By 1989, mandatory or preferred arrest policies were reported by eighty-four percent of urban police agencies. By late 1991, fifteen states and the District of Columbia had passed mandatory arrest statutes for cases in which there was probable cause to believe that misdemeanor domestic violence had occurred....

CONTROLLED EXPERIMENTS IN CRIMINAL SANCTIONS

The importance of controlled experiments in criminal law derives largely from our ignorance of the true nature of criminal deterrence. As Professor Norval Morris has observed, every criminal law system in the world (except Greenland's) has deterrence as its "primary and essential postulate." As Sir Arthur Goodhart once observed, if punishment "cannot deter, then we might as well scrap the whole of our criminal law." Yet for most of human history, the evidence of the deterrent effects of criminal law has been little more than what Morris calls "a surfeit of unsubstantiated speculation."

Excerpted from Lawrence W. Sherman, "The Influence of Criminology on Criminal Law: Evaluating Arrests for Misdemeanor Domestic Violence," *The Journal of Criminal Law and Criminology*, vol. 83, no. 1 (1992), pp. 1–45. Copyright © 1992 by Northwestern University School of Law. Reprinted by permission. Some notes omitted.

In the past quarter century, substantial strides have been made toward filling the knowledge gap about the deterrent effects of criminal sanctions. A series of theoretical treatises was followed by a prestigious National Academy of Sciences panel report on the methodological limitations of existing deterrence studies, a series of survey studies... cross-sectional analyses of the relationship of criminal sanctions to crime rates, and quasi-experimental (before and after) evaluations of the effects of sudden changes in sanctions like capital punishment, mandatory prison sentences, and police crackdowns. None of these research methods, however, has been able to resolve the lingering problems of distinguishing mere correlations from true causation. As a result, our knowledge of the deterrent or other consequences of criminal sanctions—including a possible increase in crime—remains sketchy and uncertain.

Controlled experiments are fundamentally different from all other kinds of research. They are uniquely capable of eliminating alternative causes for observed effects, or plausible rival hypotheses also consistent with the evidence. In all other research designs the scientist must specify which rival theories must be tested and eliminated. In controlled experiments, even theories that the scientist never considered can usually be eliminated automatically. By making two groups comparable with respect to virtually all characteristics (within the limits of sampling error) *except* the factor under study (like AZT or arrest), a controlled experiment leaves very little doubt about inferring causation from any observed correlations—at least within the particular sample under study. As we shall see, however, generalizing from one sample to other populations is quite another matter....

POLICE RESPONSES TO DOMESTIC VIOLENCE

The historical custom of police in the U.S. was to make arrests only rarely in cases of misdemeanor domestic violence. In the later 1960s, this custom was reinforced by federal sponsorship of training in police mediation of domestic "disturbances," including those in which minor assaults had occurred. By the late 1970s, women's advocates used litigation and legislation to press for a policy innovation: much greater use of arrest. From the 1980s to the present, the innovation many have recommended is mandatory arrest (required by state law) whenever police have probable cause to believe that a domestic assault has occurred. This recommendation clearly constitutes a substantial increase in the severity of criminal sanctions for this particular offense. What is less understood is that it constitutes a departure from, rather than an equalization with, the level of enforcement severity for most other misdemeanors and many felonies.

Under-Enforcement: Domestic and Other Violence

As recently as 1967, the leading police professional organization, the International Association of Chiefs of Police, declared in its training manual that "in dealing with family disputes, the power of arrest should be exercised as a last resort." This position was endorsed by the American Bar Association, whose 1973 *Standards for the Urban Police Function* said that police should "engage in the resolution of conflict such as that which occurs between husband and wife ... in the highly populated sections of the large city, without reliance upon criminal assault or disorderly conduct statutes." In 1977, police in three metropolitan areas were observed to take slightly longer to respond to domestic disturbance calls (4:65 minutes) than non-domestic disturbances (3.86 minutes). Police in these areas openly told observers it was the officers' policy (not the department's) "to proceed slowly in the hope that the problem would be resolved or that a disputant would have left before they arrived." The expression of such policies led many to conclude that male police officers practice discriminatory enforcement in such cases because they side with male offenders.

The evidence is far from clear, however, that police practiced *more* under-enforcement in domestic situations than in other cases in general, or in cases of interpersonal violence in particular. By the 1970s, the best evidence from observations of police work suggested that there was no less enforcement in domestic violence cases than in other cases of personal violence, although there was less enforcement in cases involving a male and a female than in cases involving two males. The evidence remains inconclusive largely because of imprecise data on the levels of injury involved in the different categories of cases.

... It is unfortunate that so many advocates cannot accept the concern of criminologists with the plight of domestic violence victims, apparently because we do not always reach politically correct conclusions.

It is even more unfortunate that the battered women's movement in Milwaukee and elsewhere has shown little concern for the evidence that arrest positively harms black women in at least one poverty ghetto, where the majority of the suspects are unemployed and unmarried. [Joan] Zorza's characterization of those results typically obscures the issue:

> [E]ven if arrest may not deter unemployed abusers in ghetto neighborhoods, arrest still deters the vast majority of abusers ... [w]e do not consider eliminating arrest for other crimes (e.g., robbery), however, because it may not deter a particular individual or class of individuals.[1]

The Milwaukee finding is not the failed deterrence of arrest, but the substantial *increases* arrest produces in the total volume of violence against victims of the ghetto poor unemployed. We have no evidence that arrest for robbery increases the total number of robbery offenses robbers commit, nor is arrest without prosecution the typical response to robbery —as it is in the realm of domestic assault. If we had evidence that the typical criminal justice response to robbery backfired, we might respond to it with longer prison sentences upon conviction in order to counteract higher recidivism rates with greater incapacitation effects. Whether such a response makes sense when applied to a crime as pervasive as domestic violence—either for the families involved or for society—is another question altogether. What seems clear is that prosecutors are generally unwilling to do much with domestic violence cases, especially in cities with high volumes of such arrests (like Milwaukee). As long as that is true, we must soberly assess the wisdom of an "arrest-and-nothing-else" policy, since that is all we seem likely to get.

The comment that "most abusers" are deterred by arrest also misses a key point. While most abusers may be white, married and employed, the abusers *coming to police attention* may not be. Most of the crime, most of the police, and most police responses to reports of domestic violence in this country are found in cities of over 100,000. Most of those cities, in turn, have substantial minority populations, in which victims disproportionately call on the police for assistance. Disregarding these facts in order to pursue a policy beneficial to women who do not live in poverty stricken ghettoes—primarily white women—displays an unfortunate racial and economic insensitivity to the overall effects of mandatory arrest. Even if most abusers coming to police attention are not ghetto dwellers, we cannot write off as unimportant the victims of those who are....

WHAT HAVE WE LEARNED?

After more than a decade of evaluating arrest for misdemeanor domestic violence, we still have much to learn. The jigsaw puzzle of diverse results in different cities has not been put together, and too many pieces are still missing. Many alternate approaches still remain untested or unreplicated, such as the impressive Omaha result that issuing warrants for *absent* offenders reduced repeat violence by fifty percent. Nonetheless, it is time we took stock of what we have learned, both about the substance of the problem and about the process of doing policy-relevant criminology.

Domestic Violence Arrests

One response to the replication results is that it is too early to reach any policy recommendations. This view implies that the burden of proof must be on any argument to undo mandatory arrest laws, or stop them from being passed. Such

a view, however, runs contrary to the principles laid down by the Federal Judicial Center's Advisory Committee on Experimentation in the Law.... The question as of 1984 was whether an innovation of greater severity should be adopted—preferred or mandatory arrest. The initial experiment supported the innovation, but with reservations. On balance, the subsequent experiments have not.

Even if we disregard the evidence of increased domestic violence caused by arrest in some cities and with some kinds of offenders, the weight of the evidence fails to justify an innovation of greater severity—at least on specific deterrent grounds alone. Yet it is those grounds, alone, which have morally justified the entire program of research....

What may ultimately be acceptable, under the existing principles of community policing, is different police policies or practices for different neighborhoods. Police discretion already varies widely by neighborhood, and community policing is trying to make it vary even more explicitly in response to community preferences. A local option approach, informed by research on the specific deterrent effects of arrest in different communities, might be the best way to develop a workable policy from the findings.

This possibility can be fully assessed, however, only after further analyses explore the neighborhood basis for the interaction effects observed to date. Whether that analysis can predict the likely effects of arrest based on census tract characteristics remains to be seen. It may well be more effective at that task, however, than we have been in predicting city-level effects so far.

Whatever approach may be taken on structuring discretion to use arrest, the key question is whether any discretion should remain in the hands of the police. This question has both a philosophical and a practical dimension. On philosophical grounds, it is clear that large segments of the legal and advocacy communities want no discretion invested in the police; they can cite legions of horror stories in support of their positions. On the practical side, no one has ever figured out how to eliminate police discretion. As Ms. Zorza quite correctly points out, we have learned that mandatory arrest laws are widely circumvented. That is all the more reason, it would seem, to develop an alternative approach.

The available research cannot say what that approach should be. All it can say is what the results of the six experiments show. Therein lies the lesson for the influence of criminology on the criminal law.

Experimental Criminology and Criminal Law

The domestic violence experiments show that criminology can provide factual information about the criminal law and its consequences. That is about all it can do. It cannot, for example, control the ways in which participants in the political process describe (or distort) research results in advancing a point of view. It cannot ensure that its recommendations will be heeded, or that its conclusions will be believed. It cannot speak to value judgments about "just deserts," even when they are conveniently raised as a fallback position when evidence of deterrence is weakened. It cannot guarantee that its findings will resonate with the prevailing ethos of the age, as the Minneapolis findings did but the replication findings did not.

The Minneapolis findings stirred enormous interest by a wide range of writers and editorialists, who hailed the results as a breakthrough. The replication results received grudging acceptance in some of those quarters, and complete silence in most others. They were even attacked editorially by the Milwaukee newspapers. It is clear that our zeitgeist in the 1990s still favors "getting tough," and that greater severity is more politically correct than lesser severity among a broad coalition of both liberal and conservative groups. This carries a sobering lesson: provisional policy recommendations made on initial research results may be widely accepted in support of that broad coalition, but subsequent findings that run against it may have far less influence. Undoing the effects of initial results may be much harder than some criminologists imagined, largely because there is less rational interest in minimizing violence than one might have assumed. It appears that preferences for punishment have more ideological than pragmatic foundations, and that criminology can only speak to the pragmatic.

This is a sad commentary for a system of criminal law founded on the presumption of deterrence. It suggests that as criminology unravels the deterrence hypothesis in its full complexity, the criminal law is unlikely to respond to that information in ways that will maximize crime control. Rather, the principle of appropriate vengeance, already so strong in the sentencing guidelines movement, may become even stronger, making deterrence irrelevant. If this keeps up, we will have no need for a JOURNAL OF CRIMINAL LAW AND CRIMINOLOGY; a Journal of Just Deserts will do just fine.

But times change, and knowledge takes a long time to accumulate. By the time we have fully assembled the puzzle of diverse effects of domestic violence arrests, perhaps the political culture may become more open to adopting columnist Ellen Goodman's point of view:

> What is progress after all in the course of sexual politics? Is it marked by an increase in the number of men in jail? Or by a decrease in the number of assaults? I don't want to choose between law

enforcement and "crime prevention," but I would chart the long run of progress by the change in men's behavior.[2]

NOTES

1. Joan Zorza. *The Criminal Law of Misdemeanor Domestic Violence, 1970–1990,* 83 J. CRIM. L. & CRIMINOLOGY 46 (1992), at 72.

2. Ellen Goodman, *I'd Have Let Him Walk,* WASH. POST, Dec. 14, 1991, at A27.

NO

Cynthia Grant Bowman

THE ARREST EXPERIMENTS: A FEMINIST CRITIQUE

Quantitative research has elicited a good deal of criticism from feminists. Quantitative methods are considered suspect because they place a greater value on "objective" and quantifiable information than on other sources of knowledge; because they assume a separation—indeed, a distance—between the researcher and the object of study; and because they isolate the factors under study from their socio-economic and historical context.[1] In the domestic violence field, moreover, survey research is greeted with particular mistrust because of early studies which were perceived as both insensitive in their design and biased in their results.[2]

The series of quantitative studies described in this symposium may, I fear, be rightfully subjected to the same criticism. In this brief comment, I will discuss how these studies may in some ways distort rather than clarify our understanding of the effect of different police responses to domestic violence (1) by isolating one factor—arrest—from the larger context of domestic violence and the response of the criminal justice system to it; (2) by reducing the subjects of the study to statistics and thus losing the important information which could be provided by the voices of the victims themselves; and (3) by analysing both the problem under study and the potential policy implications solely in individualistic, non-relational terms.

My position is not that quantitative research is without its uses. Rather, my intent is to illustrate the contribution of studies of this sort, to discuss their limitations, and to call for a more complete investigation into the appropriate police response to domestic violence based upon a genuine dialogue between the literatures of social science and feminism. The *ideal* experiment, I think, would be one which examined the impact of forceful responses by the criminal justice system within a context that also provided a broad range of supportive services—shelter, child care, therapy, employment and income support, if necessary—to the victims of domestic violence.

The arrest experiments in Milwaukee, Charlotte, Omaha and Colorado Springs attempt to correlate arrest, as contrasted with other possible responses by police to domestic violence incidents, with a number of measures

Excerpted from Cynthia Grant Bowman, "The Arrest Experiments: A Feminist Critique," *The Journal of Criminal Law and Criminology*, vol. 83, no. 1 (1992), pp. 201–208. Copyright © 1992 by Northwestern University School of Law. Reprinted by permission. Some notes omitted.

of recidivism over a six- or twelve-month period of time. Contrary to the results of the previous study in Minneapolis, which showed that arrest correlated with a reduction in subsequent violence, the authors of the newer studies conclude that arrest is no more effective a deterrent than other responses. The new studies further conclude that arrest may in some cases lead to retaliation and thus bear an inverse relationship to specific deterrence.

In order to be appropriately "scientific," the designers of these studies seek to isolate arrest as a factor in their experimental design, in order to evaluate the mandatory arrest policies which were initiated in many locales in the wake of the Minneapolis experiment. By isolating one factor, however, and by slicing into reality at one point in time, they distort it. Arrest is only one stage of response to any crime. It is preceded by the act of calling the police; it is followed, at least in theory, by charging and prosecution. In the domestic relations context, there is evidence that the mere fact of calling the police, without more, has some deterrent impact. In addition, as Joan Zorza points out, abusers and their victims cannot fail to notice that ninety-five percent of domestic violence cases are not subsequently prosecuted. Finally, even if convicted, very few abusers ever serve any time in prison. These other factors may well be more important than arrest. By simply correlating arrest with subsequent reports of abuse, there is no way of knowing which of the factors actually caused or deterred recidivism.

Second, by objectifying the subjects of the arrest experiments, reducing them to statistics classified by race, employment and socio-economic status, one is by definition deprived of the valuable infor-

mation that could be provided by these victims' voices. Given that the experiments carried out in each city included follow-up interviews, a critical source of information was bypassed. Consider, for a moment, the questions these women could have addressed: whether they had any independent source of income or place to go; whether they might have left and sought safety before subsequent attacks if supportive services had been available; whether they were reluctant to report incidents for fear of jeopardizing their spouses' jobs and family income; whether the treatment of their cases by the police and court system encouraged or deterred them from seeking assistance from the criminal justice system in the future, etc. Each of these inquiries leads potentially to quite different policy implications, implications which are unclear from a simple correlation between a particular police response and future incidents of violence.

An additional question which might be answered by in-depth interviews with the abuse victims is whether, despite the recidivism rate, they would prefer arrest to other possible police responses to domestic violence calls. The authors of the Milwaukee report implicitly assume that certain groups of women, primarily those who are Black and poor, will oppose arrest for fear of retaliation.[3] This may not be the case, however. Those women, if given a choice, might nonetheless want the validation of an arrest or the time and space it gives them. Their answers might be very different, moreover, if the choice were not posed in a vacuum. What might they say if they were offered both arrest and a variety of supportive services?

The quantitative approach not only misses the voice of the victim; it loses her perspective as well. Even amidst the seeming neutrality of statistics, the authors of these reports appear automatically to assume the male perspective from which to explain data. The unquestioned assumption is that arrest produces certain results either by deterring or failing to deter the abuser. This assumption becomes even more explicit in the conclusion that the variable effects of arrest are explained by the socio-economic class of the *man*. If the abuser is middle class, employed, and white, arrest results in reduced recidivism.

If statistics are truly neutral, however, why is it to be assumed that the effects of arrest result from its impact on the abuser rather than on his victim? Arrest may empower the victim, both because it affirms her rights and because it allows her time to make arrangements to ensure her own safety, assuming she is psychologically ready to do so. Similarly, although the authors assume that the class and employment status of the *man* are significant deterring factors (*i.e.*, whether he has much to lose from arrest), these factors can be viewed from the perspective of the woman as well. The middle-class wife may also be reluctant to sacrifice her lifestyle and status. This is a probable result either of arrest, with its attached stigma and the potentially adverse consequences upon the husband's employment, or of divorce proceedings. After an automatic arrest, a battered woman may therefore be less likely to report subsequent abuse. Thus, lower recidivism for this group could reflect *her* fear of the consequences of arrest rather than, or in addition to, any deterrent effect upon the abuser.

On the other hand, the authors assume that arrest fails to deter abusers who are poor and unemployed because arrest is a common phenomenon in the ghetto.[4]

This correlation also looks different if interpreted from the point of view of the woman. Whereas a middle-class woman may be able to take advantage of her resources to obtain support—alternate living arrangements, therapy, etc.—which allows her to escape or to prevent repeated abuse, poor women usually have no such alternatives. If they have managed to find low-cost or public housing in the inner city and to patch together support systems or social services which allow them to care for their children, they have no alternative but to remain there as sitting ducks for the abuser when he returns. In short, the perspective from which neutral statistics are analysed clearly makes a difference both in conclusions to be drawn and in the policy implications which emerge from those conclusions.[5]

Indeed, even the obvious ethical questions about conducting arrest experiments like these appear to have been analysed from the point of view of the abuser. In order to conduct these studies, women summoning the police because they feared for their own physical safety or that of their children were randomly assigned to a category determining the police's response to their calls: separation or mediation, or both; issuance of a warning; short arrest (two hours and a recognizance bond); or long arrest (eleven hours or more plus $250 bond). For members of groups for whom arrest is clearly a deterrent, random assignment to the non-arrested control group thus increased the risk of harm to the women and their children. Yet Sherman et al. reason that the ethical posture of their experiment was improved by the fact that the experiment had the effect of reducing the severity of the police response in the control group, since arrest was otherwise mandatory in

Milwaukee. I was puzzled by this explanation for quite some time, until it suddenly dawned upon me that the ethical
question was being viewed solely from
the point of view of the abusers, some of
whom were given a "break," rather than
from the perspective of their victims, who
were deprived of the response to which
they were legally entitled and were possibly endangered thereby.

Third, quantitative studies like the arrest experiments are inherently atomistic
and individualistic in their mode of analysis: they tote up the statistics and then
attempt to determine what is the greatest
good to the greatest number. This "good"
is measured in terms of the likelihood
of recidivism or retaliation by this man
against this woman, ignoring more re-
lational or communitarian values which
may be at stake. It is, for example, well established that the effects of a child's witnessing spousal abuse are a major factor
in the inter-generational transmission of
domestic violence, as well as in the development of aggressive criminal tendencies in that child as an adult; it is also
known that a large number of men who
batter their wives abuse their children as
well. Thus, the balance of benefits from
an arrest must be assessed not only from
the point of view of deterring continued
abuse within one couple but also, and
perhaps more importantly, from the point
of view of the community's critical interest in addressing the problem of domestic
violence on a societal and long-term basis. Arresting and removing the abuser
may thus be important, quite apart from
any specific deterrent effect, because arrest delivers an empowering message to
the victim and communicates society's
condemnation of the abusive behavior to
children or other witnesses.

To be fair, the authors of the Charlotte
experiment do acknowledge that considerations such as these may militate in favor of arrest even if it is not shown to
constitute a deterrent. Nonetheless, we
must be realistic about the probable effects of these studies upon policy. As Joan
Zorza describes, the police are not fond
of mandatory arrest policies because they
interfere with their usual discretion; the
mandatory arrest policies now in effect
resulted from litigation and from legislative changes brought about by pressure
from advocates for domestic violence victims. If "scientific" studies demonstrate
that arrest is not a deterrent, mandatory
and preferred arrest policies are likely
to come under substantial attack; and
many may be repealed. In fact, the type
of quantitative analysis employed is predisposed to certain types of policy outcomes because it implies by its very structure that the goal is a unitary one. The
issue is reduced to the following question: to prevent recidivism, should we
have a mandatory arrest policy or not? If
arrest does not deter recidivism, the answer appears obvious.
I submit that this analysis is too
simplistic. In fact, there are many possible
policy alternatives. In the absence of
mandatory arrest, police departments
could revert to their prior discretionary
arrest policies. Under these policies, the
police tended to arrest persons whom
the officers regarded as "riffraff" and
to let those they regarded as more
"respectable" go free, thus arresting
only those individuals least likely to
be deterred. Alternatively, the police
could, theoretically at least, be ordered
to reverse the direction of their previous
discrimination by arresting the middle
class and employed suspect instead of
the poor and Black one. As an additional

alternative, mandatory arrest policies could be extended, even if there is evidence that they may lead to retaliation and thus actually increase recidivism in many cases.

Finally, the framework of analysis may also be broadened, so as to open up the range of possibilities far beyond the question of "to arrest or not to arrest." This, I believe, is the only sensible approach. A study of the long-term consequences of police policy in abuse cases in London, Ontario showed that when the police pressed charges against abusers *and* the community provided a broad range of services, including shelters and therapy, for victims of abuse, there was a 25-fold increase in domestic violence filings, no reduction in the willingness of victims to request the help of the police, a higher level of satisfaction with the police, and a reduction in victim-reported incidents of violence. Before backing away from a forceful police response to abuse, it is certainly worth studying whether a more comprehensive approach to this problem would yield different results. Such an approach would include a commitment to arrest, prosecution, and more severe sentencing practices, coupled with the provision of supportive services for domestic violence victims.

In conclusion, I would call for more, and more sensitive, studies of the appropriate societal response to domestic violence. The current studies are useful, in particular because they have disclosed the variable effects of mandatory arrest and the ways in which the appropriate response to abuse may differ with the race and class of the victims or abusers. It is important, at the same time, to realize the limits of strictly quantitative research and not be quick to draw policy conclu-sions from its narrow findings. In short, I think a genuine dialogue is necessary—between social scientists and criminologists, on the one hand, and feminists, victim advocates, and victims, on the other —in order to achieve a fuller understanding of the most effective ways to confront this form of violence against women.[6]

NOTES

1. *See, e.g.*, Evelyn Fox Keller, GENDER AND SCIENCE (1978); Kersti Yllo, *Political and Methodological Debates in Wife Abuse Research, in* FEMINIST PERSPECTIVES ON WIFE ABUSE (Kersti Yllo & Michele Bograd, eds. 1988); Catherine A. MacKinnon, TOWARD A FEMINIST THEORY OF THE STATE 96–101 (1989).

2. The most dramatic example was the Conflict Tactics Scale (CTS) developed by Straus, Gelles and Steinmetz, which counted individual acts of violence without regard for either the severity of the injury or whether they were in self-defense, resulting in a conclusion—known to be false by feminist researchers, shelter workers, and battered women—that husband abuse was as large a problem as wife abuse. *See* Murray A. Straus et al., BEHIND CLOSED DOORS: VIOLENCE IN THE AMERICAN FAMILY (1980). . . .

3. Lawrence R. Sherman et al., *The Variable Effects of Arrest on Criminal Careers: The Milwaukee Domestic Violence Experiment*, 83 J. CRIM. L. & CRIMINOLOGY 137, 160–61 (1992).

4. Sherman et al., *supra* note 3, at 162.

5. Whether the woman was initially living with her abuser and, if so, had left by the time of the follow-up is potentially a very powerful independent variable as well, although the direction of its effect may not be clear in the aggregate. Obviously, if a woman is able completely to escape her abuser and to live in a place which is entirely safe, this fact will deter further attack. However, it is also true that the most serious attacks upon women, the ones which most frequently lead to death, occur when they have in fact separated from the men abusing them—a phenomenon which Martha Mahoney has aptly described as "separation assault."

6. This dialogue is at present unidirectional: feminist writers are aware of the quantative work, but the authors of the criminology studies appear to ignore the insights of feminist scholars. The bibliographies provided by the criminology authors are largely devoid of any references to the by now extensive literature concerning domestic violence by feminist authors, although their tentative hypotheses could be improved by incorporating

its insights. For example, while concerned about the appropriate time frame for measuring repeat attacks upon spouses, the experiment designers fail to consider Lenore Walker's description of the "cycle of violence," which would lead one to expect recidivism during some periods of time more than during others.... Moreover, the feminist critique of research methodology is now quite extensive. *See, e.g.,* Sandra Harding, Feminism and Methodology (1987); Mary Margaret Fonow & Judith A. Cook, Beyond Methodology (1991).

POSTSCRIPT

Can Traditional Criminology Make Sense Out of Domestic Violence?

One of the aspects of human behavior, including criminal behavior, that makes research both so fascinating and so exasperating is its multifaceted and multicausal nature. Simply put, there are no straightforward relationships between some specific cause and some specific effect in social relations. For instance, families living in poverty will frequently have children who participate in crime, yet many living in the meanest conditions, surrounded by vice and poverty, have children that rarely get into trouble. In many parts of the world, communities living in poverty far more terrible than we know often exhibit a crime rate far below ours. Moreover, there are many doctors, lawyers, college professors, or the like, who have children who are criminals —or who abuse *their* wives or children. No social situation *inevitably* leads to a specific outcome. In social relations, we have only at best *probabilities* that some conditions will produce certain outcomes.

Domestic violence, as has been shown in these selections, is a multifaceted issue. It includes violence of parents against their children, of husband against wife, of wife against husband, and of adult child against an elderly parent. The causes are usually obscure and complex. In short, as in many areas of human behavior, *why* anyone assaults another is problematic, as are the "cures" for such assaults. There likely is no single panacea. The initial research in the early 1980s by Sherman and Berk was based on a limited sample. Although it was full of cautions, many policymakers quickly embraced their findings because they fit in nicely with current ideological leanings.

Unfortunately, the domestic violence phenomenon, because it has multiple causes, compels multiple solutions—and no single treatment modality is considered universally effective. Yet if arrest does indeed reduce domestic assault or if the threat of arrest can prevent someone from initiating such terrible behavior to begin with, then arrests should be encouraged. Moreover, even if it is not a powerful deterrent in many cases, arrest has an important symbolic function: it signals that society will no longer tolerate this form of brutality. Certainly, Bowman would concur with this, although she would also recommend counseling and support, especially for the victim. However, it seems that we would probably know little or none of this without research. Moreover, by showing us how complicated and difficult solutions to domestic violence might be, criminological research has performed (and could continue to perform) a valuable function.

If you were to research the effects of arrest on domestic violence, which ideas from Sherman and from Bowman would you use? Why? How might you combine the two seemingly very different research strategies? "Deterrent Effects of Arrest for Domestic Assault," by L. W. Sherman and R. A. Berk, *American Sociological Review* (April 1984), remains the seminal article on this issue. Also consider reading "Handling Battering Men: Police Action in Wife Abuse Cases," by E. W. Gondolf and J. R. McFerron, *Criminal Justice and Behavior* (December 1989), and "Use of Police Services by Battered Women," by E. M. Abel and E. K. Suh, *Social Work: Journal of the National Association of Social Workers* (November/December 1987). See also K. R. Williams and R. Hawkins's "The Meaning of Arrest for Wife Assault," *Criminology* (vol. 27, 1989), and L. Sherman and E. G. Cohn's "The Impact of Research on Legal Policy," *Law and Society Review* (vol. 23, 1989). For a comparison of battering wives and husbands, see "Generalization and Containment: Different Effects of Past Aggression for Wives and Husbands," by J. Malone et al., *Journal of Marriage and the Family* (August 1989). To understand more about children of battered women, see *Ending the Cycle of Violence* edited by E. Peled et al., (Sage Publications, 1994). For an extended review of five current books on domestic violence, see D. Dutton's "Hits and Misses: The Literature of Family Violence," *Criminal Justice Review* (Autumn 1993).

For additional controversies related to this issue, see volume 11 of *Crime and Justice: An Annual Review*, a special issue on family violence edited by Lloyd Ohlin and M. Tonry (University of Chicago Press, 1989), and *Family Violence: Research and Public Policy Issues* edited by D. J. Besharov (AEI Press, 1990). For an especially acrimonious debate over both the conceptualization of domestic violence and the extent of female-initiated violence, see R. L. McNeely and G. Robinson-Simpson's "The Truth About Domestic Violence Revisited," *Social Work* (March/April 1988). Included in that issue are several articles bitterly attacking McNeely and Robinson-Simpson. For a discussion of black family violence, see *Violence in the Black Family* edited by R. L. Hampton (Lexington Books, 1987). Two sources that tend to support Bowman's approach to scientific research are B. DiChristina's *Method of Criminology* (Harrow & Hestor, 1995), in which the author argues that much of Sherman's and others' work is "privileged" or elitist criminology, and M. Hammersley's *The Politics of Social Research* (Sage Publications, 1995).

An excellent overview is Joan McCord's "Deterrence of Domestic Violence: A Critical View of Research," *Journal of Research in Crime and Delinquency* (May 1992). For an insightful look at another angle on domestic violence, see D. Island and P. Letellier's *Men Who Beat the Men Who Love Them: Battered Gay Men and Domestic Violence* (Haworth Press, 1991). An empirical study that challenges the contention that domestic violence is passed generationally is R. Simmons et al., "A Test of Various Perspectives on the Intergenerational Transmission of Domestic Violence," *Criminology* (February 1995). Also look for the journal *Violence Against Women*, edited by C. Renzetti. For a legal discussion, see A. Roberts, "Court Responses to Battered Women and Reform Legislation," in *Critical Issues in Crime and Justice* edited by A. Roberts (Sage Publications, 1994).

ISSUE 11

Is Waiver to Adult Courts a Solution to Juvenile Crime?

YES: Henry Sontheimer, from "Is Waiver to Adult Court the Best Response to Juvenile Crime?" *Juvenile Justice Update* (April/May 1995)

NO: Jennifer Vogel, from "Throw Away the Key: Juvenile Offenders Are the Willie Hortons of the '90s," *Utne Reader* (July/August 1994)

ISSUE SUMMARY

YES: Henry Sontheimer, a contributing author to *Juvenile Justice Update*, provides a straightforward summary of arguments and newly emerging legal policies in support of waiving to adult courts juveniles charged with serious crimes, which, he suggests, will help reduce crime.

NO: Writer and activist Jennifer Vogel contends that placing juveniles into adult courts and prisons is a tragic part of the increasing arrest, neglect, impoverishment, and abuse of America's young.

Records reveal thousands of years of serious tensions between youngsters and their parents. The Greek philosopher Socrates, for example, bemoaned children of his day who showed little respect for authority. To this day it is legal in some societies to stone to death children who are disobedient. In the United States, parents and children alike complain that they receive no respect from the other. Meanwhile, largely due to the spread of guns and drugs, younger and younger children (sometimes 10 or younger) are killing more, and more or being killed. Even in the wildest, most violent years in U.S. history, the rate of juvenile violence and victimization did not equal the current level, according to children's rights advocates.

Technically, since 1838, wayward or neglected youths have been subject to state protection (i.e., incarcerated in a state facility) under the doctrine *parens patriae*, literally, "the state as the parent." In the late 1890s the first juvenile court was established in Chicago. Members of the turn-of-the-century Progressive movement prided themselves on the humane treatment of youngsters. The assumption was that the criminal justice system should work to help youngsters, not to humiliate or punish them. Juveniles went before juvenile masters or magistrates instead of judges, and they had hearings instead of trials, all for the ostensible purpose of ascertaining the best way to help the youngsters, not to determine their guilt. Youth service bureaus, social workers, counselors, and many other professional youth workers sprang up for the manifest function of helping juveniles.

Unfortunately, many serious unanticipated negative consequences resulted from these early-twentieth-century reforms. Among these was the creation of the concept of "status offenders." This referred to offenses for children that, if committed by adults, would not elicit official responses and certainly not incarceration. These included running away from home and truancy. Such children would be given the label "children in need of supervision" (CINS). Some could be kept in a juvenile facility until their 21st birthday for being truant or sassy, even at age 14!

In the 1950s and 1960s, criminologists began to worry about the wisdom of spreading the criminal justice net over youths who were not being helped by the system. In fact, many thought that juveniles were probably being permanently harmed by being labeled "delinquent." As a consequence of both scholars and activists examining the juvenile justice system, at least three major legal decisions were made: *Kent v. United States* (1966), *In re Gault* (1967), and *In re Winship* (1970). These decisions restored legal rights to juveniles —the right to due process, the right to counsel, the right to notification of charges, and the right to appellate review, among others. Although many insist that these and other court decisions have had little real value for juveniles, symbolically they represented a major shift in orientation.

Another major change was the massive effort after the 1950s to keep youths out of training schools. This entailed redirecting accused delinquents to other social services; sometimes ignoring their delinquent actions; and, if shown to be guilty of serious crimes, giving them another chance.

Unfortunately, massive societal changes have occurred in the past 15 or 20 years. Arguably, no component of the legal system has seen more dramatic changes than the treatment of juveniles. Some attribute this to the increasing fear of crime and the get-tough-on-crime approach of state and national leadership. Others blame (or defend) the changes on rising rates of violence among the young.

What policies vis-à-vis juveniles charged with serious crimes make sense? The most dramatic policy emerging in the United States today is encouraging states to waive—or relinquish responsibility for—juveniles to adult courts. Defenders maintain that this is better for society, the citizens of which are now calling for whippings and even the execution of some delinquents. Critics are horrified. Some cite the example of Georgia, where 13-year-olds will soon be facing mandatory 10-year prison sentences, part of which will be in adult lockups! Some researchers, however, assert that waivers may not lead to much tougher sentences. In the following selections, Henry Sontheimer indicates that waiver to adult courts would help solve the problem of juvenile crime. Jennifer Vogel argues that the fact that officials are considering such pathways for youngsters who commit terrible crimes indicates that the issue of waivering children to adult courts is simply the tip of a far deeper, more tragic societal problem.

YES

IS WAIVER TO ADULT COURT THE BEST RESPONSE TO JUVENILE CRIME?

Juvenile courts are an invention of state government; there is no constitutional right to be tried as a juvenile. Consequently, the states have considerable latitude to change the way juveniles are prosecuted. It is estimated that as many as 200,000 juvenile cases are tried in adult courts each year. Given our current social and political environment, this number is likely to increase dramatically. Widespread media coverage of some rather heinous crimes involving juvenile offenders does nothing to alleviate the possibility that this will occur.

Recent state actions have sought to expand the use of waiver from juvenile to adult courts. They stress accountability rather than rehabilitation as the primary sentencing goal and reflect concerns for equity and proportionality as opposed to individualized justice. Given the pressure currently being brought to bear on the juvenile court, the likely result is more changes to liberalize waiver policies.

Studies Show Adult Court Processing Does Not Guarantee a More Punitive Disposition Than Juvenile Court Processing

The traditional justification for waiver—that the juvenile system does not afford the more stringent sanctions available in the adult system—presumes that these harsher sanctions will in fact be imposed if waived juveniles are convicted as adults. However, recent studies show that about one-third of waived juveniles are not incarcerated by adult courts. Many transferred juveniles are not even convicted due to decisions not to prosecute. Also, conviction rates in adult court jury trials are generally lower than juvenile court adjudication rates. Feld (1987) calls this lenient treatment of waived juveniles the "punishment gap."

Relatively lenient sentences may be imposed on transferred juveniles either because their crimes seem less serious than those typically committed by adults or because the juveniles do not have extensive prior records. Although

From Henry Sontheimer, "Is Waiver to Adult Court the Best Response to Juvenile Crime?" *Juvenile Justice Update* (April/May 1995). Copyright © 1995 by Civic Research Institute, Inc. Reprinted by permission. All rights reserved.

many waived offenders have prior juvenile adjudications, this information may not always be available to or admissible in criminal court at the point of sentencing. It is also possible that judges are reluctant to send the young transferred offenders to state prisons for fear they may be victimized there.

Best Rationale for Waiver May Be That It Symbolizes the Seriousness of Committing a Crime

Despite empirical evidence that adult court processing does not guarantee a more punitive disposition than the juvenile court could offer, some argue that waiver is appropriate. Many judges and probation officers feel that waiver serves a symbolic function by "drawing the line" and putting the child on notice that his/her behavior no longer will be afforded the protection of a special forum. Similarly, the risk that a given waiver will result in a lenient criminal court sentence is seen as acceptable, since the child will at least acquire a formal criminal record if convicted. This viewpoint particularly applies to repeat property offenders, since few single delinquent acts may seem serious enough to require waiver.

In the broadest sense, waiver is invoked when the maximum available juvenile court sanctions do not afford the level of response (i.e., social control) that is appropriate for the alleged offense(s). Judges and/or prosecutors often state that the longest allowable juvenile court sentences do not provide for enough time for the appropriate rehabilitation (or punishment) of an offender, considering the child's age and the age of maximum juvenile court jurisdiction. Juvenile court personnel may also fear that the most serious and non-amenable offenders will create management problems if commit-

ted to juvenile institutions, thus reducing the likelihood of successfully treating their more receptive counterparts. This concern may be alleviated by developing specialized juvenile institutions for more serious offenders (as has been proposed in Pennsylvania and other states).

Public Safety, Not Juvenile's Amenability, Governs Waiver Decision in One State

After several years of study, Minnesota enacted new legislation in 1994 concerning the transfer of juveniles to adult court. The new law bases the transfer decision on factors related to public safety (e.g., seriousness of offense, prior record) rather than on the youth's amenability to treatment. The new law provides for the "presumptive certification" of 16- or 17-year olds charged with serious crimes against the person. In such cases, the burden of proof is on the juvenile to show that he or she should be processed in juvenile court. Failure to prove by "clear and convincing evidence" that juvenile court handling is appropriate triggers automatic certification to adult court. In cases involving youths 14 to 17 years old who are charged with felony offenses other than those calling for presumptive certification, the burden of proof is on the prosecutor to show that transfer is required under public safety considerations (Feld, 1994).

Extension of Juvenile Jurisdiction to Age 21 Viewed as "Last Chance." Under Minnesota's old law, juvenile court jurisdiction over adjudicated delinquents ended at age 19. The new law permits juvenile courts to retain jurisdiction over some offenders until age 21. This provision applies to juveniles who are subject to presumptive certification (among others). As an alternative to certification, the court may designate them as "Extended Jurisdiction Juveniles" (EJJs). These juveniles, if adjudicated, *receive both adult and juvenile sentences.* The adult sentence is stayed, but may be implemented if the offender violates the conditions of his or her juvenile sentence. As a necessary adjunct to this provision, EJJs receive all adult due process protections at their juvenile adjudication hearing, including the right to a jury trial (Feld, 1994). The Minnesota Advisory Task Force that drafted the new provisions stated that extended jurisdiction "will give the juvenile one last chance at success in the juvenile system, with the threat of adult sanctions as an incentive not to reoffend."

Georgia: Automatic Waiver for Some 13-Year-Olds May Result in Mandatory 10-Year Prison Sentences

The Georgia Legislature also enacted significant new provisions governing juvenile waiver during 1994. The new excluded offense provisions give the Superior (adult) Court jurisdiction over defendants aged 13 to 17 who are charged with one of seven offenses (murder, voluntary manslaughter, rape, aggravated sodomy, aggravated child molestation, aggravated sexual battery, and robbery with a firearm). Juveniles convicted of lesser included offenses in adult court may have their cases transferred back to juvenile court for disposition.

The new waiver provisions took on added significance in November 1994, when the Georgia Legislature passed the "Sentence Reform Act of 1994." This act mandated minimum 10-year sentences of incarceration for adult court convictions for armed robbery, kidnapping, rape, aggravated child molestation, aggravated sodomy, and aggravated sexual battery.

Since five of these offenses are among the seven crimes subject to automatic waiver, 13-year-olds in Georgia may soon be facing mandatory minimum 10-year state prison sentences. Murder already carried a minimum sentence of life without parole.

Juveniles affected by the new provisions who are convicted of any of the seven enumerated offenses are to be confined by the Department of Corrections in a "designated youth confinement unit" until age 17, after which they may serve the balance of their sentence among the general Department of Corrections population. According to preliminary estimates from the state of Georgia, over 500 children per year may be affected by the new legislative waiver provisions.

The amendments to Georgia's juvenile code also provided that certain repeat felony offenders may be committed to a juvenile facility for an initial period of five years (up from 18 months under the old law). And, for the first time, juvenile court judges are now allowed to directly commit adjudicated delinquents to state secure institutions for up to 90 days. Previously, such commitments were made through the state Department of Children and Youth Services.

Recommendations for Waiver Policies

Unified Juvenile and Criminal Justice System Sentencing Policy; Improved Access to Juvenile Court Records. Many of the problems associated with states' attempts to change their waiver laws and practices demonstrate the need for a unified sentencing policy across their juvenile and criminal justice systems. Quick-fix solutions and politicization of the waiver issue have not achieved the desired goals of predictable and equitable sentencing policies. Criminologists have made several recommendations in this area. Feld (1987), for example, recommends "making offenses count" in juvenile court by incorporating a child's prior record into the criteria used to make the waiver decision. The new Minnesota law provides an example of this practice. Minnesota further makes offenses count by requiring that all EJJ convictions be included in adult criminal history records (Feld, 1994). States should also assure that once a juvenile is waived to adult court and convicted, the court will have access to the juvenile's prior record. At the very least, the juvenile record should be covered in the pre-sentence investigation. Accurately documenting a juvenile record is even more important in states with sentencing guidelines (such as Minnesota and Pennsylvania) where prior juvenile convictions can increase the convicted offender's "prior record score" and enable the court to impose a harsher sentence.

Juvenile Court Must Have Jurisdiction Long Enough for an Adequate Sentence to Be Imposed. Several other issues should be considered when attempting to coordinate juvenile and adult sentencing practices. The age of maximum juvenile court jurisdiction over adjudicated delinquents is an important consideration, since it determines the longest possible juvenile sentence (i.e., total time in confinement and/or on juvenile probation).

Suppose, for example, the juvenile court's jurisdiction ends at age 21 (as it does in most states). This means that the court will have a maximum of four years to work with a juvenile defendant who is age 17. In states where the juvenile court's authority over adjudicated offenders ends at age 18, waiver may be sought for a 17-year-old offender in preference to an extremely short juvenile sentence.

A higher age of durational jurisdiction at least gives juvenile court judges the ability to consider a sentence comparable in length to what a criminal court might impose on a similarly situated adult offender. However, in order for the advantage of a higher age to be realized, juvenile courts must be willing to finance longer placements and appropriate juvenile programs must be available to work with older and sometimes more serious offenders.

Practical Consideration: Waiver May Be Viewed as an Alternative to Overcrowded Juvenile Facilities. While the absolute number of annual waivers is low in most states, the numbers may be significant in relation to the total bed space in a state's juvenile correctional system. In Pennsylvania, for example, there are only about 500 beds in the nine juvenile facilities operated by the state. Currently, most of these programs are full, and there are long waiting lists.

About 300 cases are waived in Pennsylvania in a typical year. If these cases were retained in the juvenile system, where would judges be able to commit them?

New Youthful Offender Category Should Be Added for Oldest Offenders Handled by Juvenile Court and Youngest Adult Offenders. A special classification should be created for the oldest offenders traditionally handled by juvenile courts and the youngest adult offenders. New Mexico, which revised its juvenile code in 1993, provides an example of this strategy.... The revision established a new class of "youthful offenders" who, though not subject to trial as adults, may be sentenced by a juvenile court judge using either juvenile or criminal sanctions. Youthful offenders are 15- to 18-year olds charged with one of several specified serious offenses or multiple felony offenses. This dual sentencing provision appears to be functionally equivalent to traditional judicial waiver in that amenability to treatment is the primary issue considered by the court. However, the prospect of a juvenile incurring a stiff adult prison sentence as a result of a juvenile court adjudication proceeding, without the right to a jury trial and other due process protections available to adults, is disturbing.

Relationship Between Juvenile and Criminal Court Sentencing Practices. A key factor judges and prosecutors must consider when contemplating a transfer decision is the likely outcome of a waived case once it reaches criminal court. As previously mentioned, if the adult court and correctional systems are overcrowded, the cases of waived juveniles may not be vigorously prosecuted or the sentence that is imposed may be unduly lenient.

If the goal of waiving a given case is to ensure some incarceration (given a conviction or adjudication), retaining the case in juvenile court may be the preferred choice. However, if the goal is to achieve a long sentence, waiver to adult court may be the only option. In the latter case, juvenile court officials must weigh the desire for a lengthy prison term against the possibility that the defendant may avoid incarceration altogether.

Minnesota's new waiver provisions were designed to mesh juvenile court sentencing practices with those of adult courts. Thus, the sentencing guidelines stipulate that offenses eligible for presumptive waiver are the same offenses that entail presumptive incarceration for adults. This integrated sentencing policy should help reduce the "punishment gap" that occurs when youths tried as adults receive relatively lenient sentences.

National Council of Juvenile and Family Court Judges and OJJDP Endorse Juvenile Court Handling of Serious and Violent Offenders

The National Council of Juvenile and Family Court Judges has issued an action plan for dealing with violent juvenile crime. Although the plan recognizes the need to maintain the transfer mechanism for the most serious and violent offenders, the Council strongly criticizes statutory changes to restrict juvenile court jurisdiction or mandate waiver. In support of their position, the Council cites research showing that juvenile courts are "far more likely to impose some sanction that seeks to correct the behavior of the juvenile than is the criminal court."

The U.S. Office of Juvenile Justice and Delinquency Prevention (OJJDP) also endorses the ability of the nation's juvenile courts to deal with serious offenders. According to the OJJDP (1993), "effective intervention strategies and programs for serious, violent, and chronic delinquents have been documented." The OJJDP calls upon the juvenile justice system to "identify and control the small group of serious, violent, and chronic juvenile offenders." The recommended interventions for these offenders include secure correctional placement (preferably followed by intensive community-based aftercare), but not waiver to adult court.

REFERENCES

Feld, Barry C., "The Juvenile Court Meets the Principle of the Offense: Legislative Changes in

Juvenile Waiver Statutes," 78 *Journal of Criminal Law and Criminology* 3 (1987).

Feld, Barry C., "Violent Youth and Public Policy: Minnesota Juvenile Justice Task Force and 1994 Legislative Reform." Paper presented at the annual meeting of the American Society of Criminology, November 10, 1994.

Office of Juvenile Justice and Delinquency Prevention, 1993. *A Comprehensive Strategy for Serious, Violent, and Chronic Juvenile Offenders, Program Summary*. OJJDP, Washington, DC.

NO

Jennifer Vogel

THROW AWAY THE KEY:
JUVENILE OFFENDERS ARE THE
WILLIE HORTONS OF THE '90s

Judged by any number of statistical yardsticks—infant mortality, child poverty, teen suicide and incarceration—America in the '90s is doing in kids at an alarming rate. It's estimated that every day, 2,700 babies are born into poverty, more than 2,000 students drop out of school, 250 kids are arrested for violent crimes, and 1,700 are abused by their parents. Youthful America's vision of its own future has never been more dire, particularly in the cities. As one 17-year-old African-American put it on his way into court: "I been dead since I was 12, so I'm not afraid of dying. I'm just waiting to get kicked into the grave."

Watching the courts and Congress, it's easy to conclude that the country is waging a battle against its children. While schools, jobs, and the social safety net continue to erode, more kids are finding themselves caught up in an ever-expanding criminal justice system. Politicians and the major media, having discovered a boom market in the public frenzy for bigger jails and longer sentences, have made juvenile offenders the Willie Hortons of the '90s.

"Over the 1980s, the United States achieved the highest rates of incarceration in the industrialized world, moving past South Africa and the former Soviet Union," notes a 1993 study by the Milton S. Eisenhower Foundation. "Because the inmates were disproportionately young, in many ways prison building became the American youth policy of choice.... By the 1992 elections, one in every four young African-American males was either in prison, on probation, or on parole."

These are uncommonly honest observations compared to the reams of recent studies and white papers on "the juvenile problem." Generally speaking, young people themselves are far more candid than politicians and pundits about what lies ahead. When a national study compared the worries of high school seniors in 1979 to those of 1991, it found less concern about nuclear war, more about hunger and poverty. The numbers bear out their skepticism:

- Unemployment among teens was 19 percent in 1993, up from 15.3 percent five years earlier—and for black youths, the figure was twice that high. For those who do find jobs, the average hourly wage has fallen nearly 10 percent in the last decade.

- Since 1970, Aid to Families with Dependent Children benefits have declined an average of 45 percent in inflation-adjusted dollars, according to the Children's Defense Fund.

- In 1992, there were 14.6 million children living below the poverty line, the Children's Defense Fund says, about 5 million more than in 1973.

- [In 1993,] there were 3 million victims of child abuse, according to the National Committee for the Prevention of Child Abuse—a rate 50 percent higher than in 1985. Studies also indicate that the majority of prison inmates were abused as children.

- Teen suicide rates increased nearly 20 percent during the 1980s.

But numbers like these are not the stuff of legislative debate, in Washington or in state legislatures around the country. Almost without exception, the trend among lawmakers is to use highly publicized incidents of brutal violence—often charged with racial stereotypes—to push for harsher penalties. In Minnesota this year, a 16-year-old black youth who broke into a suburban home and killed a white woman and her child became the poster child for juvenile justice reform. Neighbors actually circulated a petition to have him tried as an adult; 20,000 signed on. In Minnesota as elsewhere,

legislators have decided to play to mob sentiments.

Of course this shift requires a rationale, and pundits have been quick to provide one. Juvenile justice laws weren't set up to deal with these new monsterlike children, they say, but to give kids stealing cookies from cookie jars a slap on the wrist. (The presumption here is that juvenile law just isn't tough enough; in fact, kids in some states tend to serve longer sentences in juvenile facilities than adults convicted of similar crimes.) While there already are numerous provisions for getting serious juvenile offenders into adult courts, the "reforms" sweeping the nation now seek to wipe out the protected status of juveniles as a class, making it easier to put young offenders on the road to lifelong incarceration by the age of 13 or 14.

News outlets play their part by routinely featuring images of vacant-eyed children carrying out acts of random violence. They happily parrot jacked-up statistics and stereotypes about teenagers, capping the information with headlines like "Killer Kids"—or this, from the *L.A. Times*: "Who are our children? One day, they are innocent. The next, they may try to blow your head off." One of the most prominent myths of the media is that kids are the biggest problem this country faces in its battle against crime, when in fact they make up only 16 to 17 percent of total arrests, according to one expert.

The percentage of kids arrested has remained fairly constant during the past 10 to 15 years. Though statistics is anything but an exact science, it appears that there's been a decline in juvenile property crimes such as theft, break-ins, and robberies, and an increase in murders, aggravated assaults, and other violent crimes. Even so, only a small percentage of juvenile offenses are violent crimes: about 5 percent in 1990.

Says Bob DeComo, senior program manager for the National Council on Crime and Delinquency: "I think the public perception is that [violent crime committed by juveniles] has increased much more dramatically than is really the case. It is a fact that violent crimes are up, but the extent is overstated in part because of attention to crime in general. It's still the case that the public is much more likely to be victimized by an adult."

* * *

Not that some of the numbers aren't troubling. In 1981, according to Federal Bureau of Justice statistics, youths were charged with 53,240 violent crimes; in 1992, the figure was 104,137. There's something about kids that clearly *isn't* the same as it was 20 years ago. "We're reaping the benefits of 12 years of lessening federal commitments," says Miriam Rollin, vice president for advocacy development for the National Association of Child Advocates. "I would think that if the concern was for the future, that would lead more clearly to the response that lets us invest in them. I think people are scared. I don't know that we've ever had the kind of desperation among young people, particularly in poverty, nor have we had the number of young people in poverty as we do today. I think people understand, to a certain extent, what that means. That you are potentially creating a very dysfunctional young person. There aren't enough jails and facilities to lock up all the poor kids in this country, but that's what they are on their way toward doing."

Around the country, the most popular solutions include defining new classes of juvenile crime, making juvenile records public, creating boot camps for young offenders, tightening up curfew laws (in some cases fining parents who don't keep their kids in the house at night), and installing metal detectors in schools. One state proposed trying 12-year-olds as adults, and another has sought to eliminate age guidelines altogether.

But, like deficit spending, locking up youths may only be a way to defer the problem. In a speech before Congress in March, Michael E. Saucier, national chair of the Coalition for Juvenile Justice, said the approach "looks tough but is shortsighted. It addresses the problem of serious juvenile crime by allowing youth to be dealt with in an adult setting, a setting that is almost completely bankrupt when it comes to crime prevention, rehabilitation, and reducing recidivism.

"Juveniles in adult institutions are five times more likely to be sexually assaulted, twice as likely to be beaten by staff, and 50 percent more likely to be attacked with a weapon than youths in a juvenile facility," Saucier continued. "The most revealing research is three different studies conducted over a ten-year period that show significantly higher recidivism rates for youths tried in adult courts compared to those tried in juvenile courts for the same offenses and with similar personal profiles."

It isn't that there are no workable alternatives—just that the very concept of rehabilitation has fallen out of favor. Every year the Office of Juvenile Justice and Delinquency Prevention gives awards to particularly effective programs around the country. Those honored last year include a Nebraska program in which juvenile offenders are educated and taught independent living and family reconciliation strategies. It boasts a 50 percent reduction in recidivism. In New Hampshire, juvenile offenders are offered the chance to do community service work for local businesses or nonprofit agencies in lieu of going to jail, again resulting in very low recidivism rates.

The choice is clear, says Rollin: "Would you rather have them get out after they've had some sort of program or have them grow up in an adult facility and come out better criminals, having completed the ideal criminal mentoring program?"

POSTSCRIPT

Is Waiver to Adult Courts a Solution to Juvenile Crime?

Tom Gitchoff, professor of criminal justice at San Diego State University and noted author and researcher on juveniles, insists that America's most precious asset is its youths. How does Vogel seem to feel about the way we are treating this treasure? In his survey of waiver policies and practices, does Sontheimer find that waiver would automatically entail abandoning young people charged with serious crimes to the "cruel" adult courts, followed by even crueler incarceration in adult prisons? If so, will society be better off? Why, or why not?

On the other hand, juvenile crime is skyrocketing, and other programs aimed at reducing it have not worked. According to a report entitled *Juvenile Offenders and Victims: A National Report* by the National Center for Juvenile Justice in Pittsburgh, Pennsylvania, if current trends in juvenile crime continue, the number of arrests of juveniles for violent crimes will double by the year 2010. The report notes that between 1983 and 1992, arrest rates among juveniles between the ages of 10 and 17 for violent crimes increased 100 percent. Also, the number of homicides committed by juveniles with handguns increased 500 percent between 1984 and 1993. The report suggests that juvenile crime prevention programs such as midnight basketball leagues and curfews have not been effective. Is there a viable alternative? Should the system treat more juvenile delinquents as adults?

The literature on juvenile crimes and various societal responses and policies is vast. A good legalistic review is B. Feld's *Justice for Children: The Right to Counsel and the Juvenile Courts* (Northeastern University Press, 1993). For an excellent comparison of the U.S. system with that of Sweden, see B. Feld's "Juvenile Justice Swedish Style: A Rose by Another Name?" *Justice Quarterly* (December 1994). B. Krisberg and J. Austin, in *Reinventing Juvenile Justice* (Sage Publications, 1993), explore in great depth most of the perspectives of this issue. A timely book that addresses concerns about race and juvenile justice is *Minorities in Juvenile Justice* edited by K. Leonard et al. (Sage Publications, 1995). A good discussion tracing some of the current get-tough-on-juveniles attitudes within the courts is "Hard Times for Bad Kids," by M. Curriden, *ABA Journal* (February 1995). The journal *Juvenile Justice Update* has monthly articles on the waiver issue (and most other vital juvenile justice issues). See, for instance, "Beyond Punishment and Treatment: A Restorative Model for Juvenile Justice," by G. Bazemore, *Juvenile Justice Update* (June/July 1995).

A helpful series of articles on both research and policy on delinquency can be found in "Symposium on the Future of Research in Crime and Delinquency," *Journal of Research in Crime and Delinquency* (November 1993). An additional discussion on the issue is C. McNeece's "National Trends in Offenses and Case Dispositions" and T. Armstrong and D. Altschuler's "Recent Developments in Programming for High-Risk Juvenile Parolees," both in *Critical Issues in Crime and Justice* edited by A. Roberts (Sage Publications, 1994). For a discussion of juvenile conflict resolution mediation as an alternative to crime, see "Talk, Talk, Talk... A Descriptive Study of Project Brave," by R. Monk, *Police News* (December 1993). A seminal work remains *The Child Savers* by T. Platt (University of Chicago Press, 1969).

ISSUE 12

Are Violent Criminals and Delinquents Treated Too Leniently?

YES: Albert Shanker, from "Restoring the Connection Between Behavior and Consequences," *Vital Speeches of the Day* (May 15, 1995)

NO: D. Stanley Eitzen, from "Violent Crime: Myths, Facts, and Solutions," *Vital Speeches of the Day* (May 15, 1995)

ISSUE SUMMARY

YES: Albert Shanker, president of the American Federation of Teachers, argues that parents want safe schools for their children to go to and that, to this end, the system should quit coddling troublemakers who are ruining the system for the good students, their teachers, and others.

NO: D. Stanley Eitzen, a professor emeritus of sociology at Colorado State University, acknowledges that there is a hard core of violent criminals, but he argues that the idea that America has been too lenient on violent criminals and delinquents is a myth.

In many ways this issue brings together many loose ends of criminological and criminal justice ideologies, research, and policies. The disagreement over whether or not we are too lenient on violent criminals and delinquents directly and indirectly touches on many other issues for clarification and eventual resolution. For example, some sociologists have theorized that crime is functional for society, in that it reaffirms moral boundaries and sometimes brings about necessary moral changes. But after reading the account of mayhem in our classrooms in the following selection by Albert Shanker, could anyone believe that elementary school children pointing (and even firing) loaded guns at each other is in any way functional for society? Violent acts such as these are frequently ignored out of fear, and they seem to be contributing to America's growing divisiveness. Although there is growing consensual anger (as reflected by Shanker), there is no meaningful collective moral outrage. Although local and national leaders have called for seemingly tough solutions, such as chain gangs, whippings, increased capital punishment, and waiving juveniles to adult courts, there is little sense of social solidarity as to what is right and wrong and what ought to be done to restore collective faith in American values and ideals.

In considering general theories of crime as a possible help, many would suggest that such theories are too far removed from the realities of kids killing kids. Also, practitioners and some criminologists would be bothered by sweeping explanations of violent acts that also purport to explain white-collar crimes and welfare fraud.

Some criminologists' belief that crime is rooted in biology may be apropos here. Delinquents may be acting out some surreal fantasies as a result of an intoxicating high-sugar diet, lead poisoning, or exposure to toxic waste. However, as you read the selections by Shanker and D. Stanley Eitzen, you will notice that biological causes are not even considered. Should they be? If so, how might they affect Shanker's or Eitzen's proposed solutions?

Shanker, a longtime teacher in the public schools as well as a pedagogical politician, tip-toes evasively around the issue of race. Notice what he says (and does not say) about charges of unfair and discriminatory expulsions of minority youth, teachers' lack of familiarity with poor children's problems, and so on. The sociologist Eitzen, in contrast, *blames* many of the problems on race, but he turns the issue around by contending that authoritarian or even draconian responses to delinquency, not delinquency itself, are the problem.

As you study this debate, ask yourself if disruptive youngsters are always the same 2 percent that Shanker identifies. That is, will the kids marked as troublemakers in third grade still be troublemakers when (and if) they reach high school? Are schoolroom disruptors destined to become delinquents or criminals?

Both authors recommend very specific policy changes for dealing with the identified problems. As you study them, consider which seem reasonable and practical, which seem most cost-effective, and which might fail because they ignore either possible broader cultural causes of the problem or the current political climate.

YES

Albert Shanker

RESTORING THE CONNECTION BETWEEN BEHAVIOR AND CONSEQUENCES

Delivered at the American Federation of Teachers' National School Safety Conference, Washington, D.C., February 3, 1995

... The reason that we have high levels of violence and disruption has to do with lessons that the youngsters learn—and we teach them those lessons, we, collectively who are in the school system—at a very early age. They see some youngster in kindergarten behaving in an atrocious way, and they are all sure that something is going to happen to that youngster. They're looking, and they're waiting for someone to come from heaven or from the principal's office, from somewhere, because they have some sense of justice. They have some sense that when you do something wrong, somebody comes to get you or to do something about it. But what happens? Nothing happens.

And when nothing happens, this little kid who is five or six years old turns to his or her peers and says, "Now look at that, you yellow so and so. You see what I did? You didn't have the guts to do that, did you? You were afraid that something was going to happen to me, right? Well, what happened to me? Nothing." What happens very soon is that the teacher is no longer the leader in the classroom, that youngster is. Because that youngster is now the proud leader in that peer group. The peer group is not afraid that the principal will come. Nobody's going to come. If you didn't do anything when one kid did something, what are you going to do when all of us together are doing the same thing? Now you've got a real problem. Do you kick them all out? No, you can't do that.

And so what we do, at a very early age, is teach these youngsters a very bad lesson and then that moves up all the way through the schools. Now, just think about it. You let one kid into a school with a weapon, and if you tolerate that, pretty soon half of the kids have weapons. Why? Well, the others need them to protect themselves from the first guy. That's their excuse. If you ask most of the kids, they don't want to be carrying the weapons. But they're carrying weapons because they want to protect themselves. Of course, once they've got them it doesn't turn out to be only protection. And once you get into a situation where all of the youngsters in a class or in a school are like this, whether it's with arms or with disruption, how do you change that? Then you have to close the place, redistribute the youngsters, because you've got an entire culture that says this is the way things are going to be.

... [I]f you want to talk about opportunity-to-learn standards, there are a lot of kids who've made it without the most up-to-date textbooks. It's better if you have them. There are a lot of kids who've made it without early childhood education. It's a lot better if you've got it, and we're for that. Throughout history, people have learned without computers, but it's better if you've got them. But nobody has ever learned if they were in a classroom with one or two kids who took up 90 percent of the time through disruption, violence, or threats of violence. You deprive children of an opportunity to learn if you do not first provide an orderly situation within the classroom and within the school. That come ahead of all of these other things.

... [T]he idea is not that we want to be punitive or nasty, but essentially schools must teach not only English and mathematics and reading and writing and history, but also teach that there are ways of behaving in society that are unacceptable. And when we sit back and tolerate certain types of behavior, we are teaching youngsters that certain types of behavior are acceptable, which eventually will end up with their being in jail or in poverty for the rest of their lives. We are not doing our jobs as teachers. And the system is not doing its job, if we send youngsters the message that this is tolerable behavior within society.

We are also putting at risk the education of millions of youngsters. Now, you know that's something we wouldn't do as parents. Suppose we had, let's say, four or five kids of our own, and suppose that one of these was a very dangerous and emotionally disturbed youngster, a youngster with a lot of violence. I'll bet that we would do an awful lot to separate that one youngster of ours from the other three or four because we wouldn't want the others to be harmed. We would try very hard to help this youngster, very hard. But, as parents, our first responsibility would be to say, let's make sure that these other kids don't get badly hurt or killed or have something happen to them. That's the first thing we would do. We're not sure whether all of the things that we do for this youngster will work. We're going to try. And we're going to have to do more, in many ways, for this youngster than we do for the other youngsters, who are not in such trouble. But our first responsibility is to make sure that we don't give that youngster the opportunity to be destructive with the other youngsters.

All we ask of our schools is that they behave in the same way that a caring and intelligent parent would behave with respect to their own children. I doubt very much, if you had a youngster who was a fire bug or a youngster who used weapons, whether you would say, well, I owe it to this youngster to trust him with my other children to show him that I'm not separating him out or treating him differently. Or I'm going to raise his self-esteem by allowing him to do these things. All of these nutty things that we talk about in school, we would not do....

People are paying for education and they want youngsters who are going to be able to be employed and get decent jobs. We want youngsters who are going to be as well off or in better shape than we are, just as most of us are with respect to our parents and grandparents. And the academic function is the one that's neglected. The academic function is the one that's destroyed in this notion that our job is mainly custodial.

So our central position is that we have to be tough on these issues, and we have to be tough because basically we are defending the right of children to an education. And those who insist on allowing violence and disruptive behavior in the school are destroying the right to an education for the overwhelming majority of youngsters within our schools.

Two years ago or three years ago, I was in Texas at a convention of the Texas Federation of Teachers. I didn't know this was going to happen, but either just before I got there or while I was there, there was a press conference on a position the convention adopted, and they used the phrase "zero tolerance." They said that with respect to certain types of dangerous activities in schools, there would be zero tolerance. These things are not acceptable and there are going to be consequences. There might be suspension, there might be expulsion, or there might be something else, but nevertheless, consequences will be clear....

Now what should schools do? Schools should have codes of conduct. These codes can be developed through collective bargaining or they can be mandated in legislation. I don't think it would be a bad idea to have state legislation that every school system needs to have a code of discipline that is very clear, not a fuzzy sort of thing, something that says these things are not to be done and if this happens, these are the consequences. A very

clear connection between behavior and consequences. And it might even say that, if there is a legitimate complaint from a group of parents or a group of teachers or a group of students that clearly shows the school district doesn't have such a code or isn't enforcing it, there would be some sort of financial penalty against the district for failing to provide a decent education by allowing this type of violence and disruption to continue.

Taxpayers are sending money into the district so that the kids can have an education, and if that district then destroys the education by allowing one or two youngsters to wipe out all of the effects that money is supposed to produce, what the hell is the point of sending the money? If you allow these youngsters to so disrupt that education, you might as well save the money. So there's a reason for states to do this. And, by the way, I think that you'll find a receptive audience, because the notion of individuals taking responsibility for their actions is one of the things fueling the political anger in this country—that we have a lot of laws which help people to become irresponsible or encourage them not to take responsibility for their own actions.

Now, enforcement is very important. For every crime, so to speak, there ought to be a punishment. I don't like very much judgment to be used, because once you allow judgment to be used, punishments will be more severe for some kids than for others and you will get unfairness. You will get prejudice. The way to make sure that this is done fairly and is not done in a prejudiced way is to say, look, we don't care if you're white or Hispanic or African-American or whether you're a recent immigrant or this or that, for this infraction, this is what happens. We don't have a different sanction depending upon whether we like you a little more or a little less. That's how fairness would be ensured, and I think it's very important that we insist on that.

We're talking about students taking responsibility for their own behavior, but I think we, as educators, have to take some responsibility, too. Not all youngsters, not all adults, can sit still and keep quiet for five or six hours. And if you go to Japan or China or other places, when you are finished with math, you go out and play ball for fifteen or twenty minutes, when you're finished with Chinese, you go out and run around for fifteen or twenty minutes and so forth. They know that kids need to get some of that out of their systems. We shouldn't punish youngsters for just being fidgety and moving because they can't stand doing something that they can't do physically. And so for those kids who can sit and listen and take it, fine. But before we declare a kid a major menace because he moves around and disturbs the rest of us, we ought to provide some types of programs where youngsters can move and be more active, so that we don't end up punishing them for a condition that, in a sense, we create. We can't create human beings that can sit still for six hours. We haven't figured out a way of doing that, so we need to say all right, if you can't sit still, here's a way in which you can learn English and history and mathematics in a different way, but you still have to learn. You still don't use foul language, you still don't hit anybody, you don't spit, you don't run all over the place. We don't want to create an artificial situation in which the youngster is blamed for something that is essentially a rigidity that we build into the system.

Now, this is common sense. I'm talking about the way parents would behave with respect to their own children. If my youngster does something wrong, I want my youngster to know it. My youngster is going to pay some price for it, so that he or she doesn't do it again. And I'm not doing this because I hate my youngster or because I get pleasure in punishing, but because I am afraid that if I let this go, there's going to be something else, and something else, and something else, and at some point it's going to be too late. A good school system ought to think the same way, because the schools are in the place of the parent during that period of time.

One of the big problems is school administrators. School administrators are concerned that, if there are a large number of reports of disruptions and violence in their schools, their reputations will suffer. They like to say they have none of those problems in their schools. Now, how do you prove that you have none of these problems in your school? Very simple. Just tell the teachers that if they report it, it's because they are ineffective teachers. If you tell that to one or two teachers, you will certainly have a school that has very little disruption or violence reported. You may have plenty of disruption and violence. So, in many places we have this gag rule. It's not written, but it's very well understood.

As a teacher, I myself faced this. Each time I reported something like this, I was told that if I knew how to motivate the students properly, this wouldn't happen. It's pretty universal. It wasn't just one district or just my principal. It's almost all of them. Therefore, I think that we ought to seek laws that require a full and honest reporting of incidents of violence and extreme disruption. And that would mean that, if an administrator goes around telling you to shut up or threatening you so that you're not free to report, I think that there ought to be penalties. Unless we know the extent of this problem, we're never going to deal with it adequately.

Of course, parents know what the extent of it is. What is the number one problem? It's the problem of violence and order in the schools. They know it. The second big problem and obstacle we face is, what's going to happen if you put the kid out on the streets? It reminds me of a big campaign in New York City to get crime off the streets, and pretty soon they were very successful. They had lots of policemen on the streets, and they drove the criminals away. The criminal went into the subways. Then they had a campaign about crime in the subways, and they drove them back up into the streets. So the business community, parents, and others will say, you can't just throw a kid out and put them on the streets. That's no good. But you could place some conditions on it. To return to school, students would have to bring with them a parent or some other grown-up or relative responsible for them. There is a list of ways in which we might handle it. But we can't say that we're going to wait until we build new schools, or build new classrooms, or have new facilities. The first thing you do is separate out the youngster who is a danger to the other youngsters.

Now, let me give an example. And I think it's one that's pretty close. We know that, when we arrest adults who have committed crimes and we jail them, jail will most likely not help those who are jailed. I don't think it does, and I don't think most people do. However, most of us are pretty glad when someone who has committed a pretty bad crime is jailed.

Not because it's going to do that person any good, but because that person won't be around to do the same thing for the next ten or fifteen years. And for the separation of youngsters who are destroying the education of others, the justification is the same. I'm not sure that we can devise programs that will reach those youngsters that will help them. We should try. But our first obligation is to never destroy the education of the twenty or twenty-five or thirty because you have an obligation to one. Especially when there's no evidence that you're doing anything for that one by keeping him there.

Now, another big obstacle is legal problems. These are expensive and time-consuming. If a youngster gets a lawyer and goes to court, the principal or some other figure of authority from the school, usually has to go to court. They might sit a whole day and by the end of the first day, they decide not to hear it. And they come a second day, and maybe it's held over again. It might take three or four days for each youngster. So if you've got a decent-sized school, even if you're dealing with only two or three percent of the youngsters, you could spend your full time in court, instead of being in school. Well, I wouldn't want to do that if I were the principal of the school. And then what does the court do when you're all finished? The court says, well, we don't have any better place to put him, so send him right back. So, that's why a lot of teachers wouldn't report it, because nothing happens anyway. You go through all of this, you spend all of that time and money, and when you're finished, you're right back where you started. So we need to change what happens with respect to the court, and we have two ideas that we're going to explore that have not been done before.

One of the things we need to do is see whether we can get parents, teachers, and even perhaps high school students to intervene in these cases and say, we want to come before the judge to present evidence about what the consequences are for the other children. When you go to court now, you have the lawyer for the board of education, the lawyer for the youngster, and the youngster. And the youngster, well, he's just a kid and his lawyer says, "This poor child has all of these problems," and the judge is looking down at this poor youngster. You know who is not there? The other 25 youngsters to say, this guy beats me up every day. If I do my homework, I get beat up on the way to school because he doesn't want me to do my homework. So instead of first having this one child standing there saying, "Poor me, let me back in school, they have kicked me out, they have done terrible things to me," you also have some of the victims there saying, "Hey, what about us?" You'll get a much fairer consideration if the judge is able to look at both sides, instead of just hearing the bureaucrat from the board of education. None of these board of education lawyers that I've met talk about the other students. They talk about the right of the board of education under the law to do thus, and so what you have is a humane judge who's thinking of the bureaucrat talking about the rights of the board of education as against the child. I think we need to balance that....

Now, let me point out that a lot of the tolerance for bad behavior is about to change, because we are about to have stakes attached to student academic outcomes. In other words, in the near future, we are going to have a situation where, if you don't make it up to this point, then you can't be admitted into college. Or if you don't make it here, then you will not get certified for a certain type of employment. But in Chapter I schools, this is going to start very soon. There is a provision in the new Chapter One, now called Title I, and very soon, if Title I schools do not show a substantial progress for students, the school's going to be punished. And one of the punishments is reconstitution of the school. The school will be closed down, teachers will go elsewhere, students will go elsewhere, and the school will open up with a new student body, slowly rebuild. That's one of the punishments. There are other punishments as well. So if you've got a bunch of these disruptive youngsters that prevent you from teaching and the other students from learning, it won't be like yesterday, where nobody seems to care, the kids are all going to get promoted anyway and they can all go to college, because there are no standards. There are no stakes.

Now, for the first time, there will be stakes. The teachers will know. The parents will know, hey, this school's going to close. I'm going to have to find a way of getting my kid to some other school because of the lack of learning that comes from this disruption. Teachers are going to say, hey, I'm not going to have my job in this school a couple of years from now because they're going to shut it down. I don't know what the rules are, what happens to these teachers, whether other schools have to take them or not. But we are entering a period where there will be consequences and parents and teachers are going to be a lot more concerned about achievement.

Now, one of the other issues that has stood in the way of doing something here is a very difficult one to talk about in our society, and that's the issue of race. And whenever the topic of suspension or expulsion comes up, there's always the question of race. Cincinnati is a good example. The union there negotiated a good discipline code as part of a desegregation suit. And the question was raised, "Well, is there a disparate impact, with more minority kids being suspended than others?" And who are the teachers who are suspending them? Do you have more white teachers suspending African-American kids?

Our position on that is very clear. In any given school, you may have more white kids with infractions or you may have more African-American kids, or you may have more Hispanic kids. We don't know. I don't think anybody knows. But we handle that by saying, "Whatever your crime is and whoever you are, you're going to get exactly the same punishment." If we do that, I'm sure that the number who will be punished will end up being very, very small. Because, as a young kid, if you see that there is a consequence, you will change your behavior.

In Ohio, they have a minimum competency test. When they first put it out, a huge number of students of all ethnic groups failed the exam. Now, the exam is not a very tough exam, it's like a 7th or 8th grade exam for graduating from high school, but nevertheless, about 55 to 60 percent passed it three years ago and 40 percent failed it. Now you've got up to 85 or 90 percent passing it. It shows that if you say you're going to stick to it, you're not going to graduate unless you learn this stuff, all of a sudden, all of these youngsters sit down and take it seriously. The same thing will happen if you've got a discipline code you enforce. Youngsters, who now know there are no consequences, will behave differently once they know the consequences. There's no

question about it. So we're not talking about suspending, expelling, or punishing the huge number of youngsters who are now engaged in this sort of behavior. What we're talking about is doing something that changes behavior substantially, so that what we end up with is a very, very small percentage of youngsters who really have some severe problems that you can't cope with. The overwhelming majority of youngsters, who become part of that peer culture because their leader tells them to do it, won't be doing it, because the leader is the kid who's going to be removed.

Now we have another very big problem, and we're going to try to deal with this in legislation. Under legislation that deals with disabled youngsters, we have two different standards. Namely, if a youngster in this class is not disabled and commits an infraction, you can do whatever is in that discipline code for that youngster. But if the youngster is disabled and is in that same class (for instance, the youngster might have a speech defect), you can't suspend that youngster while all of the proceedings are going on because that's a change in placement. It might take you a year-and-a-half in court, and meanwhile that youngster who is engaged in some threatening or dangerous behavior has to stay there. This makes no sense. We have a lot of support in the Congress on this, and we think we have a good chance of changing this.

I was just given this clipping today, from the *Washington Post* [1/29/95] just a couple of days ago. It's a column by Courtland Milloy called "An Education in Self-Help:"

"When seventeen-year old Selima Nelson dropped out of the eleventh grade last year, her mother was understandably upset and wanted to know why. Selima explained that she had witnessed a stabbing and that a crew of girls involved in the crime had threatened to kill her if she talked to police."

Unable to find a safe haven for Selima in the DC public schools, Edna Nelson ended up in enrolling her daughter in the GED program. Instead of receiving a high school diploma, Selima now has a special citation from the DC Board of Education congratulating her on 'overcoming tremendous obstacles for the sake of your education.' [And that's a quote. Mind you, the innocent kid had to leave school while the others stayed.] It's certainly not the way her parents planned it. But given the violent reality of life for some of today's adolescents and the chaos within the District's public school system, Nelson says it beats a death certificate from the city morgue.

"I received six summons for her to come testify in the case, but I just couldn't let her go," Nelson recalled.

At first, Nelson said, we thought Selima was exaggerating the threats, which began after a street fight among some girls in October of 1993. "After all," Nelson said, "the fight was about almost nothing—a remark one girl had made about another—and Selima had known most of the girls for most of her life."

"I just couldn't see how girls who used to run in and out of my house, calling me Ma, could turn on her," recalled Nelson, who works as a program manager for academic affairs at the University of the District of Columbia. "Besides, when I had trouble with my girlfriends, we could talk it out."

"I'd say, Ma, you just don't understand," Selima recalled. "It's not like when you were a little girl. Don't you watch the news? They mean business these days."

Nelson said that she eventually realized that "these girls are worse than the boys," when Selima's refusal to testify against the accused perpetrators still didn't result in peace. "The problem wasn't so much with the girl who did the stabbing," Nelson explained. "It was with the girls who were trying to impress the girl who did the stabbing. They were willing to do anything to prove themselves, and by hurting Selima, they thought they could win points with the leader."

DC police tried to assure Nelson that the stabber would be "put away" if Selima testified. But there was nothing they could do about the others, who were constantly approaching Selima with threats.

One night after a dance, Selima found herself encircled by the crew, who shot menacing stares at her. Feeling helpless and filled with fear, Selima went home and took a bottle of pills from her mother's medicine cabinet. She almost died of an overdose.

While Selima was in the hospital, Nelson kept trying to get her daughter transferred from the school where the crew hung out. But her efforts were in vain. "I was told by several school principals that my daughter would not be welcome because they felt trouble would follow her and they didn't want any more of that," Nelson recalled. Nelson said several meetings to resolve the matter among adults, including teachers and parents of the girls involved, degenerated into the same kind of behavior exhibited by children. There were anger and accusations and, finally, no communication at all.

After being released from the hospital, Selima remained distraught and refused to go outdoors. The saving grace appeared to be daily phone calls from her 82-year-old grandmother, Eleanor Nelson, who had a sixth sense that something was wrong. Selima did not want her grandmother to know the truth, fearing that the bad news would be too much for her to bear.

So, Nelson said, she began threatening to tell the grandmother everything if Selima didn't summon up the courage to go back to school. It worked, and with help from the DC Board of Education member, Sandra Butler-Truesdale, Selima was enrolled in the General Equivalency Diploma program in November.

Meanwhile, charges in the stabbing case were dropped because of Selima's refusal to testify, according to police. She was the only witness who was not involved in the crime, police said. The victim recovered from her wounds but reportedly has dropped out of school. She and Selima had been friends, but the two girls hardly speak to each other any more.

"I'm sorry about that, but I was just too afraid for my child," Nelson said. "All I had asked was for the police to protect my daughter, and they would not. I had asked the school system to transfer her to another school, but they wouldn't take the risk."

Nelson said it seemed as if everybody was looking out for themselves, so she had no choice but to look out for her own.

Two weeks ago, Selima was admitted to the University of the District of Columbia, having completed her GED requirements. She now goes to class under the watchful eye of her mother and her colleagues.

"This experience nearly killed me in more ways than one," Selima said. "I pray that it is over and that I'm finally on my way."

Well, that's the whole picture. And to return to the theme at the beginning, we have a cry for choice, a cry for vouchers, a cry for charters. It's not really a cry for these things. People really want their own schools, and they want their kids to go to those schools, and they want those schools to be safe and orderly for their youngsters.

It is insane to set up a system where we move 98 percent of our kids away from the two percent who are dangerous, instead of moving the two percent away from the 98 percent who are OK. We need to have discipline codes, we need to have a new legal system, we need to have one standard for all students. We need to have a system where we don't have to wait for a year or a year-and-a-half after a student has perpetrated some terrible and atrocious crime before that student is removed for the safety of the other students. How are we going to do this? We are going to do this, first of all, by talking to our colleagues within the schools. Our polls show that the overwhelming majority accepts these views.

The support of African-American parents for the removal of violent youngsters and disruptive students is higher than any other group within our society. Now very often when youngsters are removed, it's because some parents' group or some committee starts shouting and making noise, and the school system can't resist that. Now I think that it's time for us to turn to business groups, it's time for us to turn to parents' groups. When youngsters commit such acts, and when they've had a fair due-process within the system, we need to have a system of public support, just as we have in the community when someone commits a terrible crime. People say, send that person to jail, don't send him back to us. We need to have a lot of decent people within our communities, when you have youngsters who are destroying the education of all the others, who will stand up and say, "Look, we don't want to punish this kid, but for the sake of our children, you're going to have to keep that one away, until that one is ready to come back and live in a decent way in society with all of the other youngsters."

I'm sure that if we take this back to our communities, and if we work on it, the appeal will be obvious. It's common sense. And we will save our schools and we will do something which will give us the basis for providing a decent education for all of our children.

NO

D. Stanley Eitzen

VIOLENT CRIME: MYTHS, FACTS, AND SOLUTIONS

My remarks are limited to violent street crimes (assault, robbery, rape, and murder). We should not forget that there are other types of violent crimes that are just as violent and actually greater in magnitude than street crimes: corporate, political, organized, and white collar. But that is another subject for another time. Our attention this morning is on violent street crime, which has made our cities unsafe and our citizens extremely fearful. What are the facts about violent crime and violent criminals and what do we, as a society, do about them?

I am going to critique the prevailing thought about violent crime and its control because our perceptions about violent crime and much of what our government officials do about it is wrong. My discipline—sociology—knows a lot about crime but what we know does not seem to affect public perceptions and public policies. Not all of the answers, however, are always crystal clear. There are disagreements among reasonable and thoughtful people, coming from different theoretical and ideological perspectives. You may, difficult as it seems to me, actually disagree with my analysis. That's all right. The key is for us to address this serious problem, determine the facts, engage in dialogue, and then work toward logical and just solutions.

What do criminologists know about violent crime? Much of what we know is counter intuitive; it flies in the face of the public's understanding. So, let me begin with some demythologizing.

Myth 1: As a Christian nation with high moral principles, we rank relatively low in the amount of violent crime. Compared with the other industrialized nations of the world, we rank number one in belief in God, "the importance of God in our lives," and church attendance. We also rank first in murder rates, robbery rates, and rape rates. Take homicide, for example: the U.S. rate of 10 per 100,000 is three times that of Finland, five times that of Canada, and nine times greater than found in Norway, the Netherlands, Germany, and Great Britain. In 1992, for example, Chicago, a city about one-fifth the population of the Netherlands had nine times more gun-related deaths than occurred in the Netherlands.

Myth 2: We are in the midst of a crime wave. When it comes to crime rates we are misled by our politicians, and the media. Government data indicate that between 1960 and 1970 crime rates doubled, then continued to climb through the 1970s. From 1970 to 1990 the rates remained about the same. The problem is with violent crime by youth, which has increased dramatically. Despite the rise in violent crime among youth, however, the *overall* violent crime rate actually has decreased in the 1990s.

Our perceptions are affected especially by the media. While crime rates have leveled and slightly declined during the 1990s, the media have given us a different picture. In 1993, for example, the three major networks doubled their crime stories and tripled their coverage of murders. This distortion of reality results, of course, in a general perception that we are in the midst of a crime wave.

Myth 3: Serious violent crime is found throughout the age structure. Crime is mainly a problem of male youths. Violent criminal behaviors peak at age 17 and by age 24 it is one-half the rate. Young males have always posed a special crime problem. There are some differences now, however. Most significant, young males and the gangs to which they often belong now have much greater firepower. Alienated and angry youth once used clubs, knives, brass knuckles, and fists but now they use Uzis, AK47s, and "streetsweepers." The result is that since 1985, the murder rate for 18–24 year-olds has risen 65 percent while the rate for 14–17 year-olds has increased 165 percent.

The frightening demographic fact is that between now and the year 2005, the number of teenagers in the U.S. will grow by 23 percent. During the next ten years, black teenagers will increase by 28 percent and the Hispanic teenage population will grow by about 50 percent. The obvious prediction is that violent crime will increase dramatically over this period.

Myth 4: The most dangerous place in America is in the streets where strangers threaten, hit, stab, or shoot each other. The streets in our urban places are dangerous, as rival gangs fight, and drive-by shootings occur. But, statistically, the most dangerous place is in your own home, or when you are with a boyfriend or girlfriend, family member, or acquaintance.

Myth 5: Violent criminals are born with certain predispositions toward violence. Criminals are not born with a criminal gene. If crime were just a function of biology, then we would expect crime rates to be more or less the same for all social categories, times, and places. In fact, violent crime rates vary considerably by social class, race, unemployment, poverty, geographical place, and other social variables. Research on these variables is the special contribution of sociology to the understanding of criminal behavior.

Let's elaborate on these social variables because these have so much to do with solutions. Here is what we know about these social variables:

1. The more people in poverty, the higher the rate of street crime.

2. The higher the unemployment rate in an area, the higher the crime rate. Sociologist William J. Wilson says that black and white youths at age 11 are equally likely to commit violent crimes

but by their late 20s, blacks are four times more likely to be violent offenders. However, when blacks and whites in their late 20s are employed, they differ hardly at all in violent behavior.

3. The greater the racial segregation in an area, the higher the crime rate. Sociologist Doug Massey argues that urban poverty and urban crime are the consequences of extremely high levels of black residential segregation and racial discrimination. Massey says,

> "Take a group of people, segregate them, cut off their capital and guess what? The neighborhoods go downhill. There's no other outcome possible."

As these neighborhoods go downhill and economic opportunities evaporate, crime rates go up.

4. The greater the family instability, the higher the probability of crimes by juveniles. Research is sketchy, but it appears that the following conditions are related to delinquent behaviors: (a) intense parental conflict; (b) lack of parental supervision; (c) parental neglect and abuse; and (d) failure of parents to discipline their children.

5. The greater the inequality in a neighborhood, city, region, or society, the higher the crime rate. In other words, the greater the disparities between rich and poor, the greater the probability of crime. Of all the industrialized nations, the U.S. has the greatest degree of inequality. For example, one percent of Americans own 40 percent of all the wealth. At the other extreme, 14 1/2 percent of all Americans live below the poverty line and 5 percent of all Americans live below *one-half* of the poverty line.

When these social variables converge, they interact to increase crime rates. Thus, there is a relatively high probability of criminal behavior—violent criminal behavior—among young, black, impoverished males in inner cities where poverty, unemployment, and racial segregation are concentrated. There are about 5 million of these high-risk young men. In addition, we have other problem people. What do we do? How do we create a safer America?

To oversimplify a difficult and contentious debate, there are two answers —the conservative and progressive answers. The conservative answer has been to get tough with criminals. This involves mandatory sentences, longer sentences, putting more people in prison, and greater use of the death penalty. This strategy has accelerated with laws such as "three strikes and you're out (actually in)," and the passage of expensive prison building programs to house the new prisoners.

In my view, this approach is wrongheaded. Of course, some individuals must be put in prison to protect the members of society. Our policies, however, indiscriminately put too many people in prison at too high a cost. Here are some facts about prisons:

1. Our current incarceration rate is 455 per 100,000 (in 1971 it was 96 per 100,000). The rate in Japan and the Netherlands is one-tenth ours. Currently, there are 1.2 million Americans in prisons and jails (equivalent to the population of Philadelphia).

2. The cost is prohibitive, taking huge amounts of money that could be spent on other programs. It costs about $60,000 to build a prison cell and $20,000 to keep a prisoner for a year. Currently the overall cost of prisons and jails (federal, state, and local) is $29 billion annually. The willingness to spend for punishment reduces money that could be

spent to alleviate other social problems. For example, eight years ago Texas spent $7 dollars on education for every dollar spent on prisons. Now the ratio is 4 to 1. Meanwhile, Texas ranks 37th among the states in per pupil spending.

3. As mentioned earlier, violent crimes tend to occur in the teenage years with a rapid drop off afterwards. Often, for example, imprisonment under "3 strikes and you're out" laws gives life imprisonment to many who are in the twilight of their criminal careers. We, and they, would be better off if we found alternatives to prison for them.

4. Prisons do not rehabilitate. Actually, prisons have the opposite effect. The prison experience tends to increase the likelihood of further criminal behavior. Prisons are overcrowded, mean, gloomy, brutal places that change people, but usually for the worse, not the better. Moreover, prisoners usually believe that their confinement is unjust because of the bias in the criminal justice system toward the poor and racial minorities. Finally, prisoners do not ever pay their debt to society. Rather they are forever stigmatized as "ex-cons" and, therefore, considered unreliable and dangerous by their neighbors, employers, fellow workers, and acquaintances. Also, they are harassed by the police as "likely suspects." The result is that they are often driven into a deviant subculture and eventually caught—about two-thirds are arrested within three years of leaving prison.

Progressives argue that conservative crime control measures are fundamentally flawed because they are "after the fact" solutions. Like a janitor mopping up the floor while the sink continues to overflow; he or she may even redouble the effort with some success but the source

of the flooding has not been addressed. If I might mix metaphors here (although keeping with the aquatic theme), the obvious place to begin the attack on crime is *upstream*, before the criminal has been formed and the crimes have been committed.

We must concentrate our efforts on high-risk individuals before they become criminals (in particular, impoverished young inner city males). These prevention proposals take time, are very costly, and out-of-favor politically but they are the only realistic solutions to reduce violent street crime.

The problem with the conservative "after the fact" crime fighting proposals is that while promoting criminal justice, these programs dismantle social justice. Thus, they enhance a criminogenic climate. During the Reagan years, for example, $51 billion dollars were removed from various poverty programs. Now, under the "Contract for America" the Republicans in Congress propose to reduce subsidized housing, to eliminate nutrition programs through WIC (Women, Infants, and Children), to let the states take care of subsidized school lunches, and to eliminate welfare for unmarried mothers under 18 who do not live with their parents or a responsible guardian.

Progressives argue that we abandon these children at our own peril. The current Republican proposals forsake the 26 percent of American children under six who live in poverty including 54 percent of all African American children and 44 percent of all Latino children under the age of six. Will we be safer as these millions of children in poverty grow to physical maturity?

Before I address specific solutions, I want to emphasize that sociologists examine the structural reasons for crime.

This focus on factors outside the individual does not excuse criminal behavior, it tries to understand how certain structural factors *increase* the proportion of people who choose criminal options.

Knowing what we know about crime, the implications for policy are clear. These proposals, as you will note, are easy to suggest but they are very difficult to implement. I will divide my proposals into immediate actions to deal with crime now and long-term preventive measure:

Measures to protect society immediately:

1. The first step is to protect society from predatory sociopaths. This does not mean imprisoning more people. We should, rather, only imprison the truly dangerous. The criminal law should be redrawn so that the list of crimes reflects the real dangers that individuals pose to society. Since prison does more harm than good, we should provide reasonable alternatives such as house arrest, half-way houses, boot camps, electronic surveillance, job corps, and drug/alcohol treatment.

2. We must reduce the number of handguns and assault weapons by enacting and vigorously enforcing stringent gun controls at the federal level. The United States is an armed camp with 210 million guns in circulation. Jeffrey Reiman has put it this way:

> "Trying to fight crime while allowing such easy access to guns is like trying to teach a child to walk and tripping him each time he stands up. In its most charitable light, it is hypocrisy. Less charitably, it is complicity in murder."

3. We must make a special effort to get guns out of the hands of juveniles. Research by James Wright and his colleagues at Tulane University found that juveniles are much more likely to have guns for protection than for status and power. They suggest that we must restore order in the inner cities so that fewer young people do not feel the need to provide their own protection. They argue that a perceived sense of security by youth can be accomplished if there is a greater emphasis on community policing, more cooperation between police departments and inner city residents, and greater investment by businesses, banks, and cities in the inner city.

4. We must reinvent the criminal justice system so that it commands the respect of youth and adults. The obvious unfairness by race and social class must be addressed. Some laws are unfair. For example, the federal law requires a five-year, no-parole sentence for possession of five grams of crack cocaine, worth about $400. However, it takes 100 times as much powder cocaine—500 grams, worth $10,000—and a selling conviction to get the same sentence. Is this fair? Of course not. Is it racist? It is racist since crack is primarily used by African Americans while powder cocaine is more likely used by whites. There are also differences by race and social class in arrest patterns, plea bargain arrangements, sentencing, parole, and imposition of the death penalty. These differences provide convincing evidence that the poor and racial minorities are discriminated against in the criminal justice system. As long as the criminal justice system is perceived as unfair by the disadvantaged, that system will not exert any moral authority over them.

5. We must rehabilitate as many criminals as possible. Prisons should be more humane. Prisoners should leave prison with vocational skills useful in the real world. Prisoners should leave

prison literate and with a high school degree. And, society should formally adopt the concept of "forgiveness" saying to ex-prisoners, in effect, you have been punished for your crime, we want you to begin a new life with a "clean" record.

6. We must legalize the production and sale of "illicit drugs" and treat addiction as a medical problem rather than a criminal problem. If drugs were legalized or decriminalized, crimes would be reduced in several ways: (a) By eliminating drug use as a criminal problem, we would have 1.12 million *fewer* arrests each year. (b) There would be many *fewer* prisoners (currently about 60 percent of all federal prisoners and 25 percent of all state prisoners are incarcerated for drug offenses). (c) Money now spent on the drug war ($31 billion annually, not counting prison construction) could be spent for other crime control programs such as police patrols, treatment of drug users, and job programs. (d) Drugs could be regulated and taxed, generating revenues of about $5 billion a year. (e) It would end the illicit drug trade that provides tremendous profits to organized crime, violent gangs, and other traffickers. (f) It would eliminate considerable corruption of the police and other authorities. (g) There would be many fewer homicides. Somewhere between one-fourth and one-half of the killings in the inner cities are drug-related. (h) The lower cost of purchasing drugs reduces the need to commit crimes to pay for drug habits.

Long-term preventive measures to reduce violent crime:

1. The link between poverty and street crime is indisputable. In the long run, reducing poverty will be the most effective crime fighting tool. Thus, as a society, we need to intensify our efforts to break the cycle of poverty.

This means providing a universal and comprehensive health care system, low-cost housing, job training, and decent compensation for work. There must be pay equity for women. And, there must be an unwavering commitment to eradicate institutional sexism and racism. Among other benefits, such a strategy will strengthen families and give children resources, positive role models, and hope.

2. Families must be strengthened. Single-parent families and the working poor need subsidized child care, flexible work schedules, and leave for maternity and family emergencies at a reasonable proportion of their wages. Adolescent parents need the resources to stay in school. They need job training. We need to increase the commitment to family planning. This means providing contraceptives and birth control counseling to adolescents. This means using federal funds to pay for legal abortions when they are requested by poor women.

3. There must be a societal commitment to full and decent employment. Meaningful work at decent pay integrates individuals into society. It is a source of positive identity. Employed parents are respected by their children. Good paying jobs provide hope for the future. They also are essential to keep families together.

4. There must be a societal commitment to education. This requires two different programs. The first is to help at-risk children, beginning at an early age. As it is now, when poor children start school, they are already behind. As Sylvia Ann Hewlett has said:

"At age five, poor children are often less alert, less curious, and less effective at interacting with their peers than are more privileged youngsters."

This means that they are doomed to be underachievers. To overcome this we need intervention programs that prepare children for school. Research shows that Head Start and other programs can raise IQ scores significantly. There are two problems with Head Start, however. First, the current funding only covers 40 percent of eligible youngsters. And second, the positive effects from the Head Start program are sometimes short-lived because the children then attend schools that are poorly staffed, overcrowded, and ill-equipped.

This brings us to the second education program to help at-risk children. The government must equalize the resources of school districts, rather than the current situation where the wealth of school districts determines the amount spent per pupil. Actually, equalization is not the answer. I believe that there should be special commitment to invest *extra* resources in at-risk children. If we do, we will have a safer society in the long run.

These proposals seem laughable in the current political climate, where politicians—Republicans *and* Democrats—try to outdo each other in their toughness on crime and their disdain for preven-tive programs. They are wrong, however, and society is going to pay in higher crime rates in the future. I am convinced that the political agenda of the conservatives is absolutely heading us in the wrong direction—toward more violent crime rather than less.

The proposals that I have suggested are based on what we sociologists know about crime. They should be taken seriously, but they are not. The proposals are also based on the assumption that if we can give at-risk young people hope, they will become a part of the community rather than alienated from it. My premise is this: Everyone needs a dream. Without a dream, we become apathetic. Without a dream, we become fatalistic. Without a dream, and the hope of attaining it, society becomes our enemy. Many young people act in antisocial ways because they have lost their dream. These troubled and troublesome people are society's creations because we have not given them the opportunity to achieve their dreams —instead society has structured the situation so that they will fail. Until they feel that they have a stake in society, they will fail, and so will we.

POSTSCRIPT

Are Violent Criminals and Delinquents Treated Too Leniently?

Shanker's solutions for school violence are microstructural. He suggests dealing with a fairly circumscribed, bounded area of actors, which would involve interacting face-to-face with parents; educators and students going to court to testify against specific delinquents; and schools setting up arbitration boards. Eitzen's proposals are macrostructural. He proposes altering economic and family institutions at the national level. In what ways might the two sets of solutions be combined?

Neither writer seems to consider what anthropologist Oscar Lewis over 30 years ago referred to as the "culture of poverty," or radically different lifestyles and learning styles adopted by the poor as a defense against the harsh realities of poverty. These, however, may be disruptive and divisive. Should such factors be ignored?

In what ways might continuing school disruptions and delinquency be indicators of broader social disintegration? Are traditional criminological and sociological theories able to provide satisfactory explanations or solutions? Would arresting or expelling more youngsters solve the problem?

This issue is a broad one, straddling several areas within criminology and criminal justice. For an outstanding analysis of the problems identified by both Shanker and Eitzen with specific policy proposals, see J. Toby's "The Schools," in J. Q. Wilson and J. Petersilia, eds., *Crime* (ICS Press, 1995). A formal analysis of motivations to commit crime is R. Agnew's "Delinquency and the Desire for Money," *Justice Quarterly* (September 1994). A seminal work that deals with the female component of the issue is *Girls, Delinquency, and Juvenile Justice* by M. Chesney-Lind and R. Sheldon (Pacific Grove, 1992). Two discussions that take positions diametrically opposite of that of Shanker are "The Disease Is Adolescence," by D. Foster, and "The Comfort of Being Sad: Kurt Cobain and the Politics of Damage," by S. Ferguson, both in *Utne Reader* (July/August 1994). For an examination of possible causal considerations, see J. Q. Wilson, "What to Do About Crime: Blaming Crime on Root Causes," *Vital Speeches of the Day* (April 1, 1995). For ethnographies looking at the street subculture's bearing on violence and delinquency, see "The Code of the Streets," by E. Anderson, *The Atlantic Monthly* (May 1994).

Also see W. Kaminer's *It's All the Rage: Crime and Culture* (Addison-Wesley 1994); A. Peyton's *Crime and the Sacking of America: The Roots of Chaos* (1995); and a very sad report on child witnesses to violence, " 'Silent Victims' Who Witness Violence," by C. Johnson, *U.S. News & World Report* (March 27, 1995).

ISSUE 13

Is Capital Punishment Bad Policy?

YES: David Von Drehle, from "Miscarriage of Justice: Why the Death Penalty Doesn't Work," *The Washington Post Magazine* (February 5, 1995)

NO: Ernest van den Haag, from "The Ultimate Punishment: A Defense," *Harvard Law Review* (May 1986)

ISSUE SUMMARY

YES: David Von Drehle, a writer and the arts editor for the *Washington Post*, examines specific capital punishment cases, statistics, and statements made by U.S. Supreme Court justices and prosecutors reversing their support of the death penalty, and concludes that capital punishment is bad policy.

NO: Ernest van den Haag, a professor (now retired) and a psychoanalyst, analyzes a number of objections to capital punishment, ranging from its unfair distribution to its excessive costs and its brutal nature. He rejects claims that capital punishment is unfair and barbaric, and he insists that the death penalty does deter criminals and is just retribution for terrible crimes.

In 1968 only 38 percent of all Americans supported the death penalty for certain crimes. In 1972, when the U.S. Supreme Court handed down its decision in *Furman v. Georgia* stating that capital punishment violated the Eighth Amendment, which prohibits cruel and unusual punishment, many Americans were convinced that capital punishment was permanently abolished. After all, even though there were 500 inmates on death row at the time, there had been a steady decline in the number of executions in the United States: In the 1930s there were on average 152 executions per year; in 1962 there were 47 executions; and in 1966 there was 1. Polls in the late 1960s showed that most Americans opposed the death penalty, and virtually every other Western industrial nation had long since eliminated the death sentence or severely modified its use.

Polls taken in the late 1980s and 1990s have shown that 75 to 80 percent of all Americans support capital punishment. Some three dozen inmates had been executed through the first eight months of 1995. Since 1977 the highest number of criminals executed in any year was 31 (until 1995). In this century, the all-time high was 199 executions in 1935. Since the 1970s some 5,000 people have been sentenced to die. Although 2,000 sentences were rescinded, there are still over 3,000 people on death row, some of whom will wait 20 years for their appeals to be completed. Approximately 280 executions have occurred in the past 18 years.

What has happened since the 1960s? Naturally, we will probably never know the full answer to this question, but there are some clues. To begin with, in *Furman v. Georgia*, the Supreme Court did not really ban capital punishment because it was cruel and unusual in itself. It simply argued that it was unconstitutional for juries to be given the right to decide arbitrarily and discriminatorily on capital punishment. Thus, if states can show that capital punishment is not arbitrary or discriminatory and that the sentencing process is performed in two separate stages—first guilt or innocence is established, and *then* the determination of the sentence occurs—then some offenses are legally punishable by death. This was the Supreme Court's ruling in 1976 in *Gregg v. Georgia*, which effectively restored the death penalty.

Since the late 1960s, Americans have become more conservative. Fear of crime has greatly increased, although the number of crimes may not have changed. Moreover, many of the measures taken under the Omnibus Safe Streets Act to reduce crime, speed up judicial processes, and rehabilitate criminals are now viewed by professionals and laypeople alike as failures. The national mood is now solidly behind "getting tough" on criminals, especially drug dealers and murderers. Support and utilization of capital punishment make sense within the logic of the present cultural and political situation.

There is a movement among criminologists to reassess studies done before the 1960s that claimed that states in which capital punishment prevailed had homicide rates that were just as high as those in which it was not a penalty and that executions did not deter others from committing crimes. Isaac Ehrlich, for instance, in an extensive statistical analysis of executions between the years 1933 and 1967, reached very different conclusions. He contends not only that the executions reduced the murder rate but that one additional execution per year between 1933 and 1967 would have resulted in seven or eight fewer murders per year!

Many scholars have bitterly attacked Ehrlich's empirical findings. Most attempt to fault his methods, but others assert that even if he is empirically correct, the trade-off is not worth it. The state should not have the right to extract such a primitive "justice" as the murder of a human being, even a convicted killer. Other scholars emphasize the fact that there have been a disproportionate number of blacks executed (between 1930 and 1967, 2,066 blacks were executed as opposed to 1,751 whites, even though blacks constituted only 10 percent of the total population then). Some counter that this simply indicates that more whites need to be executed as well!

Is capital punishment bad policy? If not, what crimes ought it be reserved for? Murder? Rape? Espionage? Drug dealing? Kidnapping? How should it be carried out?

YES

David Von Drehle

MISCARRIAGE OF JUSTICE: WHY THE DEATH PENALTY DOESN'T WORK

As a boy of 8, the son of good, poor parents, James Curtis "Doug" McCray had limitless dreams; he told everyone he met that someday he would be president of the United States. Soon enough, he realized that poor black children did not grow up to be president, but still he was a striver. At Dunbar High School in Fort Myers, Fla., he was an all-state receiver on the football team, an all-conference guard in basketball and the state champion in the 440-yard dash. He made the honor roll, and became the first and only of the eight McCray kids to attend college.

His was a success story, but for one flaw. McCray had a drinking problem. He washed out of college and joined the Army. A year and a half later, the Army gave him a medical discharge because he had been found to suffer from epilepsy. McCray married, fathered a son, tried college again; nothing took. He wound up back home, a tarnished golden boy.

On an October evening in 1973, an elderly woman named Margaret Mears was at home in her apartment, picking no trouble, harming no one, when someone burst in, stripped and raped her, then beat her to death. A bloody handprint was matched to Doug McCray's. He insisted that he had no memory of the night in question, and his jury unanimously recommended a life sentence. But McCray had the bad fortune to be tried by Judge William Lamar Rose.

... To him, the murder of Margaret Mears was precisely the type of savagery the law was intended to punish: committed in the course of another felony, and surely heinous, surely atrocious, surely cruel. Rose overruled the jury and banged the gavel on death.

* * *

When McCray arrived at Florida State Prison in 1974, nine men awaited execution and he made 10. His case entered the appeals process, and as the years went by, McCray wept for his best friend on death row, John Spenkelink, who became the first man in America executed against his will under modern death penalty laws. He watched as a young man named Bob Graham became governor of Florida and led the nation in executing criminals. Eight years later, he watched Gov. Bob Martinez take Graham's place and sign 139 death warrants in four years. McCray saw the infamous serial killer Ted Bundy come to the row, and almost 10 years later saw him go quietly to Old Sparky.

Living on death row, McCray saw men cut, saw men burned, even saw a man killed. He saw inmates carried from their cells after committing suicide, and others taken away after going insane. He saw wardens and presidents come and go. Death row got bigger and bigger. By the time Spenkelink was executed in May 1979, Jacksonville police officers printed T-shirts proclaiming "One down, 133 to go!" ...

Doug McCray watched as death row doubled in size, and grew still more until it was not a row but a small town, Death Town, home to more than 300 killers. Nationwide, the condemned population climbed toward 3,000. The seasons passed through a sliver of dirty glass beyond two sets of bars outside McCray's tiny cell on the row, which was very cold in the winter and very hot in the summer, noisy at all times and stinking with the odor of smoking, sweating, dirty, defecating men. Four seasons made a year, and the years piled up: 5, 10, 15, 16, 17 ...

All this time, Doug McCray was sentenced to death but he did not die. Which makes him the perfect symbol of the modern death penalty.

People talk a great deal these days about getting rid of government programs that cost too much and produce scant results. So it's curious that one of the least efficient government programs in America is also among the most popular. Capital punishment is favored by more than three-quarters of American voters. And yet, in 1994, the death row population nationwide exceeded 3,000 for the first time ever; out of all those condemned prisoners, only 31 were executed. There are hundreds of prisoners in America who have been on death row more than a decade, and at least one—Thomas Knight of Florida—has been awaiting execution for 20 years. Every cost study undertaken has found that it is far more expensive, because of added legal safeguards, to carry out a death sentence than it is to jail a killer for life. Capital punishment is the principal burden on the state and federal appellate courts in every jurisdiction where it is routinely practiced. The most efficient death penalty state, Texas, has a backlog of more than 300 people on its death row. It manages to execute only about one killer for every four newly sentenced to die—and the number of executions may drop now that the U.S. Supreme Court has ordered Texas to provide lawyers for death row inmate appeals. Overall, America has executed approximately one in every 20 inmates sentenced to die under modern death penalty laws.

This poor record of delivering the punishments authorized by legislatures and imposed by courts has persisted despite a broad shift to the right in the federal courts. It has resisted legislative and judicial efforts to streamline the process. It has outlasted William J. Brennan Jr. and Thurgood Marshall, the Supreme Court's strongest anti-death penalty justices. It has endured countless campaigns by state legislators and governors and U.S. representatives and senators and even presidents who have promised to get things moving. If New York reinstates the death penalty this year, as Gov. George Pataki has promised, there is no reason to believe things will change; New York is unlikely to see another execution in this century. Congress extended the death penalty to cover more than 50 new crimes last year, but that bill will be long forgotten before Uncle Sam executes more than a handful of prisoners.

Most people like the death penalty in theory; virtually no one familiar with it likes the slow, costly and inefficient reality. But after 20 years of trying to make the death penalty work, it is becoming clear that we are stuck with the reality, and not the ideal.

* * *

To understand why this is, you have to understand the basic mechanics of the modern death penalty. The story begins in 1972.

For most of American history, capital punishment was a state or even a local issue. Criminals were tried, convicted and sentenced according to local rules and customs, and their executions were generally carried out by town sheriffs in courthouse squares. Federal judges took almost no interest in the death penalty, and even state appeals courts tended to give the matter little consideration.

Not surprisingly, a disproportionate number of the people executed under these customs were black, and the execution rate was most dramatically skewed for the crime of rape. As sensibilities became more refined, however, decent folks began to object to the spectacle of local executions. In Florida in the 1920s, for example, a coalition of women's clubs lobbied the legislature to ban the practice, arguing that the sight of bodies swinging in town squares had a brutalizing effect on their communities. Similar efforts around the country led to the centralizing of executions at state prisons, where they took place outside the public view, often at midnight or dawn.

Still, the death penalty remained a state matter, with the federal government extremely reluctant to exert its authority. Washington kept its nose out of the death chambers, just as it steered clear of the schools, courtrooms, prisons and voting booths. All that changed, and changed dramatically, in the 1950s and '60s, when the Supreme Court, in the era of Chief Justice Earl Warren, asserted more vigorously than ever that the protections of the U.S. Constitution applied to actions in the states. For the first time, federal standards of equality were used to strike down such state and local practices as school segregation, segregation of buses and trains, poll taxes and voter tests. The lengthened arm of the federal government reached into police stations: For example, in Miranda v. Arizona, the Supreme Court required that suspects be advised of their constitutional rights when arrested. The long arm reached into the courtrooms: In Gideon v. Wainwright, the high court declared that the federal guarantee of due process required that felony defendants in state trials be provided with lawyers.

Opponents of capital punishment urged the courts to reach into death rows as well. Anthony Amsterdam, at the time a Stanford University law professor, crafted arguments to convince the federal courts that the death penalty violated the Eighth Amendment (which bars "cruel and unusual punishments") and the 14th Amendment (which guarantees "equal protection of the laws"). Amsterdam's arguments won serious consideration in the newly aggressive federal courts, and on January 17, 1972, the greatest of Amsterdam's lawsuits, *Furman v. Georgia*, was heard in the Supreme Court.

Amsterdam delivered a brilliant four-pronged attack on capital punishment. He began by presenting statistical proof that the death penalty in America was overwhelmingly used against the poor and minorities. Next, Amsterdam argued that the death penalty was imposed arbitrarily, almost randomly. Judges and juries meted out their sentences without clear standards to guide them, and as a result men were on death row for armed robbery, while nearby, murderers served life, or less. Discretion in death sentencing was virtually unfettered. Amsterdam's third point was his most audacious, but it turned out to be crucial: The death penalty was so rarely carried out in contemporary America that it could no longer be justified as a deterrent to crime. In the years leading up to Amsterdam's argument, use of the death penalty had steeply declined. What made this argument so daring was that the sharp drop in executions was partly a result of Amsterdam's own legal campaign to abolish the death penalty. He was, in effect, challenging a state of affairs he had helped to create.

In closing, Amsterdam argued that the death penalty had become "unacceptable in contemporary society," that the "evolving standards" of decent behavior had moved beyond the point of legal killing. This was the weakest of his arguments, because nearly 40 states still had death penalty laws on the books, but previous Supreme Court decisions suggested that the shortest route to abolishing the death penalty would be to convince a majority of the justices that "standards of decency" had changed. Amsterdam had to try.

Behind closed doors, the nine justices of the court revealed a wide range of reactions to Amsterdam's case—from Brennan and Marshall, the court's liberal stalwarts, who voted to abolish capital punishment outright, to Justice William H. Rehnquist, the new conservative beacon, who rejected all of the arguments. Justice William O. Douglas was unpersuaded by the notion that standards of decency had evolved to the point that capital punishment was cruel and unusual punishment, but he agreed the death penalty was unconstitutionally arbitrary. Chief Justice Warren E. Burger and Justice Harry A. Blackmun both expressed personal opposition to capital punishment—if they were legislators, they would vote against it—but they believed that the language of the Constitution clearly left the matter to the states. That made three votes to strike down the death penalty, and three to sustain it.

Justice Lewis F. Powell Jr. also strongly objected to the court taking the question of the death penalty out of the hands of elected legislatures. This would be an egregious example of the sort of judicial activism he had always opposed. Though moved by Amsterdam's showing of racial discrimination, Powell believed this was a vestige of the past, and could be rectified without a sweeping decision in Furman. Powell's vote made four to sustain the death penalty. Justice Potter Stewart, painfully aware of the more than 600 prisoners whose lives were dangling on his vote, moved toward Douglas's view that the death penalty had become unconstitutionally arbitrary. Stewart's vote made four to strike down the death penalty as it existed.

That left Justice Byron R. White, known to observers of the court as a strict law-and-order man. In his brusque opinions, White backed prosecutors and police at almost every turn. But he was deeply impressed by Amsterdam's presentation; he told his law clerks that it was "possibly the best" oral argument he had ever heard. The point that had won White was Amsterdam's boldest: that the death penalty was applied too infrequently to serve any purpose. White cast the deciding vote to strike down the death penalty not because he wanted to see an end to capital punishment, but because he wanted to see more of it.

The product of these deliberations was one of the most difficult decisions in the history of the U.S. Supreme Court. The broad impact of *Furman v. Georgia*, striking down hundreds of separate laws in nearly 40 separate jurisdictions, was unprecedented. Rambling and inchoate—nine separate opinions totaling some 50,000 words—it remains easily the longest decision ever published by the court. But for all its wordy impact, Furman was almost useless as a precedent for future cases. It set out no clear legal standards. As Powell noted in his stinging dissent:

"Mr. Justice Douglas concludes that capital punishment is incompatible with notions of 'equal protection' that he finds 'implicit' in the Eighth Amendment... Mr. Justice Brennan bases his judgment primarily on the thesis that the penalty 'does not comport with human dignity'... Mr. Justice Stewart concludes that the penalty is applied in a 'wanton' and 'freakish' manner... For Mr. Justice White it is the 'infrequency' with which the penalty is imposed that renders its use unconstitutional... Mr. Justice Marshall finds that capital punishment is an impermissible form of punishment because it is 'morally unacceptable' and 'excessive'...

"I [will not] attempt to predict what forms of capital statutes, if any, may avoid condemnation in the future under the variety of views expressed by the collective majority today."

In other words, totally missing from the longest Supreme Court decision in history was any clear notion of how the death penalty might be fixed.

*   *   *

That painfully splintered 5-to-4 vote turned out to be a high-water mark of the Supreme Court's willingness to intervene in the business of the states. In Furman, the justices were willing to abolish the death penalty as it existed. But the justices were not willing to forbid executions forever. They kicked the question of whether the death penalty was "cruel and unusual" back to the state legislatures. For nearly 20 years, the states—especially the Southern states—had felt pounded by the Supreme Court. Rarely did they get the chance to answer. The court did not ask what they thought about school desegregation, or voting rights, or the right to counsel. But *Furman v. Georgia* invited the states to respond to a hostile Supreme Court decision.

Florida was the first state to craft an answer, after calling its legislature into special session. Blue-ribbon panels appointed by the governor and legislature struggled to make sense of Furman— but how? On the governor's commission, legal advisers unanimously predicted that no capital punishment law would ever satisfy the high court, but the membership turned instead to a nugget from Justice Douglas's opinion. Douglas wrote that the problem with the pre-Furman laws was that "under these laws no standards govern the selection of the penalty." Douglas seemed to be saying that judges and juries needed rules to guide their sentencing.

The legislative commission reached a different conclusion, simply by seizing on a different snippet from the Furman ruling. Figuring that Byron White was the most likely justice to change his position, commission members combed his opinion for clues. White had complained that "the legislature authorizes [but] does not mandate the penalty in any particular class or kind of case..." That phrase seemed crucial: "Authorizes but does not mandate." Apparently, White would prefer to see death made mandatory for certain crimes.

Furman was as cryptic as the Gnostic gospels. Robert Shevin, Florida's attorney general at the time, was just as confused. He summoned George Georgieff and Ray Marky, his two top death penalty aides, to explain the ruling. "I've been reading it since it came out," Marky told his boss, "and I still have no idea what it means."

Gov. Reubin Askew refused to go along with mandatory sentences—he considered them barbaric. And so it was that while rank-and-file lawmakers made interminable tough-on-crime speeches, in the last month of 1972 Florida's power brokers hashed out a deal behind closed doors. Their new law spelled out "aggravating" circumstances—such as a defendant's criminal record and the degree of violence involved in the crime—which, if proven, would make a guilty man eligible for the death penalty. The law also spelled out "mitigating" circumstances, such as a defendant's age or mental state, that might suggest a life sentence instead. After a defendant was found guilty of a capital offense, the jury would hear evidence of aggravating and mitigating factors. By majority vote, the jurors would recommend either life in prison or the death penalty. Then the judge would be required to reweigh the aggravating and mitigating factors and impose the sentence, justifying it in writing. As a final safeguard, the sentence would be reviewed by the state's highest court. In this way, perhaps, they could thread the Furman needle: setting standards, limiting discretion, erasing caprice—all while avoiding mandatory sentences.

They were a few men in a back room, trading power and guessing over an incoherent Supreme Court document. It was not a particularly promising effort. Nevertheless, their compromise passed overwhelmingly, giving America its first legislative answer to Furman. Immediately, officials from states across the country began calling Florida for advice and guidance. And very soon, lawyers and judges began to discover that the law drafted in confusion and passed in haste was going to be hell to administer.

* * *

The problem was that underneath the tidy, legalistic, polysyllabic, etched-in-marble tone of the new law was a lot of slippery mishmash. The aggravating and mitigating factors sounded specific and empirical, but many of them were matters of judgment rather than fact. A murderer was more deserving of the death penalty, for example, if his actions involved "a great risk of death to many persons"—but where one judge might feel that phrase applied to a drive-by killer who sprays a whole street with gunfire, another might apply it to a burglar who stabs a man to death while the victim's wife slumbers nearby. How much risk makes a "great" risk, and what number of persons constitutes "many"?

Another aggravating circumstance was even harder to interpret—"especially heinous, atrocious or cruel." The idea was to identify only the worst of the hundreds of murders each year in Florida. But wasn't the act of murder itself "heinous, atrocious or cruel"? Again, this aggravating circumstance was very much in the eye of the beholder: To one judge, stabbing might seem more cruel than shooting, because it involved such close contact between killer and victim. Another judge, however, might think it crueler to place a cold gun barrel to a victim's head before squeezing the trigger. One jury might find it especially heinous for a victim to be killed by a stranger, while the next set of jurors might find it more atrocious for a victim to die at the hands of a trusted friend. And so forth. It was an attempt to define the undefinable.

The imprecision was even more obvious on the side of mitigation, where it weighed in a defendant's favor if he had no "significant history" of past criminal behavior. How much history was that? "The age of the defendant" was supposed to be considered under the new law— but where one judge might think 15 was old enough to face the death penalty, another might have qualms about executing a man who was "only" 20. What about elderly criminals? Was there an age beyond which a man should qualify for mercy— and if so, what was it?

Clearly, a lot of discretion was left to the judge and jury. Even more discretion was allowed in tallying the aggravating versus the mitigating circumstances, and still more in deciding what weight to give each factor. The jury was supposed to render an "advisory" opinion on the proper sentence, death or life in prison, but how much deference did the judge have to pay to that advice? The law said

nothing. After the judge imposed a death sentence, the state supreme court was required to review it. But what standards was the court supposed to apply? The law said nothing.

These questions might have seemed tendentious and picayune, except for the fact that Doug McCray and dozens of others were quickly sent to death row, and these seemingly trivial questions became the cruxes of life-and-death litigation. The law, shot through with question marks, became a lawyer's playground. After all, laws were supposed to be clear and fixed; they were supposed to mean the same thing from day to day, courtroom to courtroom, town to town. And given that their clients were going to be killed for breaking the law, it seemed only fair for defense lawyers to demand that simple degree of reliability.

In 1976, when the U.S. Supreme Court returned to the question of capital punishment, the justices agreed that the laws must be reliable. By then some 35 states had passed new death penalty laws, many of them modeled on Florida's. In a string of rulings the high court outlawed mandatory death sentences and affirmed the complex systems for weighing specified factors in favor of and against a death sentence.

But in striking down mandatory sentences, the court made consistency a constitutional requirement for the death penalty; the law must treat "same" cases the same and "different" cases differently. The thousands of capital crimes committed each year in America raised a mountain of peculiarities—each criminal and crime was subtly unique. Somehow the law must penetrate this mountain to discern some conceptual key that would consistently identify cases that were the "same" and cull ones that were "different." Furthermore, the court decided, the Constitution requires extraordinary consistency from capital punishment laws. "The penalty of death is qualitatively different from a sentence of imprisonment, however long," Justice Potter Stewart wrote. "Because of that qualitative difference, there is a corresponding difference in the need for reliability..."

Each year, some 20,000 homicides are committed in America, and the swing justices expected the death penalty laws to steer precisely and consistently through this carnage to find the relatively few criminals deserving execution. Somehow, using the black-and-white of the criminal code, the system must determine the very nature of evil. King Solomon himself might demur.

"The main legal battle is over," declared the New York Times in an editorial following the 1976 decisions. In fact, the battles were only beginning.

* * *

After Doug McCray was sentenced to die in 1974, his case went to the Florida Supreme Court for the required review.... In October 1980, the Florida Supreme Court agreed that Doug McCray should die. The following year the U.S. Supreme Court declined to review the state court's decision.

Through all this, McCray continued to insist that he had no memory of murdering Margaret Mears. He passed a lie detector test, and though such tests are not admissible in court, there was another reason to believe what he said. It was possible that McCray's epilepsy, which had first emerged in several powerful seizures during his Army basic training, was the type known as "temporal lobe seizure disorder." This disease often emerges in late adolescence; it is known

to cause violent blackouts; and it can be triggered by alcohol. The possibility had not come out at McCray's trial, nor was it properly researched in preparation for his hearing on executive clemency. The hearing, held on December 16, 1981, went badly for McCray. An attorney, Jesse James Wolbert, had been appointed to represent him, but Wolbert did not bother to read the trial record, let alone prepare a compelling case for mercy. Perhaps he had other things on his mind: By the time McCray's death warrant was signed three months later, Wolbert had drained another client's trust fund and become a federal fugitive.

Wolbert's disappearance turned out to be a blessing for McCray, because an anti-death penalty activist named Scharlette Holdman persuaded Bob Dillinger of St. Petersburg to take the case, and Dillinger was a damn good lawyer. He filed a hasty appeal in the Florida Supreme Court asking for a stay of execution. The result was amazing: Having affirmed McCray's death sentence 18 months earlier, the justices now ordered a new trial. The sentence, they ruled, had been based on the theory that the murder had been committed in conjunction with a rape. "Felony murder," this is called—murder coupled with another felony. In 1982, the Florida Supreme Court, by a vote of 4 to 3, declared that the underlying felony, rape, had not been proven beyond a reasonable doubt. Eight years after the original sentence, Doug McCray was going back to trial.

Except that something even more amazing happened a few weeks later. The state supreme court granted the prosecution's request for a rehearing, and Justice Ray Ehrlich abruptly changed his mind. His vote made it 4 to 3 in favor of upholding McCray's death sentence.

In the course of six months, Ehrlich had gone from believing McCray's sentence was so flawed that he should have a new trial to believing that his sentence was sound enough to warrant his death. The court contacted the company that publishes all its decisions and asked that the first half of this flip-flop—the order for a new trial—be erased from history.

Gov. Bob Graham signed a second death warrant on May 27, 1983. By this time, Bob Dillinger had located his client's ex-wife in California, where she lived with her son by Doug McCray. The son was what his father had once been: bright as a whip, interested in current events, a devourer of books, good at games. The ex-wife, Myra Starks, was mystified by the course her husband's life had taken. They had been high school sweethearts, and she had married him certain that he was upward bound. When McCray had left school to join the Army, Starks had clung to that vision, picturing a steady string of promotions leading to a comfortable pension. Then came the seizures and the medical discharge, and her husband's behavior changed horribly. He drank heavily, and sometimes when he was drunk he struck out at her violently—though after each of these outbursts, he insisted he remembered nothing. Myra Starks did not make a connection between the medical discharge and the change in her man; instead, she packed up their baby boy and moved out. Within a year, McCray was on trial for murder.

In addition to locating Starks, Bob Dillinger also arranged for a full-scale medical evaluation of his client, and the doctor concluded that McCray indeed suffered from temporal lobe seizure disorder. It all came together: the violent blackouts, triggered by drink. In prison, after a number of seizures, McCray was put on a drug regimen to control his disease: Dilantin, a standard epilepsy treatment, in the mornings, and phenobarbital, a sedative, at night. When Dillinger arranged for Myra Starks to see her ex-husband, after a decade apart, she exclaimed, "He's just like the old Doug!"

But he was scheduled to die. Following established procedure, Dillinger returned to the Florida Supreme Court. It was the fifth time the court had considered McCray's case. This time, the justices concluded that the new medical evidence might be important in weighing whether death was the appropriate sentence. They ordered the trial court to hold a hearing and stayed the execution while this was done.

Doug McCray had lived on death row nine years....

In all that time, though, his case had not moved past the first level of appeals. The Florida Supreme Court had weighed and reweighed his case, and with each weighing the justices had reached a different conclusion.

* * *

McCray's case was far from unusual. Every death penalty case winds up on spongy ground, even the most outrageous. It took nearly a decade for Florida to execute serial killer Ted Bundy, and even longer for John Wayne Gacy to reach the end in Illinois. The courts routinely reverse themselves, then double back again. The same case can look different with each fresh examination or new group of judges. Defenders have learned to exploit every possible advantage from the tiniest detail to the loftiest constitutional principle. A conscientious defense attorney has no choice—especially if any question remains as to whether the condemned man actually committed the crime for which he was sentenced. The effort involves huge expenditures of time and resources, and results are notoriously uncertain....

* * *

By the time Doug McCray's case returned to the trial court for a new sentence in 1986, the hanging judge, William Lamar Rose, was gone. So many years had passed. But in his place was another stern man who was no less outraged at the enormity of McCray's crime....

McCray had, over the years, become a favorite of death penalty opponents, because he seemed so gentle and redeemable. Frequently, they argued that not all death row prisoners are "like Ted Bundy," and McCray was the sort of prisoner they were talking about. The harshest word in his vocabulary was "shucks." He read every book he could get his hands on. There was a poignant vulnerability to him.

But the new judge focused, as the old one had done, on the crime: A defenseless, innocent, helpless woman alone, terrorized, apparently raped, then killed. He sentenced McCray to death once more. And the case returned to the Florida Supreme Court for a sixth time. In June 1987, after a U.S. Supreme Court decision in favor of another Florida inmate, the justices sent McCray's case back because the judge had overruled the jury's advisory sentence. What was his justification? The judge's justification was an elderly woman savagely murdered. Once again, he imposed the death sentence.

So the case of Doug McCray returned for the seventh time to the Florida Supreme Court. Did he deserve to die? Four times, a trial judge insisted

that he did. Twice, the state's high court agreed. And four times, the same court expressed doubts. A single case, considered and reconsidered, strained and restrained, weighed and reweighed. A prism, a kaleidoscope, a rune of unknown meaning. The life of a man, viewed through the lens of a complex, uncertain, demanding law. Should he live or die?

In May 1991, after weighing his case for the seventh time in 17 years, the Florida Supreme Court reversed McCray's death sentence and imposed a sentence of life in prison. For 17 years, two courts had debated—the trial court and the state supreme court. No liberal outsiders stalled the process, no bleeding hearts intervened. Even the lawyers added little to the essential conundrum, which was in the beginning as it was in the end: Doug McCray, bad guy, versus Doug McCray, not-quite-so-bad guy. The case was far from aberrant. It was one of hundreds of such cases.

* * *

Some politicians and pundits still talk as if the confusion over the death penalty can be eliminated by a healthy dose of conservative toughness, but among the people who know the system best that explanation is losing steam. More than 20 years have passed since *Furman v. Georgia*; courts and legislatures have gotten tougher and tougher on the issue—but the results have remained negligible. The execution rate hovers at around 25 or 30 per year, while America's death row population has swelled past 3,000. It makes no real difference who controls the courts, as California voters learned after they dumped their liberal chief justice in 1986. The court turned rightward, but $7^1/_2$ years later, California had executed just two of the more than 300 prisoners on its death row. (One of the two had voluntarily surrendered his appeals.) No matter how strongly judges and politicians favor capital punishment, the law has remained a mishmash.

It is hard to see a way out. The idea that the death penalty should not be imposed arbitrarily—that each case should be analyzed by a rational set of standards —has been so deeply woven into so many federal and state court rulings that there is little chance of it being reversed. Courts have softened that requirement, but softening has not solved the problem. Proposals to limit access to appeals for death row inmates have become staples of America's political campaigns, and many limits have been set. But it can take up to a decade for a prisoner to complete just one trip through the courts, and no one has proposed denying condemned inmates one trip.

... [E]ven the most vicious killers... cannot be executed quickly. Gerald Stano, who in the early 1980s confessed to killing more than two dozen women, is alive. Thomas Knight, who in 1980 murdered a prison guard while awaiting execution for two other murders, is alive. Jesus Scull, who in 1983 robbed and murdered two victims and burned their house around them, is alive. Howard Douglas, who in 1973 forced his wife to have sex with her boyfriend as he watched, then smashed the man's head in, is alive. Robert Buford, who in 1977 raped and beat a 7-year-old girl to death, is alive. Eddie Lee Freeman, who in 1976 strangled a former nun and dumped her in a river to drown, is alive. Jesse Hall, who in 1975 raped and murdered a teenage girl and killed her boyfriend, is alive. James Rose, who in 1976 raped and murdered an 8-year-old girl in Fort Lauderdale, is alive. Larry Mann, who in 1980 cut a little girl's throat and clubbed her to death as she crawled away, is alive.

And that's just in Florida. The story is the same across the country.

In 1972, Justice Harry Blackmun cast one of the four votes in favor of preserving the death penalty in *Furman v. Georgia*, and he voted with the majority to approve the new laws four years later. For two decades, he stuck to the belief that the death penalty could meet the constitutional test of reliability. But last year Blackmun threw up his hands. "Twenty years have passed since this Court declared that the death penalty must be imposed fairly and with reasonable consistency or not all," he wrote."... In the years following Furman, serious efforts were made to comply with its mandate. State legislatures and appellate courts struggled to provide judges and juries with sensible and objective guidelines for determining who should live and who should die... Unfortunately, all this experimentation and ingenuity yielded little of what Furman demanded... It seems that the decision whether a human being should live or die is so inherently subjective, rife with all of life's understandings, experiences, prejudices and passions, that it inevitably defies the rationality and consistency required by the Constitution... I feel morally and intellectually obligated simply to concede that the death penalty experiment has failed."

Also last year, an admiring biography of retired Justice Lewis Powell was published. Powell was one of the architects of the modern death penalty. As a swing vote in 1976, he had helped to define the intricate weighing system that restored capital punishment in America. Later, as the deciding vote in a 1987 case, *Mc-Cleskey v. Kemp*, Powell had saved the death penalty from the assertion that racial disparities proved the system was still arbitrary. Now Powell was quoted as telling his biographer, "I have come to think that capital punishment should be abolished." The death penalty "brings discredit on the whole legal system," Powell said, because the vast majority of death sentences are never carried out. Biographer John C. Jeffries Jr. had asked Powell if he would like to undo any decisions from his long career. "Yes," the justice answered. "McCleskey v. Kemp."

No one has done more than Ray Marky to make a success of the death penalty. As a top aide in the Florida attorney general's office, he worked himself into an early heart attack prosecuting capital appeals. Eventually, he took a less stressful job at the local prosecutor's office, where he watched, dispirited, as the modern death penalty—the law he had helped write and had struggled to enforce —reached its convoluted maturity. One day a potential death penalty case came across his new desk, and instead of pushing as he had in the old days, he advised the victim's mother to accept a life sentence for her son's killer. "Ma'am, bury your son and get on with your life, or over the next dozen years, this defendant will destroy you, as well as your son," Marky told her. Why put the woman through all the waiting, the hearings and the stays, when the odds were heavy that the death sentence would never be carried out? "I never would have said that 15 years ago," Marky reflected. "But now I will, because I'm not going to put someone through the nightmare. If we had deliberately set out to create a chaotic system, we couldn't have come up with anything worse. It's a merry-go-round, it's ridiculous; it's so clogged up only an arbitrary few ever get it.

"I don't get any damn pleasure out of the death penalty and I never have," the prosecutor said. "And frankly, if they abolished it tomorrow, I'd go get drunk in celebration."

NO

Ernest van den Haag

THE ULTIMATE PUNISHMENT: A DEFENSE

In an average year about 20,000 homicides occur in the United States. Fewer than 300 convicted murders are sentenced to death. But because no more than thirty murderers have been executed in any recent year, most convicts sentenced to death are likely to die of old age.[1] Nonetheless, the death penalty looms large in discussions: it raises important moral questions independent of the number of executions.

The death penalty is our harshest punishment. It is irrevocable: it ends the existence of those punished, instead of temporarily imprisoning them. Further, although not intended to cause physical pain, execution is the only corporal punishment still applied to adults. These singular characteristics contribute to the perennial, impassioned controversy about capital punishment.

I. DISTRIBUTION

Consideration of the justice, morality, or usefulness, of capital punishment is often conflated with objections to its alleged discriminatory or capricious distribution among the guilty. Wrongly so. If capital punishment is immoral *in se*, no distribution among the guilty could make it moral. If capital punishment is moral, no distribution would make it immoral. Improper distribution cannot affect the quality of what is distributed, be it punishments or rewards. Discriminatory or capricious distribution thus could not justify abolition of the death penalty. Further, maldistribution inheres no more in capital punishment than in any other punishment.

Maldistribution between the guilty and the innocent is, by definition, unjust. But the injustice does not lie in the nature of the punishment. Because of the finality of the death penalty, the most grievous maldistribution occurs when it is imposed upon the innocent. However, the frequent allegations of discrimination and capriciousness refer to maldistribution among the guilty and not to the punishment of the innocent.

Maldistribution of any punishment among those who deserve it is irrelevant to its justice or morality. Even if poor or black convicts guilty of capital offenses suffer capital punishment, and other convicts equally guilty of the same crimes do not, a more equal distribution, however desirable, would merely be more equal. It would not be more just to the convicts under sentence of death.

Punishments are imposed on persons, not on racial or economic groups. Guilt is personal. The only relevant question is: does the person to be executed deserve the punishment? Whether or not others who deserved the same punishment, whatever their economic or racial group, have avoided execution is irrelevant. If they have, the guilt of the executed convicts would not be diminished, nor would their punishment be less deserved. To put the issue starkly, if the death penalty were imposed on guilty blacks, but not on guilty whites, or, if it were imposed by a lottery among the guilty, this irrationally discriminatory or capricious distribution would neither make the penalty unjust, nor cause anyone to be unjustly punished, despite the undue impunity bestowed on others.

Equality, in short, seems morally less important than justice. And justice is independent of distributional inequalities. The ideal of equal justice demands that justice be equally distributed, not that it be replaced by equality. Justice requires that as many of the guilty as possible be punished, regardless of whether others have avoided punishment. To let these others escape the deserved punishment does not do justice to them, or to society. But it is not unjust to those who could not escape.

These moral considerations are not meant to deny that irrational discrimina-tion, or capriciousness, would be inconsistent with constitutional requirements. But I am satisfied that the Supreme Court has in fact provided for adherence to the constitutional requirement of equality as much as possible. Some inequality is indeed unavoidable as a practical matter in any system.[2] But, *ultra posse neo obligatur.* (Nobody is bound beyond ability.)

Recent data reveal little direct racial discrimination in the sentencing of those arrested and convicted of murder. The abrogation of the death penalty for rape has eliminated a major source of racial discrimination. Concededly, some discrimination based on the race of murder victims may exist; yet, this discrimination affects criminal victimizers in an unexpected way. Murderers of whites are thought more likely to be executed than murderers of blacks. Black victims, then, are less fully vindicated than white ones. However, because most black murderers kill blacks, black murderers are spared the death penalty more often than are white murderers. They fare better than most white murderers. The motivation behind unequal distribution of the death penalty may well have been to discriminate against blacks, but the result has favored them. Maldistribution is thus a straw man for empirical as well as analytical reasons.

II. MISCARRIAGES OF JUSTICE

In a recent survey Professors Hugo Adam Bedau and Michael Radelet found that 7000 persons were executed in the United States between 1900 and 1985 and that 25 were innocent of capital crimes. Among the innocents they list Sacco and Vanzetti as well as Ethel and Julius Rosenberg. Although their data may be questionable, I do not doubt that, over a long enough period, miscarriages of justice will occur even in capital cases.

Despite precautions, nearly all human activities, such as trucking, lighting, or construction, cost the lives of some innocent bystanders. We do not give up these activities, because the advantages, moral or material, outweigh the unintended losses. Analogously, for those who think the death penalty just, miscarriages of justice are offset by the moral benefits and the usefulness of doing justice. For those who think the death penalty unjust even when it does not miscarry, miscarriages can hardly be decisive.

III. DETERRENCE

Despite much recent work, there has been no conclusive statistical demonstration that the death penalty is a better deterrent than are alternative punishments. However, deterrence is less than decisive for either side. Most abolitionists acknowledge that they would continue to favor abolition even if the death penalty were shown to deter more murders than alternatives could deter. Abolitionists appear to value the life of a convicted murderer or, at least, his nonexecution, more highly than they value the lives of the innocent victims who might be spared by deterring prospective murderers.

Deterrence is not altogether decisive for me either. I would favor retention of the death penalty as retribution even if it were shown that the threat of execution could not deter prospective murderers not already deterred by the threat of imprisonment.[3] Still, I believe the death penalty, because of its finality, is more feared than imprisonment, and deters some prospective murderers not deterred by the threat of imprisonment. Sparing the lives of even a few prospective

victims by deterring their murderers is more important than preserving the lives of convicted murderers because of the possibility, or even the probability, that executing them would not deter others. Whereas the lives of the victims who might be saved are valuable, that of the murderer has only negative value, because of his crime. Surely the criminal law is meant to protect the lives of potential victims in preference to those of actual murderers.

Murder rates are determined by many factors; neither the severity nor the probability of the threatened sanction is always decisive. However, for the long run, I share the view of Sir James Fitzjames Stephen: "Some men, probably, abstain from murder because they fear that if they committed murder they would be hanged. Hundreds of thousands abstain from it because they regard it with horror. One great reason why they regard it with horror is that murderers are hanged." Penal sanctions are useful in the long run for the formation of the internal restraints so necessary to control crime. The severity and finality of the death penalty is appropriate to the seriousness and the finality of murder.

IV. INCIDENTAL ISSUES: COST, RELATIVE SUFFERING, BRUTALIZATION

Many nondecisive issues are associated with capital punishment. Some believe that the monetary cost of appealing a capital sentence is excessive. Yet most comparisons of the cost of life imprisonment with the cost of execution, apart from their dubious relevance, are flawed at least by the implied assumption that life prisoners will generate no judicial costs during their imprisonment. At any rate, the actual monetary costs are trumped by the importance of doing justice.

Others insist that a person sentenced to death suffers more than his victim suffered, and that this (excess) suffering is undue according to the *lex talionis* (rule of retaliation). We cannot know whether the murderer on death row suffers more than his victim suffered; however, unlike the murderer, the victim deserved none of the suffering inflicted. Further, the limitations of the *lex talionis* were meant to restrain private vengeance, not the social retribution that has taken its place. Punishment—regardless of the motivation—is not intended to revenge, offset, or compensate for the victim's suffering, or to be measured by it. Punishment is to vindicate the law and the social order undermined by the crime. This is why a kidnapper's penal confinement is not limited to the period for which he imprisoned his victim; nor is a burglar's confinement meant merely to offset the suffering or the harm he caused his victim; nor is it meant only to offset the advantage he gained.[4]

Another argument heard at least since Beccaria is that, by killing a murderer, we encourage, endorse, or legitimize unlawful killing. Yet, although all punishments are meant to be unpleasant, it is seldom argued that they legitimize the unlawful imposition of identical unpleasantness. Imprisonment is not thought to legitimize kidnapping; neither are fines thought to legitimize robbery. The difference between murder and execution, or between kidnapping and imprisonment, is that the first is unlawful and undeserved, the second a lawful and deserved punishment for an unlawful act. The physical similarities of the punishment to the crime are irrelevant. The relevant difference is not physical, but social.[5]

V. JUSTICE, EXCESS, DEGRADATION

We threaten punishments in order to deter crime. We impose them not only to make the threats credible but also as retribution (justice) for the crimes that were not deterred. Threats and punishments are necessary to deter and deterrence is a sufficient practical justification for them. Retribution is an independent moral justification. Although penalties can be unwise, repulsive, or inappropriate, and those punished can be pitiable, in a sense the infliction of legal punishment on a guilty person cannot be unjust. By committing the crime, the criminal volunteered to assume the risk of receiving a legal punishment that he could have avoided by not committing the crime. The punishment he suffers is the punishment he voluntarily risked suffering and, therefore, it is no more unjust to him than any other event for which one knowingly volunteers to assume the risk. Thus, the death penalty cannot be unjust to the guilty criminal.

There remain, however, two moral objections. The penalty may be regarded as always excessive as retribution and always morally degrading. To regard the death penalty as always excessive, one must believe that no crime—no matter how heinous—could possibly justify capital punishment. Such a belief can be neither corroborated nor refuted; it is an article of faith.

Alternatively, or concurrently, one may believe that everybody, the murderer no less than the victim, has an imprescriptible (natural?) right to life. The law therefore should not deprive anyone of life. I share Jeremy Bentham's view that any such "natural and imprescriptible rights" are "nonsense upon stilts."

Justice Brennan has insisted that the death penalty is "uncivilized," "inhuman," inconsistent with "human dignity" and with "the sanctity of life," that it "treats members of the human race as nonhumans, as objects to be toyed with and discarded," that it is "uniquely degrading to human dignity" and "by its very nature, [involves] a denial of the executed person's humanity." Justice Brennan does not say why he thinks execution "uncivilized." Hitherto most civilizations have had the death penalty, although it has been discarded in Western Europe, where it is currently unfashionable probably because of its abuse by totalitarian regimes.

By "degrading," Justice Brennan seems to mean that execution degrades the executed convicts. Yet philosophers, such as Immanuel Kant and G. F. W. Hegel, have insisted that, when deserved, execution, far from degrading the executed convict, affirms his humanity by affirming his rationality and his responsibility for his actions. They thought that execution, when deserved, is required for the sake of the convict's dignity. (Does not life imprisonment violate human dignity more than execution, by keeping alive a prisoner deprived of all autonomy?)

Common sense indicates that it cannot be death—or common fate—that is inhuman. Therefore, Justice Brennan must mean that death degrades when it comes not as a natural or accidental event, but as a deliberate social imposition. The murderer learns through his punishment that his fellow men have found him unworthy of living; that because he has murdered, he is being expelled from the community of the living. This degradation is self-inflicted. By murdering, the murderer has so dehumanized himself that he cannot remain among the living. The social recognition of his self-degradation is the punitive essence of execution. To believe, as Justice Brennan appears to, that the degradation is inflicted by the execution reverses the direction of causality.

Execution of those who have committed heinous murders may deter only one murder per year. If it does, it seems quite warranted. It is also the only fitting retribution for murder I can think of.

NOTES

1. Death row as a semipermanent residence is cruel, because convicts are denied the normal amenities of prison life. Thus, unless death row residents are integrated into the prison population, the continuing accumulation of convicts on death row should lead us to accelerate either the rate of executions or the rate of commutations. I find little objection to integration.

2. The ideal of equality, unlike the ideal of retributive justice (which can be approximated separately in each instance), is clearly unattainable unless all guilty persons are apprehended, and thereafter tried, convicted and sentenced by the same court, at the same time. Unequal justice is the best we can do; it is still better than the injustice, equal or unequal, which occurs if, for the sake of equality, we deliberately allow some who could be punished to escape.

3. If executions were shown to increase the murder rate in the long run, I would favor abolition. Sparing the innocent victims who would be spared, *ex hypothesi*, by the nonexecution of murderers would be more important to me than the execution, however just, of murderers. But although there is a lively discussion of the subject, no serious evidence exists to support the hypothesis that executions produce a higher murder rate. Cf. Phillips, *The Deterrent Effect of Capital Punishment: New Evidence on an Old Controversy*, 86 AM. J. Soc. 139 (1980) (arguing that murder rates drop immediately after executions of criminals).

4. Thus restitution (a civil liability) cannot satisfy the punitive purpose of penal sanctions, whether the purpose be retributive or deterrent.

5. Some abolitionists challenge: if the death penalty is just and serves as a deterrent, why not televise executions? The answer is simple. The death even of a murderer, however well-deserved,

should not serve as public entertainment. It so served in earlier centuries. But in this respect our sensibility has changed for the better, I believe. Further, television unavoidably would trivialize executions, wedged in, as they would be, between game shows, situation comedies and the like. Finally, because televised executions would focus on the physical aspects of the punishment, rather than the nature of the crime and the suffering of the victim, a televised execution would present the murderer as the victim of the state. Far from communicating the moral significance of the execution, television would shift the focus to the pitiable fear of the murderer. We no longer place in cages those sentenced to imprisonment to expose them to public view. Why should we so expose those sentenced to execution?

POSTSCRIPT

Is Capital Punishment Bad Policy?

One of the most striking elements about the issue of capital punishment is that most of the public, the politicians, and even many criminological scholars seem not to be fazed by empirical evidence. Each side ritualistically marshalls empirical evidence to support its respective position. Opponents of capital punishment often draw from Thorsten Sellin's classic study *The Penalty of Death* (Sage Publications) to "prove" that the number of capital offenses is no lower in states that have the death penalty as compared to states that have abolished executions.

In the 1992 presidential election, both George Bush and Bill Clinton indicated support for the death penalty. In fact, most political candidates seem to support capital punishment nowadays. Supporters of capital punishment draw from numerous studies, including I. Ehrlich's "The Deterrent Effect of Capital Punishment," *American Economic Review* (vol. 65, 1975), pp. 397–417, and his "Capital Punishment and Deterrence: Some Further Thoughts and Additional Evidence," *Journal of Political Economy* (vol. 85, 1977), pp. 741–788. They also draw from W. Berns's *For Capital Punishment: Crime and the Morality of the Death Penalty* (Basic Books, 1979).

Generally, the empirical research indicates that the death penalty cannot conclusively be proven to deter others from committing homicides and other serious crimes. Entire scientific commissions have been charged with the responsibility of determining the deterrent effects of the death penalty (for example, the National Academy of Sciences in 1975). The gist of their conclusions was that the value of the death penalty as a deterrent "is not a settled matter."

As is typical with most aspects of human behavior, including crime and crime control, the issue is filled with much irony, paradox, and contradiction. First, clashing views over capital punishment rely largely on emotion. The public's attitudes, politicians' attitudes, and even scholarly attitudes are frequently shaped more by sentiment and preconceived notions than by rational discourse. As F. Zimring and G. Hawkins indicate in *Capital Punishment and the American Agenda* (Cambridge University Press, 1986), very few scholars have ever changed their opinions about capital punishment.

For a discussion of the controversy of executing juveniles, see "Execution at an Early Age: Should Young Killers Face the Death Penalty?" *Newsweek* (January 13, 1986) and "Should Teenagers Be Executed?" by C. Whitaker, *Ebony* (March 1988).

As we rapidly approach the twenty-first century, capital punishment should be a dead issue. Yet it is still with us and may continue into the next century.

For dissenting views, see "The Death Penalty Dinosaur," by R. C. Dieter, *Commonweal* (January 15, 1988); "A Court Divided: The Death Penalty," by P. Reidinger, *ABA Journal* (January 1, 1987); "Public Support for the Death Penalty: Retribution as Just Deserts or Retribution as Revenge?" by J. O. Finckenauer, *Justice Quarterly* (vol. 5, no. 1, 1988); *Challenging Capital Punishment: Legal and Social Scientific Approaches* edited by K. Haas and J. Inciardi (Sage Publications, 1988); and "The Symbolic Death of Willie Darden," *U.S. News & World Report* (March 28, 1988). Also see H. A. Bedau's *Death Is Different* (Northeast University Press, 1987); *When the State Kills* (Amnesty International USA, 1989); and *Facing the Death Penalty* edited by M. L. Radelet (Temple University Press, 1989).

A remarkable work that almost puts you into the death chamber and is the best description of the bureaucratization if not the trivialization of executions is R. Johnson's *Death Watch: A Study of the Modern Execution Process* (American Correctional Association, 1990). Two books of interest are *The Death Penalty in America: Current Research* edited by R. M. Bohm (Anderson, 1991) and R. Paternoster's *Capital Punishment in America* (Lexington Books, 1992). Both Bohm and Paternoster have written extensively on capital punishment.

A more recent book, written by a Catholic nun who counsels death row inmates, is H. Prejean's *Dead Man Walking: Eyewitness Account of the Death Penalty* (Random House, 1993). Two provocative works that take the death penalty to task are K. Miller, *Executing the Mentally Ill* (Sage Publications, 1993) and M. Radelet et al., *In Spite of Innocence: Erroneous Convictions in Capital Cases* (Northeastern University Press, 1993).

Two studies of the deterrence issue are "Capital Punishment and the Deterrence of Violent Crime in Comparable Countries," by D. Cheatwood, *Criminal Justice Review* (August 1993) and "Deterrence or Brutalization?" by J. Cochran et al., *Criminology* (February 1994). For a survey of the attitudes toward capital punishment among politicians, see M. Sandys and E. McGarrell, "Attitudes Toward Capital Punishment Among Indiana Legislators," *Justice Quarterly* (December 1994). A popular media account of a death penalty sentence given to a mentally impaired individual is "Untrue Confessions," by J. Smolowe, *Time* (May 22, 1995). An interesting comparison of the effects of publicized executions on whites and blacks is "The Impact of Publicized Executions on Homicide," by S. Stack, *Criminal Justice and Behavior* (June 1995). The *Bureau of Justice Statistics Bulletin* routinely updates death penalty statistics. For an outstanding description of death row, see Von Drehle's *Among the Lowest of the Dead: The Culture of Death Row* (Times Books, 1995).

PART 4

Future Trends

In the field of criminal justice, forecasting is an important device that entails extrapolating from present trends and projecting solutions to organizational problems. Criminologists supply the needed data, including the rates, frequencies, and distributions of crime. Yet even if we indeed know who commits what crimes, where, when, how, and why with any real certainty, there is no guarantee that this knowledge will hold true a few years from now. Moreover, as debatable as current policy proposals are, what we should do in the future is even more so. Drugs and gun control have been the subject of controversy for generations now, and they will more than likely be part of crime debates into the twenty-first century. By contrast, while both euthanasia and variants of community policing have been around for centuries, they have been peripheral to criminological and legal dialogue until quite recently. Finally, some 50 years after the end of the Holocaust and 20 years after the victories of the civil rights movement, widespread violations of human rights have again become manifest at century's end. Meanwhile, the past becomes the future as we once again debate as a society the appropriate response to deviants.

- Should Drugs Be Legalized?

- Will Gun Control Reduce Crime?

- Should Euthanasia Be a Crime?

- Will Community Policing Be the Answer to Crime Control?

- Are Human Rights Basic to Justice?

- Should We Get Even Tougher on Criminals?

ISSUE 14

Should Drugs Be Legalized?

YES: Arnold S. Trebach, from "For Legalization of Drugs," in Arnold S. Trebach and James A. Inciardi, *Legalize It? Debating American Drug Policy* (American University Press, 1993)

NO: James A. Inciardi, from "Against Legalization of Drugs," in Arnold S. Trebach and James A. Inciardi, *Legalize It? Debating American Drug Policy* (American University Press, 1993)

ISSUE SUMMARY

YES: Arnold S. Trebach, president of the Drug Policy Foundation in Washington, D.C., has been a persistent critic of U.S. drug policies. He argues for the immediate removal of all legal prohibitions against the use of any drug.

NO: James A. Inciardi, director of the Center for Drug and Alcohol Studies at the University of Delaware, rejects Trebach's thinking and proposal, arguing that laws against drugs must be maintained.

Throughout the twentieth century, America's problems have often been traced to dubious origins that have served primarily as scapegoats. The shifting nature of the American family, the changing behavioral patterns of the young, the broadening of opportunities for blacks, women, and other minority groups, and increasing political disenchantment—which were all partially the result of increasing modernization, an unpopular war, and other specific structural precipitants—were variously blamed on the movie industry, comic books, bolshevism, gambling, alcohol, organized crime, and, now and then, the devil himself. Currently, the continued concern with the changing nature of the American family, the increasing fear of crime, and the widening generation gap are linked with drug use. If only we could get the dealers off the streets or at least get the kids to say no to drugs, then we could restore our family system. If only we could arrest everyone who takes drugs, then we could eliminate crime, since it is drugs that cause most people to commit crimes. If only the students in our junior high schools, high schools, and colleges were not taking drugs, then they would not only do better on their academic achievement scores but once again love and obey their parents.

The entire criminal justice system, it seems, is marshalled to participate in the war on drugs. According to the *BJS Bulletin* (April 1995), not only have jail and prison populations escalated in the past 15 years, but the greatest increase in jail populations is a result of drug arrests (between 1983 and

1989, the number of drug arrests increased from 20,800 to 91,000!). Currently, over one-quarter of jail inmates are drug violators. Most were not dealers or involved in violent crimes. About one-third of prison populations since 1990 consists of those convicted of drug offenses. A significant percentage of the prison population's growth is a result of drug crackdowns.

Exactly what laws have been passed in the twentieth century to stem drug manufacturing, distribution, and consumption? Although there were a few local regulations in the late 1800s that prohibited the sale of over-the-counter drugs containing narcotics, it was not until 1906 that Congress passed the Pure Food and Drug Act, which was concerned primarily with the availability of patent medicines and with prohibiting the sale of dangerous drugs.

The Harris Act passed in 1914 and the Volstead Act (prohibiting alcohol) passed in 1919 were even broader than the Pure Food and Drug Act. Many use this as a benchmark for the first antidrug campaign in the United States. In 1937 the Marijuana Tax Act was passed, and during the 1950s stiffer penalties were legislated for the possession and sale of drugs. However, it was not until 1970, with the passage of the Controlled Substances Act (Title II of the Comprehensive Drug Abuse and Control Act), that efforts were made to standardize the many existing local and state drug laws.

In June 1986, $1.7 billion was added to the budget by Congress to fight drugs. Currently over $9 billion per year is spent on drug control. Toward the end of 1988, Congress authorized the death penalty for murders related to drug deals. It also called for considerably stiffer penalties for the manufacture, distribution, and use of illegal drugs. Between March and June of 1988, during the height of "zero tolerance," or active government interdiction, over 1,500 boats, bikes, and cars were seized. At the San Diego–Mexican border alone, over 20 drivers per week were arrested for illegal possession.

In spite of these efforts, 25 million Americans occasionally or regularly use drugs, according to some estimates. And the U.S. Justice Department estimates that 70 percent of all criminals arrested for serious offenses are regular drug users. Yet the link between crimes and drug use is problematic—there is no firm proof that all serious offenders, or even the majority, committed their crimes *because* of drugs.

Should drug dealers and users be locked up? How often has the regulation of personal conduct "worked" in America? After users are arrested, should they be imprisoned to punish them or should they receive treatment? Is the use of hard-core drugs really a "victimless" crime? Can society afford to "say yes" to drug use? These and other highly emotional issues are addressed by Arnold S. Trebach, who believes that the time for drug decriminalization has come, and by James A. Inciardi, who maintains that drugs are extremely harmful and dangerous.

YES

Arnold S. Trebach

FOR LEGALIZATION OF DRUGS

ON BECOMING RADICALIZED

This is an argument for the full legalization of currently illegal drugs for sale to adults within regulations similar to those for alcohol. Only in recent years have I become an advocate of such a radical position. . . .

In the end, the case for radical change in the matter of drugs will stand or fall on the extent to which the people of this country and of other civilized nations come to believe that drug prohibition and the drug war are simply inconsistent with the moral heart of a democratic society.

. . . During recent months, . . . I have come to believe that the urban situation in America is so desperate as to demand the nearly immediate dismantling of drug prohibition.

The change in my thinking occurred because of the excesses of the American war on drugs, some of which I saw close up in my travels throughout this country in the course of research. I observed that in the relentless and impossible pursuit of a "drug-free society," the drug warriors were filling the jails and prisons with petty drug offenders, invading personal privacy and violating constitutional rights, provoking hatred of racial minorities, wasting billions of dollars, facilitating violent drug traffickers and police corruption, and diverting resources and attention from other pressing social problems. This endless holy war has had no demonstrable effect on drug abuse but has appeared to spur record-level American crime and violence to even greater heights.

. . . As the reform movement gained in power and prestige, . . . the guardians of prohibition and of the drug war brought forth a familiar myth in its defense. They claimed that the current system was from its inception carefully planned, inherently compassionate, and ultimately rational. Change the drug laws, ease up on enforcement even a little bit, and we will become a nation of drugged zombies, they declared. Besides, some added, this country had tried legalization earlier in its history and found it unworkable.

This was followed by the charge that proponents of change were utterly irresponsible in that they had never once laid out concrete, rationally planned

From Arnold S. Trebach, "For Legalization of Drugs," in Arnold S. Trebach and James A. Inciardi, *Legalize It? Debating American Drug Policy* (American University Press, 1993). Copyright © 1993 by American University Press. Reprinted by permission. Notes and references omitted.

proposals for reform. These charges were put forth by a variety of leading authorities in several ingenious ways....

James Inciardi has been one of the most prominent scholarly proponents of the Bennett-Rangel approach to dealing with drug policy critics. In his book, *The War on Drugs* (1986), Inciardi made scathing attacks on those experts who disagreed with accepted American drug-control doctrine. For example, he wrote that Thomas Szasz's classic dissenting book, *Ceremonial Chemistry*, suffered from "numerous errors of fact, poor scholarship, and his caustic abuse of the English language" (Inciardi 1986, 203). After treating most of the drug dissenters of the past forty years, including this writer, to such assaults, Inciardi then issued this broadside:

> Although one runs the risk of being ignored, or being called "fascist" or "arch-conservative" by atavistic liberal thinkers, *it would appear that contemporary American drug-control policies, with some very needed additions and changes, would be the most appropriate approach.*

... Inciardi is wrong... in this personal attack. The power of the drug policy reform movement—not all of whose members favor complete legalization, as do I— is in the breadth of its support across all walks of life and professions. Included as supporters of the Drug Policy Foundation, for example, are many experts who have seen the horrors of drug abuse from the trenches, including doctors, psychiatrists, nurses, pharmacologists, and other treatment specialists. Some of our strongest supporters recently have been those doctors involved in the treatment of AIDS, who are joining the foundation in fighting the government ban on marijuana in medicine. That ban is viewed as a major weapon in the war on drugs, but it is contributing to the public health disaster of the AIDS epidemic.

Other supporters of reform who have seen the misery of addiction close up are priests, ministers, and rabbis. Through the organizational efforts of the Reverend Robert Sirico, a Roman Catholic priest, they have formed the Religious Coalition for a Moral Drug Policy, which advocates full legalization of drugs. The current president is another Roman Catholic priest, the Reverend Joseph Ganssle, who specializes in addiction counseling and is actively involved in Narcotics Anonymous. Contrary to what Inciardi says, these treatment experts and religious counselors view the war on drugs as harming the very people it is supposed to help the most, the addicts and the abusers —and they have very direct knowledge of that harm....

THE CASE FOR A SOVIET SOLUTION

The Illusory Line Between Legal and Illegal Drugs

It was a surprise to me and I suspect it will be to many people that there is no scientific basis for the line between legal and illegal drugs. All of the popular drugs in use today—from alcohol to heroin to marijuana to cocaine to crack to caffeine— pose threats to many users. Yet, all of them, including crack, are used without material harm by the great majority of users.

Dr. Andrew Weil summarized the little-known reality of the drug- human condition best when he observed: *"Any drug can be used successfully, no matter how bad its reputation, and any drug can be abused, no matter how accepted it is.*

There are no good or bad drugs; there are only good and bad relationships with drugs" (Weil 1983, 27; italics in original). I recognize that this view strikes many good people as an outrage, but it is irrefutably true. Drugs are not like environmental problems such as acid rain or radioactivity, where everyone is at risk merely because the condition exists. Drugs only affect people in the context of how an individual uses them, and once that human element is brought into the equation, all our well-documented foibles as a species come into play....

Prohibition, Murders, and the American Gulag

Crime and violence are inextricably intertwined with drug prohibition. During periods when alcohol or drug prohibition laws are vigorously enforced, the number of homicides and prisoners rises dramatically....

The Drug Exception to the Constitution

The essential nature of U.S. Drug enforcement has an alien tinge to it, more suited to an intrusive totalitarian society than to the democratic, capitalist culture that evolved uniquely here in the United States. That is because drug taking is for the most part a private, consensual matter. Like sexual activity, it normally takes place in the privacy of the home and involves consenting adults, although youths are sometimes involved. It follows that drug enforcement must break into this veil of privacy and intrude in the most intimate aspects of the lives of citizens, using the same tactics as communist officials once brought to bear against dissenters.

Without fully realizing the extent to which we have surrendered our rights, I suspect, we Americans have come to accept deeply intrusive practices as the norm because our leaders tell us that we all must give up some freedoms to save our people, especially our children, from the menace of drugs. Americans by the millions are now being told to urinate in front of strangers upon pain of not being hired or of losing their only means of livelihood. In addition to this increased power given to employers, with or without formal legal endorsement, the powers of police officials have been formally increased by judicial opinions, wherein the judges seem to have been deeply affected by drug war myths and rhetoric....

Huge Costs, Little Return

Drug war spending is hardly an investment in the future.... [T]he federal government [planned] to spend approximately $12.7 billion in fiscal 1993 on the drug war, much of which [would] simply be consumed on enforcement attempts and prison construction....

State and local governments can fairly be said to spend about the same amount on the drug war as the federal government from year to year, especially as the war has moved up on the national agenda. That gives a total of $20 to $26 billion a year in spending of taxpayers' dollars that virtually no one questions, much as practically no one in the recent past could find a voice to criticize the fattened defense budgets of the Cold War....

The Drug War Diverts Attention from Real Social Problems

The greatest current dangers to our society are not drugs, no matter what form they are in, but rather racial hatred, criminal violence, and AIDS. The war on drugs adds to every one of these major dangers and builds them up to the level of a searing catastrophe....

We Americans have almost always lived under the threat that racial hatred would tear us asunder. Today that threat seems worse than ever. For a whole variety of reasons—including especially poverty, discrimination, the collapse of too many black families, the workings of an economy that excludes too many blacks, and the perverse effects of drug enforcement on minority communities—blacks are involved in crime all out of proportion to their representation in the population. To even make such a statement often results in a charge, from both blacks and whites, of racism. Yet unless the problem is acknowledged, it can never be solved. The continued existence of horrendous levels of black crime perpetuates both the high toll of black victims and the fears of too many whites of even being in proximity to blacks whether on the job, in social situations, or in housing....

Bruce Alexander also discredited the standard disease-crime model of addiction that underlies the war on drugs. Alexander theorized that addiction may involve a "devotion to" or "dependence on" a wide variety of activates and substances, ranging from exercise to love to drugs. In some cases that devotion or dependence may be positive and in some cases negative in terms of the lifestyle of the addicted person. He observed that the most powerful justification for the war on drugs is the widely shared view that drugs always cause negative addiction in horrendous proportions....

Alexander could find no evidence to support this view and offered in its place the theory that for many people negative addiction to drugs

is a way people adapt to serious problems if they can find no better solution. According to this "adaptive model," the immediate cause of negative addiction is not a drug but a situation so dire that addiction is the most adaptive response a person can muster. From this viewpoint, no disease or criminality is necessarily involved. The adaptive model lends little support for the War on Drugs (Alexander 1990, 255).

Yet, the war on drugs continues to be seen as the most prominent method of dealing with urban decay, crime, and violence. It seems that we risk the danger that our leaders, supported by many scholars, will forever be blind to the reality that we can never deal with any of our worst social problems so long as drug prohibition and the war on drugs perversely are seen as major cures, rather than major aggravating causes, of those same problems....

Legal Drugs Did Not Produce Significant Crime

National drug prohibition has been in effect in the United States for over 75 years....

The writings of many conventional scholars and the stories of journalists in the popular press would lead one to believe that social chaos inevitably results when masses of people have easy access to powerful drugs. We have already seen that there is no evidence of any major type of social disruption in the known record from the turn of the century. In the following review of new data, which I and my research assistants gathered in 1992, it becomes clear that crime rates before prohibition were a small fraction of what they are today. A comparison of statistics from a century ago and today shows that crime, the most troubling side effect of drugs in our society, was not at such outrageous levels before drug prohibition as to necessitate tight controls on drugs. Free availability of narcotics, cocaine, and other substances to adults did not lead to substantial crime....

THE REPEAL OF DRUG PROHIBITION

Basic Principles of Repeal and Legalization

It follows that any sensible plan for legalization will work so long as it adheres to certain basic principles of realism about the manner in which people actually relate to drugs....

- We must stop thinking about drugs and drug users in terms of war and hate.... In the wake of the riots of 1992 and revolutionary discontent of the American public over the inability of the government to cope with harshly divisive social problems, the need for drugpeace is more vital than ever. We cannot have peace in our cities in the midst of the constant attacks and counterattacks of a drug war.

- Multitudes of people, most of them perfectly decent and respectable human beings, like drugs. Any program that demands, upon threat of criminal punishment, that these people always repress those desires so as to create a drug-free society is unrealistic and harmful. It is the equivalent of attempting to repress the natural and diverse sexual appetites of our people.... Some way must be found to allow those so inclined to obtain drugs within a set of reasonable rules. Repression of natural drives inevitably creates worse forms of the so-called vice.

- The criminal law must not be allowed to occupy the center of the new drug-control system. Police and prison keepers should not be the primary agents for controlling the admittedly bad effects of many drugs. We should attempt to put parents, educators, clergy, and cultural leaders in their place. The criminal law should operate only at the edges of the system....

- "Harm reduction" should be the overarching theme of all new drug laws and drug-control policies.... [W]e must bend our energy and ingenuity to convincing people that they must make careful choices and that in a free society they may choose no drugs at all (as most will), comparatively harmless ways of using drugs, or very destructive methods. Whatever their choices, they must be assured that they will not be treated as enemies of the state and that help will be available if they encounter trouble.

- Every civilized (meaning, in this context, nonforceful) attempt should be made to counteract any move toward more potent forms of drugs such as has taken place recently in the illicit drug market.... It is to be expected that sellers of the newly legal drugs will want to offer a wide variety of less concentrated and more natural products. They should be encouraged to do so....

- The pursuit of highs and altered states of consciousness, far from being destructive as is widely assumed, is natural and good for individuals and society. The best highs are very probably those brought about without the help of chemicals—through, for example, religion, meditation, cheering on a favorite sports team, exercise, and making love. This is because natural highs avoid the risks of drugs and demonstrate to people the powerful truth that each individual has the inherent ability to achieve internal happiness. Yet, the great majority of people who use drugs, legal or illegal, to achieve highs do so without causing observable harm to themselves or others. Only a small minority of opium, heroin, cocaine, crack, and marijuana users get into trouble with the drugs (and with other elements of their lives) and come to public attention. Sadly, the universe of drug users is defined in the public mind by that tiny percentage who draw so much attention to themselves and their troubles.

• Education and public relations campaigns should stress these principles of drug realism and harm reduction. While the Partnership for a Drug-Free America may well continue its distorted television commercials meant to scare people away from drugs (it's a free country, after all), major efforts should be made also to have on the air spot commercials and informative programs that express the different values espoused herein. The same should be true of public education. Instead of the current biased, one-sided drug-war curriculum now offered in most schools, American students should be presented with the rich array of conflicting ideas about drugs that is now available in any decent library or video center.

• As we design new drug-control systems, we should remember our revolutionary democratic roots. For centuries, the great mass of people were considered inferior clods, certainly incapable of choosing rulers, who were instead anointed by God and the accident of royal blood. In a shocking reversal of these established, hallowed truths, the Declaration of Independence declared that the people had a natural right—based upon natural law which was superior to written law—both to throw out their divinely appointed rulers by force of arms if necessary and also to choose all future rulers. If we can put faith in the people to make the awesome choice of who will rule their nation, it seems an easy step now to ask those rulers to relinquish control once again over what substances people may choose to put in their own bodies. In the end, that is all that is involved here: returning the power of individual choice to the citizens of a supposedly free country over a very intimate matter.

NO

James A. Inciardi

AGAINST LEGALIZATION OF DRUGS

THE PRO-LEGALIZATION ISSUES AND CONTENDERS

The drug legalization debate emerged in both generic and specific configurations. In its most generic adaptation, it went something like this. First, the drug laws have created evils far worse than the drugs themselves—corruption, violence, street crime, and disrespect for the law. Second, legislation passed to control drugs has failed to reduce demand. Third, you should not prohibit that which a major segment of the population is committed to doing; that is, you simply cannot arrest, prosecute, and punish such large numbers of people, particularly in a democracy. And specifically in this behalf, in a liberal democracy the government must not interfere with personal behavior if liberty is to be maintained....

Many of the arguments were insightful and important for the evolution and growth of an informed drug policy, while others were droll, naive, ludicrous, gormless [stupid], and potentially destructive.

Legalization's Troupers and Thespians
It would appear that by the onset of the 1980s, the drug legalization debate had little in its formative years that could be built upon. If anything, its progenitors had given the debate an aura of foolishness, absurdity, and extremism. But rationality and scholarship quickly came to the forefront.

Arnold S. Trebach and Harm Reduction
Perhaps most respected in the field of drug-policy reform is Arnold S. Trebach....

Briefly, his proposals for drug-policy are the following:

1. *Reverse drug-policy funding priorities....*

2. *Curtail AIDS: Make clean needles available to intravenous drug addicts....*

3. *Develop a plan for drug treatment on demand, allow Medicaid to pay for the poor, and expand the variety of treatment options available....*

4. *Stop prosecutions of pregnant drug users....*

5. *Make medical marijuana available to the seriously ill....*

From James A. Inciardi, "Against Legalization of Drugs," in Arnold S. Trebach and James A. Inciardi, *Legalize It? Debating American Drug Policy* (American University Press, 1993). Copyright © 1993 by American University Press. Reprinted by permission. Notes and references omitted.

6. Appoint a commission to seriously examine alternatives to prohibition....

Although my objections and alternatives are discussed later, let me just say that Trebach has experienced a "conversion" of sorts in recent years. There was a time when he denied endorsing the legalization of drugs. In the closing pages of his book, *The Great Drug War*, he stated:

> Up to now in this book, I have not argued that we should legalize *all* drugs nor that we should give heroin addicts *all* the heroin they want. ... *Allow me to state once again that I have never taken that position. Never. And I do not now* (Trebach 1987, 368, emphasis added).

But then in 1989, he recanted:

> ... I am now convinced that our society would be safer and healthier if all of the illegal drugs were fully removed from the control of the criminal law tomorrow morning at the start of business....

The Debate's Supporting Cast and Bit Players

An aspect of the drug-policy debates of the second half of the 1980s was a forum awash with self-defined experts from many walks of life.

The Bit Players The "bit players" were the many who had a lot to say on the debate, but from what I feel were not particularly informed positions. They wrote books, or they published papers, but they remained on the sidelines because either no one took them seriously, their work was carelessly done, or their arguments were just not persuasive....

A rather pathetically hatched entry to the debate was Richard Lawrence Miller's book, *The Case for Legalizing Drugs* (1991).... Perhaps most misleading in the book is the list of "benefits" of using illicit drugs. I'll cite but one example to provide a glimpse of the author's approach:

> Heroin can calm rowdy teenagers—reducing aggression, sexual drive, fertility, and teen pregnancy—helping adolescents through that time of life (Miller 1991, 153).

I have a teenage daughter, so I guess I'll have to remember that if she ever gets rowdy. Enough!

Cameos and Comic Relief After the great drug debate reached the United States House of Representatives, the weekly news magazines, television networks, and such well-known personages as conservative pundit William F. Buckley, Jr., Nobel laureate economist Milton Friedman, former Secretary of State George P. Shultz, journalist Anthony Lewis, *Harper's* editor Lewis H. Lapham, and even Washington, D. C., Mayor Marion Barry came forward to endorse legalization. The "legalizers" viewed the support of these notables as a legitimation of their argument, but all had entered the debate from disturbingly uninformed positions. With the exception of Marion Barry, and I say this facetiously, none had any first-hand experience with the issues....

ARGUING AGAINST LEGALIZATION

... While there are numerous arguments *for* legalization, there are likely an equal or greater number *against*.

Some Public Health Considerations

Tomorrow, like every other average day in the United States, about 11,449.3 babies will be born, 90 acres of pizza will be ordered, almost 600,000 M&M candies will be eaten, and some 95 holes-in-one will be claimed. At the same time, 171 million bottles of beer will be consumed, and almost 1.5 billion cigarettes will be smoked (Ruth 1992). In 1965, the annual death toll from smoking-related diseases was estimated at 188,000. By the close of the 1980s that figure had more than doubled, to 434,000, and it is expected to increase throughout the 1990s (Centers for Disease Control 1990, 1991b). And these figures do not include the almost 40,000 nonsmokers who die each year from ailments associated with the inhalation of passive smoke.

... [I]t is estimated that there are 10.5 million alcoholics in the United States, and that a total of 73 million adults have been touched by alcoholism (*Alcoholism and Drug Abuse Weekly*, 9 October 1991, 1). Each year there are some 45,000 alcohol- related traffic fatalities in the United States (Centers for Disease Control 1991a), and thousands of women who drink during pregnancy bear children with irreversible alcohol-related defects (Steinmetz 1992). Alcohol use in the past year was reported by 54 percent of the nation's eighth graders, 72 percent of tenth graders, and 78 percent of twelfth graders, and almost a third of high school seniors in 1991 reported "binge drinking." ... [T]he cost of alcohol abuse in the United States for 1990 has been estimated at $136.31 billion (*Substance Abuse Report*, 15 June 1991, 3).

Sophism, Legalization, and Illicit Drug Use   Keep the above data in mind, and consider that they relate to only two of the *legal* drugs. Now for some reason, numerous members of the pro-legalization lobby argue that if drugs were to be legalized, usage would likely not increase very much, if at all. The reasons, they state, are that "drugs are everywhere," and that everyone who wants to use them already does. But the data beg to differ. For example,... 56 percent of high school seniors in 1991 had never used an illicit drug in their lifetimes, and 73 percent had never used an illicit drug other than marijuana in their lifetimes.... [T]he absolute numbers in these age cohorts who have never even *tried* any illicit drugs are in the tens of millions. And most significantly for the argument that "drugs are everywhere," half of all high school students do not feel that drugs are easy to obtain.

Going further,... most people in the general population do not use drugs. Granted, these data are limited to the "general population," which excludes such hard-to-reach populations as members of deviant and exotic subcultures, the homeless, and others living "on the streets," and particularly those in which drug use rates are highest. However, the data do document that the overwhelming majority of Americans do not use illicit drugs. This suggests two things: that the drug prohibitions may be working quite well; and that there is a large population who might, and I emphasize might, use drugs if they were legal and readily available....

An interesting variety of sophist reasoning pervades segments of the pro-legalization thesis. It is argued over and over that drugs should be legalized because they don't really do that much harm.... The legalizers use... data to demonstrate that not too many people actually have adverse encounters with heroin, cocaine, and other illicit drugs, as compared with the hundreds of thousands of deaths each year linked to alcohol and tobacco use.... But interestingly, it is never stated that proportionately few people actually use illicit drugs, and that the segment of the population "at risk" for overdose or other physical complications from illegal drug use is but an insignificant fraction of that at risk for disease and death from alcohol and tobacco use.

The Problems With Illegal Drugs Considerable evidence exists to suggest that the legalization of drugs could create behavioral and public health problems that would far outweigh the current consequences of drug prohibition. There are some excellent reasons why marijuana, cocaine, heroin, and other drugs are now controlled, and why they ought to remain so....

Marijuana. There is considerable misinformation about marijuana. To the millions of adolescents and young adults who were introduced to the drug during the social revolution of the 1960s and early 1970s, marijuana was a harmless herb of ecstasy. As the "new social drug" and a "natural organic product," it was deemed to be far less harmful than either alcohol or tobacco (see Grinspoon 1971; Smith 1970; Sloman 1979). More recent research suggests, however, that marijuana smoking is a practice that combines the hazardous features of both tobacco and alcohol with a number of pitfalls of its own. Moreover, there are many disturbing questions about marijuana's effect on the vital systems of the body, on the brain and mind, on immunity and resistance, and on sex and reproduction (Jones and Lovinger 1985).

One of the more serious difficulties with marijuana use relates to lung damage.... Researchers at the University of California at Los Angeles reported... in 1988 that the respiratory burden in smoke particulates and absorption of carbon monoxide from smoking just one marijuana "joint" is some *four times greater* than from smoking a single tobacco cigarette.... [M]arijuana deposits four times more tar in the throat and lungs and increases carbon monoxide levels in the blood fourfold to fivefold.

... [A]side from the health consequences of marijuana use, recent research on the behavioral aspects of the drug suggests that it severely affects the social perceptions of heavy users. Findings from the Center for Psychological Studies in New York City, for example, report that adults who smoked marijuana daily believed the drug helped them to function better—improving their self- awareness and relationships with others (Hendin et al. 1987). In reality, however, marijuana had acted as a "buffer," enabling users to tolerate problems rather than face them and make changes that might increase the quality of their social functioning and satisfaction with life. The study found that the research subjects used marijuana to avoid dealing with their difficulties, and the avoidance inevitably made their problems worse, on the job, at home, and in family and sexual relationships.

... [W]hat has been said about cocaine also applies to crack, and perhaps more so. Crack's low price (as little as $2 per rock in some locales) has made it an attractive drug of abuse for those with limited funds. Its rapid absorption brings on a faster onset of dependence than is typical with other forms of cocaine, resulting in higher rates of addiction, binge use, and psychoses. The consequences include higher levels of cocaine-related violence and all the same manifestations of personal, familial, and occupational neglect that are associated with other forms of drug dependence....

Heroin. A derivative of morphine, heroin is a highly addictive narcotic, and is the drug historically associated with addiction and street crime. Although heroin overdose is not uncommon, unlike alcohol, cocaine, tobacco, and many prescription drugs, the direct physiological damage caused by heroin use tends to be minimal. And it is for this reason that the protagonists of drug legalization include heroin in their arguments. By making heroin readily available to users, they argue, many problems could be sharply reduced if not totally eliminated, including: the crime associated with supporting a heroin habit; the overdoses resulting from unknown levels of heroin purity and potency; the HIV and hepatitis infections brought about by needle-sharing; and the personal, social, and occupational dislocations resulting from the drug-induced criminal lifestyle.

The belief that the legalization of heroin would eliminate crime, overdose, infections, and life dislocations for its users is for the most part delusional. Instead, it is likely that the heroin-use lifestyle would change little for most addicts regardless of the legal status of the drug, an argument supported by ample evidence in the biographies and autobiographies of narcotics addicts, the clinical assessments of heroin addiction, and the drug abuse treatment literature. And to this can be added the many thousands of conversations I have had over the past 30 years with heroin users and members of their families.

The point is this. Heroin is a highly addicting drug. For the addict, it becomes life-consuming: it becomes mother, father, spouse, lover, counselor, and confessor. Because heroin is a short-acting drug, with its effects lasting at best four to six hours, it must be taken regularly and repeatedly. Because there is a more rapid onset when taken intravenously, most heroin users inject the drug. Because heroin has depressant effects, a portion of the user's day is spent in a semi-stupefied state. Collectively, these attributes result in a user more concerned with drug-taking and drug-seeking than health, family, work, relationships, responsibility, or anything else.

The Pursuit of Pleasure and Escape ... [R]esearch by professors Michael D. Newcomb and Peter M. Bentler of the University of California at Los Angeles has documented the long-term behavioral effects of drug use on teenagers (Newcomb and Bentler 1988). Beginning in 1976, a total of 654 Los Angeles County youths were tracked for a period of eight years. Most of these youths were only occasional users of drugs, using drugs and alcohol moderately at social gatherings, whereas upwards of 10 percent were frequent, committed users. The impact of drugs on these frequent users was considerable. As teenagers, drug use tended to intensify the typical adolescent problems with family and school. In addition, drugs contributed to such psychological difficulties as loneliness, bizarre and disorganized thinking, and suicidal thoughts. Moreover, frequent drug users left school earlier, started jobs earlier, and formed families earlier, and as such, they moved into adult roles with the maturity levels of adolescents. The consequences of this pattern included rapid family break-ups, job instability, serious crime, and ineffective personal relationships. In short, frequent drug use prevented the acquisition of the coping mechanisms that are part of maturing; it blocked teenagers' learning of interpersonal skills and general emotional development.

... [A]lthough we have no explicit data on whether the numbers of addicts and associated problems would increase if drugs were legalized, there are reasons to believe that they would, and rather dramatically. First, the number of people who actually use drugs is proportionately small. Second, the great majority of people in the United States have never used illicit drugs, and hence, have never been "at risk" for addiction. Third, because of the drug prohibition, illicit drugs are *not* "everywhere," and as a result, most people have not had the opportunity to even experiment with them. Fourth, alcohol *is* readily available, and the numbers of people who have been touched by alcoholism are in the dozens of millions.

Given this, let's take the argument one step further. There is extensive physiological, neurological, and anthropological evidence to suggest that we are members of a species that has been honed for pleasure. Nearly all people want and enjoy pleasure, and the pursuit of drugs—whether caffeine, nicotine, alcohol, opium, heroin, marijuana, or cocaine —seems to be universal and inescapable. It is found across time and across cultures (and species). The process of evolution has for whatever reasons resulted in a human neurophysiology that responds both vividly and avidly to a variety of common substances. The brain has pleasure centers—receptor sites and cortical cells—that react to "rewarding" dosages of many substances....

If the legalization model were of value, then ... the narcotic would just be there— attracting little attention. There would be minimal use, addiction, and the attendant social and public health problems—as long as the drug's availability was not restricted and legislated against.

... [C]onsider Poland. For generations, Poles have cultivated home-grown poppies for the use of their seeds as flavoring in breads, stews, pretzel sticks, cookies, cakes, and chocolates. During the early 1970s, many Polish farmers began transforming their poppy straw into what has become known as *jam, compote,* or "Polish heroin." Then, many Poles began using heroin, but the practice was for the most part ignored. By the end of the 1970s heroin use in Poland had escalated significantly, but still the situation was ignored. By late 1985, at a time when the number of heroin users was estimated at 600,000 and the number of heroin-dependent persons was fixed at 200,000, the Polish government could no longer ignore what was happening. The number of overdose deaths was mounting, and the range of psychosocial and public health problems associated with heroin use was beginning to affect the structure of the already troubled country. By 1986, feeling that heroin use had gotten out of hand, the Communist government in Poland placed controls on the cultivation of poppy seeds, and the transformation of poppy straw into heroin was outlawed....

Although the events in Poland have not been systematically studied, what is known of the experience suggests that introducing potent intoxicants to a population can have problematic consequences. Moreover, the notion that "availability creates demand" has been found in numerous other parts of the world, particularly with cocaine in the Andean regions of South America (see Inciardi 1992, 222).

The Legacy of Crack Cocaine

The great drug wars in the United States have endured now for generations, although the drug legalization debates have less of a history—on again, off again since the 1930s, with a sudden burst of energy at the close of the 1980s. But as the wars linger on and the debates abide, a coda must be added to both of these politically charged topics. It concerns crack cocaine, a drug that has brought about a level of human suffering heretofore unknown in the American drug scene. The problem with crack is not that it is prohibited, but rather, the fact that it exists at all.... The chemistry and psychopharmacology of crack, combined with the tangle of socioeconomic and psychocultural strains that exist in those communities where the drug is concentrated, warrant some consideration of whether further discussion of its legality or illegality serves any purpose. Focusing on crack as an example, my intent here is to argue that both the "drug wars" and "harm reduction effort" are better served by a shifting away from the drug legalization debate.

Crack Cocaine in the United States

... For the inner cities across America, the introduction of crack couldn't have happened at a worse time. The economic base of the working poor had been shrinking for years, the result of a number of factors, including the loss of many skilled and unskilled jobs to cheaper labor markets, the movement of many businesses to the suburbs and the Sun Belt, and competition from foreign manufacturers. Standards of living, health, and overall quality of life were also in a downward direction, as consequences of suburbanization and the shrinking tax bases of central cities, combined with changing economic policies at the federal level that shifted the responsibility for many social supports to the local and private sectors. Without question, by the early to mid–1980s there was a growing and pervasive climate of hopelessness in ghetto America. And at the same time, as HIV and AIDS began to spread through inner-city populations of injectable drug users and their sex partners and as funding for drug abuse treatment declined, the production of coca and cocaine in South America reached an all-time high, resulting in high-purity cocaine at a low price on the streets of urban America. As I said, crack couldn't have come to the inner city at a worse time....

I've been doing street studies in Miami, Florida, for more years than I care to remember, and during that time I've had many an experience in the shooting galleries, base houses, and open-air drug and prostitution markets that populate the local drug scene. None of these prepared me, however, with what I was to encounter in the crack houses. As part of a federally funded street survey and ethnography of cocaine and crack use, my first trip to a crack house came in 1988. I had gained entrée through a local drug dealer who had been a key informant of mine for almost a decade. He introduced me to the crack house "door man" as someone "straight but OK." After the door man checked us for weapons, my guide proceeded to show me around.

Upon entering a room in the rear of the crack house (what I later learned was called a "freak room"), I observed what appeared to be the forcible gang-rape of an unconscious child. Emaciated, seemingly comatose, and likely no older than 14 years of age, she was lying spread-eagled on a filthy mattress while four men in succession had vaginal intercourse with her. Despite what was happening, I was urged not to interfere. After they had finished and left the room, another man came in, and they engaged in oral sex.

Upon leaving the crack house sometime later, the dealer/informant explained that she was a "house girl"—a person in the employ of the crack house owner. He gave her food, a place to sleep, some cigarettes and cheap wine, and all the crack she wanted in return for her providing sex—any type and amount of sex—to his crack house customers.

That was my first trip to a crack house. During subsequent trips to this and other crack houses, there were other scenes: a woman purchasing crack, with an infant tucked under her arm—so neglected that she had maggots crawling out of her diaper; a man "skin-popping" his toddler with a small dose of heroin, so the child would remain quietly sedated and not interrupt a crack-smoking session; people in various states of excitement and paranoia, crouching in the corners of smoking rooms inhaling from "the devil's dick" (the stem of the crack pipe); arguments, fist fights, stabbings, and shootings over crack, the price of crack, the quantity and quality of crack, and the use and sharing of crack; any manner and variety of sexual activity—by individuals and/or groups, with members of the opposite sex, the same sex, or both, or with animals, in private or public, in exchange for crack. I also saw "drug hounds" and "rock monsters" (some of the "regulars" in a crack house) crawling on their hands and knees, inspecting the floors for slivers of crack that may have dropped; beatings and gang rapes of small-time drug couriers—women, men, girls, and boys—as punishment for "messing up the money"; people in

convulsions and seizures, brought on by crack use, cocaine use, the use of some other drug, or whatever; users of both sexes, so dependent on crack, so desperate for more crack, that they would do anything for another hit, eagerly risking the full array of sexually transmitted diseases, including AIDS; imprisonment and sexual slavery, one of the ultimate results of crack addiction....

Many crack users engage in sexual behaviors with extremely high frequency. However, to suggest that crack turns men into "sex-crazed fiends" and women into "sex-crazed whores," as sensationalized media stories imply, is anything but precise. The situation is far more complex than that.

... Medical authorities generally concede that because of the disinhibiting effects of cocaine, its use among new users does indeed enhance sexual enjoyment and improve sexual functioning, including more intense orgasms (Weiss and Mirin 1987; Grinspoon and Bakalar 1985). These same reports maintain, however, that among long-term addicts, cocaine decreases both sexual desire and performance.

Going further, the crack-sex association involves the need of female crack addicts to pay for their drug. Even this connection has a pharmacological component—crack's rapid onset, extremely short duration of effects, and high addiction liability combine to result in compulsive use and a willingness to obtain the drug through any means.... Prostitution has long been the easiest, most lucrative, and most reliable means for women to finance drug use (Goldstein 1979).

The combined pharmacological and sociocultural effects of crack use can put female users in severe jeopardy. Because crack makes its users ecstatic and yet is so short-acting, it has an extremely high addiction potential. Use rapidly becomes compulsive use. Crack acquisition thus becomes enormously more important than family, work, social responsibility, health, values, modesty, morality, or self-respect....

A benefit of its current criminalization is that since it *is* against the law, it doesn't have widespread availability, so proportionately few people use it.

So where does all of this take us? My point is this. Within the context of reversing the human suffering that crack has helped to exacerbate, what purpose is served by arguing for its legalization? Will legalizing crack make it less available, less attractive, less expensive, less addictive, or less troublesome? Nobody really knows for sure, but I doubt it.

Drugs-Crime Connections

For the better part of this century there has been a concerted belief that addicts commit crimes because they are "enslaved" to drugs, that because of the high prices of heroin, cocaine, and other illicit chemicals on the black market, users are forced to commit crimes in order to support their drug habits. I have often referred to this as the "enslavement theory" of addiction (Inciardi 1986, 147–49; Inciardi 1992, 263–64)....

Research since the middle of the 1970s with active drug users in the streets of New York, Miami, Baltimore, and elsewhere has demonstrated that enslavement theory has little basis in reality, and that the contentions of the legalization proponents in this behalf are mistaken (see Inciardi 1986, 115–43; Johnson et al. 1985; Nurco et al. 1985; Stephens and McBride 1976; McBride and McCoy 1982). All of these studies of the criminal careers of heroin and other drug

users have convincingly documented that while drug use tends to intensify and perpetuate criminal behavior, it usually does not initiate criminal careers. In fact, the evidence suggests that among the majority of street drug users who are involved in crime, their criminal careers were well established prior to the onset of either narcotics or cocaine use....

POSTSCRIPT

... [L]et me reiterate the major points I have been trying to make.

The arguments *for* legalization are seemingly based on the fervent belief that America's prohibitions against marijuana, cocaine, heroin, and other drugs impose far too large a cost in terms of tax dollars, crime, and infringements on civil rights and individual liberties. And while the overall argument may be well-intended and appear quite logical, I find it to be highly questionable in its historical, sociocultural, and empirical underpinnings, and demonstrably naive in its understanding of the negative consequences of a legalized drug market. In counterpoint:

1. Although drug-prohibition policies have been problematic, it would appear that they have managed to keep drugs away from most people. High school and general population surveys indicate that most Americans don't use drugs, have never even tried them, and don't know where to get them. Thus, the numbers "at risk" are dramatically fewer than is the case with the legal drugs. Or stated differently, there is a rather large population who might be at risk if illicit drugs were suddenly available.

2. Marijuana, heroin, cocaine, crack, and the rest are not "benign" substances. Their health consequences, addiction

liability, and/or abuse potential are considerable.

3. There is extensive physiological, neurological, and anthropological evidence to suggest that people are of a species that has been honed for pleasure. Nearly all people want and enjoy pleasure, and the pursuit of drugs—whether caffeine, nicotine, alcohol, opium, heroin, marijuana, or cocaine—seems to be universal and inescapable. It is found across time and across cultures. Moreover, history and research has demonstrated that "availability creates demand."

4. Crack cocaine is especially problematic because of its pharmacological and sociocultural effects. Because crack makes its users ecstatic and yet is so short-acting, it has an extremely high addiction potential. *Use* rapidly becomes *compulsive use*. . . .

5. The research literature on the criminal careers of heroin and other drug users have convincingly documented that while drug use tends to intensify and perpetuate criminal behavior, it usually does not initiate criminal careers.

6. There is also a large body of work suggesting that drug abuse is overdetermined behavior. That is, physical dependence is secondary to the wide range of influences that instigate and regulate drug-taking and drug-seeking. Drug abuse is a disorder of the whole person, affecting some or all areas of functioning. In the vast majority of drug offenders, there are cognitive problems, psychological dysfunction is common, thinking may be unrealistic or disorganized, values are misshapen, and frequently there are deficits in educational and employment skills. As such, drug abuse is a response to a series of social and psychological disturbances. Thus, the goal of treatment should be "habilitation" rather

than "rehabilitation." Whereas *rehabilitation* emphasizes the return to a way of life previously known and perhaps forgotten or rejected, *habilitation* involves the client's initial socialization into a productive and responsible way of life.

7. The focus on the war on drugs can be shifted. I believe that we do indeed need drug enforcement, but it is stressed far too much in current policy. Cut it in half, and shift those funds to criminal justice-based treatment programs.

8. Drug control should remain within the criminal justice sector for some very good reasons. The Drug Use Forecasting (DUF) program clearly demonstrates that the majority of arrestees in urban areas are drug-involved. Moreover, recent research has demonstrated not only that drug abuse treatment works, but also that coerced treatment works best. The key variable most related to success in treatment is "length of stay in treatment," and those who are forced into treatment remain longer than volunteers. By remaining longer, they benefit more. As such, compulsory treatment efforts should be expanded for those who are dependent on drugs and are involved in drug-related crime.

9. Since the "war on drugs" will continue, then a more humane use of the criminal justice system should be structured. This is best done through treatment in lieu of incarceration, and corrections-based treatment for those who do end up in jails and prisons. . . .

American drug policy as it exists today is not likely to change drastically anytime soon. Given that, something needs to be kept in mind. While the First Amendment and academic freedom enable the scholarly community to continue its attack on American drug policy, verbal assault and vilification will serve no significant purpose in effecting change. Calls for the legalization or decriminalization of marijuana, heroin, cocaine, and other illicit drugs accomplish little more than to further isolate the legalizers from the policy-making enterprise.

Finally, there is far too much suffering as the result of drug abuse that is not being addressed. Many things warrant discussion, debate, and prodding on the steps of Capitol Hill and the White House lawn. More drug abuse treatment slots, a repeal of the statutes designed to prosecute pregnant addicts and prohibit needle-exchange programs, the wider use of treatment as an alternative to incarceration—all of these are worthy of vigorous consideration and lobbying. But not legalizing drugs. It is an argument that is going nowhere.

POSTSCRIPT

Should Drugs Be Legalized?

The decriminalization (frequently referred to as the medicalization) of drugs, and the impact on society and the criminal justice system of such a policy, is very much in the forefront of the public's mind. Within criminology, it is a current preoccupation as well. Trebach and Inciardi provide us with a stimulating debate. Yet the issue goes beyond ineffective policies and prisons overflowing with narcotics violators. In addition to the question of real social and individual harm resulting from current or future policies is the issue of racial discrimination. Not only are prisons crowded with drug offenders, but the majority of the offenders are black. In addition, according to James T. Meeks in *National Rainbow Coalition* (August 17, 1995), "Ninety-one percent of those serving a five-year mandatory sentence for possession of crack cocaine are African American, yet 55% of all crack cocaine users are White." He also points out that no nonblack has been convicted of a crack cocaine offense in federal courts serving southern California. Moreover, no whites have even been prosecuted for a crack offense in federal courts in 17 states.

Clearly, even if one reflects a conservative response to these statistics (i.e., "Well, we simply have to arrest more whites along with the minorities"), it does seem that drugs, crime, and race are intricately intertwined. To understand the current scene in the United States, criminologists, criminal justice researchers, and policy formulators may have no choice but to take both drugs and race into account.

The literature on drug policies, drug control, and drug treatment has become massive. An interesting analysis of the political framing and social construction of drug policies is W. Elwood's *Rhetoric in the War on Drugs* (Praeger, 1994). A classic work that presents a variety of perspectives on this issue is *The Search for Rational Drug Control* by F. Zimring and G. Hawkins, (Cambridge University Press, 1995). For two contrasting interpretations of drugs and alcohol and the crime connection, see C. Shine and M. Mauer, *Does the Punishment Fit the Crime? Drug Users and Drunk Drivers* (The Sentencing Project, March 1993) and "Alcohol and Other Drugs," by D. Boyum and M. Kleiman, in J. Wilson and J. Petersilia, eds., *Crime* (ICS Press, 1995). For an insightful discussion of contradictions in the criminal justice system, see D. Forbes, *False Fixes: The Cultural Politics of Drugs* (State University of New York Press, 1995). A very different approach is found in the National Institute of Justice reports, which consist of forecasts, current study summaries, and helpful statistical overviews, such as the institute's annual *Drug Use Forecasting* (to get on their mailing list, call 1-800-732-3277).

ISSUE 15

Will Gun Control Reduce Crime?

YES: Josh Sugarmann, from "The NRA Is Right: But We Still Need to Ban Handguns," *Washington Monthly* (June 1987)

NO: James D. Wright, from "Ten Essential Observations on Guns in America," *Society* (March/April 1995)

ISSUE SUMMARY

YES: Josh Sugarmann, formerly with the National Coalition to Ban Handguns, identifies several problems with legal handguns, including what he describes as unacceptably high rates of suicides with guns, family homicides, and accidents.

NO: Sociologist James D. Wright offers ten "fundamental truths" about guns. While he acknowledges that there is widespread disagreement over interpretations of the facts, he concludes that most gun control laws are unfair and ineffective.

According to some estimates, one in every two households in the United States contains a gun. And because of the growing fear of crime, many citizens express increased unwillingness to give up their guns. Guns are seen as necessary to protect home and family. An excellent example of this is the complicated situation that the nationally syndicated columnist Carl Rowan confronted. A well-known supporter of strict firearm controls, he was allegedly threatened by an intruder in his own backyard. Rowan quickly produced a pistol and shot the intruder. While conservatives (who consistently support the right to bear arms and oppose most kinds of gun control) jeered Rowan for his hypocrisy, other Americans were sympathetic. Rowan was later acquitted of criminal charges in the incident. He, like approximately 50 million other Americans, continues to possess a handgun.

This reflects another paradox in our society. On the one hand, many, if not most, Americans support handgun control. On the other hand, they feel that law-abiding citizens should have the right to possess a gun, at least inside their own homes, and to use it to protect themselves and their families. The argument is that weapons are needed for simple protection.

Simple assault is the most common crime of violence, followed by aggravated assault, which is the use of or threat of a weapon to inflict bodily harm. Other than robbery, most violent crimes are not committed with a gun. Knives, fists, and blunt instruments are more likely to be the weapons of choice. Homicide is the least frequent form of assault in the United States.

However, for most years between 1960 and 1985, violent crimes as reported to the police increased. In the late 1970s and in the 1982–1984 period, there was a slight decrease, but between 1984 and 1985 there was about a 4 percent increase. According to the U.S. Bureau of Justice Statistics, the number of attempted violent crimes increased by approximately 11 percent between 1990 and 1991. Currently, over 6 million violent crimes are committed each year. (Although the rate has come down since the peak year of 1981, when 6.6 million violent crimes were reported, as compared to 6.4 million in 1991.) There are over 20,000 murders per year, and in approximately 62 percent of all murders, guns are used in the commission of the crime. Six percent of gun assaults result in death; by comparison, 1.8 percent of knife assaults are fatal, and .05 percent of fights result in death.

Traditionally, the debate over gun control has centered largely around the control of, if not the elimination of, "Saturday night specials" (inexpensive, .22-caliber pistols). However, the issue has become more complicated in the 1990s. Not only is the fear and frustration over assaults and homicides being fueled by the significant numbers of young people being arrested for possession of arms, use of arms, and threats with arms, but the power of the weapons on the streets and the types of weapons available have changed dramatically. Uzis, AK-47 assault rifles, MAC-11 assault pistols, .357 Magnums, .45-caliber semiautomatics, and other semiautomatic weapons are frequently being used in deadly assaults. The consequences are an increase of public fear and an increase in fatalities because these weapons, newer to the criminal street scene, are far deadlier than "mere" Saturday night specials.

Gun control is now very much part of the cultural war landscape. Reminiscent (only in reverse) of the charges in the 1920s that Prohibition (of alcohol) was the triumph of the conservative, mean-spirited, rural religious right over the fun-loving, ethnically diverse, liberal city dwellers, some charge today that gun control laws represent the efforts of urban politicians and scholars to suppress rural hunters and other Americans. Many gun owners nowadays interpret gun control as a deliberate attempt to export to America's heartland the violence and chaos of the cities. Certainly such sentiments pervade far right militants who openly call for war on various government agencies. It seems that this issue is spreading and growing uglier.

Josh Sugarmann of the National Coalition to Ban Handguns acknowledges that the issue is complex, but he still recommends banning handguns. Sociologist James D. Wright asserts that neither empirically nor morally can some Americans demand other Americans to give up their guns.

Do *you* own a handgun? Would you willingly give it up if a law were passed? If a burglar has been working your neighborhood, would you still forgo purchasing one? Would you be willing to be a close friend of someone who has handguns? Why, or why not? Are folks with guns safer than those without them?

YES

Josh Sugarmann

THE NRA IS RIGHT: BUT WE STILL NEED TO BAN HANDGUNS

One tenet of the National Rifle Association's faith has always been that hand-gun controls do little to stop criminals from obtaining handguns. For once, the NRA is right and America's leading handgun control organization is wrong. Criminals don't buy handguns in gun stores. That's why they're criminals. But it isn't criminals who are killing most of the 20,000 to 22,000 people who die from handguns each year. We are.

This is an ugly truth for a country that thinks of handgun violence as a "crime" issue and believes that it's somehow possible to separate "good" handguns (those in our hands for self-defense) from "bad" handguns (those in the hands of criminals).

Contrary to popular perception, the most prevalent form of handgun death in America isn't murder but suicide. Of the handgun deaths that occur each year, approximately 12,000 are suicides. An additional 1,000 fatalities are accidents. And of the 9,000 handgun deaths classified as murders, most are not caused by predatory strangers. Handgun violence is usually the result of people being angry, drunk, careless, or depressed—who just happen to have a handgun around. In all, fewer than 10 percent of handgun deaths are felony-related.

Though handgun availability is not a crime issue, it does represent a major public health threat. Handguns are the number one weapon for both murder and suicide and are second only to auto accidents as the leading cause of death due to injury. Of course there are other ways of committing suicide or crimes of passion. But no means is more lethal, effective, or handy. That's why the NRA is ultimately wrong. As several public health organizations have noted, the best way to curb a public health problem is through prevention—in this case, the banning of all handguns from civilian hands.

THE ENEMY IS US

For most who attempt suicide, the will to die lasts only briefly. Only one out of every ten people attempting suicide is going to kill himself no matter what.

The success or failure of an attempt depends primarily on the lethality of the means. Pills, razor blades, and gas aren't guaranteed killers, and they take time. Handguns, however, lend themselves well to spontaneity. Consider that although women try to kill themselves four times as often as men, men succeed three to four times as often. For one reason: women use pills or less lethal means; men use handguns. This balance is shifting, however, as more women own or have access to handguns. Between 1970 and 1978 the suicide rate for young women rose 50 percent, primarily due to increased use of handguns.

Of course, there is no way to lock society's cupboard and prevent every distraught soul from injuring him or herself. Still, there are ways we can promote public safety without becoming a nation of nannies. England, for instance, curbed suicide by replacing its most common means of committing suicide—coal stove gas—with less toxic natural gas. Fifteen years after the switch, studies found that suicide rates had dropped and remained low, even though the number of suicide *attempts* had increased. "High suicide rates seem to occur where highly lethal suicidal methods are not only available, but also where they are culturally acceptable," writes Dr. Robert Markush of the University of Alabama, who has studied the use of handguns in suicide.

Most murders aren't crime-related, but are the result of arguments between friends and among families. In 1985, 59 percent of all murders were committed by people known to the victim. Only 15 percent were committed by strangers, and only 18 percent were the result of felonious activity. As the FBI admits every year in its *Uniform Crime Reports*, "murder is a societal problem over which law enforcement has little or no control." The FBI doesn't publish separate statistics on who's killing whom with handguns, but it is assumed that what is true of all murders is true of handgun murders.

CONTROLLING THE VECTOR

Recognizing that eliminating a disease requires prevention, not treatment, health professionals have been in the forefront of those calling for a national ban on handguns. In 1981, the Surgeon General's Select Panel for the Promotion of Child Health traced the "epidemic of deaths and injuries among children and youth" to handguns, and called for "nothing short of a total ban." It is estimated that on average, one child dies from handgun wounds each day. Between 1961 and 1981, according to the American Association of Suicidology, the suicide rate for 15- to 24-year-olds increased 150 percent. The report linked the rise in murders and suicides among the young to the increased use of firearms—primarily handguns. In a 1985 report, the Surgeon General's Workshop on Violence and Public Health recommended "a complete and universal ban on the sale, manufacture, importation, and possession of handguns (except for authorized police and military personnel)." ...

Comparing the relationship between handguns and violence to mosquitos and malaria, Stephen P. Teret, co-director of the Johns Hopkins Injury Prevention Center, says, "As public health professionals, if we are faced with a disease that is carried by some type of vehicle/vector like a mosquito, our initial response would be to control the vector. There's no reason why if the vehicle/vector is a handgun, we should not be interested in controlling the handgun."

The NRA refers to handgun suicides, accidental killings, and murders by acquaintances as "the price of freedom." It believes that handguns right enough wrongs, stop enough crimes, and kill enough criminals to justify these deaths. But even the NRA has admitted that there is no "adequate measure that more lives are saved by arms in good hands than are lost by arms in evil hands." Again, the NRA is right.

A 1985 NCBH study found that a handgun is 118 times more likely to be used in a suicide, murder, or fatal accident than to kill a criminal. Between 1981 and 1983, nearly 69,000 Americans lost their lives to handguns. During that same period there were only 583 justifiable homicides reported to the FBI, in which someone used a handgun to kill a stranger—a burglar, rapist, or other criminal. In 1982, 19 states reported to the FBI that not once did a private citizen use a handgun to kill a criminal. Five states reported that more than 130 citizens were murdered with handguns for each time a handgun was justifiably used to kill a criminal. In no state did the number of self-defense homicides approach the murder toll. Last year, a study published in the *New England Journal of Medicine* analyzing gun use in the home over a six-year period in the Seattle, Washington area, found that for every time a firearm was used to kill an intruder in self-defense, 198 lives ended in murders, suicides, or accidents. Handguns were used in more than 70 percent of those deaths.

Although handguns are rarely used to kill criminals, an obvious question remains: How often are they used merely to wound or scare away intruders? No reliable statistics are available, but most police officials agree that in a criminal confrontation on the street, the handgun-toting civilian is far more likely to be killed or lose his handgun to a criminal than successfully use the weapon in self-defense. "Beyond any doubt, thousands more lives are lost every year because of the proliferation of handguns than are saved," says Joseph McNamara, chief of police of San Jose, who has also been police chief in Kansas City, a beat cop in Harlem, and is the author of a book on defense against violent crime. Moreover, most burglaries occur when homes are vacant, so the handgun in the drawer is no deterrent. (It would also probably be the first item stolen.)

Faced with facts like these, anti-control advocates often turn to the argument of last resort: the Second Amendment. But the historic 1981 Morton Grove, Illinois, ban on handgun sale and possession exploded that rationale. In 1983, the U.S. Supreme Court let stand a lower court ruling that stated, "Because the possession of handguns is not part of the right to keep and bear arms, [the Morton Grove ordinance] does not violate the Second Amendment."

CRIMINAL EQUIVOCATION

Unfortunately, powerful as the NRA is, it has received additional help from the leading handgun control group. Handgun Control Inc. (HCI) has helped the handgun lobby by setting up the perfect strawman for the NRA to shoot down. "Keep handguns out of the wrong hands," HCI says. "By making it more difficult for criminals, drug addicts, etc., to get handguns, and by ensuring that law-abiding citizens know how to maintain their handguns, we can reduce handgun violence," it promises. Like those in the NRA, HCI chairman Nelson

T. "Pete" Shields "firmly believe(s) in the right of law-abiding citizens to possess handguns... for legitimate purposes."

In its attempt to paint handgun violence solely as a crime issue, HCI goes so far as to sometimes ignore the weapon's non-crime death tally. In its most recent poster comparing the handgun murder toll in the U.S. with that of nations with strict handgun laws, HCI states: "In 1983, handguns killed 35 people in Japan, 8 in Great Britain, 27 in Switzerland, 6 in Canada, 7 in Sweden, 10 in Australia, and 9,014 in the United States." Handguns *killed* a lot more than that in the United States. About 13,000 suicides and accidents more.

HCI endorses a ban only on short-barrelled handguns (the preferred weapon of criminals). It advocates mandatory safety training, a waiting period during which a background check can be run on a purchaser, and a license to carry a handgun, with mandatory sentencing for violators. It also endorses mandatory sentencing for the use of a handgun in a crime. According to HCI communications director Barbara Lautman, together these measures would "attack pretty much the heart of the problem."

HCI appears to have arrived at its crime focus by taking polls. In his 1981 book, *Guns Don't Die—People Do*, Shields points out that the majority of Americans don't favor a ban on handguns. "What they do want, however, is a set of strict laws to control the easy access to handguns by the criminal and the violence prone—*as long as those controls don't jeopardize the perceived right of law-abiding citizens to buy and own handguns for self defense* [italics his]." Shields admits "this is not based on any naive hope that criminals will obey such laws. Rather, it is based on the willingness of the rest

of us to be responsible and accountable citizens, and the knowledge that to the degree we are, we make it more difficult for the criminal to get a handgun." This wasn't always HCI's stand. Founded in 1974 as the National Council to Control Handguns, HCI originally called a ban on private handgun possession the "most effective" solution to reducing violent crime rapidly and was at one time a member of NCBH. Michael Beard, president of NCBH, maintains that HCI's focus on crime "started with a public relations concern. Some people in the movement felt Americans were worried about crime, and that was one way to approach the problem. That's the problem when you use public opinion polls to tell you what your position's going to be. And I think a lot of the handgun control movement has looked at whatever's hot at the time and tried to latch onto that, rather than sticking to the basic message that there is a relationship between the availability of handguns and the handgun violence in our society.... Ultimately, nothing short of taking the product off the market is really going to have an effect on the problem."

HCI's cops and robbers emphasis has been endlessly frustrating to many in the anti-handgun movement. HCI would offer handgun control as a solution to crime, and the NRA would effectively rebut their arguments with the common-sensical observation that criminals are not likely to obey such laws. I can't help but think that HCI's refusal to abandon the crime argument has harmed the longterm progress of the movement.

SATURATED DRESSER DRAWERS

In a nation with 40 million handguns—where anyone who wants one can get one

—it's time to face a chilling fact. We're way past the point where registration, licensing, safety training, waiting periods, or mandatory sentencing are going to have much effect. Each of these measures may save some lives or help catch a few criminals, but none—by itself or taken together—will stop the vast majority of handgun suicides or murders. A "controlled" handgun kills just as effectively as an "uncontrolled" one.

Most control recommendations merely perpetuate the myth that with proper care a handgun can be as safe a tool as any other. Nothing could be further from the truth. A handgun is not a blender.

Those advocating a step-by-step process insist that a ban would be too radical and therefore unacceptable to Congress and the public. A hardcore 40 percent of the American public has always endorsed banning handguns. Many will also undoubtedly argue that any control measure—no matter how ill-conceived or ineffective—would be a good first step. But after more than a decade, the other foot hasn't followed.

In other areas of firearms control there has been increasing recognition that bans are the most effective solution. The only two federal measures passed since the Gun Control Act of 1968 have been bans. In each case, the reasoning was simple: the harm done by these objects outweighed any possible benefit they brought to society. In 1986, Congress banned certain types of armor-piercing "cop-killer" bullets. There was also a silver lining to last year's NRA-McClure-Volkmer handgun "decontrol" bill, which weakened the already lax Gun Control Act of 1968, making it legal, for instance, for people to transport unloaded, "not readily accessible" handguns interstate. A last-minute amendment added by pro-control forces banned the future production and sale of machine guns for civilian use.

Unfortunately, no law has addressed the major public health problem. Few suicides, accidental killings, or acquaintance murders are the result of cop-killer bullets or machine guns.

Outlawing handguns would in no way be a panacea. Even if handgun production stopped tomorrow, millions would remain in the dresser drawers of America's bedrooms—and many of them would probably stay there. Contrary to NRA fantasies, black-booted fascists would not be kicking down doors searching for handguns. Moreover, the absolute last segment of society to be affected by any measure would be criminals. The black market that has fed off the legal sale of handguns would continue for a long while. But by ending new handgun production, the availability of illegal handguns can only decrease.

Of course, someone who truly wants to kill himself can find another way. A handgun ban would not affect millions of rifles and shotguns. But experience shows that no weapon provides the combination of lethality and convenience that a handgun does. Handguns represent only 30 percent of all the guns out there but are responsible for 90 percent of firearms misuse. Most people who commit suicide with a firearm use a handgun. At minimum, a handgun ban would prevent the escalation of killings in segments of society that have not yet been saturated by handgun manufacturers. Further increases in suicides among women, for example, might be curtailed.

But the final solution lies in changing the way handguns and handgun violence are viewed by society. Public health campaigns have changed the way Americans look at cigarette smoking and drunk driving and can do the same for handguns.

For the past 12 years, many in the handgun control movement have confined their debate to what the public supposedly wants and expects to hear—not to reality. The handgun must be seen for what it is, not what we'd like it to be.

NO

James D. Wright

TEN ESSENTIAL OBSERVATIONS ON GUNS IN AMERICA

Talk of "gun control" is very much in the air these days. Emboldened by their successes in getting the Brady Act enacted, the pro-control forces are now striking on a number of fronts: bans on various so-called assault weapons, mandatory gun registration, strict new laws against juvenile acquisition and possession of guns, and on through the list. Much current gun-control activity springs from a recent and generally successful effort to redefine gun violence mainly as a public health issue rather than a criminal justice issue.

Increasingly, the ammunition of the gun control war is data. Pro-control advocates gleefully cite studies that seem to favor their position, of which there is no shortage, and anti-control advocates do likewise. Many of the "facts" of the case are, of course, hotly disputed; so too are their implications and interpretations. Here I should like to discuss ten essential facts about guns in America that are not in dispute—ten fundamental truths that all contestants either do or should agree to—and briefly ponder the implications of each for how the problem of guns and gun violence perhaps should be approached. These facts and their implications derive from some twenty years of research and reflection on the issues.

1. *Half the households in the country own at least one gun.* So far as I have been able to determine, the first question about gun ownership asked of a national probability sample of U.S. adults was posed in 1959; a similar question asking whether anyone in the household owns a gun has since been repeated dozens of times. Over the ensuing thirty-five years, every survey has reported more or less the same result: Just about half of all U.S. households own one or more guns. This is probably not the highest gun ownership percentage among the advanced industrial societies (that honor probably goes to the Swiss), but it qualifies as a very respectable showing. We are, truly, a "gun culture."

Five important implications follow more or less unambiguously from this first essential observation.

The percentage of households owning guns has been effectively constant for nearly four decades; at the same time, the total number of guns in circulation has increased substantially, especially in the last two decades. The evident implication is that the increasing supply of guns has been absorbed by population growth, with newly formed households continuing to arm themselves at the average rate, and by the purchase of additional guns by households already owning one or more of them. In fact there is fairly solid evidence that the average number of guns owned by households owning any has increased from about three in the late 1970s to about four today.

The second implication is thus that many (and conceivably nearly all) of the new guns coming into circulation are being purchased by people who already own guns, as opposed to first-time purchases by households or individuals who previously owned no guns. I think it is also obvious that from the viewpoint of public safety, the transition from N to N + 1 guns is considerably less ominous than the transition from no guns to one gun. If this second implication is correct, it means that *most of the people in the gun shops today buying new guns already own at least one gun,* a useful point to keep in mind when pondering, for example, the alleged "cooling off" function to be served by waiting periods imposed at the point of retail sale.

Furthermore, it is frequently argued by pro-control advocates that the mere presence of guns causes people to do nutty and violent things that they would otherwise never even consider. In the academic literature on "guns as aggression-eliciting stimuli," this is called the "trigger pulls the finger" hypothesis. If there were much substance to this viewpoint, the fact that half of all U.S. households possess a gun would seem to imply that there ought to be a lot more nuttiness "out there" than we actually observe. In the face of widespread alarm about the sky-rocketing homicide rate, it is important to remember that the rate is still a relatively small number of homicides (ten to fifteen or so) per hundred thousand people. If half the households own guns and the mere presence of guns incites acts of violence, then one would expect the bodies to be piled three deep, and yet they are not.

Fourth, gun ownership is normative, not deviant, behavior across vast swaths of the social landscape. In certain states and localities, it would be an odd duck indeed who did not own a gun. Surveys in some smaller southern cities, for example, have reported local gun ownership rates in excess of 90 percent.

And finally, to attempt to control crime or violence by controlling the general ownership or use of guns among the public at large is to attempt to control the behaviors of a very small fraction of the population (the criminally or violently inclined fraction) by controlling the behaviors and activities of roughly half the U.S. population. Whatever else might be said about such an approach, it is certainly not very efficient.

2. *There are 200 million guns already in circulation in the United States,* give or take a few tens of millions. It has been said, I think correctly, that firearms are the most commonly owned piece of sporting equipment in the United States, with the exception of pairs of sneakers. In any case, contestants on all sides of the gun debate generally agree that the total number of guns in circulation is on the order of 200 million—nearly one gun for every man, woman, and child in the country.

It is not entirely clear how many acts of gun violence occur in any typical year. There are 30–35,000 deaths due to guns each year, perhaps a few hundred thousand nonfatal but injurious firearms accidents, maybe 500,000 or 600,000 chargeable gun crimes (not including crimes of illegal gun possession and carrying), and God knows how many instances in which guns are used to intimidate or prey upon one's fellow human beings. Making generous allowances all around, however, the total number of acts of accidental and intentional gun violence, whether fatal, injurious, or not, cannot be more than a couple of million, at the outside. This implies that the 200 million guns now in circulation would be sufficient to sustain roughly another century of gun violence at the current rates, even assuming that each gun was used once and only once for some nefarious purpose and that all additions to the gun supply were halted permanently and at once. Because of the large number of guns already in circulation, the violence-reductive effects of even fairly Draconian gun-control measures enacted today might well not be felt for decades.

Many recent gun-control initiatives, such as the Brady Act, are aimed at the point of retail sale of firearms and are therefore intended to reduce or in some way disrupt the flow of new guns into the domestic market. At the outside, the number of new guns coming into the market yearly is a few million, which adds but a few percent to the existing supply. If we intend to control gun violence by reducing the availability of firearms to the general public, as many argue we should, then we have to find some workable means to confront or control the vast arsenal of guns already circulating through private hands. Various "amnesty," "buyback," and "please turn in your guns" measures have been attempted in various jurisdictions all over the country; in one well-

publicized effort, teenagers could swap guns for Toys R Us gift certificates. The success of these programs has been measured in units of several dozen or at most a few hundred relinquished firearms; the net effect on the overall supply of guns is far too trivial to even bother calculating.

3. *Most of those 200 million guns are owned for socially innocuous sport and recreational purposes.* Only about a third of the guns presently in circulation are handguns; the remainder are rifles and shotguns. When one asks gun owners why they own guns, various sport and recreational activities dominate the responses—hunting, target shooting, collecting, and the like. Even when the question is restricted to handgun owners, about 40 percent say they own the gun for sport and recreational applications, another 40 percent say they own it for self-protection, and the remaining 20 percent cite their job or occupation as the principal reason for owning a gun.

Thus for the most part, gun ownership is apparently a topic more appropriate to the sociology of leisure than to the criminology or epidemiology of violence. Many pro-control advocates look on the sporting uses of guns as atavistic, barbaric, or just plain silly. But an equally compelling case could be made against golf, which causes men to wear funny clothes, takes them away from their families, and gobbles up a lot of pretty, green, open space that would be better used as public parks. It is, of course, true that golf does not kill 35,000 people a year (although middle-aged men drop dead on the golf course quite regularly), but it is also true that the sport and recreational use of guns does not kill 35,000 people a year. There are fewer than a thousand fatal hunting accidents annually; death from skeet shooting, target practice, and such is uncounted but presumably very small. It is the violent or criminal *abuse* of guns that should concern us, and the vast majority of guns now in circulation will never be used for anything more violent or abusive than killing the furry creatures of the woods and fields.

Unfortunately, when we seek to control violence by controlling the general ownership and use of firearms among the public at large, it at least *looks* as though we think we have intuited some direct causal connection between drive-by shootings in the inner city and squirrel hunting or skeet shooting in the hinterland. In any case, this is the implication that the nation's squirrel hunters and skeet shooters often draw; frankly, is it any wonder they sometimes come to question the motives, not to mention the sanity, of anyone who would suggest such a thing?

4. *Many guns are also owned for self-defense against crime, and some are indeed used for that purpose; whether they are actually any safer or not, many people certainly seem to feel safer when they have a gun.* There is a fierce debate raging in gun advocacy circles these days over recent findings by Gary Kleck that Americans use guns to protect themselves against crime as often as one or two million times a year, which, if true, is hard to square with the common assumption of pro-control advocates that guns are not an efficacious defense against crime. Whatever the true number of self-defensive uses, about a quarter of all gun owners and about 40 percent of handgun owners cite defense against crime as the main reason they own a gun, and large percentages of those who give some other main reason will cite self-defense as a secondary reason. Gun owners and gun advocates insist that guns provide real

protection, as Kleck's findings suggest; anti-gun advocates insist that the sense of security is more illusory than real.

But practically everything people do to protect themselves against crime provides only the illusion of security in that any such measure can be defeated by a sufficiently clever and motivated criminal. Dogs can be diverted or poisoned, burglar bars can be breached, home alarm systems can be subverted, chains and deadbolt locks can be cut and picked. That sales of all these items have skyrocketed in recent years is further proof—as if further proof were needed—that the fear of crime is real. Most people have also realized, correctly, that the police cannot protect them from crime. So people face the need to protect themselves and many choose to own a gun, along with taking many other measures, for this purpose. Does a society that is manifestly incapable of protecting its citizens from crime and predation really have the right or moral authority to tell people what they may and may not do to protect themselves?

Since a "sense of security" is inherently a psychological trait, it does no good to argue that the sense of security afforded by owning a gun is "just an illusion." Psychological therapy provides an *illusion* of mental wellness even as we remain our former neurotic selves, and it is nonetheless useful. The only sensible response to the argument that guns provide only an illusion of security is, So what?

5. *The bad guys do not get their guns through customary retail channels.* Research on both adult and juvenile felons and offenders has made it obvious that the illicit firearms market is dominated, overwhelmingly, by informal swaps, trades, and purchases among family members,

friends, acquaintances, and street and black-market sources. It is a rare criminal indeed who attempts to acquire a gun through a conventional over-the-counter transaction with a normal retail outlet. It is also obvious that many or most of the guns circulating through criminal hands enter the illicit market through theft from legitimate gun owners. (An aside of some possible significance: Large numbers of legitimate gun owners also obtain guns through informal "street" sources.)

As I have already noted, many efforts at gun control pertain to the initial retail sale of weapons, for example, the prohibition against gun purchases by people with felony records or alcohol or drug histories contained in the Gun Control Act of 1968, the national five-day waiting period, or various state and local permit and registration laws. Since felons rarely obtain guns through retail channels, controls imposed at the point of retail sale necessarily miss the vast majority of criminal firearms transactions. It is thus an easy prediction that the national five-day waiting period will have no effect on the acquisition of guns by criminals because that is not how the bad guys get their guns in the first place.

Having learned (now more than a decade ago) that the criminal acquisition of guns involves informal and intrinsically difficult-to-regulate transfers that are entirely independent of laws concerning registration and permits, average gun owners often conclude (whether rightly or wrongly) that such measures must therefore be intended primarily to keep tabs on them, that registration or permit requirements are "just the first step" toward outright confiscation of all privately held firearms, and that mandated registration of new gun purchases is thus an unwarranted "police state" intrusion on law-abiding citizens' constitutional rights. Reasoning in this vein often seems bizarre or even psychotic to proponents of registration or permit laws, but it is exactly this reasoning that accounts for the white-hot ferocity of the debate over guns in America today.

And similar reasoning applies to the national waiting period: Since it is well known that the bad guys do not generally obtain guns through normal retail channels, waiting periods enforced at the point of retail sale can only be aimed at thwarting the legitimate intentions of the "good guys." What conceivable crime-reductive benefit will a national five-day waiting period give us? If the answer is "probably very little," then the minds of average gun owners are free to speculate on the nefarious and conspiratorial intentions that may be harbored, consciously or not, by those who favor such a thing. The distinction between ill-considered and evil is quickly lost, and the debate over guns in America gets hotter still.

That the illicit gun market is supplied largely through theft from legitimate owners erodes any useful distinction between legitimate and illegitimate guns. Any gun that can be owned legitimately can be stolen from its legal owner and can end up in criminal hands. The effort to find some way to interdict or interfere with the criminal gun market while leaving legitimate owners pretty much alone is therefore bootless. So long as anybody can have a gun, criminals will have them too, and it is useful to remember that there are 200 million guns out there—an average of four of them in every second household.

6. *The bad guys inhabit a violent world; a gun often makes a life-or-death difference to them.* When one asks felons—either adult

or juvenile—why they own and carry guns, themes of self-defense, protection, and survival dominate the responses. Very few of the bad guys say they acquire or carry guns for offensive or criminal purposes, although that is obviously how many of them get used. These men live in a very hostile and violent environment, and many of them have come to believe, no doubt correctly, that their ability to survive in that environment depends critically on being adequately armed. Thus the bad guys are highly motivated gun consumers who will not be easily dissuaded from possessing, carrying, and using guns. If sheer survival is the issue, then a gun is a bargain at practically any price. As James Q. Wilson has argued, most of the gun violence problem results from the wrong kinds of people carrying guns at the wrong time and place. The survival motive among the bad guys means exactly that the "wrong kinds of people" will be carrying guns pretty much all the time. The evident implication is that the bad guys have to be disarmed on the street if the rates of gun violence are to decline, and that implies a range of intervention strategies far removed from what gun control advocates have recently urged on the American population.

7. *Everything the bad guys do with their guns is already against the law.* That criminals will generally be indifferent to our laws would seem to follow from the definitions of the terms, but it is a lesson that we have had to relearn time and time again throughout our history. So let me stress an obvious point: Murder is already against the law, yet murderers still murder; armed robbery is against the law, yet robbers still rob. And as a matter of fact, gun acquisition by felons, whether from retail or private sources, is also already illegal, yet felons still acquire guns. Since practically everything the bad guys do with their guns is already against the law, we are entitled to wonder whether there is any new law we can pass that would persuade them to stop doing it. It is more than a little bizarre to assume that people who routinely violate laws against murder, robbery, or assault would somehow find themselves compelled to obey gun laws, whatever provisions they might contain.

8. *Demand creates it own supply.* That "demand creates its own supply" is sometimes called the First Law of Economics, and it clearly holds whether the commodity in demand is legal or illegal. So long as a demand exists, there will be profit to be made in satisfying it, and therefore it will be satisfied. In a capitalist economy, it could scarcely be otherwise. So long as people, be they criminals or average citizens, want to own guns, guns will be available for them to own. The vast arsenal of guns already out there exists in the first instance because people who own guns like guns, the activities that guns make possible, and the sense of security that guns provide. "Supply side" approaches to the gun problem are never going to be any more effective than "supply side" approaches to the drug problem, which is to say, not at all. What alcohol and drug prohibition should have taught us (but apparently has not) is that if a demand exists and there is no legal way to satisfy it, then an illegal commerce in the commodity is spawned, and we often end up creating many more problems than we have solved.

Brazil and several European nations manufacture small arms; the Brazilian lines are relatively inexpensive but decent guns. In fundamental respects, the question whether we can disarm the

American criminal population amounts to asking whether an organized criminal enterprise that successfully illegally imports hundreds of tons of Colombian cocaine into the U.S. market each year would not find the means to illegally import hundreds of tons of handguns from Brazil. And if this is the case, then it seems more or less self-evident that the supply of firearms to the criminal population will never be reduced by enough to make an appreciable difference.

9. *Guns are neither inherently good nor inherently evil; guns, that is, do not possess teleology.* Benevolence and malevolence inhere in the motives and behaviors of people, not in the technology they possess. Any firearm is neither more nor less than a chunk of machined metal that can be put to a variety of purposes, all involving a small projectile hurtling at high velocity downrange to lodge itself in a target. We can only call this "good" when the target is appropriate and "evil" when it is not; the gun itself is immaterial to this judgment.

Gun-control advocates have a long history of singling out "bad" guns for policy attention. At one time, the emphasis was on small, cheap handguns—"Saturday Night Specials"—which were thought to be inherently "bad" because no legitimate use was thought to exist for them and because they were thought to be the preferred firearm among criminals. Both these thoughts turned out to be incorrect. Somewhat later, all handguns, regardless of their characteristics, were singled out (as by the National Coalition to Ban Handguns); most recently, the so-called military-style assault weapons are the "bad guns of the month."

Singling out certain types of guns for policy attention is almost always justified on the grounds that the type of gun in question "has no legitimate use" or "is designed only to kill." By definition, however, all guns are "designed to kill" (that is, to throw a projectile downrange to lodge in a target), and if one grants the proposition that self-defense against predation and plunder is a legitimate reason to own a gun, then all guns, regardless of their type or characteristics, have at least some potentially "legitimate" application. It seems to me, therefore, that the focus in gun-control circles on certain "bad" guns is fundamentally misplaced. When all is said and done, it is the behavior of people that we should seek to control. Any gun can be used legitimately by law-abiding people to hunt, shoot at targets, or defend themselves against crime; and likewise, any gun can be used by a criminal to prey upon and intimidate other people. Trying to sort firearms into "inherently bad" and "inherently good" categories seems fundamentally silly.

10. *Guns are important elements of our history and culture.* Attempts to control crime by regulating the ownership or use of firearms are attempts to regulate the artifacts and activities of a culture that, in its own way, is as unique as any of the myriad other cultures that comprise the American ethnic mosaic. This is the American gun culture, which remains among the least understood of any of the various subcultural strands that make up modern American society.

There is no question that a gun culture exists, one that amply fulfills any definition of a culture. The best evidence we have on its status as a culture is that the single most important predictor of whether a person owns a gun is whether his or her father owned one, which means that gun owning is a tradition transmitted across generations. Most gun owners report that there were firearms in their homes when they were growing up; this is true even of criminal gun users.

The existence and characteristics of the American gun culture have implications that rarely are appreciated. For one, gun control deals with matters that people feel strongly about, that are integral to their upbringing and their worldview. Gun-control advocates are frequently taken aback by the stridency with which their seemingly modest and sensible proposals are attacked, but from the gun culture's viewpoint, restrictions on the right to "keep and bear arms" amount to the systematic destruction of a valued way of life and are thus a form of cultural genocide.

Guns evoke powerful, emotive imagery that often stands in the way of intelligent debate. To the pro-control point of view, the gun is symbolic of much that is wrong in American culture. It symbolizes violence, aggression, and male dominance, and its use is seen as an acting out of our most regressive and infantile fantasies. To the gun culture's way of thinking, the same gun symbolizes much that is right in the culture. It symbolizes manliness, self-sufficiency, and independence, and its use is an affirmation of man's relationship to nature and to history. The "Great American Gun War," as Bruce-Briggs has described it, is far more than a contentious debate over crime and the equipment with which it is committed. It is a battle over fundamental and equally legitimate sets of values.

Scholars and criminologists who speculate on the problem of guns, crime, and violence would thus do well to look at things, at least occasionally, from the gun culture's point of view. Hardly any of the 50 million or so American families that own guns have ever harmed anyone with their guns, and virtually none ever intend to. Nearly everything these families will ever do with their firearms is both legal and largely innocuous. When, in the interests of fighting crime, we advocate restrictions on their rights to own guns, we are casting aspersions on their decency, as though we somehow hold them responsible for the crime and violence that plague this nation. It is any wonder they object, often vociferously, to such slander?

POSTSCRIPT

Will Gun Control Reduce Crime?

In spite of the National Rifle Association's powerful lobbying efforts and media campaigns in support of gun ownership without restrictions, most Americans support some form of gun control. Yet the issue is confusing to many, in spite of the obvious evidence of the deadliness of gun assaults. One gun control fad that's catching on involves programs run by municipalities and even private organizations to buy back guns from gun owners in order to reduce the number in circulation. Symbolically, these actions strike a responsive chord. Citizens like to think something is being done about violent crime. However, empirical data suggests that the gun bounties may have little effect.

On a more positive note, local police are stepping up efforts to constitutionally identify and locate criminals who are illegally carrying guns. University of Maryland criminologist Lawrence W. Sherman is assisting urban police in developing such patrols. Meanwhile, both "what works" and "what is fair" in gun control remains highly problematic partly because individuals who assault with guns and their victims seem to be becoming younger and younger.

For an early discussion of the effectiveness of gun control laws, see J. Wright and P. Rossi's *Armed and Considered Dangerous: A Survey of Felons and Their Firearms* (Aldine de Gruyter, 1986) and D. McDowall, B. Wiserema, and C. Loftin's "Did Mandatory Firearm Ownership in Kennesaw Really Prevent Burglaries?" *Sociology and Social Research* (October 1989). For a thoughtful overview of the issue, see Cook and Moore, "Gun Control," in J. Wilson and J. Petersilia, eds., *Crime* (ICS Press, 1995).

Current discussions from a cultural war perspective include "The Fight to Bear Arms," by G. Witkin et al., and "The Gun Lobby," by Ted Gest, both in *U.S. News & World Report* (May 22, 1995). Also see "Extreme Prejudice: How the Media Misrepresent the Militia Movement," by M. Tanner, *Reason* (July 1995). A seminal study that challenges supporters of gun control is G. Kleck's *Point Blank: Guns and Violence in America* (Aldine de Gruyter, 1991). Two articles from the same point of view are D. Kates, Jr.'s "Shot Down" and J. D. Wright's "Bad Guys, Bad Guns," both in *National Review* (March 6, 1995). Also challenging gun control laws but for different reasons is D. Polsby's "The False Promise of Gun Control," *The Atlantic Monthly* (March 1994).

Canada's recent legislation controlling guns has generated widespread responses. For several sides of their debate, see *Canadian Journal of Criminology* (April 1995) and "Fighting Back: Canadians Against Gun Control," by M. Nemeth, *Maclean's* (June 5, 1995). For a legalistic article that looks at melting down guns, see T. Funk's "Gun Control and Economic Discrimination," *Journal of Criminal Law and Criminology* (Winter 1995).

A recent book by J. D. Wright and J. Sheley is *In the Line of Fire: Youth, Guns, and Violence in Urban America* (Aldine de Gruyter, 1995). For another side of the issue, see L. Fingerhut and J. Kleinman's *Firearm Mortality Among Children and Youth* (U.S. National Center for Health Statistics, 1989). A summary of the sad finding that many adolescent suicides and accidental deaths result from guns can be found in H. Hendin, *Suicide in America* (W. W. Norton, 1995).

On gun control and public sentiment, see "The Arms Race in Your Own Back Yard," *U.S. News & World Report* (April 4, 1988); "Furor Over Fire Arms," by R. Dolphin, *Maclean's* (January 9, 1989); "The NRA Comes Under the Gun," *Newsweek* (March 21, 1989); "The Other Arms Race," by G. J. Church, *Time* (February 6, 1989); and "Under Fire: The NRA," by R. Lacayo, *Time* (January 29, 1990).

Among the many recent contributions to this debate are T. Lesce's "Is Gun Control the Answer?" *Law Enforcement News* (January 12, 1988); "Gun Control and Rates of Firearms Violence in Canada and the U.S.," by R. J. Mundt, *Canadian Journal of Criminology* (January 1990); *Violent Crime and Gun Control* by G. Robin (Anderson, 1991); and D. McDowall's "Firearm Availability and Homicide Rates in Detroit, 1951–1986," *Social Forces* (June 1991). A different conceptualization of the debate is M. Bijefeld's "How Others Restrict Firearms" versus G. M. Gottlieb's "Better Crime Control Will Save More Lives," *USA Today* (June 21, 1990).

Finally, see N. A. Lewis, "N.R.A. Takes Aim at Study of Guns as Public Health Risk," *The New York Times* (August 27, 1995), which describes the National Rifle Association's attempts to eliminate a study of firearms as a public health issue being conducted by the Centers for Disease Control.

ISSUE 16

Should Euthanasia Be a Crime?

YES: Wesley J. Smith, from "Killing Grounds," *National Review* (March 6, 1995)

NO: Jack Kevorkian, from "A Modern Inquisition," *The Humanist* (November/December 1994)

ISSUE SUMMARY

YES: Wesley J. Smith, a lawyer for the International Anti-Euthanasia Task Force, contends that patients in a "persistent vegetative state" are being dehumanized so that they may be killed without objection. Smith argues that legitimizing euthanasia may lead to looser guidelines regarding which patients may be allowed to die.

NO: Jack Kevorkian, a retired pathologist and an activist for physician-assisted suicide, maintains that society has no right to criminalize voluntary euthanasia.

The word *euthanasia* is a combination of the Greek prefix *eu*, which means "good," and *thanatos*, meaning "death." Euthanasia therefore implies "easy death." *Webster's New Collegiate Dictionary* defines it as "the act or practice of killing individuals (as persons or domestic animals) that are hopelessly sick or injured for reasons of mercy."

Euthanasia, or "mercy killing," is technically murder. Yet in those rare cases in which charges have been made, juries and the courts have either been reluctant to convict or recommended relatively light sentences. Examples include a woman who killed her husband of 50 years because he had a painful terminal illness, and a man who killed his lover because he had an advanced case of AIDS.

Both moral and legal aspects of the problem have greatly expanded. In the Netherlands, for instance, physicians who assist patients who wish to die (even if they do not have a terminal illness) are not prosecuted, provided that the doctor followed proper guidelines. Many states in the United States currently have no laws against assisting suicides.

Not long ago, while philosophers and medical ethicists debated the issue of euthanasia, most criminologists and criminal justice scholars and practitioners ignored the practice. However, in the past few years, the widely publicized acts of now-suspended physician Jack Kevorkian in assisting suicides has, along with other shifting cultural and social patterns, created a new controversy. Many states have rushed to pass laws against assisting suicides, including Michigan, whose law (aimed partially at stopping Kevorkian) was recently upheld by the Michigan Supreme Court; the U.S. Supreme Court refused to hear the case. Other states, moving in the opposite direction, are considering policies protecting individuals' rights to be helped to die.

Of the estimated 30,000 suicides committed annually in the United States, less than 3 percent are by terminally ill people, and a very small fraction of that number are likely to have been assisted suicides. However, the number of patients who died because family members and physicians elected to withhold medicines or other life-sustaining supplies or simply failed to revive them is considerably larger.

Yet the issue of euthanasia is laden with symbolic and emotional implications. at the most basic level, euthanasia involves the taking of a human life. In addition, it is now possible to prolong the life of the severely injured and the elderly almost indefinitely, though at fantastic economic costs as well as emotional costs for relatives (seeing loved ones in a comatose or vegetative state). Also, people are now living far longer on average than in the past, though sometimes under very uncomfortable medical circumstances. Thus, the potential pool of candidates for euthanasia is vast.

In the twentieth century euthanasia has developed hideous connotations. Many still associate the concept and practice with the Nazi Holocaust and link it directly and indirectly with genocide. During World War II German physicians, with almost no resistance, followed the Nazi program of Action T-4. This involved exterminating through firing squads, gas chambers, and other means of death those who were mentally or physically disabled or otherwise perceived as "unfit."

In the United States scholars since the 1940s have been highly critical of any proposals that could be used to eliminate some specific category of people, such as the sick, the elderly, and racial or ethnic minorities. Indeed, many "progressive" social scientists of the 1920s noted with approval the eugenics movement, or the effort to improve the human race by suppressing "bad" genes. Supreme Court justice Oliver Wendell Holmes's famous 1927 decision legitimizing involuntary sterilization was initially viewed as a legal and ethical breakthrough. It was not until the 1960s that journalists and scholars began to realize that involuntary sterilization was being done primarily in the South and primarily to black people.

As you read the following perspectives on euthanasia by Wesley J. Smith and Jack Kevorkian, keep in mind the different circumstances that can surround an assisted death. Is the death a result of the patient's wishes at the time of her or his termination or of a written consent signed long before the patient became ill? Or is the decision to terminate life made by the family or doctor? Does the patient actually participate bringing about death (assisted suicide), or does death result from either passive neglect by medical staff or active steps?

YES
Wesley J. Smith

KILLING GROUNDS

Those we would kill we must first dehumanize. That truism has been demonstrated repeatedly throughout history. Today in the United States, disabled people with brain damage are being systematically dehumanized so that society will accept the "compassion" and utility of killing them. "He is an empty shell, a vegetable," a person may say of a relative in a coma. "He is no different than a corpse," another may agree, as if the disabled person were already dead.

Physicians and lawyers representing families who wish to end the lives of their disabled loved ones can be even more brutal. "They, as human beings, have long since departed from the world," Dr. Fred Plum of Cornell University Medical Center recently told the *American Medical News*. "They're stealing from the mouths of others." Or consider this statement by Paul Armstrong, a lawyer who represented the parents of Nancy Ellen Jobes in their ultimately successful quest to withdraw food and fluids from their disabled daughter. People with profound brain damage, he said, are "nonmentiative [sic] organ systems, artificially sustained like valued cell lines in cancer laboratories." The medical terminology for such patients, who are said to be in a "persistent vegetative state" (PVS), reflects this attitude.

Since the truly dead often get more respect than the disabled living, it's hardly surprising that the killing of PVS patients by starvation and dehydration has become routine. The American Medical Association [AMA] has given its blessing to the practice since 1986, when it approved starving or dehydrated terminally ill people on the brink of death and those who are "without doubt permanently unconscious." Nutrition through a feeding tube is now deemed "medical treatment" (which may be withheld) rather than "humane care" (which must be supplied).

Despite the limitations supposedly imposed by the AMA guidelines, conscious as well as comatose patients have been dehydrated to death. Nurses who cared for Nancy Cruzan—perhaps the most famous dehydration victim, because her case went all the way to the U.S. Supreme Court—insist to this day that she was conscious when her parents decided to withdraw her nutritional support. Indeed, she had been able to take food orally before a feeding tube was utilized to make her care easier. Likewise, Christine Busalacchi, whose care givers swore she smiled at jokes and responded to music, died by dehydration at the request of her father. Then there were the cases of Ronald Comeau (see "The Right to Die, the Power to Kill," *National Review,* April 4) and Michael Martin (see "Better Dead Than Fed," *National Review,* June 27). Both are indisputably conscious but judges nonetheless authorized their dehydration and starvation. Mr. Comeau was saved only because a pro-life minister succeeded in finding his relatives, who intervened. Mr. Martin's case is now before the Michigan Supreme Court.

These and many other cases fly in the face of the 1986 AMA guidelines, which require terminal illness or permanent unconsciousness. Not to worry. Last year the AMA revised its ethical rules to comport with the practices of physicians and the courts, expanding the list of those eligible for withholding of "artificial nutrition" to include the conscious but mentally incompetent, who cannot make medical decisions for themselves. "Even if the patient is not terminally ill or permanently unconscious," the AMA now says, "it is not unethical to discontinue all means of life-sustaining medical treatment in accordance with a proper substituted-judgment or best-interests analysis."

Furthermore, some who sanction the killing of the profoundly brain damaged would not limit it to patients who make their wishes known in advance or whose families choose to have nutrition withdrawn. They are pushing the nation toward a medical ethic that would eliminate the right of these patients to live—even if the family wants medical care to continue. The charge is being led by the prestigious *New England Journal of Medicine.* In a May 26, 1994, editorial, the journal's executive director, Dr. Marcia Angell, argues that doctors treating the profoundly disabled should be permitted to refuse treatment they consider futile or inappropriate. Dr. Angell describes three ways of accomplishing this.

First, death could be redefined to include permanent unconsciousness. The current definition, "brain death," was intended to permit organ harvesting. But after brain death, the body cannot be kept functioning more than a few days. By contrast, patients diagnosed as permanently unconscious can often survive without assistance, other than food and fluids, indefinitely. Dr. Angell sees a problem with redefining death to include those diagnosed as permanently unconscious: it would be unseemly to bury a breathing body. Thus, the "corpse" of an unconscious person considered "dead" would have to be killed.

Second, states could prohibit medical care for the unconscious after a specified time. The beauty of this approach, according to Dr. Angell, is that the decision to let a person die would be made in advance by society without regard to any particular case. In other words, the family would know that the decision to let their disabled relative die was nothing personal.

Third, states could create a legal presumption that people with brain damage would not want treatment after a specified time. A family that held the "idiosyncratic view" that their loved one should not be starved to death would have to prove that he had expressed a specific desire to be treated under these circumstances.

WHEN THE DOCTOR IS WRONG

The equanimity with which much of society has accepted euthanasia by dehydration of these profoundly disabled people is disturbing to those who hold the old-fashioned view that all human life is sacred. But even those who have doubts about the moral status of comatose patients should recognize that people deemed by doctors to be permanently unconscious often aren't. In more than a few cases, such people have awakened. (If the definition of death is ever changed to include supposedly permanent unconsciousness, we could say they were resurrected.)

According to a growing body of medical literature, misdiagnosis of the persistent vegetative state is a real problem. A study published in the June 1991 *Archives of Neurology* found that, of 84 patients with a firm diagnosis of PVS, 58 per cent recovered consciousness within three years. Moreover, researchers were unable to identify objective "predictors of recovery" to differentiate between those who would awaken and those who would not. So it is likely that many who would recover consciousness given sufficient time are being killed in the name of compassion, cost containment, or "quality of life."

Dr. Angell suggests that such mistakes can be prevented by allowing sufficient time to pass after the brain injury. But as the dehumanizing of the profoundly brain damaged has progressed, the urge has grown to get them out of the way as soon as possible. "What we are seeing in too many cases is a completely improper rush to judgment that a patient is suffering PVS," says Pasadena neurologist Dr. Vincent Fortanasce. "It takes at least three to six months before a firm diagnosis of

persistent vegetative state can be made. However, many doctors make such diagnoses within a week or less, often without objective testing. Eighty to ninety per cent of cases I see have been improperly diagnosed, often by doctors who are not qualified to make the diagnosis. Unfortunately, that's the real practice of medicine today."

To illustrate his point, Dr. Fortanasce describes a case in which he was involved. A sixty-year-old patient who had collapsed received a PVS diagnosis from his internist, who strongly recommended against continuing life support. The family was reluctant to see their loved one die, so they demanded a second opinion from a neurologist. "I came in and diagnosed a severe brain seizure, not PVS," Dr. Fortanasce says. "I prescribed continued life support and medication. Within a week, the patient walked out of the hospital in full possession of his faculties. If the family had listened to the internist, that man would be dead today."

And there is another twist. The Japanese may have discovered a way to wake up some patients from PVS. An article in the September 24 *St. Louis Post-Dispatch* reported that Japanese doctors have awakened seven of twenty patients diagnosed as permanently unconscious by stimulating their mid-brains with electrodes. This news comes at an awkward time. Just when society seems to have accepted brain-damaged people as disposable, it turns out they may not be "dead" after all. Indeed, Dr. Christopher M. DeGeorgio, an assistant professor of neurology at the University of Southern California, reports that some PVS patients who have awakened report that they were aware of their surroundings while "unconscious." Such findings make it more difficult to starve brain-damaged patients to death and still get a good night's sleep.

Perhaps that is why the Japanese study has received little attention among bioethicists, who increasingly focus on determining which vulnerable group will be the next to be deemed expendable. If that seems harsh, consider what the director of the Hastings Center for Bioethics, Daniel Callahan, wrote in 1983: "Denial of nutrition may in the long run become the only effective way to make certain that a large number of biologically tenacious patients actually die. Given the increasingly large pool of the superannuated, chronically ill, physically marginal elderly, it could well become the nontreatment of choice." He said the practice could be kept under control "if there remains a deep-seated revulsion at the stopping of feeding even under legitimate circumstances." But given the current trend, that revulsion is fast becoming a thing of the past.

Jack Kevorkian

A MODERN INQUISITION

This article is adapted from the speech delivered by Dr. Kevorkian
upon receiving the 1994 Humanist Hero Award from the American
Humanist Association at its annual conference in Detroit, Michigan.

This is probably the first time that this august body has been addressed by
someone under indictment on two counts of first-degree murder.

I was ignorant of many things when I graduated from college. I was uneducated; maybe I still am. All I was trained for was a craft. I think that's true
of colleges generally in this country today—they train you for a craft. But
everything of value I learned in my life I learned after college, on my own:
philosophy, music.... The one deficiency I have is literature; I'm very weak
there.

So I wasn't attuned, back then, to what life in our society is. I was put
by fortune into this position, which has given me a real deep insight into
what so-called civilized society is. And I learned one thing: that society is *not*
civilized. And I learned another thing: that we are still deeply mired in the
Dark Ages.

Superhighways crossing each other at several levels, color television sets
and compact discs, these to me don't indicate the height of civilization, and
they don't indicate enlightenment either—in fact, they're dangerous tools of
the Dark Ages.

The Inquisition is still alive and well. The only difference is that today it's
much more dangerous and subtle. The inquisitors don't burn you at the stake
anymore; they slowly sizzle you. They make sure you pay dearly for what
you do. In fact, they kill you often in a subtle way. My situation is a perfect
example of it.

This is not self-pity, understand. I don't regret the position I'm in. I am
not a hero, either—by my definition, anyway. To me, anyone who does what
should be done is not a hero. Heroes to me are very, very rare. And I still feel
that I'm only doing what I, as a physician, should do. A license has nothing to
do with it; I am a physician and therefore I will act like a physician whenever
I can. That doesn't mean that I'm more compassionate than anyone else, but
there is one thing I am that many aren't and that's honest.

From Jack Kevorkian, "A Modern Inquisition," *The Humanist*, vol. 54, no. 6 (November/
December 1994), pp. 7–9. Copyright © 1994 by The American Humanist Association. Reprinted
by permission.

To me, the biggest deficiency today and the biggest problem with society is dishonesty. It underlies almost every crisis and every problem you can name. It's almost an inevitable thing; in fact, it's unavoidable as you mature. Children are honest—born perfectly honest—and slowly learn how to become dishonest. They are trained at it. We feel that a little dishonesty greases the wheels of society, that it makes things easier for everybody if we lie a little to each other. But all this dishonesty becomes cumulative after awhile. If everyone were perfectly honest at all times, if human nature were such that it could stand that, you would find many fewer problems in the world. I know that's impractical. Maybe I'm a hopeless idealist. But at least that's looking at the problem at its root. Children, by the way, *can* handle honesty. They swear and curse at each other, and it doesn't affect them very much. But it's difficult to be perfectly honest as an adult.

I never considered myself a humanist. I'm not a joiner. I never join any organization. And yet humanism, I think, is the closest to what I think is a good way of living in society.

What is the best rule for life? I often ask myself that. Some people will tell you that "the Golden Rule is the best." Well, I don't know—is it? We spout platitudes without thinking. We're trained not to think, really; we're trained to respond to platitudes. Education does that. I think education in this society is geared toward making sure you are well brainwashed by the time you are an adult.

The Golden Rule: "Do unto others as you would have them do unto you." But that doesn't always apply. What if I met a masochist or a sadist? You see, it wouldn't work. I think the best rule for life is "Say and do what you wish, whenever you wish, so long as you do not harm another person or his or her property." Does that sound right? Now if every adult human being acted that way, this would be a much better society. We may not have color television sets, and we may not have superhighways, but we would probably be a better society. We certainly wouldn't have the Inquisition.

So all I'm doing is what a physician should do. I'm not really frightened by what's happening to me; I'm not even intimidated. I'm annoyed! In fact, I'm reinforced in what I'm doing because of the opposition, which is so irrational.

By the way, this is not a one-man operation. I keep getting all the credit, and I don't deserve it. I've got tremendous legal support in Geoffrey Fieger and Michael Swartz. You'd be amazed how much of a burden they relieve me of. I can't think of anybody else who could do it the way Geoffrey does it, and he deserves as much credit as I. He handles all the legal aspects, which, as you know, are enormous, and gives me free rein on what I should do. Credit must also go to my sister Margo and to my other sister Flora, who's now in Europe. Margo and Flora were with me during the Janet Atkins case, and I must admit that I couldn't have done it without them. I was very nervous—I was actually a little frightened—and they gave me great moral support. They were just as nervous as I, but they tried not to show it, which helped. I must also mention my other assistant, my medical technologist Neal Nichol. These people make up the nucleus of the group that deserves the credit; I'm just the figurehead here.

* * *

When we first started this work, we didn't expect the explosion of publicity that followed. We tried to keep this low key. I have been accused of grandstanding, recklessness, and publicity seeking, all of which, of course, is not true. You must understand that the entire mainstream media, especially in the first year or two, were totally against what I'm doing. Entirely! It was unanimous. They tried to make my work look very negative—they tried to make *me* look negative—so that they could denigrate the concept we're working on. They said I should not be identified with the concept, yet they strived to do just that. They insulted and denigrated me and then hoped that it would spill over onto the concept. It didn't work, however; according to the polls, people may be split 50-50 on what they think of me, but they are three-to-one in favor of the concept, and that's never changed.

Now isn't it strange that on a controversial subject of this magnitude—one which cuts across many disciplines—the entire editorial policy of the country is on one side? Doesn't that strike you as strange? Even on a contentious issue like abortion, there is editorial support for both sides. And our issue—death with dignity—as far as we're concerned, is simpler than abortion. So why is every mainstream editorial writer and newspaper in the country against us on this? Not one has come out in wholehearted support of us, even though public opinion is on our side.

As I surmise it, they're in a conspiracy, which is not a revelation to many people. But with whom? Well, let's take a look at who's against this: organized religion, organized medicine, and organized big money. Now, that's a lot of power.

Why is organized medicine against this? For a couple of reasons, I think: first, because the so-called profession—which is no longer a profession; it's

really a commercial enterprise and has been for a long time—is permeated with religious overtones. The basis of so-called medical ethics is religious ethics. The Hippocratic Oath is a religious manifesto—Pythagorean (pagan, by the way)—they don't even mind that. It is not medical. Hippocrates didn't write it; we don't know who did, but we think it's from the Pythagoreans. So, if you meet a physician who says, "Life is sacred," be careful: we didn't study sanctity in medical school. You are talking to a theologian first, probably a business person second, and a physician third.

The second reason that organized medicine is against physician-assisted voluntary euthanasia is because of the money involved. If a patient's suffering is curtailed by three weeks, can you imagine how much that adds up to in the medical and health-care field? Let's look at Alzheimer's disease. They say, "Well, that's not terminal." Well, it *is* terminal. Any process that curtails natural life is a terminal disease; the duration of the terminal process is the only difference. Some cancers last a week in their terminal phase. Alzheimer's disease is terminal. I understand that we have four million Alzheimer's cases in this country. Let's assume that one out of ten opts to end his or her life at a certain stage, just when it is getting bad. That's 400,000 people depriving some nursing homes of perhaps four or five years of care for a vegetating human being. At $30,000 a year, multiplied by 400,000, times five years—you're into billions of dollars. And that's just one disease, and one out of ten people.

How about the pharmaceutical industry? A lot of drugs are used in those last several months and years of life, which also add up to billions and billions of dollars. So you can see why they are going to oppose this.

That's what is so dismaying to me; that's what makes me cynical. You have to be cynical in life when you read about a situation that's so terrible and so incorrigible. There are certain ways to deal with it: you can go along with it, which is hard to do; you can go insane, which *is* a refuge (and some do that); or you can face it with deep cynicism. I've opted for cynicism.

In responding to the religious issues, I ask this: why not let all the religious underpinnings of medicine apply only to the ethics of religious hospitals and leave the secular hospitals alone? It's a perfect solution. We're not going to tell the religious hospitals what to do; they can perform any insanity they wish. But what they can't do is impose that insanity on the rest of us. The doctors who work in those religious hospitals can refuse to do abortions, they can refuse assisted suicide or euthanasia, they can do anything they want. But they have no right to impose what *they* call a universal medical ethic on secular institutions.

Besides, what is ethics? Can you define it? *My* definition is simple: ethics is saying and doing what is right, at the time. Does that make sense? And that changes. Notice I added "at the time."

Religion claims to have eternal truths; philosophy, too. I'm not singling out religion; you've got idiotic philosophy as well. You've got Kant with his unknowable realm. What sense does it make to hypothesize an unknowable realm? When you know it, there is no longer an unknowable realm. And if it's unknowable, you're never going to get there.

Ethics is saying and doing what is right at the time and that changes. Geoffrey

and I use the example of coal as fuel. Seventy-five years ago, if I told you that for Christmas I was going to have a truck deliver 10 tons of coal to your house, you would have been delighted. If I told you that today, you would be insulted. Doing the right thing changes with time.

That's true of human society also. There is a primitive society—I don't know which one exactly—whose members were shocked to learn that we embalm our dead, place them in boxes, and then bury them in the ground. Do you know what they do? They eat them. To them, it's ethical and moral and honorable to devour the corpse of your loved one. Now we're shocked at that, right? It's all a matter of acculturation, time, where you are, and who you are. Now if I visited this primitive society and learned that they do that, and I was a real humanist, I'd say, "Oh, that's interesting." And if the so-called savage in turn said, "Gee, that's interesting what you do," then he or she would be a humanist. I used to define maturity as the inability to be shocked. So I guess in some ways we're still immature. But if you're truly mature, and a true humanist, you can never be shocked. If they eat their dead, so be it—that's their culture. But you know what our missionaries did, don't you? That's immoral action.

I think you get the general gist of my position.

* * *

With Geoffrey at my side, I don't fear this indictment for murder. In fact, everybody I've met just scratches their heads and laughs about it. These contemporary inquisitors have made a mockery of the judicial system in Michigan. This indictment has done one good thing, however: it brazenly manifests the depth of corruption within our society. And it's not just the judiciary. Our legislature has manifested that as well with its silly law which it knew was unconstitutional. What kind of a legislature or government is it that would enact a so-called law it knew was unconstitutional? Can anybody get more depraved than that? Or more corrupt? Hardly. But that corruption permeates everything.

Our medical societies are just as corrupt; our medical boards are just as corrupt. I don't have a license any more. Did that stop me from doing what a physician should do? No! You see, the licensure is not entirely to guarantee competence. In fact, I think that's only a small part of what licensure is supposed to do. It guarantees absolute control. But they miscalculated on me. A piece of paper does not control me. They can't take away my training, my experience, or what I want to do, what I feel is right. They miscalculated, and now their anger knows no bounds. That is why they are behaving the way they are. That is why you are seeing so much negative press. They are desperate now, and that makes them dangerous. When anyone becomes that desperate, they are dangerous, and I recognize the danger.

So you see, in effect, our society is no different than primitive society—or Nazi Germany. People easily forget that. We pride ourselves in this country and the Western world, saying, "We're really enlightened and we're different." No, we're still totalitarian to a great degree.

And I'm afraid it's getting worse. When they added "under God" to the Pledge of Allegiance, they stepped in the wrong direction. When you get your feet mired in quicksand like that, you cannot extract them very easily. This society is thrashing around now. And you know what happens when you thrash around in quicksand. I am not optimistic at all.

It took two-and-a-half centuries for the Catholic church to apologize to Galileo, and you can bet it is going to take something like that long for any apology to come for what we are doing today. If an apology comes at all!

I hate to end on a pessimistic note, but I appreciate this opportunity to address you all. I thank you for your support. We are very much encouraged by it. We will keep going.

POSTSCRIPT

Should Euthanasia Be a Crime?

Clearly, the issue of euthanasia is replete with complications ranging from the moral to the macabre. Smith emphasizes the limitations of medicine, arguing that a significant percentage of those who are diagnosed as being in a persistent vegetative state (PVS) recover within three years. He also cites examples of individuals being subjected to "passive" or "soft" euthanasia against their will (their physicians simply allow them to die).

Kevorkian waxes more philosophical. He attacks established Christianity as a cesspool of backward policies based on malevolence and superstition. He calls for an ethical relativism partially discredited by the Nazi example (i.e., at one time many felt that all cultures should be studied, not judged, since actions are "relative").

Kevorkian radically parts company with many civil libertarians because not only does he provide information on suicide, but he helps patients to die too. Some members of humanistic organizations such as the Hemlock Society, who feel that sometimes suicide can be a rational response to unbearable conditions, argue that Kevorkian's extreme acts discredit their views. By contrast, others insist that people like Smith and organizations like the International Anti-Euthanasia Task Force are being absurd when they defend keeping all patients alive at all costs.

Currently, most Americans defend others' right to request that medical care be withheld in certain circumstances. However, beyond this point (and a large number are not even comfortable with *not* keeping all patients alive as long as possible), issues and opinions become extremely murky. We do not even have consensus on the proper terms, let alone their degree of legality. What exactly constitutes "physician-assisted suicide"? "Voluntary euthanasia"?

The literature on this issue is vast. The May–June 1995 *Hastings Center Report* is a special issue on assisted suicide and contains many excellent articles. E. van den Haag, in "Make Mine Hemlock," *National Review* (June 12, 1995), defends Kevorkian, while R. George and W. Porth, Jr., in "Death, Be Not Proud," *National Review* (June 26, 1995), challenge both van den Haag and Kevorkian. H. Hendin's *Suicide in America: New and Expanded Edition* (W. W. Norton, 1995) also challenges advocates of suicide. For a good legal overview of the issue, see *Euthanasia, Clinical Practice and the Law* edited by L. Gormally (Linace Center for Health Care Ethics, 1995); *Physician Assisted Death* edited by J. Humber et al. (Humana Press, 1994); and *Killing and Letting Die* edited by B. Steinbock (Fordham University Press, 1994). An early defense is in the Hemlock Society's *Assisted Suicide: The Compassionate Crime* (1982).

ISSUE 17

Will Community Policing Be the Answer to Crime Control?

YES: Patrick V. Murphy, from "Community Policing: The Only Proper Policing Method in a Free Society," *Law Enforcement News* (January 15, 1995)

NO: Raymond P. Manus, from "Misconceptions and 'Urban Village Policing,'" *Law Enforcement News* (February 28, 1995)

ISSUE SUMMARY

YES: Former New York City police commissioner Patrick V. Murphy contends that the only viable answer to the crime problem is community policing, which is not only the most effective method but also a requirement for police-citizen interactions in a democracy.

NO: New York City police detective Raymond P. Manus directly responds to Murphy's claims, dismissing most of them as impractical, contributing to police demoralization, expensive, of dubious value, or capable of being misused for self-promotion by politicians and police administrators.

Currently there are almost 400,000 sworn officers in some 12,000 local police agencies. Most police crime solving is from reactive policing (responding to a report of a crime), rather than proactive policing (initiating crime prevention or crime investigation).

In earlier times in the United States, the police did their jobs with the general support of the members of the community. The police were usually from the communities in which they patrolled, and they often functioned as an extension of the community.

An architect of early-twentieth-century policing was August Vollmer. He, along with the International Association of Chiefs of Police (IACP) and others, spearheaded the turn-of-the-century police reform movement. Among Vollmer's many contributions was his insistence on police professionalism, the recruitment of college students, and qualifying exams for recruitment and promotions. His emphasis was on scientific policing for the purpose of crime fighting. Yet, reflecting elements of some variants of community policing, he encouraged his officers to become involved with and help members of the communities being served, especially youngsters.

Toward the middle of the twentieth century, it was assumed that cops were more effective when they distanced themselves from the communities they served. Such distancing, it was theorized, functioned to enable officers to be more objective (e.g., to not side with one group over another in a dispute). It also was thought to minimize intimate relations that could lead to corruption. This attitude plus significant technological advances, such as motor vehicles and, more recently, computers, enabled far fewer officers to cover far greater areas than in the past. Thus, for several years the trend clearly was away from community policing.

In the past 20 years or so, however, due to documented conflicts between the police and the communities they served, a general perception of poor police coverage in many neighborhoods, increasing litigation against police, and a rapidly rising rate of drug-related and violent crimes, citizens have demanded that cops "return to the beat." Also, among criminologists and many police officers, there has been a growing belief that the police role should be expanded to include more than just raw law enforcement. At the same time, police in some areas openly admit that they can no longer control the crime problem. They sometimes ignore or even encourage neighborhood blockages, in which community members bar unknown drivers or pedestrians from entering their blocks (perhaps a commendable though legally dubious community response to crime).

Exactly what, then, is community policing? As you read this debate, notice how Patrick V. Murphy and Raymond P. Manus each seems to define the topic. What is "sector policing"? Why is it good, according to Manus? What objections do traditional officers seem to have to community policing, according to Murphy? In what ways do Murphy and Manus look at the same facts but arrive at totally different conclusions? How would you evaluate the kinds of policing recommended by the two protagonists?

YES

Patrick V. Murphy

COMMUNITY POLICING: THE ONLY PROPER POLICING METHOD IN A FREE SOCIETY

The discussion of New York City's community policing efforts that was begun in two commentaries in LEN [*Law Enforcement News*] (Nov. 30, 1994) should continue—if only because neither Professor Pisani nor Professor Rosenthal reaches the heart of the issue.

Motorized, so-called "preventive patrol" does not work and is unacceptable in a democracy. It separates residents from their protectors, with whom they need to interact. It deprives the people of their right to control the police as well as receive officer assistance in protecting and governing their communities. Community policing—the only proper method in a free society—is based on the reality that the police depend upon the eyes, ears, information and influence of the public to exert social control. Any departure from it leads us in the direction of a police state.

Neither Pisani nor Rosenthal believes in community policing. One disdains it as "politically correct." The other argues that it is dead but the Mayor and Police Commissioner deny that fact for political reasons. Rosenthal, a former assistant police chief, yearns for scientific evaluation of community policing, which he considers very expensive. Why in 1993 did the department attempt to evaluate community policing but not "preventive patrol," which is extremely wasteful, boring, unfulfilling and deprives an officer of the opportunity to be a real cop?

Community policing was practiced before the patrol car displaced virtually every "foot man" in the city. When the precinct captain, as well as a sergeant, held me accountable for knowing my post and generating information about who might be the neighborhood burglar, I was leveraging the eyes, ears and information that would break the case. Community policing is the only kind found in small towns. There are even large departments that never succumbed to the myth that police no longer needed the people once patrol was motorized. It is not expensive. It is cost-effective. It mobilized hundreds of partners for every officer involved.

Evaluation has shown a counterproductive dichotomy between sector officers and the 20 percent in each precinct who devote full time to community policing. The sector officers see themselves as "real cops" and their colleagues as "social workers." They are victims of a flawed thinking that can be found throughout the police service—a belief in the myth that motorized patrol creates an impression of omnipresence that deters the would-be criminal. The findings of the 1974 Kansas City preventive patrol experiment should have punctured that article of blind faith. However, myths die hard in a world that is not research-oriented.

In faulting former Commissioner Lee P. Brown's initiatives, neither Pisani nor Rosenthal acknowledges the basic problem: enormously wasteful motorized patrol, or stranger policing. The friendlier style of neighborhood police teams, cop-of-the-block and community officers has been more effective. It is a self-evident truth. They have proactively involved the people. Sector officers have been denied the opportunity to work in close partnership with residents. People are the major component of crime control, of the crime prevention machine. The police are the engine. Whatever the weaknesses in planning, training, scheduling or evaluating, officers mobilizing the eyes, ears, information and influence of residents are more productive than those limited to call response and unpreventive patrol.

The late Chief George Hansen of Fresno, Calif., indentified the fundamental failure of American policing:

"It is a cardinal principle of democratic societies that ultimate responsibility for peace, good order and law observance rests with the community of citizens of that society, not with an organized police force....

"[The police] role is to supplement and aid community efforts, not supplant them. And the powers permitted to these police must be carefully defined and limited.

"A community which abandons its basic duty to police itself, to a professional police service, will soon find that the police can hope to provide no more than a bare modicum of public order and security and this only through such repressive measures that the basic liberties of a free people are eroded, and the very democracy that the police seek to preserve is endangered....

"It is unfortunate, therefore, that the history of urban policing in America in the 20th century is a consistent record of efforts by the police service to assume a disproportionate share of the responsibility for maintaining society control, and the concurrent abandonment by American communities of their portion of this duty. The result has been an increasing lawlessness which even increasingly repressive measures have been unable to curb. The delicate balance between the traditional roles of the community and the police needs to be restored. Peacekeeping must again become a joint police-community effort to stand any reasonable chance for lasting success."

On taking office in 1990, Mayor David Dinkins was faced with the challenge of stabilizing a police department in disarray. Departing Mayor Edward Koch's second police commissioner—who had been described in a New York Times editorial as "a drunk, a womanizer and a loudmouth"—had retired after six long years in which Koch retained him despite repeated evidence that he was unqualified to direct, and unworthy to lead, the brave men and women of the Police Department.

Only one of 75 precincts experimented with community policing. At that rate of implementation, it would require 450 years to eliminate ineffective "preventive patrol."

A drug-corruption problem surfaced in a Brooklyn precinct. More ominously, as the Mollen Commission would later find, the integrity-control system was unraveling. The top command had changed from one devoted to integrity to one devoted to cover-up. A bad headline had become worse than a bad cop.

In the face of this, Mayor Dinkins brought the best chief in the country to New York. Within a year, more community policing had been implemented than in the previous six. As Commissioner, Lee P. Brown brought a wealth of experience from police service in four states. He had been chief of three major departments and broken new ground in advancing each of them. His reassuring presence, extensive knowledge and quiet, mature personality restored the confidence of New Yorkers and members of the Police Department after six years of embarrassment, falling morale and a 61-percent increase in murders. African-American police officer representation ranked 50th among the 50 largest cities. The war on crime had been fought with City Hall press conferences, exclusion of the public, and screeching rhetoric.

Tragically, Brown's potential contribution was cut short by the diagnosis of his wife's terminal illness early in his term. He served only 32 months, rather than 48. Well-formulated plans for many additional improvements never materialized.

Pisani misunderstands Roberg and Kuykendall's evaluation of the Neighborhood Police Team program begun in 1971. He says it failed. They say it would have been more favorable if organizational change had been introduced less rapidly. Well planned, carefully phased change is highly desirable. However, police commissioners inevitably face the difficult problem of accomplishing as much as possible in the limited time they may have. Corruption, brutality and racism should be eliminated abruptly without concern for the niceties of manipulating organizational behavior. The enormous waste of taxpayer dollars involved in perpetuating the theory of deterrent visibility through motorized patrol requires expeditious change.

Pisani's solution—a commissioner elected for eight years—would be as illogical as elected FBI or CIA directors. This is, after all, a democracy. Civilian control is the operating principle. Mayors can and should be held accountable for the performance of their commissioners.

Community policing in New York in 1994 is far from perfect. It is clear, however, that it is a major improvement over what existed when Lee Brown became commissioner. Commissioner William Bratton believes in community policing as well as creative, proactive strategies in every precinct that reduce crime and disorder. It is time well spent as distinguished from reactive patrolling that neither prevents nor solves problems.

Eventually, every general practitioner in every sector in every precinct deserves to be a cop of the block, with an individual "urban village" of his or her own. It should consist of 500–1,000 residents (or the equivalent in commercial sectors) depending upon crime rate calculated on a seriousness index. The model was developed by the officers of the 81st Precinct in 1971 without headquarters directions, and with little planning and minimal training. The wisdom of street experience led to the logic of involving, not excluding, the people.

Commissioner Bratton has identified the "innate idealism of police officers... which even the richest corporations may lack." He has called for "opening up the possibilities of the job ... to get them into the game. If we do that, then our goal of dramatically reducing crime, disorder and fear is as good as accomplished."

He is exactly right. Nothing can open the possibilities more than involving every generalist in community policing. That will empower the poor, who suffer most from crime, to take back control of their streets from criminals and improve their lives as full citizens. It is no exaggeration to say that stranger policing has deprived them of their sense of community.

NO

MISCONCEPTIONS AND "URBAN VILLAGE POLICING"

I have had a great deal of respect for Patrick V. Murphy, the former New York City police commissioner, so I was genuinely surprised to see his article in defense of New York's community policing ("Community policing: the only proper policing method in a free society," LEN, Jan. 15, 1995). Commissioner Murphy may have confused Lee Brown's version of community policing with his own earlier implementation of neighborhood policing. Murphy seems to have accepted Brown's writings while rejecting the obvious results of Brown's efforts.

Community policing defined a neighborhood "as an area in which people have shared values or a common focus on a community institution, shopping center or other neighborhood 'draw.'" ("Policing New York City in the 1990's.") Thus, the people who happened to converge on a shopping center on a Saturday afternoon would satisfy this definition. The Neighborhood Police Teams (NPT) had clearly articulated boundaries, and stressed responsibility and accountability. The lack of accountability that flourished under Commissioner Brown contributed to the riots in Crown Heights and the serious police misconduct uncovered by the Mollen Commission.

Several misconceptions appear in Murphy's article:

"Motorized, so-called 'preventive patrol' does not work and is unacceptable in a democracy."

Murphy is entitled to this opinion, but this is not relevant to the discussion of New York City policing. Preventive patrol had been a term from the 1950's which assumed that an officer's time, when not spent on a specific task, was to be used for some mystical type of deterrence. Even before Patrick Murphy became commissioner in 1971, the NYPD had rejected preventive patrol in favor of focused patrols directed at specific crime patterns and hazard locations. These patrols were conducted both on foot and in vehicles. Commissioner Brown resurrected the ghost of preventive patrol to provide an easy image of bad police practices which he would correct by his vision of policing.

From Raymond P. Manus, "Misconceptions and 'Urban Village Policing,'" *Law Enforcement News* (February 28, 1995). Copyright © 1995 by *Law Enforcement News*, John Jay College of Criminal Justice, New York, NY. Reprinted by permission.

By attaching the pejorative "preventive patrol" to the word "motorized," Murphy makes a similar mistake. It is unreasonable to tell a citizen who is being assaulted that the police cannot use a motorized vehicle to come to his assistance.

"Community policing was practiced before the patrol car displaced virtually every 'foot man' in the city.... It is not expensive. It is cost effective."

Here, Murphy is partly right—community policing did not originate with Lee Brown. Still, he neglected the hazards of local communities employing their own type of policing. It was the community-supported police officers confronting civil rights marchers in the South during the 1960's that led the President's Crime Commission to conclude that there were two nations: one protected, the other simply policed. In volume 13 of the "Perspectives on policing" monograph series, Murphy and Hubert Williams offer the "minority view" that those historically left out of the political process could be left behind once again.

Foot patrol is expensive, but in highly populated areas it can be cost effective. Not long before Brown accepted the job of New York City police commissioner, he wrote an article (September 1989) in which he stated that community policing did not require an increase in resources; it was merely changing the attitudes of police officers. But after just a few months on the job in New York, he produced a "Report to the Mayor: Staffing Needs of the New York City Police Department," in which he indicated a need for a force in excess of 30,000 sworn members to carry out community policing. At a cost of $1.8 billion to New York taxpayers, over 5,000 officers were added to the police ranks.

As commissioner, Murphy had the luxury of a force in excess of 31,000 sworn, thanks in part to New Yorkers' fear of the civil disorders of the 1960's. After the Newark, N.J., riots in 1967, the New York City police force grew by over 4,000 officers. The police force in 1970 had the capacity to serve neighborhood residents and to respond rapidly to citizens in crisis. The economy of the city couldn't continue to support a force that large.

The patrol car supplanted the foot cop when the fiscal crisis of 1975 forced a major reduction in police officers. From 1975 to 1981, the force shrunk to under 23,000. Police management went from one extreme to another. For those six years, the police were very much concerned with responding to citizens in crisis as crime and violence grew to a peak in 1981. There was little funding for providing non-essential services like the cop-of-the-block.

"Evaluation has shown a counterproductive dichotomy between sector officers and the 20 percent in each precinct who devote full time to community policing."

Twenty-three years ago, the Knapp Commission indicated the department had adequate procedures to direct and control the police force, but had failed to translate dogma into action. Lee Brown had 32 months (about average tenure for New York City police commissioners) and was unable to lead his department to follow the philosophy of community policing. It has always been within the authority of the police commissioner to require police officers to work within a specific sector, with a responsibility for the problems therein. Brown issued no directives to eliminate the cross-sector dispatching that destroys accountability, encourages "stranger policing by officers in sector cars, and separates the community officer from the emergency service provider.

"[T]he basic problem: enormously wasteful motorized patrol, or stranger policing. The friendlier style of neighborhood police team cop-of-the-block and community officers have been more effective."

Administrators have always had to balance effectiveness with efficiency. Foot patrol may have been more effective, but that effectiveness is achieved at a greater cost in manpower. Motorized patrol enables one officer to cover a much larger area at less cost to the taxpayer. Given that most of the people, most of the time, don't need a police officer to control their lives, a small force properly deployed can efficiently maintain public order. A force that is too small will be ineffective as it will be constantly occupied by acting to past events. It is a poor policy choice that sends police officers out of their primary sector to address non-emergency events, sacrificing effectiveness for efficiency. There is no reason why a friendly police officer can't use an auto or scooter to respond to conditions within his or her area. The NPT under Commissioner Murphy employed motorized patrol yet minimized the stranger policing by maintaining sector integrity. Officers assigned to the neighborhood sector were expected to attend community meetings, part their vehicles, walk and talk with residents, and address local concerns.

"Mayor David Dinkins was faced with the challenge of stabilizing a police department in disarray.... [T]he best police chief in the country ... Lee P. Brown ... restored the confidence of New Yorkers and members of the department."

The "Report to the Governor" regarding the four days of rioting in Crown Heights raises serious questions about the accuracy of these assertions. Prior to Brown telling everyone that traditional policing was bad, the Police Department accepted as its mission the obligations imposed by the New York City Charter. The force was focused on protecting life and property, suppressing riots and insurrections, and detecting and arresting offenders. It was Brown who muddled the police mission by refusing to enforce a court order at the Korean greengrocer boycott and tolerating four days of police inactivity in Crown Heights. Neither Dinkins nor Brown called for an investigation of the police response; it took the Governor and his top criminal justice aide to expose the lack of coordination and control of the police force.

On Dec. 27, 1993, the Mollen Commission looking into alleged police corruption issued an interim report on the state of the Police Department at that time, the waning days of the Dinkins Administration. Lee Brown had already left New York. The final report of the commission, issued the following July, did nothing to restore the confidence of New Yorkers, or members of the department.

"The war on crime had been fought with City Hall press conferences, exclusion of the public, and screeching rhetoric."

The "Report to the Governor" on Crown Heights indicates that the major print media relied upon press releases from Mayor Dinkins and Commissioner Brown rather than their own observations. On July 23, 1993, The New York Times conceded in a page 1 headline, "The Press Had Its Blind Spots Too." While the Mayor was reporting that everything was under control and editorials in the print media were praising his conduct, the "Report to the Governor" called Crown Heights the worst riot in the city in 20 years. Every administration gets its message to the public through the press, but it appears that the Dinkins/Brown administration could parade its promises without critical examination, comment or review.

"Community policing in New York in 1994 is far from perfect."

An admission that community policing has not worked, even after the addition of 5,000 police officers. The promise of the Safe Streets, Safe City program was widely advertised as "The beat cop is back!" The current administration makes no such promises in implementing its new strategies.

"Eventually, every general practitioner in every sector in every precinct deserves to be a cop-of-the-block, with an individual 'urban village' of his or her own. It should consist of 500–1,000 residents (or the equivalent in commercial sectors) depending upon crime rate calculated on a seriousness index. The model was developed by the officers of the 81st Precinct in 1971 without headquarters direction, and with planning and minimal training."

According to 1990 U.S. Census data, New York City has a resident population of more than 7.3 million. The city could have approximately 9,763 "urban villages," each averaging 750 residents. It would require more than 14,500 police officers to schedule one officer per day, 365 days a year, for each of these villages. To cover that area 24 hours a day, seven days a week, would require 44,000 police officers. Total coverage, including the routine exceptions to allow for such things

as vacation, sick leave, training, etc., would require more than 56,000 officers —approximately 25,000 more than are currently funded.

These 56,000 officers (no sergeants, lieutenants or higher ranking personnel) would be limited to the area they could cover on foot and the citizen would just have to wait until his or her beat officer was able to respond. There would be no provision for riots, parades, serious accidents or crimes in progress. If the task were too great for the single officer on duty in that area at a moment of need, the public would have to come to the officer's aid and community policing would be truly realized. When the officer made an arrest and had to present evidence at trial, the area would be without police coverage.

Given the size of such a force, the suggestion that every officer have his or her own "urban village" appears to be extremely expensive. Murphy may have misunderstood the model or misstated its application in this case. But there is a significant risk in applying any model developed without adequate planning, training and command direction.

Community policing, as implemented by Lee Brown, was doomed to fail in New York. He may have provided the vision, but he lacked the leadership to plan, train and direct the men and women of the NYPD. He told his managers that the train was leaving the station, and to get aboard or be left behind. His choice of metaphor illustrates reasons for the failure of his administration. More than any other vehicle, a train requires a great deal of planning and maintenance to carry passengers safely to their destination. Brown started the train before the tracks were firmly in place, the right-of-way clearly described. He brought the train up to full speed before the tracks could be tested and faulty sections replaced. As Brown's train took the anointed down the tracks to self-destruction, the majority of police managers were content to wait for the next train with the knowledge that they could safely make adjustments along the way.

By contrast, neighborhood police teams were the product of a well conceived plan, directed and coordinated by the top policy-makers in the department, with adequate training and guidance. While brutality and corruption must be stopped immediately, other policy changes in the police department can be accomplished incrementally. This provides managers with an opportunity to adjust the plan as necessary to achieve the desired results.

A fixed geographical area, a neighborhood, can be effectively and efficiently policed by teams of police officers. The responsibility for the area and the team can be fixed to one individual sergeant. The size of the team can be determined by the population, crime, and conditions within the area. A city of 300 square miles could have 300 neighborhood teams of approximately 30 members each. On average, each neighborhood would have 16 officers per day to provide services over three tours. One motorized, two-officer unit and three beat officers per square mile is currently attainable. Within the current patrol strength there is even room for emergency responders, special fixed conditions, and a reserve for unanticipated needs. Unfortunately for Commissioner Brown, he rejected this model as a relic of the past and attempted to design a whole new philosophy as community policing.

POSTSCRIPT

Will Community Policing Be the Answer to Crime Control?

Although both Murphy and Manus have been police officers in the New York City Police Department, they often seem to be talking about different departments. Manus is currently with the NYPD, while Murphy, a former police chief, has long since been an outsider. Might this influence their perceptions?

At the very least, it would seem that community policing is proactive. However, from there the definitional issue seems highly problematic. Does it always, sometimes, rarely, or never involve active community participation? Traditionally and until very recently, most officers jealously guarded their monopoly on patrolling neighborhoods. When neighborhood watches began, most precincts insisted on tight police control. This is less so today.

Is community policing, as Murphy suggests, little more than enhancing community or public relations by having a "cop on every block"? Should there be a combination of foot patrols and police car patrols? Does community policing mean that the police have to be social workers, educators, preachers, and counselors as well as law enforcers? What is the difference between the traditional crime-fighting model and community policing that entails stepping up patrols to address specific problems or to secure "hot spots"? Are most officers more interested in crime fighting than in community work? Should community policing encourage the assignment of officers to the neighborhoods in which they live?

The literature on community policing is rapidly expanding. From November 1994 through June 1995, *Law Enforcement News* kept the issue alive with running debates. The journal *Community Policing Exchange* is most helpful and sympathetic. See, for instance, "Community Policing Is Alive and Well!" by B. Bucquerourx (May/June 1995). A helpful article is "Community Policing and a Model of Crime Prevention in the Community," by M. Wiauowski and J. Vardalis, *Criminal Psychology* (October 1994). An excellent article on the police is L. Sherman, "The Police," in *Crime* edited by J. Wilson and J. Petersilia (ICS Press, 1995).

Two excellent overviews of the concept and practice of community policing are *The Challenge of Community Policing* edited by D. Rosenbaum (Sage Publications, 1994) and J. McElroy and C. Cosgrove's *Community Policing: The Cop in New York* (Sage Publications, 1992). An interesting account of barricades is in L. Yanez's "Barricades Put Neighbors on Opposite Sides," *Sun Sentinel* (July 10, 1995). Finally, a news report on citizen patrols is J. Loh's "Crime Statistics Fall With COP on the Beat," *The Washington Times* (May 2, 1995).

ISSUE 18

Are Human Rights Basic to Justice?

YES: Rhoda E. Howard, from "Human Rights and the Necessity for Cultural Change," *Focus on Law Studies* (Fall 1992)

NO: Vinay Lal, from "The Imperialism of Human Rights," *Focus on Law Studies* (Fall 1992)

ISSUE SUMMARY

YES: Sociology professor Rhoda E. Howard argues that human rights are both universal and basic for justice. Although she makes some allowances for "weak cultural relativism," she nevertheless insists that justice largely depends on a general acceptance of basic rights.

NO: Vinay Lal, a professor of humanities, dismisses human rights as a tool used by Western nations to legitimize brutal tactics that maintain their power over weaker nations and regions. Focusing primarily on the international level, Lal proposes that, in practice, human rights have been used as little more than a cover for injustice.

The philosophes such as Rousseau, Montesquieu, and Voltaire, the writers and thinkers of the eighteenth-century French Enlightenment, argued that women and men were the measure of all things, not religion nor the state. The influence of their ideas permanently altered the West. Their thinking formed the foundation of most modern legal and political systems, including the U.S. Declaration of Independence and the U.S. Constitution. The idea that all people had the right to "life, liberty, and the pursuit of happiness" was indeed revolutionary.

Unfortunately, from the very beginning of the U.S. government, there were built-in contradictions and hypocrisies. Slaves, for instance, simply were not entitled to any rights or freedoms. Women, too, were disenfranchised: they could not vote until 1920. The Bill of Rights itself was not viewed as applicable at the state level (where most legal action takes place) until the late 1800s. The idea of "due process" within America's criminal justice system was an alien concept until well into the twentieth century. This was often equally true in British and other European legal systems.

Yet, beginning with the ideas of the French philosophes and as written into such documents as the U.S. Constitution, the foundation and form for the establishment and respect of individual rights as the basis of justice and law were there.

While many intellectuals in the early twentieth century embraced human rights and the legal ideals of the West, others criticized Western missionaries and jingoists ("my country, right or wrong"; "America, love it or leave it") for superimposing their own views of morality on other countries, and a reaction against universal cultural standards set in. Influential American anthropologists such as Franz Boas (1858–1942) advocated what they called cultural relativism. This is the doctrine that any society's structures should be understood in terms of the functions they perform within that society, not by Western standards of correct conduct. The ethical corollary is ethical relativism, which can be broadly interpreted to mean anything is permissible when viewed within the context of a groups' values; there is no universal right or wrong.

Canadian sociologist Rhoda E. Howard maintains that human rights are necessary for positive cultural changes. Reflecting the economist Walter Rostow's notion of prerequisites needed for developing societies to pass through stages of growth before they reach a "taking off" point, she points out that democracy and justice, predicated on human rights, are necessary for change. Although she defends universal values, including specific legal rights, she also concedes that some elements of justice are more important than others. For instance, she would allow for a "weak cultural relativism" in certain areas where local traditions are supported.

Vinay Lal of Columbia University dismisses human rights as not only an imperfect ideal but also a tool used by the United States at the international level to unfairly attack others and advance its own cause.

While dwelling primarily at the international level in his discussion of human and legal rights, Lal also reflects an expanded understanding of rights. Traditionally, human rights (as Howard presents them) primarily had political and civil (legal) dimensions. Lal, though, argues for the inclusion of *social* rights as well (such as economic support of education, health, and employment). Since Lal and Howard's debate, reprinted here, reports of inhumane actions by criminal justice agencies around the world as well as by soldiers and private citizens have been widely publicized. Officials in Honduras are searching for bodies of dissenters as the civilian government there claims hundreds were killed by CIA-trained and financed Honduras army units in the 1980s. Police trained by the U.S. government in several other countries have been linked directly with both the brutalization of civilians and drug running. In Bosnia genocide is used as a solution to the "Muslim problem," according to the Yugoslav War Crimes Tribunal. Canadian soldiers were recently charged with the brutal murder of several Somalian teens. And perhaps the most tragic violation of human rights continues to occur in Rwanda. In 1994, 500,000 unarmed civilians were slaughtered in less than six months.

As you read the selections by Howard and Lal, who would you say is more pessimistic? Why? Who seems to have a more consistent respect for the concept of human rights? Why? Do you agree that respect for human rights is necessary for justice? Why, or why not?

YES

Rhoda E. Howard

HUMAN RIGHTS AND THE NECESSITY FOR CULTURAL CHANGE

Many critics of the concept of human rights argue that it undermines indigenous cultures, especially in the underdeveloped world (Cobbah, 1987; Pollis and Schwab, 1980; Renteln, 1990). I agree that the concept of human rights often undermines cultures. Cultural rupture is often a necessary aspect of the entrenchment of respect for human rights. Culture is not of absolute ethical value; if certain aspects of particular cultures change because citizens prefer to focus on human rights, then that is a perfectly acceptable price to pay.

Human rights are rights held by the individual merely because she or he is human, without regard to status or position. In principle, all human beings hold human rights equally. These rights are claims against the state that do not depend on duties to the state, although they do depend on duties to other citizens, e.g., not to commit crimes. They are also claims that the individual can make against society as a whole. Society, however, may have cultural preconceptions that certain types of individuals ought not to be entitled to such rights. Thus, culture and human rights come into conflict. The concept of cultural relativism recognizes this, but does not consider the possibility that, in such instances, perhaps the better path to choose is to change the culture in order to promote human rights.

Cultural relativism is a method of social analysis that stresses the importance of regarding social and cultural phenomena from the "perspective of participants in or adherents of a given culture" (Bidney, 1968). Relativism assumes that there is no one culture whose customs and beliefs dominate all others in a moral sense. Relativism is a necessary corrective to ethical ethnocentrism. But it is now sometimes taken to such an extreme that any outsider's discussions of local violations of human rights are criticized as forms of ideological imperialism.

In effect, this extreme position advocates not cultural relativism but cultural absolutism. Cultural absolutists posit particular cultures as of absolute moral value, more valuable than any universal principle of justice. In the left-right/North-South debate that permeates today's ideological exchanges,

From Rhoda E. Howard, "Human Rights and the Necessity for Cultural Change," *Focus on Law Studies*, vol. 8, no. 1 (Fall 1992). Copyright © 1992 by The American Bar Association. Reprinted by permission.

cultural absolutists specifically argue that culture is of more importance than the internationally accepted principles of human rights.

Cultural absolutists argue that human rights violate indigenous cultures because they are Western in origin. But the origins of any idea, including human rights, do not limit its applicability. The concept of human rights arose in the West largely in reaction to the overwhelming power of the absolutist state; in the Third World today, states also possess enormous power against which citizens need to be protected. As societies change, so ideals of social justice change.

Cultures are not immutable aspects of social life, ordained forever to be static. Cultures change as a result of structural change: secularism, urbanization and industrialism are among the chief causes of cultural change both in the West since the eighteenth century and in the underdeveloped world today (Howard, 1986, chapter 2). Cultures can also be manipulated by political or social spokespersons in their own interest. Culturalism is frequently an argument that is used to "cover" political repression, as when Kenyan President Daniel arap Moi told a female environmental activist not to criticize his policies because it is "against African tradition" for women to speak up in public. This does not mean that all aspects of culture must necessarily be ruptured in order that human rights can be entrenched. Many aspects of culture, such as kinship patterns, art or ritual, have nothing to do with human rights and can safely be preserved, even enhanced, when other rights-abusive practices are corrected. Many aspects of public morality are similarly not matters of human rights. The existence or abolition of polygamous marriage, for example, is not an international human rights issue, despite objections to it in the West. Nor is the proper degree of respect one should show to one's elders, or the proper norms of generosity and hospitality. The apparent Western overemphasis on work at the expense of family is a cultural practice that Third World societies can avoid without violating human rights. Many other such matters, such as whether criminal punishment should be by restitution or imprisonment, can be resolved without violating international human rights norms.

Jack Donnelly argues that "weak" cultural relativism is sometimes an appropriate response to human rights violations. Weak cultural relativism would "allow occasional and strictly limited local variations and exceptions to human rights," while recognizing "a comprehensive set of prima facie universal human rights" (Donnelly, 1989, p. 110). This is an appropriate position if the violation of a human right is truly a cultural practice that no political authority and no socially dominant group initiates or defends. Consider the case of female genital operations in Africa and elsewhere. Governments do not promote these violations; indeed, through education about their detrimental health consequences, they try to stop them. Nevertheless there is strong popular sentiment in favour of the operations, among women as well as (if not more so than) men (Slack, 1988). Similarly, child betrothal, officially a violation of international human rights norms, is popularly accepted in some cultures (Howard, 1986, chapter 8). And certain forms of freedom of speech, such as blasphemy and pornography, are deeply offensive to popular sentiment in many cultures, whether or not the government permits or prohibits them.

Although a weak cultural relativist stance is appropriate in some instances as a protection of custom against international human rights norms, to implement human rights does mean that certain cultural practices must be ruptured. One obvious example is the universal subordination of women as a group to men as a group, backed up by men's collective economic, political and physical power over women. If women have achieved greater access to human rights in North America since the second wave of feminism began about 1970, it is largely because they have challenged cultural stereotypes of how they ought to behave. Feminist activists no longer believe that women ought to be deferential to men or wives subordinate to their husbands. Nor do they any longer hold to the almost universal cultural belief that women's divinely ordained purpose in life is to bear children. Feminists in other parts of the world such as India or Africa are making similar challenges to their cultures in the process of asserting their rights (on women's rights as human rights, see Bunch, 1990, and Eisler, 1987.)

Many critics of human rights find them overly individualistic; they point to the selfish materialism they see in Western (North American) society. But the individualism of Western society reflects not protection but neglect of human rights, especially economic rights (Howard, "Ideologies of Social Exclusion," unpublished). In the United States, certain economic rights are regarded as culturally inappropriate. A deeply ingrained belief exists that everyone ought to be able to care for himself and his family. Since the U.S. is or was the land of opportunity (at least for white people), anyone who lives in poverty is personally responsible for his being in that state. Thus the U.S. has the worst record of provision of economic rights of any major Western democratic state. The right to health is not acknowledged, nor is the right to housing or food. Before such rights are acknowledged and provided in the U.S., the cultural belief in the virtues of hard work and pulling oneself up by one's bootstraps will have to be replaced by a more collectivist vision of social responsibility. The culturally ingrained belief that blacks are inferior people not deserving of the respect and concern of whites will also need to be ruptured.

Critics of human rights sometimes argue that cultures are so different that there is no possibility of shared meanings about social justice evolving across cultural barriers. The multivocality of talk about rights precludes any kind of consensus. The very possibility of debate is rejected. Indeed, debate, the idea that people holding initially opposing views can persuade each other through logic and reason of their position, is rejected as a form of thought typical of rationalist and competitive Western society. Western thought, it is argued, silences the oppressed.

Yet it is precisely the central human rights premises of freedom of speech, press and assembly that all over the world permit the silenced to gain a social voice. Human rights undermine constricting status-based categorizations of human beings: they permit people from degraded social groups to demand social change. Rational discourse about human rights permits degraded workers, peasants, untouchables, women and members of minority groups to articulate and consider alternate social arrangements than those that currently oppress them (see also Teson, 1985).

Human rights are "inauthentic" in many cultures because they challenge the ingrained privileges of the ruling classes, the wealthy, the Brahmin, the patriarch, or the member of a privileged ethnic or religious group. The purpose of human rights is precisely to change many culturally ingrained habits and customs that violate the dignity of the individual. Rather than apologizing that human rights challenge cultural norms in many societies, including our own, we should celebrate that fact.

This article is based in large part on my Human Rights and the Search for Community *(in progress). Unpublished papers from this project, available on request, include "Cultural Absolutism and the Nostalgia for Community," and "Ideologies of Social Exclusion in North American Society."*

REFERENCES

Bidney, David. 1968. "Cultural Relativism," in *International Encyclopedia of the Social Sciences,* Volume III. New York: Macmillan.

Bunch, Charlotte. 1990. "Women's Rights as Human Rights: Toward a Re-Vision of Human Rights." *Human Rights Quarterly* 12: 486–98.

Cobbah, Josiah A. M. 1987. "African Values and the Human Rights Debate: An African Perspective." *Human Rights Quarterly* 9: 309–31.

Donnelly, Jack. 1989. *Universal Human Rights in Theory and Practice.* Ithaca, N.Y.: Cornell University Press.

Eisler, Riane. 1987. "Human Rights: Toward an Integrated Theory for Action." *Human Rights Quarterly* 9: 287–308.

Howard, Rhoda E. 1986. *Human Rights in Commonwealth Africa.* Totowa, NJ.: Rowman and Littlefield.

Pollis, Adamantia, and Peter Schwab, "Human Rights: A Western Concept with Limited Applicability," in Pollis and Schwab, eds. 1980. *Human Rights: Cultural and Ideological Perspectives.* New York: Praeger.

Renteln, Alison Dundes. 1990. *International Human Rights: Universalism versus Relativism.* Newbury Park, CA.: Sage.

Slack, Alison T. 1988. "Female Circumcision: A Critical Appraisal." *Human Rights Quarterly* 10: 437–86.

Teson, Fernando R. 1985. "International Human Rights and Cultural Relativism." *Virginia Journal of International Law* 25: 869–98.

NO

Vinay Lal

THE IMPERIALISM OF HUMAN RIGHTS

The notion of human rights is deeply embedded in modern legal and political thought and could well be considered one of the most significant achievements of contemporary culture and civilization. Certain classes of people in all societies have, from the beginning of time, been endowed with "rights" which others could not claim. The immunity that emissaries (now diplomats) from one state to another have always received constitutes one of the norms of conduct that has guided relations between states. Likewise, most cultures have had, in principle at least, intricate rules to govern the conduct of warfare. Civilians were not to be taken hostage as a military strategy; a soldier was not to be shot as he was surrendering; and so on.

Some of these customary modes of conduct are now enshrined in the law, transmitted on the one hand into "rights" that the citizen can claim against the state, and on the other hand into restraints on the state's agenda to produce conformity and contain dissent. The individual has been given a great many more rights, and—what is unique to modern times—never before have such rights been placed under the protection of the law. States are bound in their relations to their subjects by a myriad of international agreements and laws, including the Geneva Conventions, the International Covenant on Civil and Political Rights, the United Nations Charter, the Universal Declaration of Human Rights, and the U.N. Body of Principles for the Protection of All Persons Under Any Form of Detention or Punishment.

Moreover, it is only in our times that the "international community" seems prepared to enforce sanctions against a state for alleged violations of such rights. With the demise of communism, the principal foes of human rights appear to have been crushed, and the very notion of "human rights" seems sovereign. Should we then unreservedly endorse the culture of "human rights" as it has developed in the liberal-democratic framework of the modern West, indeed even as a signifier of the "end of history" and of the emergence of the New World Order? On the contrary, I would like to suggest several compelling reasons why, far from acquiescing in the suggestion that the notion of human rights is the most promising avenue to a new era in human relations, we should consider the discourse of human rights as the most evolved form of Western imperialism. Indeed, human rights can be viewed as the latest masquerade of the West—particularly America, the torchbearer since the end of World War II of "Western" values— to appear to the world as the epitome of civilization and as the only legitimate arbiter of human values.

To understand the roots of the modern discourse of "human rights," we need to isolate the two central notions from which it is derived, namely the "individual" and the "rule of law." It has been a staple of Western thought since at least the Renaissance that—while the West recognizes the individual as the true unit of being and the building block of society, non-Western cultures have been built around collectivities, conceived as religious, linguistic, ethnic, tribal or racial groups. As the *Economist*—and one could multiply such examples a thousand-fold —was to boldly declare in its issue of 27 February 1909, "whatever may be the political atom in India, it is certainly not the individual of Western democratic theory, but the community of some sort." In the West the individual stands in singular and splendid isolation, the promise of the inherent perfectibility of man; in the non-West, the individual is nothing, always a part of a collectivity in relation to which his or her existence is defined, never a being unto himself or herself. Where the "individual" does not exist, one cannot speak of his or her rights; and where there are no rights, it is perfectly absurd to speak of their denial or abrogation.

On the Western view, moreover, if the atomistic conception of the "individual" is a prerequisite for a concern with human rights, so is the "rule of law" under which alone can such rights be respected. In a society which lives by the "rule of law," such laws as the government might formulate are done so in accordance with certain normative criteria—for example, they shall be non-discriminatory, blind to considerations of race, gender, class, and linguistic background; these laws are then made public, so that no person might plead ignorance of the law; and the judicial process under which the person charged for the infringement of such laws is tried must hold out the promise of being fair and equitable. As in the case of "individual," the "rule of law" is held to be a uniquely Western contribution to civilization, on the two-fold assumption that democracy is an idea and institution of purely Western origins, and that the only form of government known to non-Western societies was absolutism. In conditions of "Oriental Despotism," the only law was the law of the despot, and the life and limb of each of his subjects was hostage to the tyranny of his pleasures and whims. In the despotic state, there was perhaps only one "individual," the absolute ruler; under him were the masses, particles of dust on the distant horizon. What rights were there to speak of then?

Having briefly outlined how the notions of the "individual" and the "rule of law" came to intersect in the formulation of the discourse of human rights, we can proceed to unravel some of the more disturbing and unacceptable aspects of this discourse. Where once the language of liberation was religion, today the language of emancipation is law. Indeed, the very notion of "human rights," as it is commonly understood in the international forum today, is legalistic. Proponents of the "rule of law," convinced of the uniqueness of the West, are not prepared to concede that customs and traditional usages in most "Third World" countries have functioned for centuries in place of "law," and that even without the "rule of law" there were conventions and traditions which bound one person to respect the rights of another. We expect rights to be protected under the law and the conformity of states to the "rule of law." Many obvious and commonplace objections to such a state of affairs come to mind. By what right, with what authority, and with what consequences do certain states brand other states as "outlaw" or "renegade" states, living outside the pale of the "rule of law," allegedly oblivious to the rights of their subjects, and therefore subject to sanctions from the "international community?"

There is, as has been argued, one "rule of law" for the powerful, and an altogether different one for those states that do not speak the "rational," "diplomatic," and "sane" language that the West has decreed to be the universal form of linguistic exchange. It is not only the case that when Americans retaliate against their foes, they are engaged in "just war" or purely "defensive" measures in the interest of national security, but also that when Libyans or Syrians do so, they are transformed into "terrorists" or ruthless and self-aggrandizing despots in the pursuit of international dominance. The problem is more acute: who is to police the police? The United States claims adherence to international law, but summarily rejected the authority of the World Court when it condemned the United States for waging undeclared war against Nicaragua. More recently, the U.S. Supreme Court, in an astounding judgment barely noticed in the American press, upheld the constitutionality of a decision of a circuit court in Texas which, by allowing American law enforcement officers to kidnap nationals of a foreign state for alleged offenses under American law to be brought to the United States for trial, effectively proclaims the global jurisdiction of American law. As a noted Indian commentator has written, "We are thus back in the 15th, 16th, and 17th century world of piracy and pillage" (Ashok Mitra, "No Holds Barred for the U.S.," *Deccan Herald*, 3 July 1992). Were not the Libyans and Sandinistas supposed to be the pirates?

There are, however, less obvious and more significant problems with the legalistic conception of a world order where "human rights" will be safeguarded. The present conception of "human rights" largely rests on a distinction between state and civil society, a distinction here fraught with hazardous consequences. The rights which are claimed are rights held against the state or, to put it another way, with the blessing of the state: the right to freedom of speech and expression, the right to gather in public, the right to express one's grievances within the limits of the constitution, and so forth. The state becomes the guarantor of these rights, when in fact it is everywhere the state which is the most flagrant violator of human rights.

Not only does the discourse of "human rights" privilege the state, but the very conception of "rights" must of necessity remain circumscribed. The right to a fair hearing upon arrest, or to take part in the government of one's country, is acknowledged as an unqualified political and civil right, but the right to housing, food, clean air, an ecologically-sound environment, free primary and secondary education, public transportation, a high standard of health, the preservation of one's ethnic identity and culture, and security in the event of unemployment or impairment due to disease and old age is not accorded parity. When, as in the United States, certain communities are in a systematic and calculated fashion deprived of the basic amenities required to sustain a reasonable standard of living, when an entire economy is designed on a war footing, does not that constitute a gross and inexcusable infringement of the "human rights" of those who are most disempowered in our society? Is it not ironic that in the very week this year when rebellious demonstrators in Thailand were being hailed in the Western media as champions of human rights, martyrs to freedom, and foes of tyranny, the insurrectionists in Los Angeles were contemptuously dismissed by the same media as "rioters," "hooligans," "arsonists," and "murderers?" No doubt some were just exactly that, but that admission cannot allow us to obfuscate the recognition that the action of the insurrectionists was fueled by a deep-seated resentment at the violation of their social, economic, and cultural rights.

Certainly there are organizations, such as the Minority Rights Group (London) and Cultural Survival (Boston), which have adopted a broader conception of "human rights," and whose discourse is as concerned with the numerous rights of "collectivities," whether conceived in terms of race, gender, class, ethnic or linguistic background, as it is with the rights of "individuals." But this is not the discourse of "human rights" in the main, and it is emphatically not the discourse of Western powers, which have seldom adhered to the standards that they expect others to abide by, and would use even food and medicine, as the contin-

uing embargo against Iraq so vividly demonstrates, to retain their political and cultural hegemony even as they continue to deploy the rhetoric of "human rights." Never mind that state formation in the West was forged over the last few centuries by brutally coercive techniques—colonialism, genocide, eugenics, the machinery of "law and order"—to create homogeneous groups. One could point randomly to the complete elimination of the Tasmanian Aboriginals, the extermination of many Native American tribes, the Highland Clearances in Scotland, even the very processes by which a largely Breton-speaking France became, in less than a hundred years, French-speaking. We should be emphatically clear that what are called "Third World" countries should not be allowed the luxury, the right if you will, of pointing to the excesses of state formation in the West to argue, in a parody of the ludicrous evolutionary model where the non-Western world is destined to become progressively free and democratic, that they too must ruthlessly forge ahead with "development" and "progress" before their subjects can be allowed "human rights."

The idea of "human rights" is noble and its denial an effrontery to humankind. But it is only as an imagined idea that we can embrace it, and our fascination with this idea must not deflect us from the understanding that, as an ideological and political tool of the West, and particularly of the only remaining superpower, "human rights" is contaminated. Perhaps, before "human rights" is flaunted by the United States as what most of the rest of the world must learn to respect, the movement for "human rights" should first come home to roost. As Noam Chomsky has written, people in the Third World "have never understood the deep totalitarian strain in Western culture, nor have they ever understood the savagery and cynicism of Western culture." Could there be greater testimony to this hypocrisy than the fact that inscribed on the marble wall of the main lobby at CIA headquarters in Virginia is this quotation from John (VIII: 32): "And Ye Shall Know the Truth/And the Truth Shall Make You Free?"

POSTSCRIPT

Are Human Rights Basic to Justice?

On the surface, the debate between Howard and Lal appears rooted as much in philosophy as criminology. Yet their attempt to link human rights with basic justice (or the lack of it) clearly shows the primacy of the issue for both criminology and criminal justice.

Lal says that the "idea of 'human rights' is noble and its denial an effrontery to humankind," but does he not seem to be throwing them out with his attack on how they are misused? Although Howard appears to be an advocate of human rights as a basis for justice, could her endorsement of a "weak" relativism lead to the intellectual sanctioning of abuses that one would not be able to associate with "justice"? For example, although it is illegal throughout India, the practice of suttee still occurs sometimes in rural areas. This is the custom of a Hindu widow willingly being cremated on her husband's funeral pyre as an indication of her devotion. Should Western scholars and others be concerned about this? Lal would probably argue that the "Contract with America" of Representative Newt Gingrich (R-Georgia), which proposes a reduction in or deemphasis of poverty programs, affirmative action, and other social programs, is a human rights violation. Why do you think Lal might make such a case?

There is an enormous literature on human rights and justice in philosophy, ethnicity, and feminism, as well as in law and criminal justice. For a comparison of Canada's human rights policies with those of other countries, see *Ethnicity and Human Rights in Canada*, 2d ed., by E. Kallen (Oxford University Press, 1995). A good comparative discussion of victimology and justice is R. Mawby and S. Walklate's *Critical Victimology* (Sage Publications, 1995). For a radically different formulation of rights, see C. Young's *It's All the Rage: Crime and Culture* (Addison-Wesley, 1994). Also see N. Hooyman and J. Gonyea's *Feminist Perspective on Family Care: Policies for Gender Justice* (Sage Publications, 1995).

For interesting accounts of several state-initiated violations of human rights, see the April 10, 1995, issue of *U.S. News & World Report*. For a more analytical delineation of state terror, see G. Barak's "Crime, Criminology, and Human Rights," in G. Barak, ed., *Varieties of Criminology* (Praeger, 1994). For two criminology texts reflecting a human rights perspective, see R. Quinney and H. Pepinsky, eds., *Criminology as Peacemaking* (Midland Books, 1992) and H. Bianchi, *Justice as Sanctuary* (Indiana University Press, 1994). For a stimulating extension of Howard's ideas, see her *Human Rights and the Search for Community* (Westview Press, 1995).

ISSUE 19

Should We Get Even Tougher on Criminals?

YES: George Allen, from "The Courage of Our Convictions: The Abolition of Parole Will Save Lives and Money," *Policy Review* (Spring 1995)

NO: John Irwin and James Austin, from *It's About Time: America's Imprisonment Binge* (Wadsworth, 1994)

ISSUE SUMMARY

YES: George Allen, governor of Virginia, recently elected to office on the promise of getting tougher on criminals, insists that such a policy reduces crime, serves justice, and, in spite of the costs of incarceration and building new prisons, is economically a bargain.

NO: Professor of criminology John Irwin and James Austin, executive vice president of the National Council on Crime and Delinquency, argue that getting tougher on criminals has not reduced crime or made America safer. Instead, more petty offenders are being locked up for longer periods of time, which increases racial discrimination and is threatening to bankrupt state budgets.

The preeminent sociologist Peter Berger observed in *The Heretical Imperative* (1979), "Modern man finds himself confronted not only by multiple options of possible courses of action, but also by multiple options of possible ways of thinking about the world." In terms of the seemingly "easiest" if not necessarily the most rational or logical response to crime, getting tough, there are indeed multiple ways of thinking. Throughout much of the twentieth century, the drift of sentiment among criminologists and others (especially in the 1950s and 1960s) was toward more rehabilitation programs. The feeling was that criminals should not be incarcerated as vengeance or to punish them. Instead, they should be institutionalized to be treated through educational programs, counseling, and so on. The scientific world view was invoked, along with healthy dosages of moral sympathy by scholars and activists for society's prisoners, disproportionately consisting of minorities. Ironically, a minor skirmish of the cultural wars was fought out, as politicians and the public have almost always been sympathetic toward corporate and white-collar criminals and hostile toward street criminals. For many intellectuals, the reverse was true.

However, a strange thing happened on the highway toward a rational, enlightened approach to crime control based on rehabilitation instead of punishment or getting tough. The road disappeared.

The following debate, with George Allen on one side and John Irwin and James Austin on the other, represents explicitly what had been formerly an implicit argument between the public and the intellectuals. Yet the discourse now flies a little higher than in the past. Both sides, for instance, support their positions with science—they provide statistics instead of relying primarily on raw emotions or overt prejudices.

Both sides include race in their respective equations. Yet their respective framing of the race-crime nexus is radically different. Notice in both selections that although the protagonists are diametrically opposed, both portray the race-crime connection as a race-victim one to partially justify their perspectives.

Both Allen and Irwin/Austin, however indirectly, reflect the reformulated cultural backdrop that has changed the conversation on crime. What a few years ago Irwin and Austin would have taken for granted (e.g., getting tough does not help, is often racist, etc.), they now seem to feel they have to justify. Allen's arguments, by contrast, appear "at home" in the 1990s. Indeed, they have widespread political and intellectual support.

How did such changes come about so quickly? One factor may have been the Martinson report *Nothing Works* in 1974, which, based on an in-depth survey of prison rehabilitation programs, claimed that none of them could be shown scientifically to really change post-release behavior. Also, in the 1970s and 1980s members of the feminist movement, with access to deplorable statistics on the rate of spouse and child abuse, often assumed a get-tough-on-abusers posture.

The drug trade, which has spawned not only a rising tide of users but an increase in violent crime by juveniles and others, has significantly added to the despair. Furthermore, many black leaders and intellectuals, noting that the number of black homicides by black murderers has risen tremendously in the last decade, are rapidly abandoning a "soft" approach to what they see as their neighborhoods' being decimated.

Finally, although they are generally far less likely than others to be victims of violent crimes, nonblacks' fear of crime is rising. And prisons are seen by blacks and whites alike as hotels that coddle hard-core criminals who are receiving short sentences for committing horrible acts.

In spite of all this, it appears obvious that even with the prison population doubling since 1980, many crimes—including violent ones—continue to skyrocket. How is this possible? Could it be that the crime situation would be even worse without the additional prisons, or is it that the manifest policy of "getting tough" is simply not working?

YES

George Allen

THE COURAGE OF OUR CONVICTIONS: THE ABOLITION OF PAROLE WILL SAVE LIVES AND MONEY

On Father's Day 1986, Richmond Police Detective George Taylor stopped Wayne DeLong for a routine traffic violation. DeLong, recently released from prison after serving time for murder, shot and killed the policeman.

Leo Webb was a divinity student at Richmond's Virginia Union University who liked helping people. One of those he helped was a man named James Steele, on parole for a malicious wounding. One day in 1991, Steele entered the bakery where Webb worked part time, shot him to death, took his money, and went out partying.

Tragic as such stories are, what makes these two particularly disheartening is that both could have been easily prevented. Both killers, jailed earlier for violent crimes, spent only a fraction of their sentences in prison. We are now paying the dividends of a liberal justice system that refuses to take punishment seriously: Virginia has witnessed a 28 percent increase in criminal violence over the last five years. Three out of every four violent crimes—murder, armed robbery, rape, assault—are now committed by repeat offenders (see Figure 1).

This is why my administration pushed through legislation, which took effect on January 1, 1995 that will impose penalties for rape, murder, and armed robbery more than twice the national average for those crimes. We have abolished parole, established the principle of truth-in-sentencing, and increased as much as five fold the amount of time that violent offenders will actually spend in jail. Experience vindicates what commonsense has always told us: The only foolproof crime-prevention technique is incarceration.

Our new system is attempting to unravel 30 years of paper-tiger laws based on the questionable philosophy that people can change, criminals can be rehabilitated, and every violent criminal—even a murderer—deserves a second chance. The new law in Virginia will prevent thousands of crimes, save lives, save money, and restore trust in the criminal justice system. Despite this, we now face entrenched opposition from liberals in the General Assembly, who hope to thwart reform by withholding funds to build the minimal number of prison facilities needed to house Virginia's most violent inmates.

A few weeks after taking office in January 1994, I created the Commission on Parole Abolition and Sentencing Reform. It was a bipartisan commission of prosecutors, judges, crime victims, law-enforcement officers, business leaders, and legal scholars. William Barr, a former attorney general of the United States, and Richard Cullen, a former U.S. Attorney for the Eastern District of Virginia, co-chaired the commission. They had a daunting task.

I called for a special session of the General Assembly in September 1994 to focus the public's and the legislature's attention on this issue. I gave the commission six months to demonstrate the need for change, develop a detailed plan, and explain its costs and implementation.

We were quickly able to show why a complete overhaul was necessary. Convicted felons were serving about one-third of their sentences on average, and many served only one-sixth. Violent criminals were no exception. First-degree murderers were given average sentences of 35 years, but spent an average of only 10 years behind bars. Rapists were being sentenced to nine years and serving four. Armed robbers received sentences averaging 14 years and served only about four (see Figure 2).

Amazingly, a prior conviction for a violent crime did not affect this phenomenon. Even murderers, rapists, and armed robbers who had already served time for similar offenses were receiving the same sentences and serving the same amount of time as first offenders.

Statewide, the violent crime rate had risen 28 percent in five years, even though the crime-prone age bracket (15 to 24 years) was shrinking. Criminologists widely regard trends in the size of this demographic group as the best predictor of criminal activity. Unfortunately for Virginians, the crime-prone-age population is expected to rise sharply in the state beginning in 1996—all the more reason to press forward with reform. The peak age for murder and armed robbery has been dropping steadily; by 1993, it stood at 18 years for both crimes. More than three-quarters of all violent criminals in the system in 1993 had prior convictions.

THE PLAN

Only a multi-pronged approach can begin to turn these numbers around. Virginia's new law means, first of all, eliminating discretionary parole, in which a parole board can release an offender after he has served only part of his sentence. In Virginia, this policy clearly was being abused: offenders received 30 days of good time for every 30 days they served —effectively cutting their sentences in half as soon as they came in the door.

But this is not all. We need to eliminate "good time" as well. In order to encourage good behavior among inmates and allow correctional officers to maintain order, the commission proposed a system of earned-sentence credits. This system would allow inmates to earn a maximum of 54 days per year—a dramatic reduction from the average of 300 days they had been given in the past.

Long before our bill became law, we held town meetings across the state to solicit advice from citizens, and discussed the plan's details with prosecutors, victims-rights groups, corrections experts, and criminologists. The need for more prison space became a primary con-

Figure 1

Repeat Offenders

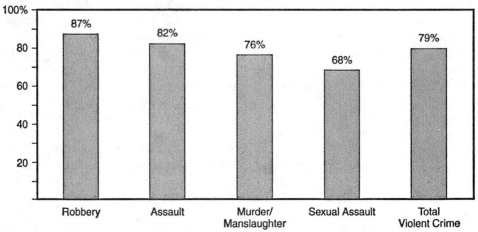

Percent of Convicted Felons in Virginia with Prior Convictions

Source: Criminal Justice Research Center.

cern. Even before I took office, Virginia was expected to double its prison population by the year 2005. The state was facing a shortfall of 7,100 prison beds by 1999. At the same time, opponents of the plan were already carping about too little spending on crime prevention and education and too much on building prisons.

Obviously, judges need some mechanism to guide their sentencing decisions. A system with no parole and no "good time" could not afford 70-year sentences for drug dealers or 150-year sentences for armed robbers. But how much do we increase the time served for violent offenders? Our commission found an answer by evaluating the relationship of recidivism to time served and age of release. The data showed that the longer an offender remained behind bars, the less likely he is to commit another crime after finishing his sentence. Similarly, the older the offender upon release, the less his propensity to commit more crime. In fact, after 37 years of age, the likelihood of violent crime drops dramatically.

Although preventing criminals from committing further acts of violence was the primary goal, the increases had to reflect the notion of retribution as well. We wanted Virginia to send a message to violent criminals: We will not tolerate violence, and if you commit a violent crime, you will stay in prison until you're too old to commit another one.

Virginia increased prison time for violent criminals as follows:

- 100 percent increase for first-time offenders.
- 125 percent for first-time murders, rapists, and armed robbers.
- 300 percent for those with previous convictions for assault, burglary, or malicious wounding.
- 500 percent for those with previous convictions for murder, rape, or armed robbery.

Figure 2
Revolving-Door Justice

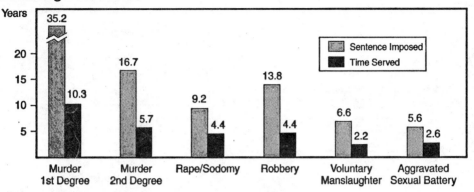

Average Sentences vs. Actual Time Served by Criminals in Virginia
Source: Criminal Justice Research Center.

To target the young violent offender, we counted comparable juvenile offenses as felony convictions when determining a sentence. For example, if John Smith is found guilty in a juvenile court of armed robbery at age 14, and was convicted of another armed robbery at age 19, the sentencing guidelines call for a 500 percent increase in the time he normally would have served under the old system.

By abolishing a bankrupt parole system, and by drastically reforming the "good time" credit provisions, Virginia courtrooms are redefining what the truth-in-sentencing debate is really about. Under our system, every inmate convicted of a violent crime will serve a minimum of 85 percent of his or her sentence. Nationwide, criminals on average serve well below 50 percent of their sentences. There is simply no surer way for the state to protect its citizens from society's most dangerous members.

SAVING LIVES AND MONEY

Had the law been in effect nine years ago, it would have saved the life of Detective Taylor. Had it been in effect four years ago, Leo Webb would be alive today.

The most conservative estimates show that more than 4,300 felony crimes would have been prevented between 1986 and 1993 if the current system had been in place. That number is based on actual convictions—real cases, not projections.

Over the next 10 years, the new law will prevent at least 119,000 felonies, including 26,000 violent crimes (see Figure 3.) Because of those averted violent crimes, an estimated 475 lives will be saved, 3,700 women will be spared from rape, and more than 11,300 aggravated assaults will not be committed. As a result, citizens will save more than $2.7 billion in direct costs.

Back in September, when it became clear that the legislation would pass with overwhelming support, some vocal opponents claimed that abolishing parole was a declaration of war on young

Figure 3

Preventing Crime Pays

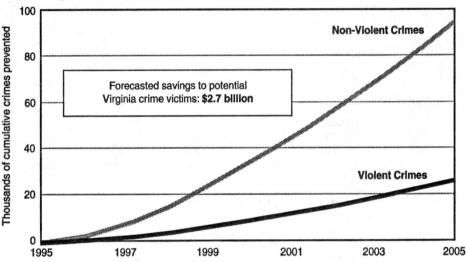

Forecast of Preventable Felony Cases Under the Governor's No-Parole Plan

Source: Criminal Justice Research Center.

black males. They demanded that the Commonwealth spend more money on prevention programs, and charged that, by focusing on punishment, we were merely catering to "white fear." Their arguments fell on deaf ears.

The crime prevented as a result of the new law will benefit the African-Amerian community—one-fifth of Virginia's population—more than any other group. Of the preventable murders that occurred between 1986 and 1993, about 65 percent involved black victims. For assaults during that same period, about 60 percent of the victims were black. Taylor and Webb were both African Americans.

Of all the crimes committed by recidivists during that same period, 60 percent would have been prevented if the current law had been in place. There is no other prevention program that can show even a fraction of this success. That is not to say that other prevention programs are not

valid or important. However, it is clear that when it comes to violent offenders, incarceration is the most just and the most efficient.

Virginia has been spending an average of $658 million in taxpayers' money each year on handling recidivists. This is the cost of new investigations, new arrests, and new trials. The total cost of the prison construction needs for the next 10 years is about $750 million. The new law will force us to build more prisons— but not many more. Virginia would have doubled its prison population in the next 10 years anyway.

The difference is that under the old system, the ratio of violent criminals among the prison population to non-violent has been 50:50. Marijuana dealers, embezzlers, and petty thieves have been serving time in the same $40,000-per-year hard cells as murderers, rapists, and armed robbers. Under the new guidelines, the inmate ratio will be 70 percent violent, 30 percent non-violent. This is obviously a more cost-effective use of medium- and maximum-security prison space.

Try telling that, however, to the liberals in the General Assembly. I asked lawmakers in February for $402.6 million as a first installment in revamping our prison system. They voted to provide only $104.4 million. They are shortchanging prison construction, making it more likely that dangerous criminals will be released early—and be back in our neighborhoods. Increasing prison terms without increasing prison capacity is precisely the mistake that too many other states have already made.

Part of the problem with the current system of incarceration is its near inability to distinguish between dangerous criminals and the more routine, petty offenders. Under our plan, we are building low-cost work centers to house first-time and non-violent offenders. These work centers operate at about half the cost per inmate as a standard prison, and they ensure that the inmates get work opportunities while incarcerated. The average length of stay at a work center will be about 10 to 18 months. We can build these facilities quickly, freeing up bed space in the prisons for violent criminals.

The abolition of parole and establishment of truth-in-sentencing rules was the centerpiece of my campaign for governor in 1993. During that campaign, critics claimed my approach was too drastic and too costly. Pundits and politicians still doubt that Virginia can overhaul its entire criminal-justice system without breaking the bank. Those naysayers failed to hear the public's demand for change. The people of Virginia—particularly crime victims and their families—are tired of seeing criminals walk free after serving only a fraction of their sentences. Businessmen can't afford to watch deals collapse because potential clients are concerned about crime. Prosecutors and police are frustrated that their hard work often amounts to abbreviated prison stints for criminals.

In order to overturn the status quo approach to crime reduction, we listened to all those people and presented extensive research to show that what we had been doing was not working. Public safety is the primary responsibility of government. Without it, nothing else can succeed. Education, economic development, and health care all suffer when people feel threatened.

Virginians came together to formulate and implement this reform. We looked at what North Carolina, Texas, Florida, and the federal government had done in the area of sentencing reform. We borrowed some of the best aspects of those systems and avoided some of the mistakes they made. In the end, we did it the Virginia way.

The principle that guided this effort, and should guide policymakers in all issues, is honesty. Easy-release rules prevent judges and juries from preempting the community's judgment about the proper punishment for illegal conduct. Under the new law, judges will not have to play guessing games when imposing sentences. Police officers will not have to see the same criminals out on the streets only a year after their last arrest. Criminals will know that they cannot beat the system. Crime victims and their families will finally see justice done. Virginia's citizens can now trust that their government is working to make this Commonwealth a safe place to live, to work, and to raise families.

NO

John Irwin and James Austin

IT'S ABOUT TIME: AMERICA'S IMPRISONMENT BINGE

For the last ten years, we have been witnessing the national tragedy and disgrace of America's imprisonment binge. We, as sociologists/criminologists, have kept in close contact with America's "prison systems," including their administrators, staffs, policy makers, and, most of all, clients—the prisoners. During the 1980s, we nervously listened to our political leaders (both Republicans and Democrats) and special interest groups advocate their simplistic but appealing message that in order to solve the crime problem we needed to escalate the use of imprisonment. We were equally dismayed to witness many of our colleagues pursue government financed studies that would justify the conservative "war on crime" agenda. Then, we watched, incredulously, the unparalleled explosion of the prison populations....

* * *

The United States has been engaged in an unprecedented imprisonment binge. Between 1980 and 1992, the prison population has more than doubled, from 329,821 to 883,593—a rise of 168 percent. The increase was so great that by 1991, the number of citizens incarcerated exceeded the population of six states and was larger than that of some of our major cities, including San Francisco, Washington, D.C., or Boston. The incarceration rate (number of persons in prison on any given day per 100,000 population) increased during the same time period from 138 to 329, as compared to only 26 in 1850 (Figure 1). We now imprison at a higher rate than any nation in the world, having recently surpassed South Africa.

And there is little evidence that America's imprisonment campaign will end soon. The National Council on Crime and Delinquency (NCCD) forecasts that under the present criminal justice policies, the nation's prison population will reach 1 million inmates by 1994. In 1991, 42 states reported that they were planning to build over 100,000 prison beds at a cost of over $5 billion. Yet even this massive construction program represents a futile effort to catch up with the increasing prison populations.

... [M]ore Americans experience jail time than any other form of correctional control. In 1988, the U.S. Department of Justice reported over 9.7 million admissions to the nation's 3,300 plus jails. Assuming that approximately 75 percent of these 9.7 million admissions represents mutually exclusive adults, this means that nearly one out of every twenty-five adults in America go to jail each year.

Those under the control of correctional authority do not represent a cross-section of the nation's population. They tend to be young African-American and Latino males who are uneducated, without jobs, or, at best, marginally employed in low-paying jobs. According to one recent study, the average daily populations of those in prison, parole, probation, and jail revealed that:

- Almost one in four (23 percent) African-American men in the age group 20–29 is either in prison, jail, probation, or parole on any given day.
- Sixty years ago, less than one-fourth of prison admissions were nonwhite. Today, nearly half are nonwhite.
- Over one out of every ten Hispanic men (10.4 percent) in the same age group is either in prison, jail, probation, or parole on any given day.
- For white men the ratio is considerably lower—one in 16 (or 6.2 percent).
- The number of young African-American men under control of the criminal justice system (609,690) is greater than the total number of African-American men of all ages enrolled in college as of 1986 (436,000).

* * *

... [M]ost of the unprecedented numbers of people we are sending to prison are guilty of petty property and drug crimes or violations of their conditions of probation or parole. Their crimes or violations lack any of the elements that the public believes are serious or associates with dangerous criminals. Even offenders who commit frequent felonies and who define themselves as "outlaws," "dope fiends," crack dealers, or "gang bangers" commit mostly petty felonies. These "high-rate" offenders, as they have been labeled by policy makers and criminologists, are, for the most part, uneducated, unskilled (at crime as well as conventional pursuits), and highly disorganized persons who have no access to any form of rewarding, meaningful conventional life. They usually turn to dangerous, mostly unrewarding, petty criminal pursuits as one of the few options they have to earn money, win some respect, and avoid monotonous lives on the streets. Frequently, they spend most of their young lives behind bars.

What may be more surprising is that a majority of all persons sent to prison, even the high-rate offenders, aspire to a relatively modest conventional life and hope to prepare for that while serving their prison sentences. This should be considered particularly important because very little in the way of equipping prisoners for a conventional life on the outside is occurring in our prisons. In preceding decades, particularly the 1950s and 1960s, a much greater effort was made to "rehabilitate" prisoners. Whatever the outcome of these efforts (as this is a matter of some dispute), rehabilitation has been all but abandoned. Prisons have been redefined as places of punishment. In addition, rapid expansion has crowded prisoners into physically inadequate institutions and siphoned off most available funds from all services other

Figure 1

Incarceration Rates, 1850–1991

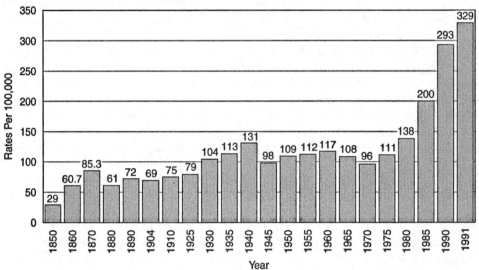

Source: Margaret Werner Cahalan, *Historical Corrections Statistics in the United States, 1850–1984.* Rockville, MD: Westat, Inc., 1986, Bureau of Justice Statistics, *Sourcebook of Criminal Justice Statistics, 1991.* Washington, D.C.: U.S. Department of Justice, 1992, and Bureau of Justice Statistics, *Prisoners in 1991.* Washington, D.C.: U.S. Department of Justice, 1992.

than those required to maintain control. Prisons have become true human warehouses—often highly crowded, violent, and cruel.

THE FINANCIAL COST

We must consider the costs and benefits of increased imprisonment rates.... [P]revious estimates routinely cited by public officials have dramatically underestimated the amounts of money spent on housing prisoners and building new prisons....

Although there is considerable variation among the states, on the average prison officials claim that it costs about $20,000 per year to house, feed, clothe, and supervise a prisoner. Because this estimate does not include indirect costs,

the true annual expenditure probably exceeds $30,000 per prisoner.

The other enormous cost is prison construction. Prisons are enclosed, "total" institutions in which prisoners are not only housed, but guarded, fed, clothed, and worked. They also receive some schooling and medical and psychological treatment. These needs require—in addition to cellblocks or dormitories—infirmaries, classrooms, laundries, offices, maintenance shops, boiler rooms, and kitchens. Dividing the total construction costs of one of these institutions by the number of prisoners it houses produces a cost per "bed" of as low as $7,000 for a minimum-security prison to $155,000 for a maximum-security prison.

Instead of using current tax revenues to pay directly for this construction, however, the state does what most citizens do when they buy a house—that is, borrow the money, which must be paid back over several decades. The borrowing is done by selling bonds or using other financing instruments that may triple the original figure. The costs of prison construction are further increased by errors in original bids by contractors and cost overruns caused by delays in construction, which seem to be the rule rather than the exception. A recent survey of 15 states with construction projects revealed that cost overruns averaged *40 percent* of the original budget projections.

Consequently, when a state builds and finances a typical medium-security prison, it will spend approximately $268,000 per bed for construction alone. So in the states that have expanded their prison populations, the cost per additional prisoner will be $39,000 a year. This includes the cost of building the new cell amortized 30 years. In other words, the 30-year cost of adding space for one prisoner is more than $1 million.

These enormous increases in the cost of imprisonment are just beginning to be felt by the states. Budgetary battles in which important state services for children, the elderly, the sick, and the poor are gutted to pay for prisons have already begun. In coming years, great cutbacks in funds for public education, medical services for the poor, highway construction, and other state services will occur.

CRIME REDUCTION

Those who are largely responsible for this state of affairs—elected officials who have harangued on the street crime issue and passed laws resulting in more punitive sentencing policies, judges who deliver more and longer prison terms, and government criminal justice functionaries who have supported the punitive trend in criminal justice policies —promised that the great expansion of prison populations would reduce crime in our society....

To support the proposition that increases in incarceration reduce crime, senior U.S. Department of Justice officials have compared Uniform Crime Reports (UCR) violent crime rates (homicides, robbery, assault, rape, and kidnapping) with imprisonment rates between 1960 and 1990 in ten-year increments. By selectively using these ten-year increments, the Justice Department's bar chart shows that, during the 1960s, imprisonment rates dropped by 19 percent while reported violent crime rates *increased* 104 percent. During the 1970s violent crime rates continued to *increase* again, but by only 47 percent, whereas imprisonment rates increased by 39 percent. And in the 1980s, as imprisonment rates increased by 99 percent, violent crime rates again *increased*, but by only 11 percent.

In other words, although violent crime rates have *steadily increased* over the past three decades, the rates of increase were lowest during the 1980s, when imprisonment rates were at their highest levels. These data have led a Justice Department spokesperson to claim that violent crime will decline even more if more persons are imprisoned....

We suggest... that these arguments are invalid and that there has been no increase in public safety produced by the imprisonment binge. On the contrary, a careful examination of all available information supports the conclusion that more imprisonment has not had any significant impact on crime rates. Most tellingly, crime rates have not declined despite the massive increases in prison and jail populations. Figure 2 summarizes the percent

Figure 2

Annual Changes in UCR, Crime and Prison Rates

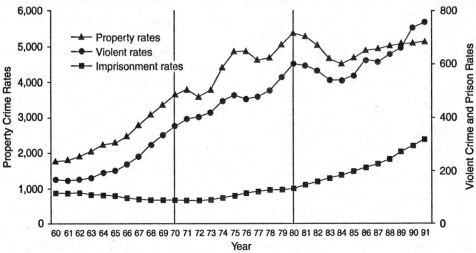

Source: James Austin and John Irwin, *Does Imprisonment Reduce Crime? A Critique of Voodoo Criminology.* San Francisco, Calif. National Council on Crime and Delinquency, February, 1993.

changes in UCR crime rates and imprisonment rates from 1960 to 1991....

State-by-State Comparisons.

The *best* test of the proposition that increasing prison populations has reduced crime is a comparison between the 50 states and the District of Columbia, which serve as experiments on this issue. This is because they not only differ in their crime and imprisonment rates, but they have also undergone dramatically different changes in these over the last fifteen years.

The period 1980 to 1991 is ideal for this comparison. The national crime rate peaked in 1980, as it did individually in all but 13 states. (These peaked in 1981 or 1982.) Also, after increasing slowly for several years, the national rate of incarceration began to rise steeply. All the states increased their prison populations in that 12-year period, but

they did so by very different amounts, from 26 to 742 per 100,000. The states and D.C., in a sense, are 51 different "petri dishes" (used in biological experiments), each with its unique array of factors that could be related to changes in crime rates, into which the experimental variable—increases in imprisonment—is introduced. If a causal relationship existed, we would see a consistent pattern —namely, states that increased their imprisonment rates the most would show the largest reductions in crime rates. Conversely, states that increased their imprisonment rates more slowly would show higher increases in crime rates.

Actually, there is no pattern....

Most states (34) experienced a decline in crime rates. However, there is no tendency for those that increased their prison populations the most to have greater decreases in crime. In fact, the opposite is true. The states that increased their prison populations by less [than] 100 per 100,000 were more likely to have experienced a decrease in crime than those that increased imprisonment rates by more than 200....

The California Imprisonment Experiment.

If we were to pick a state to test the imprisonment theory, California would be the obvious choice, for this state's prison population has increased from 19,623 in 1977 to over 110,000 by 1992....

[T]he size of the prison population increased by 237 percent (from 29,202 to 97,309) and the jail population increased by 118 percent (34,064 to 74,312). Prison operating costs increased by 400 percent, and jail operating costs increased by 265 percent. As of 1990, Californians were paying nearly $3 billion per year to operate the state's prisons and jails.

What has been the impact of this substantial investment in violent crime? Contrary to the claim that the violent crime rate (homicide, rape, robbery, and assault) has dropped, the rate actually *increased* by 21 percent. Substantial declines did occur, but only for burglary and larceny theft—a phenomenon that, as we noted earlier, was at least partially attributable to growth in illegal drug trafficking and shifts in the at-risk population. More interesting is the fact that after 1984 the overall crime rate, and especially violent crimes and auto theft, have grown despite a continued escalation of imprisonment.

California is now so strapped for funds that it must dramatically reduce the number of its parole officers and has been unable to open two brand new prisons, capable of holding 12,000 inmates. The state now has the most overcrowded prison system in the nation (183 percent of rated capacity) and spends millions of dollars each year on court cases challenging the crowded prison conditions. Despite the billions of dollars now being spent each year in locking up offenders, the public is as fearful of crime as it was a decade ago. Clearly, the grand California imprisonment experiment has done little to reduce crime or the public's fear of crime.

CUTTING OUR LOSSES ON THE PRISON SOLUTION

The past decade has witnessed the uncritical adoption of a national policy to reduce crime by increasing the use of imprisonment. That policy has failed. Despite a more than doubling of the correctional industrial complex and a tripling of criminal justice system costs, crime in general has not been reduced. Though there is evidence that property crimes committed against households have declined, all measures of crime are increasing. Moreover, it appears that crime is likely to increase in the near future. This is not news to the American public, which is increasingly apprehensive about personal safety even as their taxes are increased to pay for the failed imprisonment policy.

For these reasons, the grand imprisonment experiment, which has dominated America's crime reduction policy for the past 15 years, should not only be severely questioned but abandoned. It has simply failed to produce its primary objective—reduced crime. This is not to say that certain offenders should not be imprisoned and, in some cases, for lengthy periods; a few individuals are truly dangerous and need to receive long sentences. But to argue that all offenders should be so treated is misguided and ineffective.

Reducing crime means addressing those factors that are more directly related to crime. This means reducing teenage pregnancies, high school drop-out rates, unemployment, drug abuse, and lack of meaningful job opportunities. Although many will differ on how best to address these factors, the first step is to acknowledge that these forces have far more to do with reducing crime than escalating the use of imprisonment.

The "prison reduces crime" theory has not worked. Crime, especially violent crime, is not declining. We need to cut our losses and try crime prevention policies that will work. It may well take a decade before the fruits of such an effort are realized, but we can no longer afford to keep investing in a widespread crime reduction policy that has failed so ubiquitously.

POSTSCRIPT

Should We Get Even Tougher on Criminals?

Is Allen right or are Irwin and Austin? Have past efforts at rehabilitation really failed? Or is it true that, as one criminologist has observed, "Rehabilitation has not failed. It, like Christianity, simply was never really tried." Meanwhile, some claim that the very terms of the debate are obscene. In terms of crime, they ask if we would be willing to continue our current way of life at the expense of easily available guns for teenagers to kill each other or themselves (the vast majority of teenage suicide is gun-inflicted); a yearly rate of homicides that is approximately three times the total number of lynchings that have occurred throughout U.S. history; a criminal justice system with one-third to one-half of all black males between the ages of 17 and 26 either in its jails, in its prisons, or under street supervision; and a greater likelihood of minority males in the United States to be in prison than in college.

Critics acknowledge that crime is a real problem. However, they believe that it is time to change the dialogue. As well meaning as Allen and Irwin/Austin are, is their level of discourse reinforcing the existing problems? That is, Allen greatly simplifies crime control realities, and Irwin and Austin, some would claim, misunderstand the extent of vicious harm that is pervasive in many communities. Perhaps we need new ways of looking at the problem.

Two recent studies linking new policies with incarceration results are T. Marvell and C. Moody, "The Impact of Enhanced Prison Terms for Felonies Committed With Guns," and S. D'Alessio and L. Stolzenberg, "The Impact of Sentencing Guidelines on Jail Incarceration in Minnesota," both in *Criminology* (May 1995). Studies reflecting shifting cultural backdrops in reframing the controversy are *Criminal Justice? The Legal System Versus Individual Responsibility* edited by R. Bidinotto (Foundation for Economic Education, 1994) and J. Staddon, "On Responsibility and Punishment," *The Atlantic Monthly* (February 1995).

A criticism of the fantastic costs of building new prisons is "Get-Tough Stance Draws Fiscal Criticism," by R. Reuben, *ABS Journal* (January 1995). Nils Christie's *Crime Control as Industry* is now available in its second edition (Routledge, 1995). For an interesting interpretation of punishment from a feminist perspective, see A. Howe, *Punish and Critique: Towards a Feminist Analysis of Penalty* (Routledge, 1995). Further discussion of the debate can be found in T. Gest et al., "Crime and Punishment," *U.S. News & World Report* (July 3, 1995) and B. Gavzer, "Life Behind Bars," *Parade Magazine* (August 13, 1995).

CONTRIBUTORS
TO THIS VOLUME

EDITOR

RICHARD C. MONK is a professor of criminal justice at Coppin State College in Baltimore, Maryland, where he has been teaching sociology, criminology, and criminal justice since 1993. He received a Ph.D. in sociology from the University of Maryland in 1978, and he has taught anthropology, sociology, criminology, and criminal justice at undergraduate and graduate levels at Morgan State University, San Diego State University, and Valdosta State College. His more recent work includes an article on project BRAVE for *Police News* (December 1993) and the forward for and a chapter in *Crimes of the Criminal Justice System* edited by J. Henderson and David Simon (1994). He is currently coediting a special issue on "Police Training and Violence" for the *Journal of Contemporary Criminal Justice,* and in addition to editing this anthology, he edits Dushkin Publishing Group/Brown & Benchmark Publishers' *Taking Sides: Clashing Views on Controversial Issues in Race and Ethnicity,* soon to be available in its second edition.

STAFF

Mimi Egan   Publisher
Brenda S. Filley   Production Manager
Libra Ann Cusack   Typesetting Supervisor
Juliana Arbo   Typesetter
Lara Johnson   Graphics
Diane Barker   Proofreader
David Brackley   Copy Editor
David Dean   Administrative Editor
Richard Tietjen   Systems Manager

AUTHORS

ADALBERTO AGUIRRE, JR., is a professor of sociology at the University of California, Riverside. His research interests focus on sociolinguistics, the sociology of education, and race and ethnic relations, and he has written extensively for such professional journals as *Social Problems, Social Science Journal, Social Science Quarterly,* and the *International Journal of Sociology of Language.* His publications include *Race, Racism and the Death Penalty in the United States* (Vande Vere, 1991) and *Sources: Notable Selections in Race and Ethnicity* (Dushkin Publishing Group/Brown & Benchmark Publishers, 1995), coedited with David V. Baker.

GEORGE ALLEN is the governor (R) of Virginia (term expires January 1998).

JAMES AUSTIN is affiliated with the National Council on Crime and Delinquency in San Francisco, California, an organization of correction specialists and others interested in the prevention, control, and treatment of crime and delinquency.

DAVID V. BAKER is an associate professor of sociology and the chair of the Department of Behavioral Sciences at Riverside Community College in Riverside, California, where he has been teaching since 1987. His research interests focus on social inequality, with an emphasis on race and ethnic relations, and on racism in the American criminal justice system. His work has been published in the *Journal of Ethnic Studies, Social Justice, Justice Professional,* and *Criminal Justice Abstracts,* and he is the coeditor, with Adalberto Aguirre, Jr., of *Sources: Notable Selections in Race and Ethnicity* (Dushkin Publishing Group/Brown & Benchmark Publishers, 1995).

ALFRED BLUMSTEIN, a former president of the American Society of Criminology, is the dean of the H. John Heinz III School of Public Policy and Management at Carnegie Mellon University in Pittsburgh, Pennsylvania.

CYNTHIA GRANT BOWMAN is an associate professor of law at the Northwestern University School of Law in Chicago, Illinois. She received a Ph.D. in political science from Columbia University and a J.D. from Northwestern University. Her current research focuses upon issues involving women and the law, and she has been a reporter for the Illinois Task Force on Gender Bias in the Courts. She is a coauthor, with Mary Becker and Morrison Torrey, of *Cases and Materials on Feminist Jurisprudence: Taking Women Seriously* (West, 1993).

JACQUELINE COHEN is the associate director of the Urban Systems Institute in the School of Urban and Public Affairs at Carnegie Mellon University in Pittsburgh, Pennsylvania.

EMILE DURKHEIM (1858–1917) was a French sociologist and one of the founders and leading figures of modern sociology. He was a professor of philosophy at the University of Bordeaux and a professor of sociology and education at the University of Paris. He worked to establish a proper scientific method for the study of society, and he believed in the importance of social order, or cohesion, in society. Two of his major works in sociology are *The Division of Labor in Society* (1893) and *The Elementary Forms of the Religious Life* (1915).

D. STANLEY EITZEN is a professor emeritus of sociology at Colorado State University in Fort Collins, Colorado, where he taught criminology, social problems, and the sociology of sport. His publications include *Crime in the Streets and Crime in the Suites: Perspectives on Crime and Criminal Justice* (Allyn & Bacon, 1989), coauthored with Doug A. Trimmer, and *Society's Problems: Sources and Consequences* (Allyn & Bacon, 1989). He received a Ph.D. from the University of Kansas.

JEFF FERRELL is an associate professor of criminal justice at Northern Arizona University in Flagstaff, Arizona. He is the author of *Crimes of Style: Urban Graffiti and the Politics of Criminology* (Garland, 1993).

MICHAEL GOTTFREDSON is a professor in and the chair of the Department of Management and Policy at the University of Arizona in Tucson, Arizona.

W. BYRON GROVES (1953–1990) was an associate professor of humanistic studies at the University of Wisconsin–Green Bay. He received a Ph.D. in criminal justice from the State University of New York at Albany in 1982.

MARK S. HAMM is a professor of criminology at Indiana State University in Terre Haute, Indiana. He is the author of *American Skinheads: The Criminology and Control of Hate Crime* (Greenwood, 1993).

RICHARD J. HERRNSTEIN is the Edgar Pierce Professor of Psychology at Harvard University in Cambridge, Massachusetts, and a trustee for the Cambridge Center for Behavioral Studies. His research focuses on the effects of rewards and punishment on behavior and on the implications that human individu-ality has on how societies work and organize themselves. He is the coauthor, with James Q. Wilson, of *Crime and Human Nature* (Simon & Schuster, 1985)

TRAVIS HIRSCHI is a professor in the Department of Sociology at the University of Arizona in Tucson, Arizona.

RHODA E. HOWARD is a professor of sociology at McMaster University in Hamilton, Ontario, Canada. She is the author of *Human Rights and the Search for Community* (Westview Press, 1995).

JAMES A. INCIARDI is the director of the Center for Drug and Alcohol Studies at the University of Delaware in Newark, Delaware; an adjunct professor in the Comprehensive Drug Research Center at the University of Miami School of Medicine in Miami, Florida; and a member of the South Florida AIDS Research Consortium. He has extensive research, clinical, field, teaching, and law enforcement experience in substance abuse and criminal justice, and he has published over 24 books and more than 100 articles and chapters in the areas of substance abuse, criminology, criminal justice, history, folklore, social policy, AIDS, medicine, and law.

JOHN IRWIN is a professor emeritus of criminology at San Francisco State University in San Francisco, California.

C. R. JEFFERY is a professor of criminology and criminal justice at Florida State University in Tallahassee, Florida. His research interests include crime prevention through environmental design and the psychobiological foundations of human behavior. He is a former president of the American Society of Criminology and a recipient of their Sutherland Award, and he is the author of *Criminology: An Interdisciplinary Approach* (Prentice Hall, 1990).

JACK KEVORKIAN, a well-known activist for the cause of physician-assisted voluntary euthanasia, is a Michigan pathologist who has helped over 20 people commit suicide. He is very outspoken in his criticism against the medical establishment, politicians, theologians, and all who would actively resist a comprehensive, rational, and compassionate program of euthanasia. He is the recipient of the 1994 Humanist Hero Award.

ED KOCH, a former mayor of New York City, is a partner in the law firm of Robinson, Silverman, Pearce, Aronsohn, and Berman.

VINAY LAL is the William R. Kenan Fellow of the Society of Fellows in the Humanities at Columbia University in New York City.

ALICE LEUCHTAG is a freelance writer living in Houston, Texas, and the vice president of the Humanists of Houston. She is a former instructor of sociology at Indiana University, and she has also worked as a community education specialist, a counselor, and a program coordinator. Her articles have been published in *Journal of Human Stress* and *The Humanist*.

MICHAEL J. LYNCH is a professor in the Department of Criminology at Florida State University in Tallahassee, Florida. He is the coauthor, with E. Britt Patterson, of *Race and Criminal Justice* (Harrow & Heston, 1991).

RAYMOND P. MANUS is a lieutenant–special assignment in the Office of Management Analysis and Planning with the New York City Police Department.

DENNIS R. MARTIN is the former president of the National Association of Chiefs of Police in Arlington, Virginia, an organization of directors of national, state, provincial, and municipal law enforcement departments that provides consultation and research services on all phases of police activity.

DANIEL PATRICK MOYNIHAN is the senior U.S. senator (D) from New York (1976–present, term ends 2001). He received a Ph.D. and an LL.D. from the Fletcher School of Law and Diplomacy, and he has held academic appointments at Cornell University, Syracuse University, and Harvard University.

PATRICK V. MURPHY is the director of the police policy board of the U.S. Conference of Mayors. He has held numerous other positions in his 50-year career, including president of the Police Foundation and police commissioner of New York City.

TONY PLATT is a professor in the School of Criminology at the University of California, Berkeley, where he has been teaching since 1968. He is the coeditor, with Paul Takagi, of *Crime and Social Justice* (B & N Imports, 1981).

STEPHEN POWERS is a doctoral candidate in political science at Brandeis University in Waltham, Massachusetts. He received a B.A. in philosophy from the University of Maine and an M.A. in political science from Boston College. He is the author or coauthor of several articles on motion pictures and the coauthor of *Hollywood's America: Social and Political Themes in Motion Pictures* (Westview Press, 1996).

JEFFREY REIMAN is the William Fraser McDowell Professor of Philosophy at

American University in Washington, D.C. An expert on moral philosophy and applied ethics, he is the author of over 40 articles and numerous books on moral, political, and legal philosophy, including *In Defense of Political Philosophy* (Harper & Row, 1972) and *Justice and Modern Moral Philosophy* (Yale University Press, 1992). He is also a member of the American Society of Criminology.

STANLEY ROTHMAN is the Mary Huggins Gamble Professor Emeritus of Government at Smith College in Northampton, Massachusetts, and the director of the Center for the Study of Social and Political Change. He is the author or coauthor of numerous books and articles on society and politics, including *American Elites* (Yale University Press, 1996).

JEREMY SEABROOK is a London-based journalist and the author of *Pioneers of Change: Living Experiments for a Humane Future* (New Society, 1993) and *Victims of Development: Resistance and Alternatives* (Routledge, Chapman & Hall, 1993).

ALBERT SHANKER is the president of the American Federation of Teachers in Washington, D.C., an organization that works with teachers and other educational employees at the state and local levels in organizing, collective bargaining, research, educational issues, and public relations. A leader in the educational reform movement, he is recognized as the first labor leader elected to the National Academy of Education.

LAWRENCE W. SHERMAN is a professor of criminology in the Institute of Criminal Justice at the University of Maryland in College Park, Maryland, and the president of the Crime Control Institute in Washington, D.C. He is an experimental criminologist who has designed and directed over 15 randomized experiments in criminal sanctions, including the Minneapolis Domestic Violence Experiment. His publications include *Policing Domestic Violence: Experiments and Dilemmas* (Free Press, 1992).

WESLEY J. SMITH, a former civil trial lawyer, is a writer and legal commentator living in Los Angeles, California, who specializes on health care and medical ethics issues and on euthanasia. He has appeared on over 600 radio and television talk shows and has authored or coauthored eight books, including *Collision Course: The Truth About Airline Safety* (McGraw-Hill, 1993), coauthored with Ralph Nader.

HENRY SONTHEIMER is a contributor to *Juvenile Justice Update.*

NADINE STROSSEN is a professor in the School of Law at New York University in New York City and a general counsel for the American Civil Liberties Union.

JOSH SUGARMANN, a former communications director of the National Coalition to Ban Handguns, is the executive director of the New Right Watch, a nonprofit educational foundation that issues reports on topics dealing with the New Right in America.

PAUL TAKAGI is an associate professor of sociology at the University of California, Los Angeles.

CHARLES R. TITTLE is a professor of sociology at Washington State University in Pullman, Washington.

ARNOLD S. TREBACH is the founder and president of the Drug Policy Foundation in Washington, D.C., an independent think tank devoted to promoting peaceful and effective drug policy reform, including the legalization and medicalization of some drugs. He is also a professor in the Department of Justice, Law, and Society in the School of Public Affairs at the American University in Washington, D.C., and he has been a consultant to the U.S. Department of Justice, to Congress, and to other national agencies. His publications include *The Heroin Solution* (Yale University Press, 1982) and *The Great Drug War: And Radical Proposals That Could Make America Safe Again* (Macmillan, 1987).

ERNEST VAN DEN HAAG is a distinguished scholar at the Heritage Foundation in Washington, D.C., a public policy research and education institute whose programs are intended to apply a conservative philosophy to current policy questions. He has contributed more than 200 articles to magazines and sociology journals in the United States, England, France, and Italy, and he is the coauthor, with John P. Conrad, of *The Death Penalty: A Debate* (Plenum, 1983).

JENNIFER VOGEL is an investigative reporter for the Minneapolis–St. Paul alternative weekly *City Pages*.

DAVID VON DREHL is the art editor for the *Washington Post*. His publications include *Among the Lowest of the Dead* (Times Books, 1995).

JAMES Q. WILSON is the James Collins Professor of Management and Public Policy at the University of California, Los Angeles, where he has been teaching since 1985. He is also the chair of the board of directors of the Police Foundation and a member of the American Academy of Arts and Sciences. He has authored, coauthored, or edited numerous books on crime, government, and politics, including *Bureaucracy: What Government Agencies Do and Why They Do It* (Basic Books, 1989).

JAMES D. WRIGHT is the Charles and Leo Favrot Professor of Human Relations in the Department of Sociology at Tulane University of Louisiana in New Orleans, Louisiana. He is the author of 12 books, including 2 about the homeless, and over 140 journal articles, book chapters, essays, and reviews. His research interests include firearms acquisition and use among juveniles, the effectiveness of alcohol and drug treatment programs for homeless people, and the health and social problems of homeless street children in Latin America.

INDEX